Travels

PAUL BOWLES

ACKNOWLEDGMENTS

In compiling and editing this book, I am indebted to many of the Bowles fraternity. Kenneth Lissenbee, who runs the excellent Paul and Jane Bowles website (paulbowles.org), was enormously generous in helping to locate articles, providing leads to photographs and their copyright holders, and encouraging the project. I am also grateful for their knowledge and comments to Rodrigo Rey Rosa (Paul and Jane Bowles' literary executor), Philip Ramey, Jeffrey Miller, Daniel Halpern, Barnaby Rogerson, and Theo Collier and Charles Buchan at the Wylie Agency. Thanks for photo research to Jaime Margalotti, Rebecca Johnson Melvin, Stacy Hopping, Nick Homenda and Linda Briscoe Myers. For design, proofing and inputting, thanks to Henry Iles, Susanne Hillen and Gabriella Jaffe. And special thanks to Paul Theroux for the introduction and Dan Halpern for the Chronology.

CREDITS

We are grateful for permission to reproduce the following photographs and mansucripts: Harry Ransom Humanities Research Center at the University of Texas at Austin (p.178, 258, 486); Paul Bowles Papers, University of Delaware Library, Newark, Delaware (p.154, 436, 509); Paul Bowles photo archives at Fotostiftung Schweiz, Winterthur, Switzerland (front cover, inside front cover, p.15, 44, 69, 78, 83, 88, 94, 149, 200, 248, 276, 406, 428, 449); Karl Bissinger/Catherine Johnson (p.1/back cover flap); Magnum Photo Library (p.8); Allen Ginsberg/Corbis (inside back cover); Cherie Nutting (luggage on cover flap). All other photographs are courtesy of the Paul Bowles Estate.

Published in 2010 by Sort Of Books

PO Box 18678, London NW3 2FL

www.sortof.co.uk

Distributed by Profile Books
3a Exmouth House, Pine Street
London, EC1R 0JH

10 9 8 7 6 5 4 3 2 1

Typeset in Berkley Old Style and Sun Light to a design by Henry Iles

512pp

A CIP catalogue record for this book is available
from the British Library

ISBN 978-0956003874

Travels

COLLECTED WRITINGS, 1950-93

PAUL BOWLES

Editor's Note

The articles in this collection are arranged by date of publication – with a few exceptions. The first two pieces, "17 Quai Voltaire" and "Paris! City of the Arts", cover Paul Bowles' first travels as a teenage student, and although written some years later, they seem best placed opening this book. Similarly, "Passport", a short journal piece that was published at the end of Bowles' life, appears in its 'natural' sequence, after a longer article about travelling in south India. And the remarkable prose poem – 'Paul Bowles, His Life' – seems to have no other place than at the close of this collection.

Bowles enthusiasts will note that eight of the forty pieces appeared in his own selection of travel writing, *Their Heads Are Green and Their Hands Are Blue* (published in 1963), in which he revised a number of articles originally published in magazines. These appear in order of their original magazine publication, but the revised texts have been adopted. The original glossary from *Their Heads are Green* appears at the end of the book, and is followed by a *Chronology of Paul Bowles* by Daniel Halpern.

I have taken the term 'travel writing' loosely, in order to encompass travel-oriented journals, introductions to photographic books (Bowles was a generous contributor), even an enthusiastic glossary of kif terms for a 1960s book on cannabis. All of them showcase the unfailing quality of Bowles' prose – as well as how central a role travel played in his life and work.

Mark Ellingham, London, 2010

Contents

Paul Bowles in front of his cases, Tangier 1952

Paul Bowles' Travels

PAUL THEROUX

Paul Bowles of the stereotype is the golden man, the enigmatic exile, elegantly dressed, a cigarette holder between his fingers, luxuriating in the Moroccan sunshine, living on remittances, occasionally offering his alarming and highly polished fictions to the wider world. This portrait has a grain of truth, but there is much more to know. Certainly, Bowles had style, and a success with one book. But a single book, even a popular one, seldom guarantees a regular income. And, quite apart from money, Bowles' life was complicated emotionally, sexually, geographically, and without a doubt creatively.

A resourceful man – as the exile or expatriate tends to be – Bowles had many outlets for his imagination. He made a name for himself as a composer, writing the music for a number of films and stage-plays. He was a music ethnologist, an early recorder of traditional songs and melodies in remote villages in Morocco and Mexico. He wrote novels and short-stories. He wrote poems. He translated novels and poems from Spanish, French and Arabic, and created more than a dozen books with the Moroccan storyteller Mohammed Mrabet. So the louche languid soul of the stereotype turns out to have been a very busy man, highly productive, verging on a drudge.

He wrote travel essays, too, a whole book of them, which appeared as *Their Heads are Green and Their Hands are Blue* (1963). And as this new and valuable collection shows, he wrote vastly more travel pieces than are represented there, more than 30 of them that have never been collected before or reprinted. These range from journal entries and near prose-poems, a long autobiographical poem ("Paul Bowles, His Life"), polemical essays, political commentaries, and magazine pieces for glossy travel magazines, as well as magisterial introductions to books, such as I am attempting to do now.

He was handsome and hard to impress, watchful, solitary, and knew his own mind, his mood of acceptance, even of fatalism, made him an ideal traveler. He was not much of a gastronome – as his fiction shows, the disgusting meal (fur in the rabbit stew) interested him much more than haute cuisine. He was passionate about landscape and its effects on the traveler, as "The Baptism of Solitude" demonstrated, he was fascinated by the moods of the sky; and he was animated by the grotesque, wherever its mis-shapen form can be found. (He would have loved this observation by Augustus Hare in *The Story of My Life*: "It used to be said that the reason why Mrs. Barbara had only one arm and part of another was that Aunt Caroline had eaten the rest.") Contemptuous of what passes for progress or technology, he speaks in one of these pieces about Colombo being afflicted with "the Twentieth Century's gangrene," by which he means modernity.

As these newly disinterred pieces show over and over, Bowles was far from the dandy-dilettante that he is sometimes perceived to be. In the 62 years they represent, from 1931 to 1993, Bowles was a serious and extremely hard-working writer, trying to make a living; for, after the success of *The Sheltering Sky* (1948), his books were not brisk sellers. This is a salutary as well as an enlightening collection, demonstrating that the prudent writer, if he or she wishes to be spared the indignities of a real job, and the oppressions of a tetchy boss, has to keep writing. Bowles was fortunate in writing at a time (not long ago, but now gone) when travel magazines still welcomed long thoughtful essays. He wrote for the American *Holiday* magazine. The frivolous name masked a serious literary mission. The English fiction writers, V S Pritchett and Lawrence Durrell also traveled for this magazine; so did John Steinbeck after he won the Nobel Prize for literature, when he crisscrossed the United States with his dog. Bowles wrote for *The Nation* and *Harpers* too, and contributed to essay collections. As we see here, Bowles wrote a piece for *Holiday* about hashish, another of his enthusiasms, since he was a life-long stoner.

He knew what he enjoyed in travel, and what bored him: "If I am faced with the decision of choosing between visiting a circus and a cathedral, a café and a public monument, or a fiesta and a museum, I am afraid I shall normally take the circus, the café, and the fiesta."

No matter who he is writing for – travel magazine or pompous quarterly – he is never less than felicitous, and often funny. Of the Algerian hinterland: "When you come upon a town in such regions, lying like the remains of a picnic lunch in the middle of an endless parking lot, you know it was the French who put it there." Or in the desert, drinking "piping hot Pepsi Cola", or seeing "locust ravaged date palms whose branches look like the ribs of a broken umbrella," or the unforgettable Monsieur Omar, "lying in his bed smoking, clad in only his shorts, a delighted and indestructible Humpty Dumpty."

One of the oddities not to say weird anachronisms in some of these pieces is his casual mention of slaves or slavery: "If there is no slave or servant handy..." he writes in *Holiday* in 1950. In a piece the same year, about Fez, he writes, "Sidi Abdallah has a slave girl by whom he had a child. The slave market has been abolished by the French but the institution still persists." – stating it flatly, without details. Nine years later, another off-hand remark, in a piece about hospitality in "Africa Minor" – "only the guard, an old Sudanese slave, had the keys." Where the reader might expect outrage, Bowles simply deadpans.

He wrote about Paris at a time when he was footloose and a Francophile; the Costa del Sol while the coast was still stylish and unspoiled; Ceylon (where he owned an entire offshore island); Thailand (he hated it), Istanbul ("disorder is the visual keynote"), Kenya in the Mau-Mau period (where he was strongly, unfashionably anti-colonial), Madeira, India, and other places to which he was sent or happened to be journeying.

Morocco was his preferred place, its cities, its hinterland, and in particular Tangier. But it is Bowles' peculiar Tangier, not the tourist's, or the hippie's; nor even the city of William Burroughs or Barbara Hutton or Truman Capote, though he knew all three and wrote well about them. Tangier for Bowles is not as decadent as it is usually depicted; it is friendly and unrestrained; cheap, not beautiful, a farrago of architectural styles; off the beaten track, with no center, blighted with "a dearth of cultural life." Bowles says he feels infantilized by it, and he affectionately disparages it, "Tangier is a city where everyone lives in a greater or lesser degree of discomfort."

But Tangier had its eccentrics. They interested Bowles much more than the millionaires or the Beats. Mr Black, and his unusual drink, is like a Bowles fiction: "There was the somewhat sinister Mr Black, whom I never met, but who, I am told, kept an outsize electric refrigerator in his sitting room, in which there was a collection of half-pint glass jars. Occasionally he would open the refrigerator door, inspect the labels on the bottles and select one. Then in front of his guests he would pour its contents into a glass and drink. A lady I know, who was present one day when he did this, innocently inquired if what he had in the glass were a combination of beet and tomato juice. 'This is blood,' he said. 'Will you have some? It's delicious chilled, you know.' The lady, who had lived in Tangier for many years and was thus determined to show no astonishment at anything, replied, 'I don't think I will right now, thank you. But may I see the jar?' Mr Black handed it to her. The label read Mohammed. 'He's a Riffian boy,' explained Mr Black. 'I see,' she said, 'and the other jars?' 'Each one is from a different boy,' her host explained. 'I never take more than a half pint at a time from any one of them. That wouldn't do. Too debilitating for them.'"

In a number of pieces in this collection, Bowles unambiguously approves of Tangier's drug culture, the smoking of the narcotic kif, the eating of majoun, cannabis jam. "Cannabis, the only serious world-wide rival to alcohol, reckoned in millions of users, is always described in alcoholic countries as a social menace" [from "Kif," an essay that he wrote for *The Book of Grass*]. He is not a drinker at all, and anything but a hellraiser, but he has his pleasures.

Though some of the pieces are purely political, and others as elegant as any he wrote, his general outlook is much more relaxed here than in his fiction, or even of those essays Bowles selected for *Their Heads are Green*, many of them with the tone of Letters Home (another paradox, because for most of his life he did not really have a home outside of Tangier), informative, direct, familiar in tone, casual, sometimes abrupt, "So I'm off tomorrow; I can't stand this rain any longer." He is associated with one city, but he casually lets drop the fact that in six months of 1959 he traveled 25,000 miles – and what makes this extraordinary is that Bowles, who had a fear of flying, was traveling by ship and bus and train.

His rich experience of the world equipped him to write about travel, and one of the best essays here ("The Question of Identity") analyzes travel literature: "What is a travel book? For me it is the story of what happened to one person in a particular place, and nothing more than that; it does not contain hotel and highway information, lists of useful phrases, statistics, or hints as to what kind of clothing is to be needed by the intending visitor. It may be that such books form a category which is doomed to extinction. I hope not, because there is nothing I enjoy more than reading an accurate account by an intelligent writer of what happened to him away from home."

Bowles' long and full life is captured in these pieces, which also shed light on his brilliant fictions. It was a life of his choice. He never compromised, and thoroughly admirable in going his own way, writing what he wished, he never did anything he did not want to do; he kept at it until he died.

The melancholy lines in his autobiographical poem tell something about his last two decades. After his wife Jane died in 1973, he lived another 26 years. Jane had had a number of passionate affairs with women, and was deeply monogamously attached to a Moroccan woman called Cherifa, whom Bowles suspected to be a witch and a poisoner. Bowles too had his male attachments. Yet the death of this seemingly semi-detached wife, a dedicated lesbian, devastated him and put him in limbo:

After that it seemed to him that nothing more happened
He went on living in Tangier,
  translating from Arabic, French and Spanish.
He wrote many short stories, but no novels.
There continued to be more and more people in the world.
And there was nothing anyone could do about anything.

Travels

COLLECTED WRITINGS, 1950-93

17 QUAI VOLTAIRE

JOURNAL; MEMOIR OF PARIS, 1931–32*

I F I REMEMBER CORRECTLY, the apartment, at 17 Quai Voltaire, consisted of a very high-ceilinged studio with a balcony along one side. I slept up there. Harry Dunham, just out of Princeton, had rented the studio. He had the small bedroom downstairs. It was January, and the mornings were very cold. I could look out of the bathroom window on the balcony at the tracery of branches against the sky, and at the touts going up and down the river at my feet. This was the winter of 1931–1932; there were not many cars passing in the street below. I assume there are more now.

In Marrakesh Harry had thought it a good idea to import Abdelkader, a fifteen-year-old Moroccan who worked in the hotel there, and who could, thought Harry, be trained to act as his valet and as a general factotum. This proved to be not a successful venture.

There must have been some sort of heating apparatus in the place, or it would have seen untenable, and as a matter of fact I recall Abdelkader's journeys down the narrow back stairway to the basement in order to fetch fuel. Whether this was wood or

---

*17 Quai Voltaire is a memoir of Paul Bowles' stay in Paris in 1931–32, written some time in the 1980s. It was published after his death, initially as a monograph in French, and later in English by the magazine Open City (#20; 2005).

Paul Bowles took this photo-booth picture in Paris in 1930 and sent it to his
friend, Bruce Morrissette; the phrase he has inked in the background reads
"et qui voit le mystère" ("and who sees the mystery")

coal I have no idea. I know that it was on this staircase where one day he met someone he enthusiastically described as "*comme ma mère, je te jure*", and to whom he subsequently presented me (also on these back stairs). The voluble lady's name was Lucie Delarue-Mardrus. She invited me in to her apartment for a cup of coffee, and introduced me to Dr. Mardrus, who had much less to say than she. I was almost mute, not having read, or even known of the existence of his translation of *The Thousand and One Nights*. It was here that I first heard of Isabella Eberhardt, whom Mme. Mardrus described with great relish. They had met in Algeria.

The previous month I had been staying at an Italian ski-resort. I was not in the best of health, and I wrote this to Gertrude Stein, who insisted that I return to Paris. But in the meantime someone (there were so many gossip spreaders on the Left Bank in those days) went to her and told her that I was with a French girl there in the Alps. The girl and I were merely friends, but Gertrude Stein drew her own conclusions.

She disapproved of liaisons between the young men she was interested in and members of the opposite sex. Thus when I returned to Paris and thought I'd go around to the Rue de Fleurus and visit the Misses Stein and Toklas, I telephoned.

There was cold at the other end of the line.

"So you're back in Paris," said Gertrude Stein.

"Yes."

"Why don't you go to Mexico? I think that's where you belong. You'd last about two days."

That was the end of the conversation. She was a Californian: Mexico was her idea of a truly lethal place. I did not see her again until the following summer.

Strange, but it's impossible to remember where I ate my lunches and dinners. I was not interested in gastronomy; I was striving to make a small amount of money last as long as possible, without suffering from indigestion. It seems to me that there was a quite good, medium-priced restaurant in the Rue Bonaparte where I often went.

Two years earlier on my first visit to Paris, I had fallen in love with the Métro. It got one around the city without the rush and roar of the New York subway, which seemed always to be engaged in a race against time. On the subway one compulsively looked at one's watch; on the Métro one looked for DUBO–DUBON–DUBONNET instead. The smell of the New York subway was one of hot metal laced with harbor sewage; the Métro gave off a distinctive odor that escaped from the stations into the street. I had never smelled that particular scent anywhere else, and for me it was a symbol of Paris. Years later in a Tangier *droguerie* I discovered a disinfectant which came in three perfumes: Lavande, Citron and Parfum du Métro.

Bernard Fay, who lived in the Rue St. Guillaume, occupied a chair in Franco-American relations. What his political ideas were I have no idea, but as a result of having exposed them he was imprisoned for several years after the Second World War. It was at his house that I had met Virgil Thomson who, inasmuch as he lived at 17 Quai Voltaire, had been responsible for getting the studio there for Harry and me. Virgil also saw to it that I met various people whom he thought I ought to know, such as Marie-Louise Bousquet, Pavel Tchelitchew and Eugène Berman, whom everyone called Génia. He took me one day to see Max Jacob, a strange little man with a head like an egg. Henri Sauguet was there. But I had never read a line of Max Jacob's, nor heard a note of Sauguet's, so that these introductions were somewhat beside the point.

There were two places where I loved to go: the Bal Nègre in the Rue Blomet, and the Théâtre du Grand Guignol. I'd never before seen blacks dancing, and was of course highly impressed by their proficiency and grace. The repertory at the Grand Guignol was necessarily limited, and one had to be careful to choose a program that was not composed entirely of pieces one had already seen. Often during a performance there would be a disturbance among the spectators, and a person would be taken out by nurses in white uniforms. I never believed in the authenticity of these heart attacks and epileptic seizures. The plays did not seem horrible enough to provoke such reactions, although I was assured that the effects were bonafide, since the theater attracted invalids and neurotics. I thought it was all great fun, including the dramatic removal of the hypersensitive spectators.

Whenever a friend came to Paris and suggested that we eat together, I would choose La Mosquée, not because of its culinary excellence, but simply because the food and the ambiance were Moroccan. (I still dreamed of returning to Fez, which I'd left only a few months earlier.) And now that I recall it, it seems to me that the couscous was not at all bad. Certainly it was better than what one can get nowadays in a restaurant in Morocco. I'm told that now, more than half a century later, La Mosquée's food has deteriorated, but this is not surprising, considering what has happened to everything else.

One day at a friend's flat in Montparnasse I was introduced to Ezra Pound. He and I went out to lunch in the neighborhood. He was tall and had a reddish beard. I recalled a poem of his I'd read in a little magazine several years earlier; it was an excoriation of old people who he apparently thought owed it to society to die before they became senile. It was a cruel little poem. I had shown it to my mother, who said: "Obviously that man doesn't know much about life." Several times during lunch I was on the point of asking Mr. Pound if he still felt the same way about the elderly, but I held my tongue because I thought the question would embarass him. At the time he was one of three editors of a literary magazine called *The New Review*, the other two being Samuel Putnam and Richard Thoma. He had an appointment with Putnam that afternoon, and suggested I go with him.

We boarded a bus and stood on the back platform all the way to Fontenay-aux-Roses. I remembered that Gertrude Stein had said she couldn't have him at her house any more because he was so clumsy and careless. If he went near a table, she said, he knocked over the lamp. If he sat down, the chair broke under him. It cost her too much money to have him as a guest, so she made 27 Rue de Fleurus off-limits to him. I asked her if she thought he minded being excluded. "Oh, no. He has plenty of other people to explain things to." She called him The Village Explainer, which was fine, she said, if you were a village.

My literary activities in Paris that winter were confined to the search for missing issues of certain defunct and moribund magazines of which I wanted to have a complete collection. This took more time and energy than one might expect. The publications of particular interest were *Minotaure*, *Bifur* and *Documents*, a short-lived review edited by Carl Einstein. These were not to be found at the stalls along the quays, but in small second-hand bookshops scattered across the city, so that in my search for them I was obliged to do a good deal of walking. This however suited me perfectly, as there was nothing I enjoyed more than wandering on foot through the less frequented streets of Paris, which I continued to find mysterious and inexhaustible.

The regions which I particularly loved to explore were far from the Opéra, far from the Place de la Concorde or the Arc de Triomphe, all of which seemed too official to be of interest. On a gray winter's day the humble streets of Belleville and Ménilmontant struck me as infinitely more poetic; I could spend hours exploring those quarters, taking snapshots of courtyards piled with ladders and barrels (taking care that no person was included in the picture) and getting temporarily lost, rather as one does in a Moroccan *medina*. The food in the restaurants of these parts was not much to my liking; I recall the very red and sweetish horsemeat they served, generally with gritty spinach.

But there was one "official" building which delighted me: this was the Trocadéro with its wide staircases going down to the Seine. Am I wrong to associate it with Lautréamont? Surely it was ugly enough to have aroused his admiration, with the two unforgettable life-size rhinoceroses. Apparently these were removed at the time of the building's cosmetic surgery. I can't help wondering what happened to those two enormous animals. Do they still exist somewhere, or have they been destroyed? It seems to me that the French might have cast two more identical statues and placed all four of them at the corners of the Tour Eiffel, with which they had something in common.

Lest I be suspected of harboring perverse tastes in architecture, I should remark that I admired the Palace of Versailles. The openness of the landscape spread out before it, stretching away into the distance, provided an antidote to the occasional feeling of claustrophobia I had in Paris. I assumed that I shared a more or less universal admiration for the place, so that I was really shocked when one afternoon I saw four English tourists stand looking up at the wide façade with an expression of derision on their faces, while one woman said, in a broad Cockney accent: "Talk about ugly!"

One night I was invited to dinner at Tristan Tzara's flat. It was somewhere on the way up to Montmartre – perhaps the Rue Lepic. He had a beautiful Swedish wife, his salon was full of African sculptures and masks, and there was a splendid Siamese cat. In spite of (or possibly because of) their generally insane behavior, I'm particularly fond of these animals.

The food seemed excellent to me, but they apologized for it. They had a temporary cook, explained Tzara, since their usual cook had left earlier in the week in a state of great agitation, saying that he would under no circumstances set foot in the Tzara establishment again. It all had to do with the cat, which had never been on good terms with the cook. Perhaps the man had neglected on occasion to feed it. In any case he did not want it in the kitchen when he was working, and thus pushed it out with his foot, an insult which the cat, a huge male, obviously considered unforgivable.

The cook slept in a servant's room at the back at the apartment, and always shut his door upon retiring. But one night he failed to shut it completely, and the cat silently pulled it open. Making certain that the man was asleep, the animal crouched and sprang, landing on the cook's throat, which it began to rip open with its powerful hind feet. Clearly it had every intention of doing away with its enemy. The cook was taken to hospital, and in the morning he appeared at the door of the Tzara flat to deliver his ultimatum: if they wanted to keep him as a servant, the cat had to go immediately. He would not enter the apartment until they had got rid of it. They refused to do this, and the cook went away, threatening to start legal proceedings at once. I asked how the cat got on with the present cook. "Oh, she's a woman," said Tzara. "He doesn't mind women." The cat was sitting on a bookcase next to an African mask, watching us while we ate. Even though I had a strong desire to go over and caress his head and scratch his jowls, I was careful not to approach him at any time during the evening.

The walls of the studio at 17 Quai Voltaire were decorated with several large monochromatic drawings by Foujita. These belonged either to our landlady, Mme. Ovise, or had been left behind by a previous tenant. In spite of the presence of beautifully rendered Siamese cats in certain of the pictures, these works of art seemed unworthy of the studio, which I felt needed something more arresting. Harry was of the same opinion. The Galerie Pierre, which was nearby (probably in the Rue de Seine), was holding an exhibit of "constructions" by Joan Miró. These were made of wood, plaster, and bits of rope, somewhat reminiscent of parts of Kurt Schwitters' *Merzbau*, but conceived with an eye to please. Harry visited the Galerie Pierre and came back with three of these Mirós. They livened up the place, and made me feel that I was really in Paris and that it was the year 1932. The Foujitas had suggested another era – the preceding decade. (When one is twenty years old, a decade is a long time.) We put the Foujitas into a closet.

Scarcely a fortnight later I came home one afternoon to find that the studio seemed unusually dim. It took only a few seconds for me to realize that the Foujitas were back in their accustomed places on the wall, and that the Mirós had disappeared. The maid would not have done this; it could only have been the concierge or Mme. Ovise herself. I rushed downstairs to speak with the concierge. At first she had no idea of what I was talking about (or pretended to have none.) This was because I described the missing Mirós as pictures.

Eventually she did understand, saying: "Monsieur means those old pieces of wood that someone had put on the wall? I threw them out. I thought monsieur would be glad to be rid of them."

A search of the cellar was undertaken, and the constructions, to which I kept referring as works of art, much to the concierge's bewilderment, were found in a corner with a pile of kindling wood. They were not in prime condition, and had to be taken back to the Galerie Pierre for repairs. It was finally Miró himself who rebuilt them.

PARIS! CITY OF THE ARTS

HOLIDAY, APRIL 1953

PARTICULARLY I REMEMBER the winters in Paris – not with pleasure, not with displeasure – just the blank impressions, meaningless but powerful, of the hushed, intense cold that lay over the Seine in the early morning, the lavender-gray daylight that filtered down from the damp sky at noon; even on clear days the useless, impossibly distant, small sun up there above. I remember arranging my walks home from work so that I would get to the Tuileries in the wistful dimness of twilight.

To be seventeen and in Paris, free to do as one liked – that was an ideal state of affairs for any aspiring artist or writer a generation ago. It was ideal even without money. Perhaps especially without money. If you had money you were somewhat suspect, since it was almost an axiom that money and artistic ability could not belong to the same person; in that case, therefore, you were expected to help keep alive those who had only artistic ability.

But at seventeen one has energy: one can walk a few miles to save bus fare, one can run up six or seven flights to a room under the roof, one can live on a meal a day if one is not working, by staying in bed most of the time and eating bread. I went for months without a bath, washed my own clothes, was gnawed by bedbugs every night, and put up with a hundred inconveniences (any one of which, had I had to endure it in America, would have been downright hell) and loved it all, because I was in Paris.

I suppose it was because I felt that everybody was there. I was sharing the town with them all. Picasso was just going into his rag, bone and hank-of-hair period; Gertrude Stein was busily preparing to publish her own works in the Plain Edition; Stravinsky was writing the *Symphonie des Psaumes*; Joyce was in the middle of his *Work in Progress*; Diaghilev was there with his magnificent troupe. Then, too, it seemed to me that the struggles and scandals that went on in the art world there were of supreme importance: in a way it was like living within sight of the front during a war in whose outcome you were vitally interested. The Surrealists were regularly staging pitched battle in their own night clubs: the presence of a few policemen was almost a necessity at any artistic manifestation. It was the culmination of an era of aesthetic violence, in which the basic desire of the creative artist was to shock.

For artists, would-be artists and those numberless people for whom association with art of some sort, and with those who practice it, is a necessity, Paris is much more than a splendid city of boulevards, cafés, shops, bright night spots, parks, museums and historical monuments. It is a complete continent in itself, every region of which must be explored on foot. I wonder how many thousands of miles I myself must have covered, walking in the streets there, from the Bois de Vincennes to the Buttes-Chaumont, from Auteuil to Charenton, always seeking to penetrate, understand, participate in the sense of mystery that enveloped the city, looking for lost quarters that nobody knew, unearthing strange little alleys that were like nothing I had ever seen before, and many of which still remain intact as images in my mind's eye. Infinite variety in a harmonious whole, the certainty of discovering something new and poignant each day – such things give the artist who lives in Paris a sense of satisfaction and spiritual well-being. I think it is they, rather than the more tangible benefits Paris provides, that make it the principal gathering place for artists from every part of the world.

In the past those tangible benefits have doubtless been greater than they are today. There was a time when it seemed as though the entire Left Bank existed primarily for the artist. He was the one who was at home there, the rhythm of life was set by him, and the hotel rooms, cafés and restaurants were accessible to him for a sum he could usually manage to raise. Not so today, with food prices at astronomical levels, and Paris in the grip of one of the worst housing shortages in Europe. Now the average artist's life has little in common with the traditional *vie de bohème* of the attic studio lit by a candle stuck into a wine bottle. It used to be shabby; now it is grim. The studios are not for him; they have been moved into long since by prosperous bourgeois who consider it chic to live in places with an "artistic" atmosphere. Even the servants' rooms at the tops of the apartment houses are too expensive for him. He is literally being forced from the center of Paris out into the slums, and his life has become pretty desperate. When he eats he cooks the food himself in his tiny room, and he often has to carry his water up several flights in a pail from the tap in the courtyard below.

It is not surprising that recently there has been inaugurated a kind of "return to the soil" movement. A number of people practicing the various arts get together and rent a small house out in the suburbs. This they can get without key money. (Key money has nothing to do with rent; it is an extra bonus you must give the proprietor for the privilege of moving in, and the key money for an average studio in Paris is in the neighborhood of one thousand dollars.) Then they divide up the house to suit their requirements, plant a vegetable garden and settle in, using bicycles when they want to get into town. The garden is a great aid to the budget. This kind of life is a far cry from the traditional idea of the life of an artist in Paris, and it is conceivable that such a movement could eventually have far-reaching aesthetic repercussions, perhaps in line with the recent tendency to forsake abstraction and non-objectivism for representational painting. In any case, the average artist in Paris (and of painters alone it is estimated that the city now has approximately 46,800) is not faring too well these days.

Art students are even worse off, because in order to attend the academies they must live in the middle of town in furnished rooms, and they must depend more upon restaurants for their food, despite the fact that they generally have very little money left by the time they have paid their rent. There is a student foyer for them, near the Beaux Arts, where they can eat meals composed principally of soup and starches for 70 francs (about twenty cents), and that is a help. But the academies, which are useful above all as training centers for pedagogues, do not hold students with true creative talent for very long: these break away and work on their own, in collective studios and in their rooms.

Marc Raimbault is a good example of such a student. He is twenty-three. When he first came to Paris two years ago he was enrolled as an architectural student at the Beaux Arts, but that was only a ruse designed to get him away from his family in Poitiers, who would not hear of his becoming a painter. Now he lives as he likes, pursuing a life completely to his taste. It is a precarious life, to be sure, and often a difficult one; both ingenuity and hard work are required to keep going on the meager allowance his family sends him. Only when the former fails, however, does he resort to the latter, which consists in walking at three in the morning from Montparnasse to Les Halles and spending five or six hours unloading crates of vegetables from the trucks that come in from the country. It's not that he dislikes hard work, but it takes a lot of time and energy, and he wants to pull all that he has of both into the one thing which interests him – painting. His rent is not too high: he has managed to get a tiny room in the Rue Boissonade, in the apartment of a nice old lady who crochets scarves for a smart shop on the Right Bank. She used to paint landscapes in watercolor herself, and likes to think of herself as an artist, and so she rents him the room for very little.

If he is living according to his normal routine, and not unloading vegetables at the market, he gets up at about eight, makes himself a black coffee on his gas burner, dresses and goes out to the *Atelier de la Grande Chaumière*, where at the beginning of the season he has paid a small sum for the privilege of coming daily and working, using the models provided by the studio. On the way there he makes a pointof passing by the Dôme. He scans the *terrasse* in the hope of finding a friend who may be sitting there – a foreigner preferably, for a foreigner may ask him to sit down and have a drink. It is out of the question, naturally, for Marc to sit down on the *terrasse* of any cafè and order himself a drink. Friends are extremely important to him not only because they perform the mundane function of helping him keep within his budget but because life without them would be unthinkable. The three or four really close friends he has are all art students like himself, although they prefer to think of themselves as painters. For each one of them the little group they form is the social core of his life. Each can count on the other to provide moral, intellectual and even temporary material support. More important than actual cash loans are introductions to influential or wealthy persons. Such little brotherhoods of reciprocal aid are almost a *sine qua non* of any young artist's life.

The *Atelier de la Grande Chaumière*, smelling of cigarette smoke and turpentine, is a refuge from the chill and damp which seem always to be in the streets. There Marc exchanges a few brief words of greeting with his colleagues, and resumes the work he left the previous day. His concentration is intense, and it is only after he has been acutely hungry for some time that he becomes aware of his hunger. Still he continues to work: one can never get back into the feeling of a thing after a meal. When he can bear the strain no longer he goes out. If he has a little money in his pocket, he walks perhaps to the Restaurant Wadja, which has been a landmark in the Quarter for many years, and where the art-loving Polish proprietress gives her clientele of artists and models a nourishing meals for a minimum of francs. The place is pleasant, and conducive to slow eating and sitting over coffee afterward, but Marc has not the time for that. His afternoon is all planned: there are at least three exhibitions he wants to see before he goes home to spend an hour or so painting a still life on which he is working.

He gets a friend to go along to the exhibits with him. They walk in leisurely fashion through the streets, talking, discussing, arguing ceaselessly. He arrives back in his room in the Rue Boissonade at about half past five and sits down to work. At quarter to seven he goes out to buy food for dinner: two friends are coming to eat with him. He buys a half kilo of tomatoes, several loaves of bread and a liter of wine. It has been agreed that the other two will bring a good-sized steak. When they arrive, the steak proves to be not quite so large as he had expected, but in any case, there is enough. Over the meal they talk interminably about art and literature, as usual. If the weather permits, they may walk very slowly up toward the Seine, continuing their talk as though they were scarcely conscious of having left the room.

But suddenly Marc Raimbault says a hurried good night and dashes precipitately down a side street. He has a date with Nicole. He has known her almost a year now. One magnificent day last spring he had gone to the Jardin du Luxembourg to sit a while in the sun after lunch, changing chairs every so often, whenever the guardian approached, so as not to have to pay, and there she had been, playing the same game. So far he has not met her family: for one thing, they live way out by the Porte Maillot. Now Marc goes rapidly toward the Boulevard Saint-Michel. Nicole is standing on the curb in front of a café on the corner of the Rue Soufflot. He takes her arm and they walk toward the Luxembourg. For once Marc does not talk – only a word now and then. There is no need for many words. When they come to the Rue Auguste-Comte their pace slackens. In the shadows, touching the iron grill-work of the fence, they stand quietly. Passers-by pay them no attention: not even a stray *agent de police* arrives to bother them. A few times during the year, when he knew his landlady was going to be absent, Marc has dared to take Nicole home to his little room, but it is very risky: the old lady has already expressed her views only too clearly on that subject. Marc's predecessor was put out for just such behavior, and losing a cheap room is a major tragedy. So Marc and Nicole remain standing in the shadows of the Rue Auguste-Comte.

Eventually they start to walk again, more slowly now, toward the *Metro* station of Notre-Dame-des-Champs. The last train leaves at 12:45, and it is imperative that Nicole catch it. At the *guichet* he buys two tickets. They go down into the tunnel, and there on the end of the platform, while the sweeper cries: "*Balai! Balai!*" they make their adieux. The rumble of the arriving train covers their final words. They run along the platform after the train, Nicole gets into the last car alone, Marc stands a moment looking after her, and then goes back up the stairs into the street, to return to the Rue Boissonade and sleep.

APART FROM THE ACTUAL PHYSICAL HARDSHIPS involved in becoming or being an artist in Paris, the city provides some very definite advantages. As might be expected, these are primarily psychological, which is precisely why they are of such great importance to artists. For one thing, in Paris any kind of artist is a respected citizen, not a social exception. His civil status is on a par with that of any professional man. And this sensible attitude on the part of the populace has its practical concomitants as well. For instance, when I was a composer in Paris and wanted to send manuscript music through the mail, I was allowed to mark it *papiers d'affaires*, which meant that it received first-class handling without costing anything like the first-class rate. A music manuscript is extremely heavy, and the difference was enormous.

Then, too, the French are so accustomed to the extravagant behavior of artists and their friends that it takes something fairly excessive to call forth their disapproval. Whether this is true tolerance or merely indifference is not important to the artist. He is left alone to live, dress and love as he likes. It is taken for granted by the French that everyone is an individual and that the artist is likely to express an individuality somewhat different from the norm, and that is that.

THERE IS ANOTHER PHENOMENON which serves to keep the affections of artists turned upon Paris, and that is the fact that if one succeeds, the returns are well worth the investment. It is extraordinary how much money the so-called modern masters of Paris manage to earn. Well-known painters in America consider themselves fortunate if they take in $10,000 a year. In Paris it is not unusual for them to make several times that amount. A certain Latin-American painter, not yet what one would call a "modern master," and not particularly well-known either in America or in Europe, earned over $75,000 in Paris last year. And that despite the fact that it is a distinct disadvantage for a painter not to be French, since the French are surprisingly nationalistic when it comes to buying pictures. Thus one can imagine the incomes of French painters like Braque, Rouault, Matisse or Dufy. All of which is a way of saying that once a painting career gets going in Paris it really goes. The buying of pictures by the French is done largely on a speculative basis. It is big business, and it's the signature that counts.

Speaking of signatures, I am reminded of an amusing incident which recently occurred. There is always a group of Spanish painters living in Paris, and they usually form a little nucleus of their own, apart from the others, with whom they do not get on too well. Recently they have been gathering at the Dôme, headed by the ex-surrealist Dominguez. One of their number, a young man named Ortiz, one day found himself a little more broke than usual. In fact, he had nothing – nothing but a lump of gold which he had been saving for a long time against just such an emergency. The obvious person to sell it to, they all agreed, was Picasso; he was a fellow Spaniard, a fellow painter and fortunately a very rich man. But when Ortiz took the gold to the master, Picasso told him that he had no use for it. "However," he added, seeing the expression on Ortiz' face, "leave it with me for a few days and I'll see what I can do."

Ortiz went away just about as unhappy as when he had come, sat down despondently once again on the *terrasse* of the Dôme, and waited. In the meantime, Picasso was feverishly studying the essentials of the goldsmith's craft, one of the few which he had until then neglected. He smelted the gold, made it into a small, rather Aztec-looking mask, with features in relief, and engraved his signature on the back. When Ortiz called at his studio to see whether the master had found a buyer for his gold, Picasso handed him the mask, saying: "I think you can get exactly three times as much for this as you would have gotten for your gold." The estimate proved to be quite accurate.

The fierce competition among painters in Paris is somewhat offset by the great consumption of artistic by-products. Such things as show windows, posters, packaging and even stage sets are done not by specialists in these lines but by professional painters. Then there is the fact that many more people in France are interested in painting, to the point of investing in it, than in most other countries. There is a great, long list of French painters whose names are unknown outside France, but whose canvases bring good prices in Paris because people like to have them hanging on their walls. You are likely to find these adorning the offices of your doctor, dentist or lawyer. And the buyer is also an amateur collector, keenly aware of the value of his acquisitions, and has a sharp eye out for fluctuations in the market price of the works of those who interest him. This sort of purchaser seldom buys the work of the very young: if the beginner sells at all, it will usually be to foreigners visiting Paris, and not to the French.

As to the American painters living in Paris, one can safely say that they sell exclusively to Americans. The French are almost wholly ignorant of, and uninterested in, American painting: it has no value on the Paris exchange. This, of course, is not of any great interest to the many American painters who live in Paris: it is not why they are there in any case. Nor are they there to study. Of the 3000 students at the Beaux Arts, only about two dozen are Americans. Generally they have chosen La Ville Lumière as a home for one of two reasons: they like the life there (they live more pleasantly than they could at home on the same amount of money) or they want an exhibit in a Paris gallery.

It means a great deal for an American painter or sculptor, once he has got back home, to have had a one-man show in Paris at a reputable gallery. Having shown in Paris is like having had an official seal of approval placed on one's product, because it would seem to mean that the work has passed muster in the halls of the highest artistic criteria. In reality it means no such thing. It means primarily that the artist has been able to raise the cash for such an exhibit. If there are reviews at all they will be good, and that means that he has been able to afford them as well. There is probably no other metropolis where criticism is quite so venal as in Paris. (The reverse of the medal is that the public has a healthy distrust of all criticism, so that it is pretty much without effect in any case.) But to the American artist it is all-important. The reviews of such a show are an open-sesame to exhibits of his own in American galleries, and they also help tremendously in selling his work in the States.

A FRIEND OF MINE, a partner in one of the more important galleries on the Right Bank, told me an absurd story the other day. A newspaper critic they were expecting had failed to put in an appearance at a certain exhibition, either before, during or after the *vernissage*, and the gallery was perplexed. Then a favorable review was published in the critic's paper, and the gallery was still further perplexed. A few days later, the critic came into the gallery, picked up an expensive art book, and putting it under his arm, was about to go out again. An attendant asked if there was not some mistake. "Oh, no," he said airily. "There's no mistake. I gave this show a good review last week. Remember?" And he walked off with the book, which he probably took around the corner and sold.

If you want your work exhibited in Paris you must be prepared to pay through the nose for the privilege. The critics must be entertained, wined and dined, and the show itself will cost anywhere from 50,000 to 300,000 francs at an average gallery, and more than that at certain particularly elegant places. If you happen to be an American, a pretext will very likely be found for increasing the price. The French feel that it is a distinct injustice for an American to get anything for the same price as a Frenchman.

To avoid this sort of exploitation – indeed, to make it possible to show their works in Paris at all – a group of American painters banded together and rented a small shop not far from Notre-Dame, in the Rue Saint-Julien-le-Pauvre. They made it into a gallery and named it Galerie 8. I don't know how many were involved in the venture at the beginning, but at present there are more than twenty. There they show not only their own things but those of artists outside the co-operative as well. (So far they have shown only Americans.) In this way they have cut down the cost of a show to about 18,000 francs, and the saving makes a great difference to the artist, you may be sure. And, being in a neighborhood that American tourists are likely to visit because it is written up in the guidebooks and has night clubs like Le Caveau de la Bolée, the place has been successful.

PARIS IS ALMOST constantly the scene of some artistic scandal or other, in which everyone gets very much excited and nothing happens. Last year there was another theft of famous pictures, this time not from the Louvre but from the Musée d'Art Moderne. The two young men who engineered the thing had chosen well: their loot included the famous *Woman Ironing* of Picasso and a 40,000,000-franc Renoir (which even with the franc where it is today is still over $100,000). Nevertheless, when questioned by the police they stoutly maintained that their project had been motivated solely by affection for the pictures and not by desire for gain. (In America they would probably have claimed they had done it for kicks.) There is supposed to be a diabolically clever forger loose in Paris, painting and selling long-lost masterpieces right and left. Everyone says he is a well-known figure, but cannot be brought to justice because of his high connections. If you try to discover just what the pictures are and whose work they purport to be, the trail becomes vague and leads into the dark. However, it goes far enough to show in what direction the Parisian imagination goes when it decides to create a legend.

Recently the Place de la Concorde was the scene of a short scandal that would have been worthy of an early René Clair film. A bearded and distinguished elderly gentleman carrying a brief case appeared one morning at the foot of the obelisk in the middle of the vast square and began to make preparations for a climb to the top. Immediately the police came up and informed him that such a thing was not only expressly forbidden but unheard of. The gentleman took from his pocket a bundle of official-looking papers. He had been, he said, to the proper authorities to ask permission to study the hieroglyphs on the top of the obelisk, and after some surprise at hearing that there were such marks (since everyone had always thought that all the hieroglyphs were on the *sides* of the obelisk and had been deciphered long ago), they had decided in the interests of science and art to grant his unusual request.

There was no mistaking the authenticity of the papers, so somewhat reluctantly the police let him continue with his scholarly preparations. Still, remarked one of the dubious *agents de police*, in all the years the monument had been standing there, no one had ever attempted such a thing.

"Yes, yes, I know," said the old gentleman, giving order to his subordinates for the proper placing of the ladder.

By the time everything was set, and the bearded savant was ready to climb, it was noon and there was a good crowd watching. The old gentleman, still carrying his brief case, scaled to the top of the needle with astonishing alacrity and proceeded, piece by piece, to divest himself of his articles of clothing, throwing them to the four winds. In the meantime his subordinates had removed the ladder and disappeared into the rapidly growing crowd. The policemen said to each other that they had known all along he was a maniac, and they waved their arms and shouted up at him. When all the clothing was gone except for a pair of underdrawers, the old Egyptologist reached into his brief case, withdrawing a folding umbrella and a larger banner. When he had opened the umbrella he held it over his head. Then he let the banner unroll down the side of the obelisk, and the populace read: *When you buy a Fountain Pen insist on an Obelisk.*

The gentleman was finally brought to earth by means of fire hoses, but not before several thousand delighted Parisians had enjoyed their lunch hour more than usually. And while I am on the subject, that lunch hour, which lasts not one hour but two or even three, is a very important feature of French culture. It gives the poorer employee time to go home and have a leisurely meal; it provides the more affluent with the opportunity to stop at a café for *apéritifs*, go on to a restaurant and eat slowly (to the accompaniment of conversation, not a program of canned music), and to proceed afterward to another café for coffee; or perhaps, weather permitting, even to stroll in a park. For Paris is a city whose customs have evolved from a serious application of the theory that life is meant above all to be lived, and not dedicated to some ulterior abstract concept. It is a city designed to be lived in, not to be used as a market or workshop. And since living, no matter on how much or how little money, is always an art, it is not surprising that the artists should appear to have mastered it more successfully than any other group.

I HAVE ALWAYS believed that Paris is most strongly itself during twilight. At that hour, whatever the weather or season, the vast range of grays in the stone of which it is built becomes fully visible: appearance and essence concur for a few exquisite moments. Why is it called "gay Paree?" I have no idea. If you look you can see the open soul of the city anywhere along the Seine from the Quai de Javel to the Quai Saint-Bernard. It is there, along the banks of the river and among the bridges, that you touch the spirit of Paris, and while that spirit is not a tragic one, surely it has little to do with gaiety. Rather, it bears witness to an essential consciousness of the need in life for beauty, and to an understanding of the use of proportion and harmony in the achievement of beauty. It provides the artist with heartening, ever-present proof that man-made beauty is attainable, and does so in such a natural fashion that when one thinks of the banks of the Seine one thinks simultaneously of artists, for the two belong together.

Fez

Holiday, July 1950

F EZ IS A CITY whose site was chosen purely for aesthetic
reasons. Before its founding there was no village –
nothing but a cup-shaped valley of pleasing proportions
nestling at the edge of the place where the fertile plain goes
slightly mad, drops off into tortured, eroded, semidesert country.
Idriss II came down out of the Djebel Zerhoun one day at the
beginning of the 9th Century, saw the spot, admired the way the
river broke into many separate streams as it rushed downward
through the little valley and, with the uncomplicated simplicity
of that heroic age, determined to build a city there which would
outshine the one his father had founded among the Berbers
to the north. As the homes, mosques and universities grew in
splendor the inhabitants came to have a fierce pride in their
city, a pride which is still justified, since the place is virtually
unchanged. Many of the Fassi believe that the Western world is
about to disintegrate; obviously it can only be Islam which will
triumph! This very narrowness of ideas has kept the place pure,
kept it medieval. For the Westerner does not so much feel in
a distant place here: the removal is rather in time. A thousand
years ago the cities of Europe must have been very much like
this; from all accounts there is little difference save in detail.

There are elderly men in the town who have never to this
day seen an automobile. It is a self-imposed rule, a kind of

protest, of course, since by walking to one of the many gates and peering through they could see clusters of ancient trucks and buses outside. Sidi Driss el Yacoubi, for instance, a delightful old gentleman who looks as so many Fassi do, rather like Santa Claus, spends his time between his home, the Djamaa Andalus (the mosque with the great façade, which is at the top of the hill in his quarter), the homes of his friends, and his little garden; all of these places are well within the surrounding walls. Years ago he moved about occasionally from town to town like most Moroccans, but that was before the advent of the French.

It is a small excursion to the garden; the servant carries along tea, sugar and teapot. The charcoal, mint and water are already there. Toward sunset, when the many storks have stopped circling and making their ratchet-like calls, a little fire is built in an earthen brazier, tea is brewed, and Sidi Driss el Yacoubi asks the servant to play a while on his lute. The conversation is likely to center around the taxes collected by the French – very small taxes by our standards, but hotly resented by the Moroccans, who consider themselves a sovereign people, not colonials in any sense.

Ask Sidi Driss why he is not interested in seeing an automobile. He replies: "What good is it? The wheels go round fast, yes. The horn is loud, yes. You arrive sooner than on a mule, yes. But why should you want to arrive sooner? What do you do when you get there that you couldn't do if you got there later? Perhaps the French think if they go fast enough death won't catch up with them." And he laughs, because he thinks that Western civilization is attempting to escape from a fate which is predetermined, "written" as they put it in Arabic; any such effort naturally is doomed to failure.

Fez is pastoral. On all sides the sheep graze beneath the olive trees, right down to the city walls, and it is forbidden to build outside the wall. Even in the center of town one does not manage to shake off the impression of being in a limitless village rather than a city, perhaps because of the constant presence of rustic things – bare earth, straw, the ceilings of reed latticework over the alleys, the white herons and storks wading by the banks of the rivers, and the odors in the air; cedar and thuya wood, the ubiquitous mint, ripe figs or orange blossoms, depending on the season, and the familiar smells of the stable. No passageway is paved. One can take only a few short steps without rubbing up against a donkey, a mule or a horse.

The great wall surrounding the city is intact; certain of the gates, such as Bab Mahrouk (where until recently the heads of the Sultan's enemies were exposed on pikes), are still locked at sundown, and many of the inner gates across the passageways that serve as streets are regularly closed at night, so that the man who has stayed out late and wants to take short cuts to get home often finds he must go all the way back to where he started and try another route.

But a polite host will never let his guest depart unaccompanied. If there is no slave or servant handy he will go himself until he comes across one of the public guardians curled up asleep at the side of the passageway, and entrust his guest to this ragged phantom. Or if he happens to meet a younger acquaintance he will ask him to see that the guest arrives home safely. It may be several miles and one may complain that one prefers to go alone; there is no escape; the other will be adamant. He remains until the end, and you both go uphill and down in the darkness – through tunnels, across bridges, nearly always accompanied in the nocturnal silence by the faint sound of running water behind the walls, until you reach your door.

THERE ARE NO true streets in the city, and neither automobiles nor wagons can enter; because the passageways are not flat, but often turn into stairways, not even bicycles can be used. Everything that moves inside the walls moves on legs, so one hears no horns or bells. What rises from the city by day is a humming: two hundred thousand human voices blended into one sound. At night there is absolute silence, unless the women of some house have gone upstairs to the terrace and are beating drums. Five times a day the muezzin calls from the tower of each mosque, as in all Moslem towns; but there are more than a hundred mosques, and they can all be heard at once from the surrounding hills. There is a custom peculiar to Fez whereby, shortly before the daybreak call to prayer, the muezzins sing for half hour or more. If one can imagine a hundred powerful flamenco singers at varying distances, projecting their songs from the minarets over the silent city, one can understand that the effect is electrifying.

In the hearts of the Fassi there is a great nostalgia for the golden age of Spain; like the *janna* of the Koran, Andalusia is supposed to have been a collection of palaces whose gardens were watered with rushing streams; fountains played eternally in the rooms and the courtyards were planted with trees so that the rustle of leaves could be heard behind the music of the lutes. Fez calls its music Andalus, because the idiom was evolved in Spain at the time of the Khalifat of Cordoba and brought back here when that country had to be evacuated. The Fassi are firm believers in the importance of satisfying the senses: they love perfumes, colors, rich textiles. If at the same time they place a high value on the accumulation of money, it is only so that they may surround themselves with things that will give them sensual pleasure; they mistrust and ridicule miserliness. When they romanticize about the past I remark that Fez has all those things that Andalusia once had. "Ah, but it is more beautiful there." Of course.

It is important to know when to agree and when to disagree. Conversation seems sometimes to be a game whose principal object is to catch the other person off his guard and make him commit a *faux pas*. If your host says to you: "I am a Cherif; there are six thousand Chorfa in Morocco; that is a *great* many," you will not be invited again if you agree. The Chorfa are the descendants of Ali, Mohammed's son-in-law, and form the country's aristocracy.) You must exclaim, "Only six thousand! That is very few. I thought there were many more." However, if he says: "We want to be Americans. It is better to be American than Moroccan," you must agree briefly, and thank him, because if you protest politely you will show him that you actually believe he means what he says, which of course is impossible, and you will prove yourself extremely ill-bred.

Once when I wanted to go to Karia in the mountains and had been told vaguely there was a bus that made the trip, I asked the waiter in a native restaurant what time and from where the bus left. The boy said simply that there was no such bus. But the manager of the restaurant heard me reply that there must be a bus to Karia. He pushed the boy aside impatiently, "Of course there is," he said. "It leaves from Bab el Guissa at half past six in the morning." The next day after a three-and-a-half-hour wait I went around to the restaurant to inquire again, probably somewhat peevishly, just when the bus usually made its appearance. The manager looked startled. "You've been waiting since half past six? But there's no bus, monsieur." It took a certain amount of self-control for me to point out to him that this information was not completely in accordance with what he had told me the day before. "Oh, yesterday," he smiled, "I just said that to please you."

The modern-minded, bourgeois Fassi are very different from old Sidi Driss el Yacoubi. Sidi Abdallah Lalami lives in a house whose main patio was originally two hundred feet square. At the death of his father he and his brother built a wall across the middle of the court, making a separate house for each of them. As usual, from the outside there is nothing to see but a windowless, crumbling gray wall rising high above the dirt-floored passageway. Inside, the court is paved with mosaics; there are fountains, grape arbors, orange trees. Twenty-four stone columns support the galleries that line the three original sides of the patio. Silk awnings twenty-five feet square are let down to cover the doorways of the enormous rooms inside, if the womenfolk happen to be there. An unexpected call can precipitate great excitement when the ladies are in the court. Slaves rush to hide them by holding up an old sheet kept outside for that purpose.

Once I glanced inadvertently to the side as I passed through, and saw the women cowering against the walls, their hands over their faces; they were making absurd little moans of simulated fright.

I WAS APOLOGETIC to Sidi Abdallah for my behavior.

"Not at all," he said. "It's silly, all this hiding. Next time you come, I shall present you not only to my wife but to my daughters." This incredible thing he did, to the surprise and, I suspect, disapproval of the ladies concerned. Since that time he always

The bellboys at the Hotel Belvedere, where Bowles lived in Fez in 1947. "I never returned to the hotel until night time, and it was always locked, the lights were out... I would knock at the door and hear a giggling inside. It was these two; they had already gone to bed. And then they had to get up and open the door..." (PB)

made a point of calling his wife and mother in at some point during my visit – only occasionally a daughter.

Sidi Abdallah has a slave girl by whom he has had a child. The slave market has been abolished by the French, but the institution of slavery still persists. There is no distinction made by Koranic law between a legitimate child and one of the same father by a concubine – even in matters relating to heritage. However, it does not take much perception to see that little Hajja, although she is treated kindly, belongs much more to her mother's world than to her father's: she is the errand-runner for the entire household.

Dinner in Fez is a complex ritual. It is essential to plan to devote at least five hours of your evening to it. At the innumerable dinners I have eaten with Sidi Abdallah in his home never once has the meal been shared with any of the women. That would be going too far! There are always several other male guests, however, often as many as twenty. The slave carries out one course, brings in the next on another huge tray. Everyone eats out of the same mass of food with his fingers, using only the thumb and first two fingers of the right hand. Sometimes Sidi Abdallah hires a small orchestra (rebab, lute, tambourine, hand drum) to divert his guests, "to make the stomach happier."

A MERCHANT from Ouezzane brings forth a little tin box and offers me some of his hashish. I scoop the black paste out with my finger and eat it. Soon afterward the last course is cleared away and a massive samovar is brought in. The food the men have left is scraped together in the kitchen for the women to eat.

By the third glass of tea there is no doubt that the hashish has begun to take effect. I laugh, perhaps a little strangely, since the others also laugh. All at once the great room, the seated figures, the shoes ranged by the door, the fountain beyond, are remote and unlikely, although I remain quite aware of each word being spoken. I lie back on the cushions and announce: "*Safi ... el majoun.*" They laugh some more, continue talking. Certain of them fall asleep, stretching out on the gaudy mattresses that line the four walls of the room. I wish violently to be back home in my own bed because I know how many strange and agonizing months it is going to take to navigate the three miles of passageway and tunnels which lie between Derb el Heurra and my home. And I should like to be alone when the visions start.

I find myself standing up, looking down at my distant feet, saying I must go. The protests are endless, but eventually I get out into the night, a servant having been sent with me. My only thought then is to escape him by darting into a doorway. Obviously it is impossible. The moon is full, unbelievably bright; the city looks like an early movie, when in order to make a night sequence they printed scenes shot in sunlight on blue film. The expedition lasts forever, but I do get home somehow, even though it is not before the visions have already begun to project themselves on the moonlit walls around me as I stumble along.

With the growth of Casablanca, Fez has lost much of its commercial importance, even during the few years I have known it. It is no longer the great market of Northern Morocco. Thus the vast crowds that used to gather outside the walls and in the immense Mechouar near the Sultan's palace, attracting all the ambulant dancers, musicians and fakirs in the region, are no more.

The barbaric side of Moroccan life is to be found elsewhere – not here. As if further to make Fez the purely religious and academic center which every good Musulman desires it to be, the Sultan in 1937 issued an edict forbidding public demonstrations of the two dissident religious sects which have been much in evidence here: the Gnaoua and the Aïssaoua. This does not mean that the cults have been abolished. On certain occasions one has only to travel an hour from Fez to see the Aïssaoua eating their scorpions and serpents, lacerating themselves and drinking their own blood while the women scream and dance themselves into unconsciousness. The Gnaoua are Negroes and the Aïssaoua are Berbers; both have adapted the Islamic faith in such ways as to suit their emotional needs, but the orthodox Moslem population of Morocco will allow them no latitude.

This disapproval of the indigenous elements in the culture is carried to an extreme in the case of the students who attend the college of Moulay Idriss and the various *médersas* (theological seminaries). These young bourgeois object to Moroccan music and customs, even to Moroccan clothing. Their overwhelming obsession is to do away as speedily as possible with whatever is specifically Moroccan. However, their loyalties remain wholly within the Moslem world; they are not interested in becoming Westerners. Cairo is their idea of a really civilized place. They sit for hours under the willow trees in the outdoor cafés by the river, dressed in clothing more or less European, listening to the latest records by Abd el Wahab, Om Kalsoum or Farid el Atrache; they patronize the Cinema Bou Jeloud because it shows Egyptian films. Perhaps one viable excuse for this attitude is the great disparity between the social liberty they know exists elsewhere and the complete lack of it here.

On Friday, the day of rest, the town goes to stroll along the paths around the lake in Bou Jeloud. Here sometimes a group of young men will hazard some fleeting remarks to a ground of veiled female figures; apart from such meetings, which are viewed with distaste by the older people going by, there is strict segregation between the sexes; the marriages still take place without the groom's ever having seen the bride "There is no love in Morocco," say the young men bitterly.

THE FRENCH QUARTER, built, thanks to the discernment of Marshal Lyautey, at a distance of several miles from Fez itself, is the most changed of all since prewar days. The buildings, hastily erected in typical colonial-exposition style, are in a lamentable condition. Civic pride, which existed to a certain extent at least while things were new, appears to have disappeared entirely, and the place looks like a slum. The flimsy edifices, being of European build, require European materials for repairs; these are still not available. It is a depressing spot, a potpourri of broken windows, peeling paint, cracking concrete, wheezing old automobiles, short-tempered Frenchmen and begging native children – a hideous contrast to the soothing homogeneous beauty of the old city.

The Fassi have always known how to live – they still do. And a good many of them, far more than one would expect, have the means to live well. There is a complete lack of nervous tension in the life, an utter ignorance of what it means to be bored, all of which makes for a satisfaction in existence, a thing that very few Westerners are able to attain. At the same time, I suppose the average American would consider the life of even the wealthiest Fassi shocking in its absolute disregard of the principles of hygiene. The Moroccan, educated or otherwise, simply does not believe in germs. Every aspect of his daily life gives eloquent proof of this. One of the most amusing is the lollipop rental stand in the quarter of Guerniz, where the children pay according to the length of time they keep the lollipop in their mouths.

"But germs exist," you expostulate. "You can see them under a microscope." Your unruffled companion will reply: "For you they exist, therefore they can hurt you. For us there is only the will of Allah." And that is the stone wall against which any such argument inevitably crashes. The heavy casualties of the cholera epidemic in 1944 could have been avoided if the Moroccans had not refused to report their cases to the authorities.

Little by little, things do change. There is less vermin in the homes than there was in 1931; I can attest that DDT is exhibited in certain shops so someone must buy it. Yet the following passage from *El H'aoudh*, a somewhat simplified version of the Koranic laws written in Berber for Moroccans a few centuries ago, still makes perfectly good sense today: "One may be excused from Friday prayers and from praying with the Imam if there is a great deal of mud or if it is raining very hard. One may also be excused because of elephantiasis, leprosy or old age, or if one has no clothes to put on, or is waiting to be pardoned for a crime, or if one has eaten onions. These are valid excuses. A wedding feast is not an excuse, nor is blindness if one can feel one's way to the mosque."

FISH TRAPS AND
PRIVATE BUSINESS

JOURNAL (1950); THEIR HEADS ARE GREEN, 1963

WELIDENIYA ESTATE, CEYLON, MAY, 1950

THE LANDSCAPE IS RESTLESS – a sea of disorderly hills rising steeply. In all directions it looks the same. The hills are sharp bumps with a thin, hairy vegetation that scarcely covers them. Most of this is rubber, and the rubber is wintering. Mr. Murrow, the planter, says that in another week or two the present brownish-yellow leaves will be replaced by new ones. Where the rubber stops the tea begins. There the earth looks raw. The rocks show between the low bushes; here and there a mulberry tree with lopped branches, planted for shade.

On top of one of these steep humps is the bungalow, spread out all along the crest. Directly below to the southwest, almost straight down, is the river with its sandy banks. But in between, the steep declivity is terraced with tea, and by day the voices of the Tamil pickers are constantly audible. At night there are fires outside the huts on the opposite bank of the river.

The air is hot and breathless, the only respite coming in the middle of the afternoon, when it rains. And afterward, when it has stopped, one has very little energy until night falls. However, by then it is too late to do anything but talk or read. The lights work on the tea-factory circuit. When everyone is in bed, Mr. Murrow calls from under his mosquito net through the open door of his bedroom to a Tamil waiting outside on the lawn. Five minutes later all the lights slowly die, and the house is in complete darkness save for the small oil lamps on the shelves in the bathrooms. Nothing is locked. The bedrooms have swinging shutters, like old-fashioned barroom doors, that reach to within two feet of the floor. The windows have no glass – only curtains of very thin silk. All night long a barefoot watchman shouldering a military rifle pads round and round the bungalow. Sometimes, when it is too hot to sleep, I get up and sit out on the verandah. Once there was no air even there, and I moved a chair to the lawn. On his first trip around, the watchman saw me, and made a grunting sound which I interpreted as one of disapproval. It may not have been; I don't know.

The nights seem endless, perhaps because I lie awake listening to the unfamiliar sounds made by the insects, birds and reptiles. By now I can tell more or less how late it is by the section of the nocturnal symphony that has been reached. In the early evening there are things that sound like cicadas. Later the geckos begin. (There is a whole science of divination based on the smallest details of the behavior of these little lizards; while the household is still up they scurry silently along the walls and ceiling catching insects, and it is only well on into the night that they begin to call out, from one side of the room to the other.) Still later there is a noise like a rather rasping katydid. By three in the morning everything has stopped but a small bird whose cry is one note of pure tone and unvarying pitch. There seem always to be two of these in the rain tree outside my room; they take great care to sing antiphonally, and the one's voice is exactly a whole tone above the other's. Sometimes in the morning Mrs. Murrow asks me if I heard the cobra sing during the night. I have never been able to answer in the affirmative, because in spite of her description ("like a silver coin falling against a rock"), I have no clear idea of what to listen for.

We drink strong, dark tea six or seven times a day. No pretext is needed for Mr. Murrow to ring the bell and order it. Often when it seems perfectly good to me, he will send it back with the complaint that it has been poorly brewed. All the tea consumed in the bungalow is top-leaf tea, hand-picked by Mr. Murrow himself. He maintains that there is none better in the world, and I am forced to agree that it tastes like a completely different beverage from any tea I have had before.

The servants enter the rooms bowing so low that their backs form an arch, and their hands are held above their heads in an attitude of prayer. Last night I happened to go into the dining room a few minutes before dinner, and old Mrs. Van Dort, Mrs. Murrow's mother, was already seated at her place. The oldest servant, Siringam, suddenly appeared in the doorway of the verandah leading to the kitchen, bent over double with his hands above his head, announcing the entrance of a kitchen maid bearing the dog's meal. The woman carried the dish to the old lady, who sternly inspected it and then commanded her in Singhalese to put it down in a corner for the animal. "I must always look at the dog's food," she told me, "otherwise the servants eat part of it and the poor dog grows thinner and thinner."

"But are the servants that hungry?"

"Certainly not!" she cried. "But they like the dog's food better than their own."

Mrs. Murrow's son by a former marriage came to spend last night, bringing his Singhalese wife with him; she had already told me at some length of how she resisted the marriage for three years because of the girl's blood. Mrs. Murrow is of the class which calls itself Burgher, claiming an unbroken line of descendency from the Dutch settlers of two centuries ago. I have yet to see a Burgher who looks Caucasian, the admixture of Singhalese being always perfectly discernible. It is significant that the Burghers feel compelled to announce their status to newcomers; the apparent reason is to avoid being taken for "natives." The tradition is that they are Europeans, and one must accept it without question. The son is a tall, gentle man who wears a gray cassock and keeps his hands folded tightly all the time, a habit which makes him look as though he were prey to a constant inner anguish. He is a minister of the Anglican church, but this does not keep him from being of the extreme left politically. His joy is to stir up dissension among his parishioners by delivering sermons in which Communists are depicted as holding high posts in heaven. He has told me some amusing anecdotes of his life as a teacher in the outlying provinces before he was ordained. Of these the ones I remember have to do with the strange faculty the children have for speaking passable English without knowing the meaning of the words they use. One boy, upon being asked to answer which he would prefer to be, a tailor or a lawyer, was unable to reply. "You know what a tailor is, don't you?" said Mr. Clasen. The boy said he did, and he also knew the functions of a lawyer, but he could not answer the question. "But why?" insisted Mr. Clasen, thinking that perhaps some recondite bit of Buddhist philosophy was about to be forthcoming. But the boy finally said, "I know tailor and I know lawyer, but please, sir, what is be?" Another boy wrote, "The horse is a noble animal, but when irritated will not do so."

When you ask a question of a Singhalese who does not know English, he is likely to react in a most curious fashion. First he looks swiftly at you, then he looks away, his features retreating into an expression of pleasant contemplation, as if your voice were an agreeable but distant memory that he had just recalled and thought it worthwhile to savor briefly. After a few seconds of giving himself up to this inward satisfaction he goes on about his business without ever looking your way again – not even if you insist, or wait a bit and make your inquiry afresh. You have become invisible. At the resthouses in the country, where the members of the personnel feel they must put up some sort of front, they say, "Oh, oh, oh," in a commiserating tone ("oh" is "yes"), as if they understood only too well, and were forbearing to say more for the sake of decorum. Then they wag their heads back and forth, from side to side, a gesture which reminds you of a metronome going rather too quickly, keeping their bright eyes on you, listening politely until you have finished speaking, whereupon they smile beautifully and walk away. The servants who do speak English insist upon calling you "master," which is disconcerting because it seems to imply responsibility of some sort on your part. They also use the third person instead of the second: "Master wishing eat now?" The youngest generation, however, has almost unanimously adopted the more neutral "sir" (pronounced "sar"), as a substitute for the too colonial-sounding "master."

There is a long, thin, green adder that likes to lie in the sun on top of the tea bushes; one of these bit a woman recently while she was picking. Mr. Murrow hurried to the scene and, taking up a pruning knife, cut off the tip of her finger, applying crystals of potassium permanganate to the flesh. She was saved in this way, but as soon as she regained consciousness, she went to the police and filed a complaint, accusing Mr. Murrow of causing irreparable damage to her finger. When the investigator came to the estate, he heard the details of the case and told the woman that thanks to Mr. Murrow's quick action she was still alive; without it she would have been dead. The woman's husband, who was present at the hearing, jumped up and drew a knife on the investigator, but was prevented from hurting him. When they had subdued the man, he wailed across at the investigator: "You have no sense! I could have collected plenty of rupees for that finger, and I would have given you half."

The public toilets in the villages, instead of being marked *Ladies* or *Women*, bear signs that read: *Urinals for Females.*

A sign on the side of a building in Akmimana: *Wedding Cakes and other thing Supplied for Weddings in Convenient Times.*

Another, in Colombo: *Dr. Rao's Tonic – a Divine Drug.*

A Burgher who works in the travel agency of the Grand Oriental Hotel and who had seen me when I first arrived, said to me a few weeks later when I stopped in, "You're losing your color." "What?" I cried incredulously. "After all this time in the sun? I'm five shades darker than I was." He looked confused, but continued patiently, "That's what I say. You're losing your color."

K<small>ADUWELA</small>

T<small>HE</small> L<small>UNAWA</small> <small>RESTHOUSE</small> was a disagreeable place to stay, being directly opposite the railway station in the middle of a baking and unshaded patch of dried-up lawn. In the concrete cell I was given it was impossible to shut out the sounds made by the other guests, who happened to be extremely noisy. The room next to mine was occupied by a party of eight men, who spent the entire afternoon and evening giggling and guffawing. When I would walk past their door I could see them lying in their sarongs across the two beds which they had pushed together. In the dining room the radio never ceased blaring at maximum volume. The food was ghastly, and there was no mosquito net available for my bed and, therefore, no protection against the tiny insects that constantly brushed against my face in the dark, seeking to get under the sheet with me. When I finally got into the state of nerves they had been trying to induce, I jumped up, dressed and rushed out, to the horror of the boy lying on his mat across the front doorway. He too sprang up, went to an inner room to fetch the keeper, and together they cried out after me across the dark lawn: "Master going?"

"Coming back, coming back!" I called, and began to walk quickly up the road toward the lagoon. When I got to the bridge I stood awhile. The water was absolutely still, and there were dozens of pinkish flames guttering in lamps placed just at the surface, each with its unmoving reflection. And each lamp illumined a complex scaffolding of bamboo poles; these pale constructions scattered across the black expanse of water looked like precarious altars, and the fact that I knew they were fish traps made them no less extraordinary, no less beautiful. To break the silence a drum began to beat on the far shore. Presently a man came riding by on a bicycle; as he passed me he turned his flashlight into my face. The sight of me standing in that spot startled him, and he pedaled madly away across the bridge.

I walked on to Lunawa Junction, where I stood in the road listening to a radio in a corner "hotel" play Tamil music. (What the Singhalese call hotels are merely teahouses with three or four tables and a tiny space back of a screen or partition where there are mats on the floor for those who wish to rest.) People wandered past now and then and stared at me; I was clearly an object of great interest. Europeans never appear at night in such places. When I sat down on a culvert I was soon the center of a semicircle of men, some clad only in G-strings and with hair that reached halfway down their backs. It was no use talking to me in Singhalese, but they went right on trying. One who spoke English finally arrived and asked me if I would like to race him down the road. I declined, saying I was tired. This was true; it was after midnight, and I was beginning to wish there were some comfortable place in the neighborhood where I could lay my head. The English-speaking man then told me that they had all been asleep but had got up because someone had arrived with the news that a stranger was standing in the road.

While I sat there doing my best to make some sort of polite conversation, three older men in white robes came by and, seeing the crowd, stopped. These were obviously of a higher social station, and they were most disapproving of what they saw. One of them, who had rapidly been delegated as spokesman, stepped forward, indicated the band of wild-eyed, long-haired individuals, and said: "Hopeless people." I pretended not to understand, whereupon all three set to work repeating the same two words over and over, accenting equally each syllable. I was so fascinated with their performance that nearly all the nudists had disappeared into the dark before I realized they were leaving, and all at once I was sitting there facing only these three serious, chanting men. "Come," said the leader, and he took me by the arm and helped me up and started me walking – I won't say *forcing* me to walk, because his firmness was expressed with

Bowles included this image, captioned 'Peasant, Central Ceylon' in *Their Heads are Green*. The 'peasant', and the men 'clad only in G-strings' mentioned in this piece, are probably Vedhas – descendants of the island's indigenous tribal people (PB)

too much gentleness for that – but seeing to it that I did walk, with him and his friends, back to the road intersection where bats dipped in the air under the one street light. "Now you go to resthouse," he said, showing that he knew more English than the two-word refrain which had sufficed him until then. But then a second later, "Hopeless people," he sang, and the others, looking still more grave beneath the light, agreed with him once more. Lamely I protested that I should go back presently, when I felt like it, but they were adamant; it was clear that my personal desires were quite beside the point. They called to a boy who stood under a tree near the "hotel" and charged him to walk the mile with me back to the resthouse. For perhaps a minute I argued, half laughingly, half seriously, and then I turned and started up the road. They called good night and went on their way. The boy kept close beside me, partly out of fear, I imagine; and when I got to the bridge and stood still for a moment to look at the water and the lights, he pressed me to go on quickly, pretending there were crocodiles in the lagoon and that they came out of the water at night. I don't think he believed it at all, but he wanted to accomplish his mission and get to the safety of the resthouse as fast as he could. Trees harbor spirits here; the older and larger ones have niches carved into their trunks where the people put long-burning altar candles. The flickering lights attract the spirits, like moths, and keep them from leaving the tree and doing harm beyond its immediate vicinity. At the resthouse the man and the boy were waiting up for me. My road companion had no intention of augmenting his ordeal by going back across the lagoon unaccompanied; he curled up on the floor of the verandah and spent the night there. The gigglers had gone to sleep and there was quiet at last, but the insects were more numerous and active than they had been earlier. I did not have a very successful night.

I had already made arrangements to spend the next night at Homagama, where the resthouse is, or at least appears to be, somewhat superior. When the elderly resthouse keeper showed me his rooms there, he tried to get me to take an extension of the dining room, on the pretext that it would be quieter. The only other available room was next to his quarters, and that, he said apologetically, he was sure Master would not like at all. Since the room he was trying to give me had only three complete walls, the fourth being merely a wooden screen about five feet high over which I could see two gentlemen drinking ginger beer at a table, I unwisely decided upon the room adjoining his quarters. Once I was settled, with my luggage partially unpacked, and the servants had hung the mosquito net and brought in a very feeble oil lamp, I discovered my error. This room also was only a section of another room; in the part not inhabited by me a baby began to wail, and presently the voice of an extremely old woman rose in incantation. Whether it was a lullaby, a prayer, or merely a senile lamentation, I am still too unfamiliar with the culture of the land to tell. But it went on intermittently until dawn, when the sounds of the poultry, the crows in the mango trees, and the locomotives which passed by the doorway, blotted it out. Whenever the old lady would stop, the infant would wake her up; as soon as the baby ceased crying, she would start afresh and awaken the baby.

In the morning I discovered that there was a third room but that it was due to be occupied any moment by what is euphemistically called a "honeymoon couple." At six-thirty in the morning they arrived, and when they had left in the late afternoon, I was allowed to take it. It was vastly better, and I kept it for the next two nights, much to the keeper's disgust, since he had to put all the couples that arrived during that time into the other rooms. Given the fact that by far the larger part of his personal revenue comes in the form of gratuities from such parties, it is understandable that he should like to provide them with the best accommodations. Another expression used by resthouse keepers to refer to their honeymoon couples is "private business." Those concerned do not sign their names in the register, and for that privilege leave relatively large tips. The keeper at Kesbewa informed me that his rooms were all reserved for private business for the next six weeks.

During the late afternoon of the third day I had to leave. Unless one has special permission from the government to remain longer, one's stay in a resthouse is strictly limited to three nights, which is presumably ample time for whatever private business one may wish to conduct.

I engaged a bullock-cart with the body of an old-fashioned buggy, drawn by a small beige-colored *zebu*, and with the driver, who had never heard the English words "yes" and "no," started along the back roads through the forest for Kaduwela. There were a good many small villages on the way, and we had to stop at one so that the luggage, which was constantly slipping and falling out into the dust, could be rearranged and tied more securely. The driver brought a great length of thick but feeble rope for the purpose, and we went ahead. The incredible jolting became unbearable after a while; I had pains everywhere from my knees to my neck. The rope, of course, kept breaking, and the valises continued to slip and fall out. The charm of the landscape however had induced in me such a complete euphoria that nothing mattered. I only wanted it to stay light as long as possible so I could go on being aware of my surroundings. The forest was not constant; it opened again and again onto wide stretches of green paddy fields where herons waded. Each time we plunged again into the woods it was darker, until finally I could no longer distinguish areca palms from bamboo. People walking along the road were carrying torches, made of palm leaves bound tightly together that burned with a fierce red flame, they held them high above their heads, and the sparks dropped behind them all along the way. In one village, cinnamon bark had been piled against the houses. The odor enveloped the whole countryside. Now every ten minutes or so the driver stopped, got down, and put a new wax taper into one or the other of the two little lamps at the sides of the buggy. It was very late when we got to Kaduwela.

Here the resthouse is on the river, the Kelani Ganga, which flows by at the base of the rocks, just a few feet below the verandah. At night in the quiet I can sometimes hear a slight gurgle out there, but I am never sure whether it is a fish or merely the current. Occasionally a whole string of bamboo barges floats swiftly by without a sound; if one did not see the moving red spots, the braziers where the members of the crew are cooking their food, one would not know it was there.

HIKKADUWA

IN CEYLON the Christmas-tree light is a favorite decoration. They use thousands of them at once, string them across the fronts of the houses and shops, through the trees, and up and down the *dagobas* of the temples. If there is a religious procession, whatever is carried through the streets is covered with colored electric bulbs. During Perahera in Kandy as many as eighty elephants parade at night, wearing strings of lights which take the place of the emeralds, rubies and diamonds that cover the beasts in the daytime processions. Last week while I was in Kandy the Moslems had a festival, and they carried a pagoda-like tower, every square inch of whose area was ablaze with tiny colored lights. It looked rather like a colossal, glittering wedding cake. I followed it up and down Trincomalee Street and Ward Street, and then I went to bed. Until then I had not realized that there was a mosque across the garden from my room (they seem to have dispensed with muezzins here – at least, one never hears them), but that evening there was magnificent music coming from a courtyard behind the mosque. It went on all night, like a soft wind in the trees. I listened until nearly three, and then it carried me off into sleep.

Last night there was a *pirith* ceremony at a house across the road. The family that lived next door to the one holding the ceremony had offered their verandah for the installation of a generator, for there had to be electric light and a great deal of it. So, the clanking of the motor all but covered the chanting of the men. In one corner of the main room they had built a small cubicle. Its walls were of translucent paper, cut into designs along the edges of the partitions, so that each section looked like the frame of a fancy valentine. There were lights everywhere, but the greatest amount of light came from inside the cubicle. Earlier in the evening I had noticed two men winding or unwinding a white silk thread between them; now there was a decanter full of an unidentified liquid on the table, and the thread connected its neck with a part of the ceiling that was invisible from where I stood. The table was surrounded by men sitting pressed close to one another, chanting. One of the onlookers who stood with me in the road said that the chanting was being done in Pali, not in Singhalese. As if it were necessary to excuse the use of such an ancient language, he added that Catholic services were conducted in Latin, not in English, and I said I understood.

I asked what the white silk thread meant and was told that it was a decoration; but since everything in the ceremony had been arranged with show-window precision, and since the thread, shooting upward at its crazy angle toward the ceiling, was clearly not an adornment to anything, I was not inclined to accept that version of its function. The men shouted in a desperate fashion, so that they were obliged to lean against the table for support. All night long they kept it up. When I awoke at quarter to five they were still at it, but the sound now had a different contour; one could say that in a way it had subsided, being now a succession of short wails with a *tessitura* never exceeding a major third, a sequence that repeated itself exactly, again and again, with no variation. I was told today that the pirith chant is allowed four distinct tones and no more, since the addition of a fifth would put it into the category of music, which is strictly forbidden. Perhaps the celebrants are too much preoccupied with observing the letter of the law. In any case, within the allowed gamut they hit every quarter-tone they could find. The dogs of the resthouse objected now and then with howls and yapping, until the guard silenced them with a shout.

A young Buddhist who had been standing outside the house while I was there offered to explain a few details about the ceremony to me. "You see the women?" he said. They were sitting in the outer part of the room, conversing quietly. "They are not allowed inside." The chanting begins, he said (in this case it was at nine in the evening), with all the men shouting together. Then as they tire, only the two strongest continue, while the others gather their forces. At daybreak once again everyone joins in, after six hours or so of alternating shifts. Purpose of ceremony: to keep evil in abeyance. The young man did not hold the custom in very high esteem and suggested that I visit a monastery four miles away on an island where the *bhikkus* behaved in a really correct manner. Even Buddhism is riddled with primitive practices. Practically speaking, the pirith is merely a quiet variation of devil-dancing.

COLOMBO

THE PETTAH is the only part of the city where the visitor can get even a faint idea of what life in Colombo might have been like before the twentieth century's gangrene set in. It is at the end of a long and unrewarding walk across the railroad tracks and down endless unshaded streets, and no one in Ceylon seems to be able to understand how I can like it. It is customary to assume an expression of slight disgust when one pronounces the word Pettah.

The narrow streets are jammed with zebu-drawn drays which naked coolies (no one ever says "laborers") are loading and unloading. Scavenging crows scream and chuckle in the gutters. The shops specialize in unexpected merchandise: some sell nothing but fireworks, or religious chromolithographs depicting incidents in the lives of Hindu gods, or sarongs, or incense. With no arcades and no trees the heat is more intense; by noon you feel that at some point you have inadvertently died and are merely reliving the scene in your head. A rickshaw or taxi never passes through, and you must go on and on until you come out somewhere. Layers of dried betel spit coat the walls and sidewalks; it looks somewhat like dried blood, but it is a little too red. The pervading odor is that of any Chinese grocery store: above all, dried fish, but with strong suggestions of spices and incense. And there are, indeed, a few Chinese here in

Pettah, although most of them appear to be dentists. I remember that one is named Thin Sin Fa and that he advertises himself as a Genuine Chinese dentist. The mark of their profession is painted over the doorway: a huge red oval enclosing two rows of gleaming white squares. If there is a breeze, pillars of dust sweep majestically through the streets, adding an extra patina of grit to the sweat that covers your skin. In one alley is a poor Hindu temple with a small *gopuram* above the entrance. The hundreds of sculpted figures are not of stone, but of brilliantly painted plaster; banners and pennants hang haphazardly from criss-crossed strings. In another street there is a hideous red brick mosque. The faithful must wear trousers to enter.

There are Hindus and Moslems in every corner of Ceylon, but neither of these orthodoxies seems fitting for the place. Hinduism is too fanciful and chaotic, Islam too puritanical and austere. Buddhism, with its gentle agnosticism and luxuriant sadness, is so right in Ceylon that you feel it could have been born here, could have grown up out of the soil like the forests. Soon, doubtless, it will no longer be a way of life, having become, along with the rest of the world's religions, a socio-political badge. But for the moment it is still here, still powerful. And in any case, *après nous le déluge!*

No More Djinns

The American Mercury, June 1951

R AIN, which ordinarily gladdens the hearts of everyone but the tourists, has recently fallen in such quantities all over this part of the continent that even the natives wonder if it will ever dry off again. Lower roads have been blocked again and again by inundations. The muddy streams have swept down from the mountains with violence, destroying the villages along their banks. The professional prayer-makers have had to brush up a bit on their incantations, since people are now paying them to perform the unusual service of praying for the rain to stop.

As for the mental climate here, the absurd story which follows is a faithful reporting of a conversation I had here a while ago with two native policemen. It was night and they were off duty, strolling on the beach. These were enlightened young men, very slick and glib, taking all of Western civilization, from penicillin to television, in their stride. Soon they were squatting in the sand telling humorous stories, as these people are likely to do, about their own less enlightened countrymen. Finally one of them said: "I'll tell you a very funny story about us, when we first went on to the force. We went on together. That was two years ago, when we didn't know anything. We had to patrol the beach every night. We didn't like that much. You know, all alone, the two of us, on the beach at night, way out beyond the Balneario."

I didn't know, inasmuch as I had often walked by myself much further than that; the idea of danger had never occurred to me.

"And sure enough," he continued, "one night we see a light moving on the beach. We sneak up quietly and yell: 'Stop!' And all of a sudden a big white figure began moving up and down in the air and going: 'Ayayayay!' So what would you think if you didn't know any better? You'd think it was a *djinn*, and you'd get out fast. But then every night when we got near that part of the beach, we'd see this *djinn* jumping up and down and making an awful noise. So finally we thought we'd better tell the captain about it; he's a tough old man, and very smart, too. But when we told him about it he got very angry. 'So you saw a *djinn*, did you? Hah!' he said. 'Anybody but two nitwits like you would know there hasn't been a *djinn* around Tangier for at least ten years'."

At this point I laughed, thinking that was the point and the end of the story. But they both remained completely serious.

He continued, "I said to the old man: 'Excuse me, my captain. I didn't know.' He said: 'You're going back out to the beach tomorrow night and catch the *djinn*, you understand?' We were really scared then. But anyway, the next night when we went back we saw the light, and we sneaked up and yelled: 'Stop!' and the spirit began to go up in the air and moan the same as always. And then instead of running away we pulled out our guns and said: 'Come here or we'll shoot.' And then, – " he chuckled, "it began to cry, and it was nothing but a woman. A lousy woman! And she said: 'Oh, please, sirs! I have to come every night to take food to my husband who is fishing up the beach.' So we were pretty angry, and we said: 'What's the idea of trying to make fools of us?' And she said: 'I thought if I did that, nobody'd bother me. I'm all alone –'. So we said – " here they both began to laugh loudly with the recollection, and I knew that the point of the story was about to be reached. "We said: 'You'll see whether anybody'll bother you or not, you slut!' And we knocked her down and had a fine time with her. Afterward we ate the food she had with her and sent her back home yelling her head off. So then we had to think up something to tell the captain."

"What did you tell him?" I asked.

They were still laughing, "Oh, we said we shot at the *djinn* and it just disappeared in the air by magic, like an airplane."

"Did he believe you?"

"Of course he believed us," he said reproachfully. "He knows no man on his force would lie to him. You never lie to your captain; that's one thing you can't do. He just said: 'All right. Don't come to me with any more *djinn* stories'."

I let the matter drop. But a few minutes later I said: "Is it really true there's such a thing as a *djinn*, then?"

They laughed scornfully. "With all the electric lights and automobiles there are around Tangier? Hah! Those are women's stories to scare kids with. Listen, my friend. You have to go at least a hundred kilometers up into the mountains before you'll find a *djinn*, and even then you might not see any. This isn't like the old days. Everything's different now, since the war."

"I guess you're right," I said.

TANGIER GOES ON GROWING; it is the boom-town par excellence. In 1947 people seemed to feel that the peak had been reached, that real-estate prices simply couldn't go on rising. With the hundreds of apartment-houses that were going up, some of them actually in the open country without even a finished road nearby, everyone began to foresee a crash. Bankruptcies *en masse* were predicted; there would never be enough people to fill all the apartments. But not at all. Roads were built across the sand dunes, through the meadows, up and down the hills, suburbs sprang up which almost immediately became part of the city itself, a great many bus lines were inaugurated and today the process goes on with more impetus than ever.

Since the new war scare one has the impression that practically everyone with any money wants to leave whatever European country he is in and settle here in the International Zone. The great thing of course is to manage to transfer your capital here. There are no restrictions, no taxes, the climate is better than anywhere in Europe (despite this last winter's inclemency), and the belief is rampant that America somehow would prevent anyone else from occupying the Zone in the event of war. So at the moment anything is considered a good investment; you can buy part of a ruined wall on the ramparts, dig out three rooms, install a bathroom and electricity, and be pretty sure of making money on the resale. The only trouble is that everyone is in such a hurry to buy, build, and sell that there is no time to see that anything is properly done. And so, you open the door of your bedroom and it falls over on top of you; you turn on the water and the wash-basin collapses; you sit down to dinner and the chandelier overhead crashes into the middle of the table. The walls of the buildings crack open, the elevators don't move, the roofs leak, and one has the uneasy suspicion that in another decade many of the big new buildings of which Tangier is now so proud will no longer be standing.

Everyone complains bitterly, but to no avail, of course. A new, well-constructed building is unthinkable here today. "That's Tangier," people say with a sigh, as they put pails in the middle of their living-rooms to catch the stream of rain coming through, or telephone to have a new window fitted because the other one has fallen out into the street. "It could happen only in Tangier," they tell each other, not without a certain satisfaction at the thought of living in this unique city where everything can safely be counted on to go wrong.

BUT ALL THIS is only Tangier. Once you have left behind the last sad apartment house, standing in solitary state among goats, cactus, cows, and native shacks, the countryside is just as beautiful as ever.

Morocco is the ideal country for motoring: the scenery is magnificent and varied, the roads are excellent, and there is no traffic. Gasoline prices range from seventeen cents a gallon in the Spanish Zone to about twenty-eight cents in the French, with those of the International Zone falling halfway between. (In Algeria you pay forty-eight cents a gallon, while in France it is still higher.) The few Americans who live in Morocco are constantly making trips; one would think to hear them talk that they had all set themselves the same stunt – that of knowing every town in the land. "Here's a place I'll bet you've never been ... Let's see, what's it called? Hey, what was the name of that place we went last October, when we made the side-trip from Béni Mellal and it took all day and we had to go back and sleep in the tents again that night? You know, where the chain was across the road, and the soldier with the wooden leg had to telephone fifty miles away to his superior to get permission to let us through? Azilal! That's it! Azilal. I'll bet you've never been to Azilal. What a place!"

To the European, Morocco, southern Morocco particularly, is a vast and forbidding place (it is officially called "The Zone of Insecurity" by the French military), while to the average American it is a sort of exotic Utah whose touristic value is greatly enhanced by the fact that its southern border is non-existent and that there are whole regions as yet unseen by tourists of any nationality. What with our new Moroccan air-bases and their large technical personnel, all this may change rapidly in the near future, so that after driving six days to get to some place like Tata or Tindouf one will find a party of one's countrymen already there, complete with Coca Cola and light-meters.

There is another sort of American whom one sees here nowadays with increasing frequency. He is usually in his early twenties, sometimes wears a beard, and often goes in for clothing which is almost belligerently informal. The new "lost generation" which America turned loose on the world after the recent war is so thoroughly lost that the generation which came before seems undeserving of the epithet. Paris is still their proving ground, but this time it is the Paris of the little Algerian joints behind the Bastille, incredibly sordid spots where they gather to study the preparation, use and effects of the drug called *cannabis sativa*, known in its various forms as hashish, kif, and *majoun*.

Casbah at Ouarzazate in southern Morocco (PB)

Although a good many members of this new elite are connected with the arts in one way or another, it is a matter of common agreement that the fundamental aim in life is not self-expression, but the attainment of an indescribable and very personal state of ecstasy which is not (and must not be) related in any way to intellectual or artistic endeavor. It is a phenomenon worth considering, this new generation of nihilist mystics living on Veterans' Administration checks, Fulbright Fellowships, gifts from casual acquaintances, and occasional scraps from home. And it is of particular interest to us here because invariably they arrive in Tangier, which I suppose is the perfect place for them. Here they can get on their various kicks publicly and no one will object in the least; on the contrary, the quickest way to make friends in places where Moslems gather is to bring out your *sebsi* and light up.

If your initiate has managed to achieve a state of illumination he can maintain it night and day, indefinitely, stretched out for hours in his favorite native café or lying on the beach in the sun. No one will register the slightest disapproval or surprise; after all, he is enjoying life the way the majority of people around him enjoy it. And since in general the members of the new lost generation are chronically low in funds (to work is an absurdity – almost a sacrilege), the extremely reasonable local prices of the drugs is a great drawing-card. For the equivalent of six cents they can buy enough *majoun* in the Calle Gzennaïa to transport them to an all-night nirvana.

Each week more new faces haunt the native cafés behind the Zoco Chico; while a few may be French, most of them are Americans, and they are in passionate pursuit of one thing: an absolute detachment from what is ordinarily called reality. (Sex they consider a very "low-grade kick.") Most of them are still faithful to be-bop as the most highly perfected musical expression of the desired spiritual state. For some reason (perhaps a purely physical one, since the drug, while it momentarily activates the mental faculties, is inclined to cause great bodily inertia), they seldom continue inland to other parts of Morocco, remaining instead indefinitely in Tangier. The adepts mind their own business, they talk very little, and they are not trying to prove anything. As cults go, it's a rather sympathetic one.

UNFORTUNATELY there is an increasing tendency, led by the Nationalists here in Morocco, to suppress, both by law and propaganda, all aspects of the native life which make the country picturesque to the visitor. It looks as if they hope to discourage tourists from coming, and, indeed, when one talks with them, one finds that this is perfectly true. For these Arab fanatics are firmly convinced that Westerners visit Morocco only to scoff at the customs and behavior of a backward people. It happens that the things which are of particular interest in Morocco are not of Arab importation, but indigenous to the country – that is, Berber. From the Nationalist point of view the Berbers are little better than animals, improperly Islamized and stubborn in their insistence upon clinging to their ancient rituals. Thus a great puritanical purge has been in progress for the past fifteen years or so, and will probably continue to go on, until every vestige of spontaneous pleasure in religious observances has been destroyed.

This year for the first time the celebration of the festival of Mouloud, the anniversary of Mohammed's birthday, was forbidden in Tangier. What always has been a three-day carnival with parades, fireworks, public dancing, music and crowds of native visitors from all parts of the country, was annihilated by one disapproving stroke of the pen. Reason (among the populace): the offerings of money carried by the celebrants to the mosques are appropriated by a few wealthy families – the Chorfa, or descendants of Mohammed. But since this has always been the case and no one has ever objected before, the argument does not hold water. Reason (among the informed): the Nationalists disapproved of the women in the festivities, because it encouraged immorality! Religious dancing, the principal means of spiritual expression among the Berbers, is forbidden all over Morocco now; the Nationalists saw to that several years ago.

One wonders whether, if they were given free rein, they might not go as far as Ibn Saud in Arabia, who has carried his blue-nosed proclivities to the extent of prohibiting phonographs and radios (except for use in listening to news broadcasts) all over Arabia, because they play music. Music is evil. (One interesting clause in his code is that the police shall break the phonograph record over the head of the person who is found with it. If this seems merely amusing, let me add that the law is by no means benign. In the case of the person caught with a bottle of beer or any other alcoholic concoction, the punishment is the same: the offending bottle must be destroyed against the head of the miscreant.)

The Moslem thinks of Communism about the way the city-dweller thinks of hoof-and-mouth disease: a dangerous malady, but not one by which he himself could possibly be affected. For him Communism is a disease peculiar to the Christian world; protected by the fortifications of his religion he feels secure from it.

Here in Morocco, as everywhere else, there is a Communist Party, but its adherents are French, Spanish, Corsican. When you find a Moslem member, he is usually from Algeria. (Algerians, unlike Moroccans, are French citizens.) If you talk with a Mohammedan Communist, he will usually end up by telling you that his interest in the movement is purely opportunistic. Once the colonial regimes are extirpated, he says, the Communist Party will have done its work. Then the local Nationalists will take over, and all will be well.

What is much more important is that a great many educated Moroccans, resenting the semi-colonial status of their country, unwittingly adopt an attitude which makes them singularly vulnerable to Stalinist propaganda. *Le Petit Marocain*, which has the largest circulation of any daily newspaper in Morocco, follows the party line closely, never lets an opportunity slip for pointing out both the real and imagined injustices suffered by the people under the present government. The Communists support the Nationalists because any Nationalist gain upsets the status quo; a Nationalist coup would delight them. They could count on ensuing chaos, first of all because there are three distinct Nationalist parties which would be sure to disagree more violently than they do at present, but particularly because the Berbers, who form the majority of the population, are anti-Nationalist on the grounds that the movement is purely pro-Arab, and not interested in the Berbers at all.

It is always easy enough to induce the Berbers to form mass-demonstrations. The French did it a fortnight ago when they were trying to get the Sultan to remove certain members of the Istiqulal – the most powerful and radical of the three Nationalist parties – from among his advisors. Several thousand tribesmen riding their horses through the streets of Fez would seem to have made an impression. There was also the advice given the Sultan by El Glaoui, Pacha of Marrakesh, who is the Berbers' particular defender. In any case, the offending individuals were removed. But you can be sure the Nationalists will not take it lying down; their method is not that of passive resistance. To me the whole thing is just one more bit of madness in an already mad world.

THESE POLITICAL CONSIDERATIONS remind me of a ridiculous little adventure I had recently. I was walking along a country road several miles from Fez. Out of a dusty lane which led back into an olive grove came three Moroccans, one of whom I immediately recognized as an acquaintance. We exchanged greetings and I was presented to the others. Instead of continuing their walk, they pressed me to return with them to a house which was somewhere back in the grove, and have tea. The house, which belonged to a plump young man with thick glasses, was vast, ancient, and almost in ruins, but on an upper floor there proved to be one room that had been kept in comparative repairs, and there we sat, drank tea, and talked at great length.

When we had exhausted America as a topic, we turned to Morocco. I had been reading several books of Moroccan history in French, and it was natural that I should bring up the subject of Bou Hamara, the rebel chieftain who dared defy two sultans,

Abd el Aziz and Moulay Hafid, and who for seven years held all of eastern Morocco. It is a generally accepted fact that when Sultan Moulay Hafid seized Bou Hamara in 1909 he put him into a cage that was too small for him either to stand or sit in, had him carted about through the streets of Moroccan cities for two years, during which time he was constantly tortured by the populace, and finally fed him to his pet lions. I had seen Bou Hamara's cage many time in the Batha, and I had also seen the empty lions' cages in the courtyard of the Sultan's palace. When I touched on the story, which everyone here knows by heart, I added that I thought it just as well that a sultan like Moulay Hafid should have been replaced by someone less blood-thirsty and savage. "He must have been a very peculiar man," I said. "Do you know anything about him?"

"A little," replied my host, removing his glasses. "He was my father."

And while I attempted to stammer some sort of apology, the son of the former sultan delivered me a lengthy lecture on the inadvisability of believing anything I read in French histories of Morocco. The French, he said, always attempted to justify their occupation of the country by pointing out that the inhabitants were barbarians and incapable of governing themselves, all of which sounded perfectly logical. But three nights ago I told the story as a joke on myself to an Arab here in Tangier. When I had finished, instead of laughing, he said very seriously: "Oh, but you were perfectly right. Moulay Hafid did throw Bou Hamara to the lions. I know, because it was my father who was sent to Hagenbeck in Hamburg to buy the animals for the occasion. Only they were so tame and well-fed that they wouldn't eat him."

So I am off for the south tomorrow; I can't stand this rain any longer.

BAPTISM OF SOLITUDE

HOLIDAY, JANUARY 1953; THEIR HEADS ARE GREEN, 1963

I MMEDIATELY WHEN YOU ARRIVE in the Sahara, for the first or the tenth time, you notice the stillness. An incredible, absolute silence prevails outside the towns; and within, even in busy places like the markets, there is a hushed quality in the air, as if the quiet were a conscious force which, resenting the intrusion of sound, minimizes and disperses sound straightway. Then there is the sky, compared to which all other skies seem faint-hearted efforts. Solid and luminous, it is always the focal point of the landscape. At sunset, the precise, curved shadow of the earth rises into it swiftly from the horizon, cutting it into light section and dark section. When all daylight is gone, and the space is thick with stars, it is still of an intense and burning blue, darkest directly overhead and paling toward the earth, so that the night never really grows dark.

You leave the gate of the fort or the town behind, pass the camels lying outside, go up into the dunes, or out onto the hard, stony plain and stand awhile, alone. Presently, you will either shiver and hurry back inside the walls, or you will go on standing there and let something very peculiar happen to you, something that everyone who lives there has undergone and which the French call *le baptême de la solitude*. It is a unique sensation, and it has nothing to do with loneliness, for loneliness presupposes memory. Here, in this wholly mineral landscape lighted by stars like flares, even memory disappears;

nothing is left but your own breathing and the sound of your heart beating. A strange, and by no means pleasant, process of reintegration begins inside you, and you have the choice of fighting against it, and insisting on remaining the person you have always been, or letting it take its course. For no one who has stayed in the Sahara for a while is quite the same as when he came.

Before the war for independence in Algeria, under the rule of the French military, there was a remarkable feeling of friendly sympathy among Europeans in the Sahara. It is unnecessary to stress the fact that the corollary of this pleasant state of affairs was the exercise of the strictest sort of colonial control over the Algerians themselves, a regime which amounted to a reign of terror. But from the European viewpoint the place was ideal. The whole vast region was like a small unspoiled rural community where everyone respected the rights of everyone else. Each time you lived there for a while, and left it, you were struck with the indifference and the impersonality of the world outside. If during your travels in the Sahara you forgot something, you could be sure of finding it later on your way back; the idea of appropriating it would not have occurred to anyone. You could wander where you liked, out in the wilderness or in the darkest alleys of the towns; no one would molest you.

At that time no members of the indigent, wandering, unwanted proletariat from northern Algeria had come down here, because there was nothing to attract them. Almost everyone owned a parcel of land in an oasis and lived by working it. In the shade of the date palms, wheat, barley and corn were grown, and those plants provided the staple items of diet. There were usually two or three Arab or Negro shopkeepers who sold things such as sugar, tea, candles, matches, carbide for fuel, and cheap European cotton goods. In the larger towns there was sometimes a shop kept by a European, but the merchandise was the same, because the customers were virtually all natives. Almost without exception, the only Europeans who lived in the Sahara were the military and the ecclesiastic.

As a rule, the military and their aides were friendly men, agreeable to be with, interested in showing visitors everything worth seeing in their districts. This was fortunate, as the traveler was often completely at their mercy. He might have to depend on them for his food and lodging, since in the smaller places there were no hotels. Generally he had to depend on them for contact with the outside world, because anything he wanted, like cigarettes or wine, had to be brought by truck from the military post, and his mail was sent in care of the post, too. Furthermore, the decision as to whether he was to have permission to move about freely in the region rested with the military. The power to grant those privileges was vested in, let us say, one lonely lieutenant who lived two hundred miles from his nearest countryman, ate badly (a condition anathema to any Frenchman), and wished that neither camels, date palms, nor inquisitive foreigners had ever been created. Still, it was rare to find an indifferent or unhelpful comandante. He was likely to invite you for drinks and dinner, show you the curiosities he had collected during his years in the *bled*, ask you to accompany him on his tours of inspection, or even to spend a fortnight with him and his *peloton* of several dozen native *meharistes* when they went out into the desert to make topographical surveys. Then you would be given your own camel – not an ambling pack camel that had to be driven with a stick by someone walking beside it, but a swift, trained animal that obeyed the slightest tug of the reins.

More extraordinary were the Pères Blancs, intelligent and well-educated. There was no element of resignation in their eagerness to spend the remainder of their lives in distant outposts, dressed as Moslems, speaking Arabic, living in the rigorous, comfortless manner of the desert inhabitants. They made no converts and expected to make none. "We are here only to show the Moslem that the Christian can be worthy of respect," they explained. One used to hear the Moslems say that although the Christians might be masters of the earth, the Moslems were the masters of heaven; for the military it was quite enough that the *indigène* recognize European supremacy here. Obviously the

Paul Bowles and his shadow – photographed in the Tafilalt area of the Sahara, 1963

White Fathers could not be satisfied with that. They insisted upon proving to the inhabitants that the Nazarene was capable of leading as exemplary a life as the most ardent follower of Mohammed. It is true that the austerity of the Fathers' mode of life inspired many Moslems with respect for them if not for the civilization they represented. And as a result of the years spent in the desert among the inhabitants, the Fathers acquired a certain healthy and unorthodox fatalism, an excellent adjunct to their spiritual equipment, and a highly necessary one in dealing with the men among whom they had chosen to live.

With an area considerably larger than that of the United States, the Sahara is a continent within a continent – a skeleton, if you like, but still a separate entity from the rest of Africa which surrounds it. It has its own mountain ranges, rivers, lakes and forests, but they are largely vestigial. The mountain ranges have been reduced to gigantic bouldery bumps that rise above the neighboring countryside like the mountains on the moon. Some of the rivers appear as such for perhaps one day a year – others much less often. The lakes are of solid salt, and the forests have long since petrified. But the physical contours of the landscape vary as much as they do anywhere else. There are plains, hills, valleys, gorges, rolling lands, rocky peaks and volcanic craters, all without vegetation or even soil. Yet, probably the only parts that are monotonous to the eye are regions like the Tanezrouft, south of Reggane, a stretch of about five hundred miles of absolutely flat, gravel-strewn terrain, without the slightest sign of life, or the smallest undulation in the land, nothing to vary the implacable line of the horizon on all sides. After being here for a while, the sight of even a rock awakens an emotion in the traveler; he feels like crying, "Land!"

There is no known historical period when the Sahara has not been inhabited by man. Most of the other larger forms of animal life, whose abode it formerly was, have become extinct. If we believe the evidence of cave drawings, we can be sure that the giraffe, the hippopotamus and the rhinoceros were once dwellers in the region. The lion has disappeared from North

Africa in our own time, likewise the ostrich. Now and then a crocodile is still discovered in some distant, hidden oasis pool, but the occurrence is so rare that when it happens it is a great event. The camel, of course, is not a native of Africa at all, but an importation from Asia, having arrived approximately at the time of the end of the Roman Empire – about when the last elephants were killed off. Large numbers of the herds of wild elephants that roamed the northern reaches of the desert were captured and trained for use in the Carthaginian army, but it was the Romans who finally annihilated the species to supply ivory for the European market.

Fortunately for man, who seems to insist on continuing to live in surroundings which become increasingly inhospitable to him, gazelles are still plentiful, and there are, paradoxically enough, various kinds of edible fish in the water holes – often more than a hundred feet deep – throughout the Sahara. Certain species which abound in artesian wells are blind, having always lived deep in the subterranean lakes.

An often-repeated statement, no matter how incorrect, takes a long time to disappear from circulation. Thus, there is a popular misconception of the Sahara as a vast region of sand across which Arabs travel in orderly caravans from one white-domed city to another. A generalization much nearer to the truth would be to say that it is an area of rugged mountains, bare valleys and flat, stony wasteland, sparsely dotted with Negro villages of mud. The sand in the Sahara, according to data supplied by the Geographical Service of the French Army, covers only about a tenth of its surface; and the Arabs, most of whom are nomads, form a small part of the population. The vast majority of the inhabitants are of Berber (native North African) and/or Negro (native West African) stock. But the Negroes of today are not those who originally peopled the desert. The latter never took kindly to the colonial designs of the Arabs and the Islamized Berbers who collaborated with them; over the centuries they beat a constant retreat toward the southeast until only a vestige of their society remains, in the region now known as the Tibesti.

They were replaced by the more docile Sudanese, imported from the south as slaves to work the constantly expanding series of oases.

In the Sahara the oasis – which is to say, the forest of date palms – is primarily a man-made affair and can continue its existence only if the work of irrigating its terrain is kept up unrelentingly. When the Arabs arrived in Africa twelve centuries ago, they began a project of land reclamation which, if the Europeans continue it with the aid of modern machinery, will transform much of the Sahara into a great, fertile garden. Wherever there was a sign of vegetation, the water was there not far below; it merely needed to be brought to the surface. The Arabs set to work digging wells, constructing reservoirs, building networks of canals along the surface of the ground and systems of subterranean water-galleries deep in the earth.

For all these important projects, the recently arrived colonizers needed great numbers of workers who could bear the climate and the malaria that is still endemic in the oases. Sudanese slaves seemed to be the ideal solution of the problem, and these came to constitute the larger part of the permanent population of the desert. Each Arab tribe traveled about among the oases it controlled, collecting the produce. It was never the practice or the intention of the sons of Allah to live there. They have a saying which goes, "No one lives in the Sahara if he is able to live anywhere else." Slavery has, of course, been abolished officially by the French, but only recently, within our time. Probably the principal factor in the process by which Timbuktu was reduced from its status of capital of the Sahara to its present abject condition was the closing of the slave market there. But the Sahara, which started out as a Negro country, is still a Negro country, and will undoubtedly remain so for a long time.

The oases, those magnificent palm groves, are the blood and bone of the desert; life in the Sahara would be unthinkable without them. Wherever human beings are found, an oasis is sure to be nearby. Sometimes the town is surrounded by the trees, but usually it is built just outside, so that none of the fertile ground will be wasted on mere living quarters. The size of an oasis is reckoned by the number of trees it contains, not by the numbers of square miles it covers, just as the taxes are based on the number of date-bearing trees and not on the amount of land. The prosperity of a region is in direct proportion to the number and size of its oases. The one at Figuig, for instance, has more than two hundred thousand bearing palms, and the one at Timimoun is forty miles long, with irrigation systems that are of an astonishing complexity.

To stroll in a Saharan oasis is rather like taking a walk through a well-kept Eden. The alleys are clean, bordered on each side by hand-patted mud walls, not too high to prevent you from seeing the riot of verdure within. Under the high waving palms are the smaller trees – pomegranate, orange, fig, almond. Below these, in neat squares surrounded by narrow ditches of running water, are the vegetables and wheat. No matter how far from the town you stray, you have the same impression of order, cleanliness, and insistence on utilizing every square inch of ground. When you come to the edge of the oasis, you always find that it is in the process of being enlarged. Plots of young palms extend out into the glaring wasteland. Thus far they are useless, but in a few years they will begin to bear, and eventually this sun-blistered land will be a part of the green belt of gardens.

There are a good many birds living in the oases, but their songs and plumage are not appreciated by the inhabitants. The birds eat the young shoots and dig up the seeds as fast as they are planted, and practically every man and boy carries a sling-shot. A few years ago I traveled through the Sahara with a parrot; everywhere the poor bird was glowered at by the natives, and in Timimoun a delegation of three elderly men came to the hotel one afternoon and suggested that I stop leaving its cage in the window; otherwise there was no telling what its fate might be. "Nobody likes birds here," they said meaningfully.

It is the custom to build little summerhouses out in the oases. There is often an element of play and fantasy in the architecture of these edifices which makes them captivating. They are small

Saharan people, 1948. Bowles recalled: "You only had to walk a few steps, go to the car, and people would come and say: Take a photo of us!" (PB)

toy palaces of mud. Here, men have tea with their families at the close of day, or spend the night when it is unusually hot in the town, or invite their friends for a few hands of ronda, the favorite North African card game, and a little music. If a man asks you to visit him in his summerhouse, you find that the experience is invariably worth the long walk required to get there. You will have to drink at least the three traditional glasses of tea, and you may have to eat a good many almonds and smoke more kif than you really want, but it will be cool, there will be the gurgle of running water and the smell of mint in the air, and your host may bring out a flute. One winter I priced one of these houses that had particularly struck my fancy. With its garden and pool, the cost was the equivalent of twenty-five pounds. The catch was that the owner wanted to retain the right to work the land, because it was unthinkable to him that it should cease to be productive.

In the Sahara as elsewhere in North Africa, popular religious observances often include elements of pre-Islamic faiths in their ritual; the most salient example is the institution of religious dancing, which persists despite long-continued discouragement of the custom by educated Moslems. Even in the highly religious settlement of the M'Zab, where puritanism is carried to excessive lengths, the holding of dances is not unknown. At the time I lived there children were not allowed to laugh in public, yet I spent an entire night watching a dozen men dance themselves into unconsciousness beside a bonfire of palm branches. Two burly guards were necessary to prevent them from throwing themselves into the flames. After each man had been heaved back from the fire several times, he finally ceased making his fantastic skyward leaps, staggered, and sank to the ground. He was immediately carried outside the circle and covered with blankets, his place being taken by a fresh adept. There was no music or singing, but there were eight drummers, each one playing an instrument of a different size.

In other places, the dance is similar to the Berber *ahouache* of the Moroccan Atlas. The participants form a great circle holding hands, women alternating with men; their movements are mea-

sured, never frantic, and although the trance is constantly suggested, it seems never to be arrived at collectively. In the performances I have seen, there has been a woman in the center with
her head and neck hidden by a cloth. She sings and dances,
and the chorus around her responds antiphonally. It is all very
sedate and low-pitched, but the irrational seems never very far
away, perhaps because of the hypnotic effect produced by the
slowly beaten, deep-toned drums.

The Touareg, an ancient offshoot of the Kabyle Berbers of
Algeria, were unappreciative of the "civilizing mission" of the
Roman legions and decided to put a thousand miles or more of
desert between themselves and their would-be educators. They
went straight south until they came to a land that seemed likely
to provide them the privacy they desired, and there they have
remained throughout the centuries, their own masters almost
until today. Through all the ages during which the Arabs domi-
nated the surrounding regions, the Touareg retained their rule
of the Hoggar, that immense plateau in the very center of the
Sahara. Their traditional hatred of the Arabs, however, does
not appear to have been powerful enough to keep them from
becoming partially Islamized, although they are by no means a
completely Moslem people. Far from being a piece of property
only somewhat more valuable than a sheep, the woman has an
extremely important place in Targui society. The line of succession is purely maternal. Here, it is the men who must be veiled
day and night. The veil is of fine black gauze and is worn, so
they explain, to protect the soul. But since soul and breath to
them are identical, it is not difficult to find a physical reason, if
one is desired. The excessive dryness of the atmosphere often
causes disturbances in the nasal passages. The veil conserves
the breath's moisture, is a sort of little air-conditioning plant,
and this helps keep out the evil spirits which otherwise would
manifest their presence by making the nostrils bleed, a common
occurrence in this part of the world.

It is scarcely fair to refer to these proud people as Touareg.
The word is a term of opprobrium meaning "lost souls," given

them by their traditional enemies the Arabs, but one which, in the outside world, has stuck. They call themselves *imochagh*, the free ones. Among all the Berber-speaking peoples, they are the only ones to have devised a system of writing their language. No one knows how long their alphabet has been in use, but it is a true phonetical alphabet, quite as well planned and logical as the Roman, with twenty-three simple and thirteen compound letters.

Unfortunately for them, the Touareg have never been able to get on among themselves; internecine warfare has gone on unceasingly among them for centuries. Until the French military put a stop to it, it had been a common practice for one tribe to set out on plundering expeditions against a neighboring tribe. During these voyages, the wives of the absent men remained faithful to their husbands, the strict Targui moral code recommending death as a punishment for infidelity. However, a married woman whose husband was away was free to go at night to the graveyard dressed in her finest apparel, lie on the tombstone of one of her ancestors, and invoke a certain spirit called Idebni, who always appeared in the guise of one of the young men of the community. If she could win Idebni's favor, he gave her news of her husband; if not, he strangled her. The Touareg women, being very clever, always managed to bring back news of their husbands from the cemetery.

The first motor crossing of the Sahara was accomplished in 1923. At that time it was still a matter of months to get from, let us say, Touggourt to Zinder, or from the Tafilelt to Gao. In 1934, I was in Erfoud asking about caravans to Timbuktu. Yes, they said, one was leaving in a few weeks, and it would take from sixteen to twenty weeks to make the voyage. How would I get back? The caravan would probably set out on its return trip at this time next year. They were surprised to see that this information lessened my interest. How could you expect to do it more quickly?

Of course, the proper way to travel in the Sahara is by camel, particularly if you're a good walker, since after about two hours of the camel's motion you are glad to get down and walk for four. Each succeeding day is likely to bring with it a greater percentage of time spent off the camel. Nowadays, if you like, you can leave Algiers in the morning by plane and be fairly well into the desert by evening, but the traveler who gives in to this temptation, like the reader of a mystery story who skips through the book to arrive at the solution quickly, deprives himself of most of the pleasure of the journey. For the person who wants to see something the practical means of locomotion is the trans-Saharan truck, a compromise between camel and airplane.

There are only two trails across the desert at present (the Piste Impériale through Mauretania not being open to the public) and I should not recommend either to drivers of private automobiles. The trucks, however, are especially built for the region. If there is any sort of misadventure, the wait is not likely to be more than twenty-four hours, since the truck is always expected at the next town, and there is always an ample supply of water aboard. But the lone car that gets stuck in the Sahara is in trouble.

Usually, you can go to the fort of any town and telephone ahead to the next post, asking them to notify the hotelkeeper there of your intended arrival. Should the lines be down – a not unusual circumstance – there is no way of assuring yourself a room in advance, save by mail, which is extremely slow. Unless you travel with your own blankets this can be a serious drawback, arriving unannounced, for the hotels are small, often having only five or six rooms, and the winter nights are cold. The temperature goes to several degrees below freezing, reaching its lowest point just before dawn. The same courtyard that may show 125° when it is flooded with sun at two in the afternoon will register only 28° the following morning. So it is good to know you are going to have a room and a bed in your next stopping place. Not that there is heating of any sort in the establishments, but by keeping the window shut you can help the thick mud walls conserve some of the daytime heat. Even so, I have awakened to find a sheet of ice over the water in the glass beside my bed.

These violent extremes of temperature are due, of course, to the dryness of the atmosphere, whose relative humidity is often less than five percent. When you reflect that the soil attains a

Taghit, Algeria: Bowles described this in his autobiography, *Without Stopping*,
as "Probably the most intensely poetic spot I had ever seen." (PB)

temperature of one hundred and seventy-five degrees during the summer, you understand that the principal consideration in planning streets and houses should be that of keeping out as much light as possible. The streets are kept dark by being built underneath and inside the houses, and the houses have no windows in their massive walls. The French have introduced the window into much of their architecture, but the windows open onto wide, vaulted arcades, and thus, while they do give air, they let in little light. The result is that once you are out of the sun you live in a Stygian gloom.

Even in the Sahara there is no spot where rain has not been known to fall, and its arrival is an event that calls for celebration – drumming, dancing, firing of guns. The storms are violent and unpredictable. Considering their disastrous effects, one wonders that the people can welcome them with such unmixed emotions. Enormous walls of water rush down the dry river beds, pushing everything before them, often isolating the towns. The roofs of the houses cave in, and often the walls themselves. A prolonged rain would destroy every town in the Sahara, since the *tob*, of which everything is built, is softer than our adobe. And, in fact, it is not unusual to see a whole section of a village forsaken by its occupants, who have rebuilt their houses nearby, leaving the walls and foundations of their former dwellings to dissolve and drop back into the earth of which they were made.

In 1932 I decided to spend the winter in the M'Zab of southern Algeria. The rattletrap bus started out from Laghouat at night in a heavy rain. Not far to the south, the trail crossed a flat stretch about a mile wide, slightly lower than the surrounding country. Even as we were in it, the water began to rise around us, and in a moment the motor died. The passengers jumped out and waded about in water that soon was up to their waists; in all directions there were dim white figures in *burnouses* moving slowly through the flood, like storks. They were looking for a shallow route back to dry land, but they did not find it. In the end they carried me, the only European in the party, all the way to Laghouat on their backs, leaving the bus and its luggage to drown out there in the rain. When I got to Ghardaia two days later, the rain (which was the first in seven years) had made a deep pond beside an embankment the French had built for the trail. Such an enormous quantity of water all in one place was a source of great excitement to the inhabitants. For days there was a constant procession of women coming to carry it away in jugs. The children tried to walk on its surface, and two small ones were drowned. Ten days later the water had almost disappeared. A thick, brilliant green froth covered what was left, but the women continued to come with their jugs, pushing aside the scum and taking whatever fell in. For once they were able to collect as much water as they could store in their houses. Ordinarily, it was an expensive commodity that they had to buy each morning from the town water-sellers, who brought it in from the oasis.

There are probably few accessible places on the face of the globe where one can get less comfort for his money than the Sahara. It is still possible to find something flat to lie down on, several turnips and sand, noodles and jam, and a few tendons of something euphemistically called chicken to eat, and the stub of a candle to undress by at night. Inasmuch as it is necessary to carry one's own food and stove, it sometimes seems scarcely worth while to bother with the "meals" provided by the hotels. But if one depends entirely on tinned goods, they give out too quickly. Everything disappears eventually – coffee, tea, sugar, cigarettes – and the traveler settles down to a life devoid of these superfluities, using a pile of soiled clothing as a pillow for his head at night and a *burnous* as blanket.

Perhaps the logical question to ask at this point is: Why go? The answer is that when a man has been there and undergone the baptism of solitude he can't help himself. Once he has been under the spell of the vast, luminous, silent country, no other place is quite strong enough for him, no other surroundings can provide the supremely satisfying sensation of existing in the midst of something that is absolute. He will go back, whatever the cost in comfort and money, for the absolute has no price.

LETTER FROM TANGIER

LONDON MAGAZINE, JULY 1954

THIS CITY HAS CHANGED to such an extent since I first settled here in 1931 that if my strongest memories from that period were not inextricably connected with its climate and weather, I should no longer recognize it as the same place. The air and the wind are really about all that is left. Tangier's strange warm air with the pockets of coolness in it even under the searing sun! One day the air is crystalline, so that the mountains of Spain stand out as if they were across the street; the next day it is like a luminous gas, so that even the freighters in the harbor below are made equivocal by its white glare. And the wind is present – *ech cherqi* – the impossible *levante* that rushes in from the Mediterranean between the Pillars of Hercules with the force of a gale, and can keep blowing day after day without respite. These things are still here. Practically everything else is gone with the boom, that period of frenzied activity that started shortly before the war of 1939 and continued until the Riots of 1952. Even in the Casbah there is scarcely an alley that has not undergone a change: the Moslems of Tangier, no less than anyone else, have a passion for building and remodelling.

It was not so long ago when the Place de France was at the edge of town, and you could stand there at noon and hear the cicadas screaming from the eucalyptus trees. The Zoco de Fuera was, among other things, a grove of trees that provided shade for the performances of cobras, acrobats and dusty little apes

from the mountains. To go to Sidi Amar, instead of a municipal bus, you took a carriage with a torn beige canopy, drawn
by two horses laden with jangling bells. Instead of the rasp of
radios and the noise of traffic you heard the shrill sound of *rhaitas* being played, and there were torchlight processions in the
Medina where the bride was carried to her new abode doubled
up in an *almería* on the back of a donkey. Now she goes in a taxi
like any Christian or Jew.

'*Tous les agréments de Tangier ont disparu*', people are fond
of saying. There is nowhere to walk, unless you like shops
and motor traffic. The automobile has taken over; Tangier has
become a city, a miniature one if you like, but still a city. It
seems to me that the principal difference between a town and a
city is that while one can generally get out of a town by walking
on one's two legs, to escape from a city requires the use of some
other means of locomotion. If it weren't for a few corners of the
Casbah, the Old Mountain, the beaches and the nearby Spanish
Zone, there wouldn't really be much reason for people who have
no business interests here to bother coming, in spite of the lack
of cold weather, the absence of government, and other peculiari-
ties, most of them of a negative character, which are normally
considered to be advantages.

It is true that there is no levying of taxes and no official
interference in financial matters. You can pay for what you buy
in whatever currency you choose. No visa is needed to enter
the Zone, and once you are here you can stay on indefinitely
without ever being annoyed by thoughts of *permis de séjour* and
visits to the police. All this is, I suppose, as near to freedom as
one can get in the world of 1954. In the past six or seven years
the cost of living has risen considerably, but not in proportion to
what it has done in most parts of the world. A maid-servant who
can cook costs about a pound a week, food (with the exception
of good meat) is cheap in the market, charming little Arab
houses can be rented for anything from two to eight pounds a
month, depending on their size, location and sanitary facilities,
and petrol sells for only a shilling and eightpence a gallon, in

contrast to the astronomical sums one has to pay for it on the
Continent. In the past year all prices have dropped, and there
are indications that they will continue to do so, at least in the
immediate future. This would all be very fine for the foreign
resident with leisure on his hands, if it were not an indication
of the direction that life here is taking. The sad truth is that the
city has gone into a serious slump. The riots of March 1952,
although they were carried out by urchins at the instigation of
a few paid agitators, set people to thinking, an activity which
is often fatal to faith. The result was that gold began to leave
Tangier, bankers moved their businesses to South America, and
real-estate hit an air-pocket. From boom town to ghost town can
be a short way; the unceasing campaign of the Nationalists to
disrupt the life of French Morocco (via the bomb and the hand
grenade) certain does nothing to calm the fears of investors here.
Equally discouraging is the news that labor organizers have
arrived in the International Zone, intent upon forming unions
to raise the level of wages. The very concept of organized labor,
if disseminated, would spell death to the present economy. So
there is no cause for celebration on the part of foreign residents
in this precarious little paradise.

It would be hard to find a city the size of Tangier where the
inhabitants have less civic pride, or where there is such an utter
dearth of cultural life. An important reason for this is that very
few of those who came here during the great influx had any firm
intention of remaining. Tangier was the new El Dorado; one
would arrive, find a way to make one's killing, and get out as fast
as possible. But as in Hollywood, where the soda-jerkers and
shopgirls all seem to be *vedettes manquées* who can't bear to go
back to their farms and factories, the people somehow have not
made that quick million, and have stayed on anyway, loath to
abandon hope or to admit defeat. Besides, life for the unsuccessful prospector is no more unpleasant here than it would be
anywhere else. He can sit on the *terrasse* of one of the cafés on
the Place de France until half past eight, join the vast parade of
Spaniards taking their night *paseo* along the Boulevard Pasteur

Ahmed Yacoubi in Fez, 1955; Yacoubi became a protegé and close friend of Bowles
and accompanied him on trips to Europe, Turkey and Ceylon (PB)

until nine or so, have dinner and go to the cinema at half past ten, quite as if he were back in Marseille or Madrid or Rome, instead of a quarter of a mile from the dim fondouks of the Souk ez Zra, where the Berbers from the mountains lie wrapped in their *djellabas* among the donkeys. And, in the summer, which is Tangier's season (despite the English and American tourists who insist on coming here in January and then do nothing but complain of the rain) the beaches are frequented, but fortunately never crowded, and there are Sunday afternoon *corridas* in the bull-ring. I doubt that the absence of cultural life is noticed by many Tangerines, since most of them were not conscious of the presence of any such thing in the places from which they came.

What may be a sign of an awakening interest in art is the opening last week of Tangier's first art gallery. The inaugural exhibit was devoted to the work of the leader of young Moroccan painters, Ahmed El Yacoubi. This twenty-three-year-old Moslem artist is the son of a religious healer of Fez, which may have something to do with the fact that his work, which at first glance would seem to be a rather formalized and primitive surrealism, deals largely with the subject-matter of magic. Thus, what looks like arbitrary fantasy proves on closer inspection to be an illustration of a popular legend or an interpretation of a regional belief. Magic, incantations, the casting of spells, love-potions and even death-potions, are still a very important part of the fabric of Tangier's life, and it is not surprising that the young Moroccan artists (who, although they still believe implicitly in the efficacy of such medicine, are by virtue of their non-Islamic profession sufficiently exterior to it to observe it with a certain detachment), should draw upon this facet of the indigenous culture for their inspiration. It remains to be seen whether Tangier is large enough and cultured enough to support such an institution as the new Galería Provensa.

What is really extraordinary is that all the fantastic amount of expensive construction which has gone on here has served only to make the city look more improvised, chaotic and shabby. There was a certain ramshackle unity in the architectural style twenty years ago; now there is none. The place is frankly hideous. It is like a piece of jewellery whose setting far outshines its stone. The blue sky, the blue sea and the blue mountains are still here, but the town, not blue now save for the houses of a few recalcitrant Moors, no longer complements their combined charm. Instead, like most things of today, it rises in unlovely defiance of the laws of nature and beauty.

Yet if one lives here, one is bound to be ambivalent in one's feelings about the place. Its character, too strong to be overlooked, is like that of the little girl with the curl in the middle of her forehead. One is convinced that it is good to be in No Country, to feel, in this world of swiftly increasing social organization and hypertrophied governments, that anarchy is still a possibility. There is a spiritual healthiness in the absence of patriotic emotion, indifference to tribal loyalties, and even rampant opportunism. It is a pleasant thing to be in a place where one can at least have the illusion that the individual still has charge. The delight in freedom from bureaucratic intervention, deeper than the desire for gain, no doubt explains the fact that even when the possibilities for making a sudden fortune are gone, people are continuing to stay on.

I, who have always been an interested, if not totally involved, spectator of Tangier's evolution, shall stay on because the place has a strange and only partially explained fascination for me. I think it appeals particularly to those with a strong residue of infantilism in their character. There is an element of make-believe in the native life as seen from without (which is the only viewpoint from which we can ever see it, no matter how many years we may remain). It is a toy cosmos whose costumed inhabitants are playing an eternal game of buying and selling. The Casbah and the Medina below are a great pile of child's building blocks strewn carelessly over the side hill; when you huddle or recline inside the miniature rooms of the homes you are immediately back in early childhood, playing house, an illusion which is not dispelled by the tiny tables and tea glasses, the gaudy cushions and the lack of other furniture. The beggars come by and sing outside the door, each one with his own little song, and the forgotten but suddenly familiar sensation of being far *inside* is complete.

Certainly it's not that the Moslems of Morocco are more clever or charming than the people of any other country. In their own devious way they can be as difficult to live with as anyone else, and one can be just as ambivalent about them as about Tangier. I am not quick to see group characteristics. It has taken me more than two decades, for instance, to realize that the Moslem's incredible aptitude for putting mechanical things out of order was due to something other than simple failure to understand the principles of physics, or that his disinclination to think in any way of the future was other than the result of a childlike preoccupation with the present moment, combined with an unusually carefree nature. But of course I was quite mistaken. If Ali disables a machine ten seconds after touching it, it is because deep in his subconscious he *wants* to break it, the proper condition for all mechanical instruments is: not working. When some gadget that should function refuses to do so, you see the suppressed glee on every face. It is written in the Koran that man's inventions are falsehoods and must one day cease to be of use. Or if Mustapha regularly neglects to buy sufficient sugar for the morrow when he knows that more will be needed before the bacals are open, it is not because he is frivolous or conscious only of the existing instant as it passes: it is because he refuses to tempt Allah, who may strike at him for his presumptuousness in assuming that he will live to *see* tomorrow. For all he knows, the Supreme Being has other plans, and it would be inviting disaster to display any sense of security in life, even if he felt one, which he is not likely to do. The true Moslem attitude demands that one act always as though death loomed immediately ahead.

And to judge from the way things look at the moment, sudden death may lie ahead for a good many Moroccans. They are just beginning to awaken to the fact that the difference between their world and the world outside is not one in kind, but in

time. It is a dangerous discovery, because they are going to disregard many vital things in their haste to catch up. As long as the
discrepancies could be counted a matter of taste, everything was
all right; there were two coexistent worlds with distinctive aims.
But now that they have decided to go in our direction they are
dismayed to see how far behind us they come in the procession.
Not knowing where we are trying to go or why we want to go
there, being merely determined to go along with us, they imagine that they can do so merely by ignoring the historical distance that separates our two cultures. But sheer insistence is not
enough. Democracy is an empty word to the average Moroccan;
indeed, by his temperament and conditions he is more inclined
to totalitarianism. For this reason anti-Soviet arguments, which
are generally based on humanitarian considerations, mean
very little to them, while the most thinly disguised Communist
propaganda is often warmly received. At every turn one hears
intimations of the basic 1954 line: America is to blame. If
Moroccans are dying in Indo-China, if it rains too much or not
enough, if there is no work, if one's wife is sick and penicillin is
expensive, or if the French are still in Morocco, it is all the fault
of America. She could change everything if she chose, but she
does nothing because she does not love the Moslems.

So far, the mounting rebellion in the French Zone has not
touched Tangier directly. There have been a few murders, but
only policemen and natives known to be informers for the
French. And there has been none of the indiscriminate throwing
of bombs that characterizes the daily life of Casablanca. But
as the Moslems say: "There is fire in the Costa, and you can
feel the heat here". At the moment a concerted effort is being
made, and with success, by unofficial individuals to stop the
native populace from smoking, because tobacco is distributed
by the French. If a man is seen with a cigarette, he may be
approached by a pair or a group, who will ask him politely what
his religion is. If he answers "Moslem", they will upbraid him
and suggest that henceforth he refrain from smoking. This is a
warning. If they catch him again he will probably come away

from the second confrontation with his face slashed. Then his troubles begin, since if he reports the incident to the police, he runs the risk of a more serious, perhaps fatal, attack as a result. However, if he does not report it, and the police discover it, he will certainly be jailed as a suspected Nationalist sympathizer. Participation in this little war is not a matter of personal option.

In spite of these shadows cast by coming events, the character of the city is one so intimate that it is somehow difficult to consider them seriously. "We'll probably all be murdered in our beds", people say smiling: and nobody believes it for a minute.

There is a leering little Arabic ditty of questionable political intentions which comes over the radio from time to time. To make it chic they have given it a recurrent French refrain, which goes:

"Il y a une chose magnifique;
C'est la bombe atomique.
Ca vient de l'Amérique.
Ca arrête le trafic.
C'est leur bombe pacifique!"

Windows on
the Past

Holiday, January 1955

O NE DAY IN LATE July, 1955, a young man with a paperbound book under his arm will step out of the glare of Seville's Plaza de la Falange Española into the shade of the Calle Sierpes, walk along under the canvas tenting stretched high above the street, and turn into the Restaurant Los Corrales. Once inside, he will order a *gazpacho andaluz*, the best cold soup in the world, and then he will open his book, which he will have bought only an hour earlier, and begin to slit its pages with the butter knife. *Romancero Gitano*, the title page will say, and although he knows quite well who Garcia Lorca was, having seen productions of two of his plays in college, he finds a particular thrill in opening one of his books and seeing the neat verses in Spanish for the first time. He is so completely engrossed that the gypsy girl peering at him through the window that gives onto the back street has to hiss three times before he notices her. She is holding a pack of Pall Malls in the thin brown hand she has squeezed through the grillwork. He will in all likelihood smile at her, hold up his own pack of Chesterfields and return to his book.

The young man is doing something that is very important to him. He is not reading the book, since he understands only about half the words used in it. His mind is filled with confused images of the things he has seen in the past few days: the golden splendor of the great *retablo* in the Cathedral, the patio of orange trees viewed from the parapet of the Giralda, the gypsy who danced for him in a little café across the river in Triana, the greenness of the gardens behind the Alcázar. The book is not much more than a point of departure, a catalyzing agent. But like the fortune teller's crystal globe, it serves to focus the attention and induce the almost trancelike state he needs in order to feel that he is participating in the cultural life of the place. He wants to know this strange flat city of gardens and burning sunlight, make a part of it his own, and take it back with him to the United States. The place may not be Seville – it may be Florence or Lausanne or Killarney or Avignon or one of a thousand others in Europe where Americans will be – but the desire and the experience will be the same. The American will be seeking to capture something he feels he needs, and when he returns home it will be intangible trophies of this sort which he will prize above all his others.

THE TREND OF THIS CENTURY is being set by America for the entire world. (Even Lenin on his deathbed is reported to have said, "Americanize yourselves.") Whether or not we are as yet truly fitted for the task, we Americans are now fairly used to considering ourselves the leaders. We manage pretty well in undertakings which demand organization, perseverance, industriousness and, of course, technique. In cultural matters, however, we often find ourselves still looking across the Atlantic for guidance. To attribute this backward-glancing to mere aesthetic snobbery is to explain away some of it, I admit, but not all of it. There are deeper reasons why Europe still holds something important for us.

I think it is the business of technique that stands in the way of our own culture's complete and unimpeded flowering. In the rush to learn how we have forgotten that first we must know *what*. And we are becoming increasingly aware that an overemphasis on technique produces an unsatisfying artistic result. Unconsciously or otherwise we demand something better, we are uneasy, we suspect that we have missed some element vital to the fashioning of a culture. Why otherwise are we so consistently fascinated by Europe – slightly contemptuous of her oldness, of course, but drawn back to explore her, year after year, decade after decade, in ever increasing numbers – unless it be that our intuition tells us we shall find what we need there, among the visible vestiges of our immediate tribal past?

For some the search leads to specific museums, cathedrals, festivals – the neatly packaged evidences of Europe's culture. Not long ago I went to see *Tosca* at the Terme di Caracalla in Rome; the moon shone down from overhead, there was an audience of ten thousand people, the production and performance were superb, and no microphones were used. At the same time another annual opera season was in progress, at the vast Roman Arena of Verona, and just as that would draw to a close, the XIVth International Film Festival was scheduled to open in Venice. The visitor to Italy, or to practically any part of Europe, can be sure of finding plenty of organized culture. By timing his travels to gratify his tastes, he can catch the Shakespeare Festival at Stratford-on-Avon, or the Royal Danish Ballet Festival at Copenhagen, or the miracle play *Petrus de Dacia* on Gotland Island off the coast of Sweden, and any of innumerable music festivals, of which some celebrate the work of a single composer (Sibelius at Helsinki, Wagner at Bayreuth), others offer more general fare (Salzburg, Strasbourg, Granada), and still others specialize severely (the Dolmetsch Festival of Early English Music at Halsmere, Surrey, or the Carillon Concerts at Bruges in Belgium). Particularly in summer, Europe teems with such activities.

That is excellent. But I believe that what we Americans are searching for, and thus the most important thing we can bring back with us, is something more all-embracing. I should call it a childhood – a personal childhood that has some relationship to the childhood of our culture. The overwhelming majority of us are transplanted Europeans of one sort or another. Culturally speaking, the short time we have been in America is nothing compared to the infinitely longer time we have spent in Europe, and we seem to have forgotten this true past, lost contact with the psychic soil of tradition in which the roots of culture must be anchored.

Our gadget civilization has no visible connection with the past; it is not the continuation or outgrowth of any deep-seated myth, and however much the rational section of the mind may approve of it, the other part of the mind, the part that actually determines preferences rather than explaining them, is dissatisfied with it. What we want is to experience that glow which comes to an individual when he feels beyond a doubt that he is an integral, if infinitesimal, part of historical continuity. And Europe, if we approach it without preconceived ideas as to what constitutes its "culture" – simply with a little humility and a little imagination – provides us with that lost childhood, the childhood which never happened, but whose evocation can be so instrumental in helping us to locate ourselves in time and space. It is the first step, the indispensable one, in the direction of knowing what we are to ourselves and what we are in the world.

CULTURE IS ESSENTIALLY a matter of using the past to give meaning to the present. A man's culture is the sum of his memories. It will not consist of a wealth of facts, names and dates which he has at his finger tips, but will be rather the sum of everything that he has thought and felt – that is, *known*.

If I am faced with the decision of choosing between visiting a circus and a cathedral, a café and a public monument, or a fiesta and a museum, I'm afraid I shall normally take the circus, the café and the fiesta, trusting to luck that I shall manage to see the others later. I suppose I'm simply not what today is called culture-minded. Perhaps that is because to me the culture of a land at any given moment is the people who live in it and the lives they lead in it, not the possessions they have inherited from those who came before. They may or may not profit by their legacy. If they do, so much the better for them; but whether they do or do not, their culture is represented by them and not by their history.

I moved around Europe a good deal during my teens and twenties, and by moving around I mean constant displacement, often every day, all year round, an occupation which I pursued with an intensity I find difficult to understand now. With the usual omnivorousness of the footloose American in Europe, I wandered into hundreds of museums, chapels, galleries, cathedrals, parks, ruins and cemeteries, all the places where tangible evidence of what it pleases us to call culture could still be found. But probably because I was a young man of abysmal ignorance in such matters, the objects of culture themselves seldom impressed me as much as the general atmosphere enveloping each particular place. Always, as I stepped into one of these cultural sanctuaries, I felt that at the same time I was stepping almost entirely out of life, out of the world of reality.

With such an attitude, it is not surprising that I remember very little of what I saw in these dim places, and that in my memory they have become collectively merely an atmospheric part of the whole, whose brighter points are inevitably streets, cafés, railway stations, theaters, village squares, markets and rural landscapes.

Yet, understood and appreciated or not, the dim places remain in my mind; they are the dark, mysterious core of my European memories, and it is this core which in some unexplained fashion – perhaps precisely because of its element of mystery – now gives meaning and direction to the memories I carry.

The mind has a strange way of selecting a few details from among millions, and presenting them to us as tokens of experience. It is as if it said to us: "These are the only keepsakes you are to have, these irrelevant memories. The rest I am sweeping out." And then, doubtless just because there are so few of them, these flashes of past reality grow in intensity, the light that illumines them is no longer simple sunlight or moonlight, but ore our own making, and the illogical little vignettes become symbols in themselves, etched indelibly on our memory.

Thus a week spent in Munich for a music festival may eventually yield only the milkiness of the River Isar, the ever-present choking smell of burning coke in the air, and the Deutsches Museum, which fascinated me to such an extent that I preferred to eat a ghastly lunch there in its basement rather than go out for a good one and return. (I might add that the museum was full of automata which could be set in motion by pushing buttons.) Or the Alps in winter can be reduced to the mingled smell of melting snow and barnyards; the Alps in spring to hyacinths and ice along the road, and going to sleep nights in country inns to the sound of waterfalls; the Alps in summer to funiculars, bunches of lavender picked on the hillsides, and the cold breath of glaciers that creak in the still, hot sunlight. Of Heidelberg I can recall only crawling around the Schloss alone at night, being brushed against by startled bats and nearly breaking my neck – that and an Ascension Day morning spent sitting on a hill watching a battle between two varieties of ants, while the church bells rang. Of Salzburg, the castle on the hill slowly shedding its morning coat of mist. Of Venice the fact that living there is slightly disquieting; one feels like a personage in a painting – so much so that the paintings there seem less exciting than they should. Of Berlin, the shortness of the summer nights; in June you could go to *Götterdämmerung* at the old Kroll Oper, and when you came out there would still be daylight in the west. Then you would sit an hour in a café, and before you got home dawn would be breaking, the sparrows twittering. And of Mont Saint Michel, besides the omelettes of Mère Poulard, the plight of some unfortunate medieval gentleman, described by the guide as he dragged his flock through a particularly dark dungeon: *"On l'a jeté ici, où il a été r-r-rongé par les r-r-rats!"*

The entire French populace is often credited with having unerring taste and understanding in matters of art: this is unfortunately a gross exaggeration. One winter in Paris I lived in a large studio on the Quai Voltaire. On the walls I had placed, with care and a certain pride, three huge "constructions" by Miró, made of wood, plaster and rope. They were the only objects of art in the place, and it was a shock to return one evening to the studio and find them gone. I rushed downstairs to the concierge, who with her sister had charge of cleaning the apartment, and announced the disappearance of the Mirós, and at the same time I asked her for the address of the nearest police station. She looked mystified. "But monsieur has never had any pictures in his studio," she said. I described them. "Oh!" she laughed. "Those old pieces of wood you had tacked against the wall. I threw them in the cellar with the firewood. I thought monsieur would be pleased to get rid of them. They took up so much room." The three constructions had to be sent back to the Gallery for repairs, which I was told could be done only by the *maître* when he returned from Barcelona.

THERE WAS A *MUSIKFEST* in a spa of Westphalia one spring. I remember it, probably, because it required a concentrated participation which I was unable to give it; it is normal not to forget an incident which impresses one with a sense of one's inadequacy. The cherry trees were in bloom, the grass was lush, one crunched along the gravel sidewalks of the resort always in the shade of the carefully manicured lindens. The air was incredibly sweet, and there was an atmosphere of unsmirchable cleanliness about the town and the neighboring countryside.

The first night I got off on the wrong foot by having an argument with the hotelkeeper. On the register, under Nationality, I had written *Amerikaner*, and under Profession, I had put *Komponist*. A half hour later, passing by the desk, I happened to glance at the register again, and discovered that my host had supplied the gratuitous word *Jazz* before *Komponist*. Being at an age when such a thing constitutes a grave affront to one's honor, I promptly crossed out *Jazz* but unfortunately the proprietor saw me and hurried out to inform me that it was forbidden to change anything on the register once the authorities had been given the information contained therein. "*Polizeilich verboten!*", he barked. This led to a discussion about the nature of my work, a subject which he loudly insisted was of no interest whatever to him. An American composer was a jazz composer (he pronounced it "yatz," of course) and that was that. This put me in a fury, and as one is wont to do in such cases, I transferred most of my annoyance with him to the festival in general.

The next morning I determined to change dwelling places, and I chose a pension with a pretty garden. This place was full of musicians. From the moment I moved in until three days later when I left for Hanover the only lapses in the stream of purely musical conversation were those engendered by linguistic difficulties. Otherwise it was all Schnabel, Hindenith Gieseking, Szigeti, Bartók, Furtwängler, *cadenze*, *tutti*, *rubati*, and that strange, highly inflected but utterly unmellifluous tongue that is comprehensible only to the musicians, in which they quote themes to each other: "Paw paw paw *paw*, dzing dzing dzing-a-dzing *poom*, paw paw paw *paw*, BOM!"

Early in the game it was decided that I was a very peculiar fish. What was I, an American *jüngling*, doing all alone out here on this sacred pilgrimage? Where were my parents, and why was I not studying? The men were a little more indulgent, but the women were fierce about it.

Afternoons we would sit at cafés in the deep shade along the Hauptstrasse, drinking beer or eating ice cream topped with *Schlagsahne*. Evenings were spent, of course, at the concert hall, with everyone who had access to scores or manuscripts following them studiously. Then the real fun began, when the listeners joined the participants and composers back at the cafés afterward and let fly with their endlessly ramified opinions. But when finally everyone went to bed there was the deep silence of the country night, and in the early morning the smell of wood smoke filled the air.

Because I had been put on the defensive by these people, I felt more or less duty-bound to stick it out: the long concerts of modern music that was largely dull, the conferences afterward, and the eternal conversations at mealtimes. However, when Sunday morning dawned bright and beautiful, I had to choose between a special ten-o'clock symposium on the contemporary Czech art song and a stroll, preferably through the orchards up the hill overlooking the town and its valley. I could foresee just what sort of mournful and dissonant sounds would be filling the dark auditorium, and I took the walk. Even so, I was not without music; the birds and the village church bells provided me with a concert far more in keeping with the day and the spot.

I came late to luncheon, and was greeted with reproachful glances. I was accused of not being a serious person. Then someone had the novel idea of attributing my obviously frivolous nature to my nationality, and everyone hastened to agree. If a man were not *able* to be serious, this constitutional inferiority made him a pitiable rather than a censurable character. This reflection brought cheer to them all, and I found myself back in their good graces, where I stayed until I sneaked away to the station the next morning and caught the early train out. And that was the end of the one music festival whose events I can recall.

MY FIRST VISIT to the Prado took place twenty-two years ago on a cold rainy afternoon in November. I was passing through Madrid on my way from Marrakesh to Paris, and with me I had Abdelkader, a savage little fifteen-year-old Moroccan who was being exported to the Quai Voltaire to be broken in to domestic service in the house of a friend. In his short life Abdelkader had not had much opportunity to learn about Europeans and their culture; he had never seen or heard of such a thing as a painting.

Our first confrontation was a very large Greco. "It's broken," remarked Abdelkader, after a moment.

"What do you mean, broken?" I asked him.

"It's stuck. It's not moving."

I explained carefully that this was not a cinema, and we went into a room full of pictures by Bosch, or *El Bosco*, as the Spanish like to call him. Here were most of the famous examples of the Flemish master's intimate visions of punishment, doom and destruction. We paused in front of the *Temptation of Saint Anthony*, complete with a case of the most malevolent little demons ever depicted in paint. Abdelkader needed no previous knowledge of Christian dogma to understand the nature of the monsters that swarmed across these tortured canvases. Now he exhibited distinct signs of panic.

"It's not a cinema?" he whispered, and I assured him again that it was not.

"Then," he went on, his voice rising in volume and pitch, "that is real fire and blood, and those are real devils. Come on!"

We went hurriedly into another *sala*, hung with peaceful Flemish interiors and landscapes. He signed with relief. "Ah, no, my friend. I'm not going to stay in there with those things. They're very bad. The Spanish are crazy to leave such things around in the open."

As the afternoon wore on, his courage returned somewhat, and I think he began to feel pangs of shame for his earlier reactions. At one point he approached a particularly vivid crucifixion and tentatively touched a portion of it with his forefinger, calling my attention to his exploit. "Look! The blood doesn't come off! It's dried on." This preliminary experiment encouraged him to further daring, and he began to dart from picture to picture, rubbing flesh, tree trunks, bones, clouds and water, until a guard caught sight of him and reprimanded him severely.

"*Prohibido. Está prohibido*," the guard insisted, wagging his index finger back and forth in front of the offender's face.

"What's he saying?" asked Abdelkader. I told him, and explained that the picture might be damaged by being touched.

"But all the people are dead and dried up," he said scornfully. "How could it hurt them? The Spanish are crazy."

A somewhat similar thing happened recently when my Moorish chauffeur, on his first visit away from his native Morocco, drove me to the Cathedral in Córdoba. "Hm," he said with satisfaction as we approached the great, unmistakably Eastern edifice, "this is ours." My mistake was in saying "Yes," for he took my agreement to mean that the building was still a mosque. This illusion was not dispelled, either by the vast outer courtyard or by the interior. When he got inside, like any good Moslem, he went in search of water. Before I knew what was happening, he had installed himself before a fount of holy water,

rolled up his sleeves, immersed his face and was gargling, spit-
ting, splashing and scrubbing quite as his forebears had done in
the same place of worship a thousand years ago. Happily this
part of the Cathedral is fairly dark, and was deserted at that
moment of the afternoon, so that I got to him before anyone
heard or saw him, otherwise we might both have ended the day
at the *Comisaria de Policía*. Few citizens of Córdoba would have
taken a light-hearted view of his innocent sacrilege.

IF I DWELL upon Spain here, it is because I think Spain has the most
to offer the American in Europe. Since this is an opinion and not
a provable thesis, I can only fall back upon personal reactions to
its surpassing beauty in order to fortify my statement. It is an easy
country to "get into," the people are friendly and hospitable, and,
which is quite as important, exceedingly conscious and proud of
their *cultura hispánica*. Visually it is the most dramatic country in
Western Europe. Contrasts are always easy to seize and remember;
almost every aspect of Spain owes its character to a contradiction.
The most important single element in the landscape is an impression of fertility in the midst of barrenness, the architecture is both
an agreement and a clashing of Western and Eastern concepts of
proportion and form, the people are in general either very rich
or very poor, and since there have been relatively few changes
wrought in the economic and social fabric of the nation between
the era of Spain's glory and the present century, the past is still
powerfully alive in the land today. Just turn off the main road and
drive over the hill, and you are in a country whose spirit has not
yet been broken by the mechanical age.

Since childhood I had admired the music of Manuel de Falla,
the great latter-day Spanish composer. Thus, on my second trip
to Spain (I have since made seventeen exploratory journeys
through the country, every one fully rewarding) I determined to
catch sight of him at the very least. In Cádiz I had already seen
the house where he was born. It seemed right that he should
have chosen Granada as his home – a little house with a shady
garden on the sun-baked hill of the Alhambra, almost within

hearing distance of the fountains of the Generalife, where across the narrow valley were the caves of Sacro Monte to which he could go and listen to the *gitanos* make their magnificent music. I did see him, several times, a thin little figure in black, hurrying along the narrow back lanes of the village under the high trees, on his way to noonday Mass. He would be respectfully pointed out to me by the citizens: "*Ahí va el maestro.*" One day I decided to call on him. He and his sister lived alone in the house. They were solemn and hospitable. We sat a long while in a small patio eating fruit and discussing music. At the end of the afternoon when I left I promised to return, but somehow I never did.

In Elche, which with its palm groves looks exactly like a Saharan oasis, the proprietor of the hotel set a new low in undistinguished behavior. After I had paid the bill and tipped the porter, my host dashed out into the street in his long black mohair duster and began to run along behind the carriage, for a while almost able to keep up with the horses' gait, calling piteously after me: "*Una propinita para mí tambien, señor!*" ("A little tip for me, too, sir!").

Of Barcelona I remember the gloomy Cathedral, Gaudi's mushroom apartment house on the Paseo de Gracia, the improbable façade of the Sagrada Familia, and the beautiful black-and-gold interior of the little church of Nuestra Señora de Belén (now, alas, less beautiful as a result of Mussolini's bombs). I remember all these things, yes, but I have a far more vivid picture of the little plaza into which I stumbled one hot afternoon to find fifty or more serious-faced people in a circle, dancing a stately *sardana* to the strident sounds of the *fluviol* and the *gralla*; or of the cable car in which I swung, high over the harbor spread out below, to be transported to Montjuich for lunch; or of the fair at twilight up on Tibidabo, with the silly music going, to the east the million lights of the city being lighted one by one, and to the west the pine-covered hills losing their green and falling back into silence and darkness.

For sheer experience, pure as music, there is the night I found a small door, left open by an oversight, in the west wall of a vegetable garden attached to the Alhambra. There was a full moon; no one was in sight. I stepped in. The vegetable garden led to formal gardens, patios, into the palace itself. The sound of a fountain dribbling into its basin in the Hall of the Two Sisters was strangely loud, releasing tiny liquid echoes that played overhead in the dark. Young frogs chirped hopefully from the shadows in the Court of Myrtles. Descending stairways, tiptoeing along grilled passageways, I stopped to listen to the sound of the running water which is everywhere in the palace grounds, and leaning from a window in the Hall of the Ambassadors I heard, coming up from somewhere below in the darkness of the Albaicin, a lone voice, fragments of a song. "*Tu misma tienes la cu-u-u-u-ulpa.*" The Spaniard singing the words might have been addressing them to the entire vanquished race of the Moors. I had been to the Alhambra before, and I have been there many times since, but the two hours or so I passed there that night have nothing to do with all the other visits; they are apart, in another category, to be evaluated by other units of weight.

HALF THE PEOPLE in Seville are asleep. The color of the few strips of sunlight that fall into the Calle Sierpes between the awnings has changed from the yellow of midday to the gold of midafternoon. The young American, in a slightly somnolent state from a long and heavy meal, sallies forth into the street, his book once again under his arm, and in his mind hovers the vague project of wandering through the Barrio de Santa Cruz. Whether he will do that or not will depend upon his strength of character, for another image keeps creeping into his head: that of the cool bed back in the dimness of his shuttered hotel room. It would be pleasant to sleep awhile. *Ya es la hora de la siesta.* It will all go back with him to America, nothing will have been wasted. Each hour he has spent with open eyes and mind will have carried him a little further along the path to understanding the world, and that, after all, is the truest measure for culture we have been able to find.

A MAN MUST NOT
BE VERY MOSLEM

HOLIDAY, MAY 1955; THEIR HEADS ARE GREEN, 1963

ABOARD M/S TARSUS, TURKISH MARITIME LINES
SEPTEMBER 25, 1953

W HEN I ANNOUNCED my intention of bringing Abdeslam along to Istanbul, the general opinion of my friends was that there were a good many more intelligent things to do in the world than to carry a Moroccan Moslem along with one to Turkey. I don't know. He may end up as a dead weight, but my hope is that he will turn out instead to be a kind of passkey to the place. He knows how to deal with Moslems, and he has the Moslem sense of seemliness and protocol. He has also an intuitive gift for the immediate understanding of a situation and at the same time is completely lacking in reticence or inhibitions. He can lie so well that he convinces himself straightway, and he is a master at bargaining; it is a black day for him when he has to pay the asking price for anything. He never knows what is printed on a sign because he is totally illiterate; besides, even if he did know he would pay no attention, for he is wholly deficient in respect for law. If you mention that this or

Paul Bowles and Ahmed Yacoubi (the real life Abdeslam of this piece), on his right,
on the boat from Tangier to Istanbul, 1953 (PB)

that thing is forbidden, he is contemptuous: "Agh! a decree for the wind!" Obviously he is far better equipped than I to squeeze the last drop of adventure out of any occasion. I, unfortunately, can read signs but can't lie or bargain effectively, and will forgo any joy rather than risk unpleasantness or reprimand from whatever quarter. At all events, the die is cast: Abdeslam is here on the ship.

My first intimation of Turkey came during tea this afternoon, as the ship was leaving the Bay of Naples. The orchestra was playing a tango which finally established its identity, after several reprises, as the "Indian Love Call," and the cliffs of Capri were getting in the way of the sunset. I glanced at a biscuit that I was about to put into my mouth, then stopped the operation to examine it more closely. It was an ordinary little arrow-root tea-biscuit, and on it were embossed the words *hayd park*. Contemplating this edible tidbit, I recalled what friends had told me of the amusing havoc that results when the Turks phoneticize words borrowed from other languages. These metamorphosed words have a way of looking like gibberish until you say them aloud, and then more likely than not they resolve themselves into perfectly comprehensible English or French or, even occasionally, Arabic. *skoç tuid* looks like nothing; suddenly it becomes Scotch Tweed. *Tualet, trençkot, ototeknik* and *seksoloji* likewise reveal their messages as one stares at them. Synthetic orthography is a constantly visible reminder of Turkey's determination to be "modern." The country has turned its back on the East and Eastern concepts, not with the simple yearning of other Islamic countries to be European or to acquire American techniques, but with a conscious will to transform itself from the core outward – even to destroy itself culturally, if need be.

TARABYA, BOSPORUS

THIS AFTERNOON it was blustery and very cold. The water in the tiny Sea of Marmara was choppy and dark, laced with froth; the ship rolled more heavily than it had at any time during its three days out on the open Mediterranean. If the first sight of Istanbul was impressive, it was because the perfect hoop of a rainbow painted across the lead-colored sky ahead kept one from looking at the depressing array of factory smokestacks along the western shore. After an hour's moving backward and forward in the harbor, we were close enough to see the needles of the minarets (and how many of them!) in black against the final flare-up of the sunset. It was a poetic introduction, and like the introductions to most books, it had very little to do with what followed. "Poetic" is not among the adjectives you would use to describe the disembarkation. The pier was festive; it looked like an elegant waterside restaurant or one of the larger Latin American airports – brilliantly illumined, awnings flapping, its decks mobbed with screaming people.

The customs house was the epitome of confusion for a half-hour or so; when eventually an inspector was assigned us, we were fortunate enough to be let through without having to open anything. The taxis were parked in the dark on the far side of a vast puddle of water, for it had been raining. I had determined on a hotel in Istanbul proper, rather than one of those in Beyoğlu, across the Golden Horn, but the taxi driver and his front-seat companion were loath to take me there. "All hotels in Beyoğlu," they insisted. I knew better and did some insisting of my own. We shot into the stream of traffic, across the Galata Bridge, to the hotel of my choosing. Unhappily I had neglected, on the advice of various friends back in Italy, to reserve a room. There was none to be had. And so on, from hotel to hotel there in Istanbul, back across the bridge and up the hill to every establishment in Beyoğlu. Nothing, nothing. There are three international conventions in progress here, and besides, it is vacation time in Turkey; everything is full. Even the M/S Tarsus, from which we just emerged, as well as another ship in the harbor, has been called into service tonight to be used as a hotel. By half past ten I accepted the suggestion of being driven twenty-five kilometers up the Bosporus to a place, where they had assured me by telephone that they had space.

"Do you want a room with bath?" they asked.

I said I did.

"We haven't any," they told me.

"Then I want a room without bath."

"We have one." That was that.

Once we had left the city behind and were driving along the dark road, there was nothing for Abdeslam to do but catechize the two Turks in front. Obviously they did not impress him as being up-to-the-mark Moslems, and he started by testing their knowledge of the Koran. I thought they were replying fairly well, but he was contemptuous. "They don't know anything," he declared in Moghrebi. Going into English, he asked them: "How many times one day you pray?"

They laughed.

"People can sleep in mosque?" he pursued. The driver was busy navigating the curves in the narrow road, but his companion, who spoke a special brand of English all his own, spoke for him. "Not slep in mosque many people every got hoss," he explained.

"You make sins?" continued Abdeslam, intent on unearthing the hidden flaws in the behavior of these foreigners. "Pork, wine?"

The other shrugged his shoulders. "Moslem people every not eat pork not drink wine but maybe one hundred year ago like that. Now different."

"*Never* different!" shouted Abdeslam sternly. "You not good Moslems here. People not happy. You have bad government. Not like Egypt. Egypt have good government. Egypt one-hundred-percent Moslem."

The other was indignant. "Everybody happy," he protested. "Happy with Egypt too for religion. But the Egypts sometimes fight with Egypts. Arab fight Arabs. Why? I no like Egypt. I in Egypt. I ask my way. They put me say *bakhshish*. If you ask in Istanbul, you say I must go my way, he can bring you, but he no say give *bakhshish*. Before, few people up, plenty people down. Now, you make your business, I make my business. You take your money, I take my money. Before, *you* take *my* money. You rich with *my* money. Before, Turkey like Egypt with Farouk." He stopped to let all this sink in, but Abdeslam was not interested.

"Egypt very good country," he retorted, and there was no more conversation until we arrived. At the hotel the driver's comrade was describing a fascinating new ideology known as democracy. From the beginning of the colloquy I had my notebook out, scribbling his words in the dark as fast as he spoke them. They express the average uneducated Turk's reaction to the new concept. It was only in 1950 that the first completely democratic elections were held. (Have there been any since?) To Abdeslam, who is a traditionally minded Moslem, the very idea of democracy is meaningless. It is impossible to explain it to him; he will not listen. If an idea is not explicitly formulated in the Koran, it is wrong; it came either directly from Satan or via the Jews, and there is no need to discuss it further.

This hotel, built at the edge of the lapping Bosporus, is like a huge wooden box. At the base of the balustrade of the grand staircase leading up from the lobby, one on each side, are two life-sized ladies made of lead and painted with white enamel in the hope of making them look like marble. The dining room's decorations are of a more recent period – the early 'twenties. There are high murals that look as though the artist had made a study of Boutet de Monvel's fashion drawings of the era; long-necked, low-waisted females in cloches and thigh-length skirts, presumably picnicking on the shores of the Bosporus.

At dinner we were the only people eating, since it was nearly midnight. Abdeslam took advantage of this excellent opportunity by delivering an impassioned harangue (partly in a mixture of Moghrebi and Standard Arabic and partly in English), with the result that by the end of the meal we had fourteen waiters and bus boys crowded around the table listening. Then someone thought of fetching the chef. He arrived glistening with sweat and beaming; he had been brought because he spoke more Arabic than the others, which was still not very much. "Old-fashioned Moslem," explained the headwaiter. Abdeslam immediately put him through the *chehade*, and he came off with flying colors, reciting it word for word along with Abdeslam: "*Achhaddouanlaillahainallah.* . . ." The faces of the younger men expressed unmistakable admiration, as well as pleasure at the approval of the esteemed foreigner, but none of them could perform the chef's feat. Presently the manager of the hotel came in, presumably to see what was going on in the dining room at this late hour. Abdeslam asked for the check, and objected when he saw that it was written with Roman characters. "Arabic!" he demanded. "You Moslem? Then bring check in Arabic." Apologetically the manager explained that writing in Arabic was "dangerous," and had been known on occasion to put the man who did it into jail. To this he added, just to make things quite clear, that any man who veiled his wife also went to jail. "A man must not be *very* Moslem," he said. But Abdeslam had had enough. "I *very very* Moslem," he announced. We left the room.

The big beds stand high off the floor and haven't enough covers on them. I have spread my topcoat over me; it is cold and I should like to leave the windows shut, but the mingled stenches coming from the combined shower-lavatory behind a low partition in the corner are so powerful that such a course is out of the question. The winds moving down from the Black Sea will blow over me all night. Sometime after we had gone to bed, following a long silence during which I thought he had fallen asleep, Abdeslam called over to me: "That Mustapha Kemal was carrion! He ruined his country. The son of a dog!" Because I was writing, and also because I am not sure exactly where I stand in this philosophical dispute, I said: "You're right. *Allah imsik bekhir.*"

WE ARE INSTALLED at Sirkeci on the Istanbul side, in the hotel I had first wanted. Outside the window is a taxi stand. From early morning onward there is the continuous racket of men shouting and horns being blown in a struggle to keep recently arrived taxis from edging in ahead of those that have been waiting in

line. The general prohibition of horn-blowing, which is in effect
everywhere in the city, doesn't seem to apply here. The alterca-
tions are bitter, and everyone gets involved in them. Taxi drivers in Istanbul are something of a race apart. They are the only
social group who systematically try to take advantage of the foreign visitor. In the ships, restaurants, cafés, the prices asked of
the newcomer are the same as those paid by the inhabitants.
(In the bazaars buying is automatically a matter of wrangling;
that is understood.) The cab drivers, however, are more actively
acquisitive. For form's sake, their vehicles are equipped with
meters, but their method of using them is such that they might
better do without them. You get into a cab whose meter registers seventeen liras thirty kuruş, ask the man to turn it back to
zero and start again, and he laughs and does nothing. When
you get out it registers eighteen liras eighty kuruş. You give him
the difference – one lira and a half. Never! He may want two
and a half or three and a half or a good deal more, but he will
not settle for what seems equitable according to the meter. Since
most tourists pay what they are asked and go on their way, he
is not prepared for an argument, and he is likely to let his temper run away with him if you are recalcitrant. There is also the
prearranged-price system of taking a cab. Here the driver goes
as slowly and by as circuitous a route as possible, calling out the
general neighborhood of his destination for all in the streets to
hear, so that he can pick up extra fares en route. He will, unless
you assert yourself, allow several people to pile in on top of you
until there is literally no room left for you to breathe.

The streets are narrow, crooked and often precipitous; traffic
is very heavy, and there are many tramcars and buses. The result
is that the taxis go like the wind whenever there is a space of a
few yards ahead, rushing to the extreme left to get around obsta-
cles before oncoming traffic reaches them. I am used to Paris and
Mexico, both cities of evil repute where taxis are concerned, but
I think Istanbul might possibly win first prize for thrill-giving.

One day our driver had picked up two extra men and merci-
fully put them in front with him, when he spied a girl standing

on the curb and slowed down to take her in, too. A policeman saw his maneuver and did not approve: one girl with five men seemed too likely to cause a disturbance. He blew his whistle menacingly. The driver, rattled, swerved sharply to the left, to pretend he had never thought of such a thing as stopping to pick up a young lady. There was a crash and we were thrown forward off the seat. We got out; the last we saw of the driver, he was standing in the middle of the street by his battered car, screaming at the man he had hit, and holding up all traffic. Abdeslam took down his license number in the hope of persuading me to instigate a lawsuit.

Since the use of the horn is proscribed, taxi drivers can make their presence known only by reaching out the window and pounding violently on the outside of the door. The scraping of the tramcars and the din of the enormous horse-drawn carts thundering over the cobbled pavements make it difficult to judge just how much the horn interdiction reduces noise. The drivers also have a pretty custom of offering cigarettes at the beginning of the journey; this is to soften up the victim for the subsequent kill. On occasion they sing for you. One morning I was entertained all the way from Sulemaniye to Taksim with "Jezebel" and "Come On-a My House." In such cases the traffic warnings on the side of the car are done in strict rhythm.

Istanbul is a jolly place; it's hard to find any sinister element in it, notwithstanding all the spy novels for which it provides such a handsome setting. A few of the older buildings are of stone; but many more of them are built of wood which looks as though it had never been painted. The cupolas and minarets rise above the disorder of the city like huge gray fungi growing out of a vast pile of ashes. For disorder is the visual keynote of Istanbul. It is not slovenly – only untidy; not dirty – merely dingy and drab. And just as you cannot claim it to be a beautiful city, neither can you accuse it of being uninteresting. Its steep hills and harbor views remind you a little of San Francisco; its overcrowded streets recall Bombay; its transportation facilities evoke Venice, for you can go many places by boats which are continually making stops.

(It costs threepence to get across to Üsküdar in Asia.) Yet the streets are strangely reminiscent of an America that has almost disappeared. Again and again I have been reminded of some New England mill town in the time of my childhood. Or a row of little houses will suggest a back street in Stapleton, on Staten Island. It is a city whose aesthetic is that of the unlikely and incongruous, a photographer's paradise. There is no native quarter, or, if you like, it is all native quarter. Beyoğlu, the site of the so-called better establishments, concerns itself as little with appearances as do the humbler regions on the other side of the bridges.

You wander down the hill toward Karaköy. Above the harbor with its thousands of caïques, rowboats, tugs, freighters and ferries, lies a pall of smoke and haze through which you can see the vague outline of the domes and towers of Aya Sofia, Sultan Ahmet, Süleyimaniye; but to the left and far above all that there is a pure region next to the sky where the mountains in Asia glisten with snow. As you descend the alleys of steps that lead to the water's level, there are more and more people around you. In Karaköy itself just to make progress along the sidewalk requires the best part of your attention. You would think that all of the city's million and a quarter inhabitants were in the streets on their way to or from Galata Bridge. By Western European standards it is not a well-dressed crowd. The chaotic sartorial effect achieved by the populace in Istanbul is not necessarily due to poverty, but rather to a divergent conception of the uses to which European garments should be put. The mass is not an ethnically homogeneous one. The types of faces range from Levantine through Slavic to Mongoloid, the last belonging principally to the soldiers from eastern Anatolia. Apart from language there seems to be no one common element, not even shabbiness, since there are usually a few men and women who do understand how to wear their clothing.

Galata Bridge has two levels, the lower of which is a great dock whence the boats leave to go up the Golden Horn and the Bosporus, across to the Asiatic suburbs, and down to the islands in the Sea of Marmara. The ferries are there, of all sizes and shapes, clinging to the edge like water beetles to the side of a floating stick. When you get across to the other side of the bridge there are just as many people and just as much traffic, but the buildings are older and the streets narrower, and you begin to realize that you are, after all, in an oriental city. And if you expect to see anything more than the "points of interest," you are going to have to wander for miles on foot. The character of Istanbul derives from a thousand disparate, nonevident details; only by observing the variations and repetitions of such details can you begin to get an idea of the patterns they form. Thus the importance of wandering. The dust is bad. After a few hours of it I usually have a sore throat. I try to get off the main arteries, where the horses and drays clatter by, and stay in the alleyways, which are too narrow for anything but foot traffic. These lanes occasionally open up into little squares with rugs hanging on the walls and chairs placed in the shade of the grapevines overhead. A few Turks will be sitting about drinking coffee; the *narghilehs* bubble. Invariably, if I stop and gaze a moment, someone asks me to have some coffee, eat a few green walnuts and share his pipe. An irrational disinclination to become involved keeps me from accepting, but today Abdeslam did accept, only to find to his chagrin that the narghileh contained tobacco, and not kif or hashish as he had expected.

Cannabis sativa and its derivatives are strictly prohibited in Turkey, and the natural correlative of this proscription is that alcohol, far from being frowned upon as it is in other Moslem lands, is freely drunk; being a government monopoly it can be bought at any cigarette counter. This fact is no mere detail; it is of primary social importance, since the psychological effects of the two substances are diametrically opposed to each other. Alcohol blurs the personality by loosening inhibitions. The drinker feels, temporarily at least, a sense of participation. Kif abolishes no inhibitions; on the contrary it reinforces them, pushes the individual further back into the recesses of his own isolated personality, pledging him to contemplation and inaction. It is to be expected that there should be a close relationship between the culture of a given society and the means used by its members to achieve release and euphoria. For Judaism and Christianity the means has always been alcohol; for Islam it has been hashish. The first is dynamic in its effects, the other static. If a nation wishes, however mistakenly, to Westernize itself, first let it give up hashish. The rest will follow, more or less as a matter of course. Conversely, in a Western country, if a whole segment of the population desires, for reasons of protest (as has happened in the United States), to isolate itself in a radical fashion from the society around it, the quickest and surest way is for it to replace alcohol by cannabis.

OCTOBER 2

TODAY IN OUR WANDERINGS we came upon the old fire tower at the top of the hill behind Süleymaniye, and since there was no sign at the door forbidding entry, we stepped in and began to climb the one hundred and eighty rickety wooden steps of the spiral staircase leading to the top. (Abdeslam counted them.) When we were almost at the top, we heard strains of Indian music; a radio up there was tuned in to New Delhi. At the same moment a good deal of water came pouring down upon us through the cracks above. We decided to beat a retreat, but then the boy washing the stairs saw us and insisted that we continue to the top and sit awhile. The view up there was magnificent; there is no better place from which to see the city. A charcoal fire was burning in a brazier, and we had tea and listened to some Anatolian songs which presently came over the air. Outside the many windows the wind blew, and the city below, made quiet by distance, spread itself across the rolling landscape on every side, its roof tiles pink in the autumn sun.

Later we sought out Pandeli's, a restaurant I had heard about but not yet found. This time we managed to discover it, a dilapidated little building squeezed in among harness shops and wholesale fruit stores, unprepossessing but cozy, and with the best food we have found in Istanbul. We had *pirinç çorba,* beyendeli kebap, barbunya fasulya and other good things. In the middle of the meal, probably while chewing on the *taze makarna*, I bit my lip. My annoyance with the pain was not mitigated by hearing Abdeslam remark unsympathetically, "If you'd keep your mouth open when you chew, like everybody else, you wouldn't have accidents like this." Pandeli's is the only native restaurant I have seen which doesn't sport a huge refrigerated showcase packed with food. You are usually led to this and told to choose what you want to eat. In the glare of the fluorescent lighting the food looks pallid and untempting, particularly the meat, which has been hacked into unfamiliar-looking cuts. During your meal there is usually a radio playing ancient jazz; occasionally a Turkish or Syrian number comes up. Although the tea is good, it is not good enough to warrant its being served as though it were nectar, in infinitesimal glasses that can be drained at one gulp. I often order several at once, and this makes for confusion. When you ask for water, you are brought a tiny bottle capped with tinfoil. Since it is free of charge, I suspect it of being simple tap water; perhaps I am unjust.

In the evening we went to the very drab red-light district in Beyoğlu, just behind the British Consulate General. The street was mobbed with men and boys. In the entrance door of each house was a small square opening, rather like those through which one used to be denied access to American speakeasies, and framed in each opening, against the dull yellow light within, was a girl's head.

The Turks are the only Moslems I have seen who seem to have got rid of that curious sentiment (apparently held by all followers of the True Faith), that there is an inevitable and hopeless difference between themselves and non-Moslems. Subjectively, at least, they have managed to bridge the gulf created by their religion, that abyss which isolates Islam from the rest of the world. As a result the visitor feels a specific connection with them which is not the mere one-sided sympathy the well-disposed traveler has for the more basic members of other cultures, but is something desired and felt by them as well. They are touchingly eager to understand and please – so eager, indeed, that they often neglect to listen carefully and consequently get things all wrong. Their good will, however, seldom flags, and in the long run this more than compensates for being given the breakfast you did not order, or being sent in the opposite direction from the one in which you wanted to go. Of course, there is the linguistic barrier. One really needs to know Turkish to live in Istanbul and because my ignorance of all Altaic languages is total, I suffer. The chances are nineteen in twenty that when I give an order things will go wrong, even when I get hold of the housekeeper who speaks French and who assures me calmly that all the other employees are idiots. The hotel is considered by my guidebook to be a "de-luxe" establishment – the highest category. Directly after the "de-luxe" listings come the "first-class" places, which it describes in its own mysterious rhetoric: "These hotels have somewhat luxury, but are still comfortable with every convenience." Having seen the lobbies of several of the hostelries thus pigeonholed, complete with disemboweled divans and abandoned perambulators, I am very thankful to be here in my deluxe suite, where the telephone is white so that I can see the cockroaches on the instrument before I lift it to my lips. At least the insects are discreet and die obligingly under a mild blast of DDT. It is fortunate I came here: my two insecticide bombs would never have lasted out a sojourn in a first-class hotel.

OCTOBER 6

SANTA SOPHIA? Aya Sofya now, not a living mosque but a dead one, like those of Kairouan which can no longer be used because they have been profaned by the feet of infidels. Greek newspapers have carried on propaganda campaigns designed to turn the clock back, reinstate Aya Sofya as a tabernacle of the Orthodox Church. The move was obviously foredoomed to failure; after having used it as a mosque for five centuries the Moslems would scarcely relish seeing it put back into the hands of the Christians.

And so now it is a museum which contains nothing but its own architecture. Sultan Ahmet, the mosque just across the park, is more to my own taste; but then, a corpse does not bear comparison to a living organism. Sultan Ahmet is still a place of worship, the imam is allowed to wear the classical headgear, the heavy final syllable of Allah's name reverberates in the air under the high dome, boys *dahven* in distant corners as they memorize *surat* from the Koran. When the tourists stumble over the prostrate forms of men in prayer, or blatantly make use of their light meters and Rolleiflexes, no one pays any attention. To Abdeslam this incredible invasion of privacy was tantamount to lack of respect for Islam; it fanned the coals of his resentment into flame. (In his country no unbeliever can put even one foot into a mosque.) As he wandered about, his exclamations of indignation became increasingly audible. He started out with the boys by suggesting to them that it was their great misfortune to be living in a country of widespread sin. They looked at him blankly and went on with their litanies. Then in a louder voice he began to criticize the raiment of the worshipers, because they wore socks and slippers on their feet and on their heads berets or caps with the visors at the back. He knows that the wearing of the *tarboosh* is forbidden by law, but his hatred of Kemal Ataturk, which has been growing hourly ever since his arrival, had become too intense, I suppose, for him to be able to repress it any longer. His big moment came when the imam entered. He approached the venerable gentleman with elaborate salaams which were enthusiastically reciprocated. Then the two retired into a private room, where they remained for ten minutes or so. When Abdeslam came out there were tears in his eyes and he wore an expression of triumph. "Ah, you see?" he cried, as we emerged into the street. "That poor man is very, very unhappy. They have only one day of Ramadan in the year." Even I was a little shocked to hear that the traditional month had been whittled down to a day. "This is an accursed land," he went on. "When we get power we'll soak it in petrol and set it afire and burn everyone in it. May it forever be damned! And all these dogs living in it, I pray

Allah they may be thrown into the fires of Gehennem. Ah, if we only had our power back for one day, we Moslems! May Allah speed that day when we shall ride into Turkey and smash their government and all their works of Satan!" The imam, it seems, had been delighted beyond measure to see a young man who still had the proper respect for religion; he had complained bitterly that the youth of Turkey was spiritually lost.

Today I had lunch with a woman who has lived here a good many years. As a Westerner, she felt that the important thing to notice about Turkey is the fact that from having been in the grip of a ruthless dictatorship it has slowly evolved into a modern democracy, rather than having followed the more usual reverse process. Even Ataturk was restrained by his associates from going all the way in his iconoclasm, for what he wanted was a Turkish adaptation of what he had seen happen in Russia. Religion was to him just as much of an opiate in one country as in another. He managed to deal it a critical blow here, one which may yet prove to have been fatal. Last year an American, a member of Jehovah's Witnesses, arrived, and as is the custom with members of that sect, stood on the street handing out brochures. But not for long. The police came, arrested him, put him in jail, and eventually effected his expulsion from the country. This action, insisted my lunch partner, was not taken because the American was distributing Christian propaganda; had he been distributing leaflets advocating the reading of the Koran, it's likely that his punishment would have been more severe.

OCTOBER 10

AT THE BEGINNING of the sixteenth century, Selim the Grim captured from the Shah of Persia one of the most fantastic pieces of furniture I have ever seen. The trophy was the poor Shah's throne, a simple but massive thing made of chiseled gold, decorated with hundreds of enormous emeralds. I went to see it today at the Topkapi Palace. There was a bed to match, also of emerald-studded gold. After a moment of looking, Abdeslam ran out of the room where these incredible objects stood into the courtyard, and could not be coaxed back in. "Too many riches are bad for the eyes," he explained. I could not agree; I thought them beautiful. I tried to make him tell me the exact reason for his sudden flight, but he found it difficult to give me a rational explanation of his behavior. "You know that gold and jewels are sinful," he began. To get him to go on, I said I knew. "And if you look at sinful things for very long you can go crazy; you know that. And I don't want to go crazy." I was willing to take the chance, I replied, and I went back in to see more.

OCTOBER 16

THESE LAST FEW DAYS I have spent entirely at the covered souks. I discovered the place purely by accident, since I follow no plan in my wanderings about the city. You climb an endless hill; whichever street you take swarms with buyers and sellers who take up all the room between the shops on either side. It isn't good form to step on the merchandise, but now and then one can't avoid it.

The souks are all in one vast anthill of a building, a city within a city whose avenues and streets, some wide, some narrow, are like the twisting hallways of a dream. There are more than five thousand shops under its roof, so they assure me; I have not wondered whether it seems a likely number or not, nor have I passed through all its forty-two entrance portals or explored more than a small number of its tunneled galleries. Visually the individual shops lack the color and life of the *kissarias* of Fez and Marrakesh, and there are no painted Carthaginian columns like those which decorate the souks in Tunis. The charm of the edifice lies in its vastness and, in part, precisely from its dimness and clutter. In the middle of one open space where two large corridors meet, there is an outlandish construction, in shape and size not unlike one of the old traffic towers on New York's Fifth Avenue in the 'twenties. On the ground floor is a minute kitchen. If you climb the crooked outside staircase, you find yourself in a tiny restaurant with four miniature tables. Here you sit and eat, looking out along the tunnels over the heads of the passers-by. It is a place out of Kafka's *Amerika*.

The antique shops here in the souks are famous. As one might expect, tourists are considered to be a feebleminded and nearly defenseless species of prey, and there are never enough of them to go around. Along the sides of the galleries stand whole tribes of merchants waiting for them to appear. These men have brothers, fathers, uncles and cousins, each of whom operates his own shop, and the tourist is passed along from one member of the family to the next with no visible regret on anyone's part. In one shop I heard the bearded proprietor solemnly assuring a credulous American woman that the amber perfume she had just bought was obtained by pressing beads of amber like those in the necklace she was examining. Not that it would have been much more truthful of him had he told her that it was made of ambergris; the amber I have smelled here never saw a whale, and consists almost entirely of benzoin.

If you stop to look into an antiquary's window you are lost. Suddenly you are aware that hands are clutching your clothing, pulling you gently toward the door, and honeyed voices are experimenting with greetings in all the more common European languages, one after the other. Unless you offer physical resistance you find yourself being propelled forcibly within. Then as you face your captors over arrays of old silver and silk, they begin to work on you in earnest, using all the classic clichés of Eastern sales-patter. "You have such a fine face that I want my merchandise to go with you." "We need money today; you are the first customer to come in all day long." A fat hand taps the ashes from a cigarette. "Unless I do business with you, I won't sleep tonight. I am an old man. Will you ruin my health?" "Just buy one thing, no matter what. Buy the cheapest thing in the store, if you like, but buy something … " If you get out of the place without making a purchase, you are entitled to add ten to your score. A knowledge of Turkish is not necessary here in the bazaars. If you prefer not to speak English or French or German, you find that the Moslems love to be spoken to in Arabic, while the Jews speak a corrupt Andalusian version of Spanish.

Today I went out of the covered souks by a back street that I had not found before. It led downward toward the Rustempaşa Mosque. The shops gave the street a strange air: they all looked alike from the outside. On closer inspection I saw that they were all selling the same wildly varied assortment of unlikely objects. I wanted to examine the merchandise, and since Abdeslam had been talking about buying some rubber-soled shoes, we chose a place at random and went into it. While he tried on sneakers and sandals I made a partial inventory of the objects in the big, gloomy room. The shelves and counters exhibited footballs, Moslem rosaries, military belts, reed mouthpieces for native oboes, doorhooks, dice of many sizes and colors, *narghilehs*, watchstraps of false cobraskin, garden shears, slippers of untanned leather hard as stone, brass taps for kitchen sinks, imitation ivory cigarette holders ten inches long, suitcases made of pressed paper, tambourines, saddles, assorted medals for the military and plastic game counters. Hanging from the ceiling were revolver holsters, lutes and zipper fasteners that looked like strips of flypaper. Ladders were stacked upright against the wall, and on the floor were striped canvas deck chairs, huge tin trunks with scenes of Mecca stamped on their sides, and a great pile of wood shavings among whose comfortable hills nestled six very bourgeois cats. Abdeslam bought no shoes, and the proprietor began to stare at me and my notebook with unconcealed suspicion, having decided, perhaps, that I was a member of the secret police looking for stolen goods.

OCTOBER 19

MATERIAL BENEFITS may be accrued in this worldwide game of refusing to be oneself. Are these benefits worth the inevitable void produced by such destruction? The question is apposite in every case where the traditional beliefs of a people have been systematically modified by its government. Rationalizing words like "progress," "modernization," or "democracy" mean nothing because, even if they are used sincerely, the imposition of such concepts by force from above cancels whatever value they might otherwise have. There is little doubt that by having been made indifferent Moslems the younger generation in Turkey has become more like our idea of what people living in the twentieth century should be. The old helplessness in the face of *mektoub* (it is written) is gone, and in its place is a passionate belief in man's ability to alter his destiny. That is the greatest step of all; once it has been made, anything, unfortunately, can happen.

Abdeslam is not a happy person. He sees his world, which he knows is a good world, being assailed from all sides, slowly crumbling before his eyes. He has no means of understanding me should I try to explain to him that in this age what he considers to be religion is called superstition, and that religion today has come to be a desperate attempt to integrate metaphysics with science. Something will have to be found to replace the basic wisdom which has been destroyed, but the discovery will not be soon; neither Abdeslam nor I will ever know of it.

YALLAH

INTRODUCTION TO PHOTOGRAPHIC BOOK ON THE
SAHARA BY PETER W. HAEBERLIN,1956

THE WESTERN SAHARA is one of the last great terrae
incognitae left on this shrinking planet – a vast,
mysterious lunar land which seems almost to possess
natural laws of its own. It could scarcely be nearer to Europe
without being in Europe, and yet the traveler there could not
feel himself farther from the world he knows, even if he were
to lose himself in the deepest jungle of the Mato Grosso. Since
it is fashionable at the moment to believe that man has more or
less completed his conquest of nature, people speak confidently
of having "subdued" the Sahara because they have managed
to scratch three tiny trails across its surface, and because they
have succeeded, temporarily at least, in persuading certain of
the inhabitants not to engage in their time-honored pursuit of
pillaging the voyager's camp. But let the rising tide of Moslem
desire for independence from European domination move
a little farther south from Algeria, a little farther north from
the Senegal, and the three narrow ribbons of trail would be
useless; the Sahara would then have to be flown across rather
than ridden across, the sand-covered trails would no longer be
visible even from low-flying planes, and conditions all over the
western Sahara would again be what they were in Rio de Oro
two decades ago. On paper Rio de Oro belonged to Spain, but

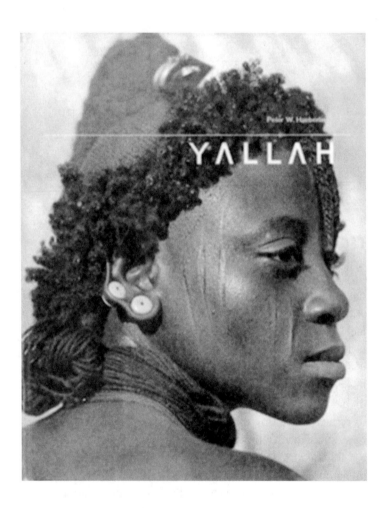

Yallah (the title means 'Let's go' in Arabic): this book of photographs of the Sahara by Peter Haeberlin was initially published in German in 1956 and a year later in English.

in fact it belonged to the men who lived there; the holes shot in the wings of any plane which flew too low to please the natives proved that. It is one thing to "own" land, and another to be able to set foot on it.

But at the moment of writing there are, between the Nile valley and the Atlantic, three trails along which motor vehicles regularly pass, and they are referred to as the lifelines of the French Empire. The most recently opened and least frequented of these is the ancient Piste Imperiale, which leads from Morocco to Senegal, passing through Mauritania. Next, to the east, there is the Oran-Gao trail which follows the dry Zousfana-Saoura river valleys as far as it can, and then plunges straight across one of the most formidable regions in all the Sahara, the Tanezrouft. And finally, farthest east, there is the original and classic route from Algiers southward, passing through the Territory of the M'Zab and the principal towns of the north Sahara: Ghardaïa, El Goléa and In Salah, through the Hoggar Mountains, and into the Niger Colony to Zinder. Except for the final section of the trail, this is the route taken by the Haardt Audouin Expedition in 1923, which accomplished the first crossing of the Sahara using automotive power. And this is also the itinerary followed by Peter Haeberlin.

The course of each of these trails was determined many centuries ago by the inhabitants of the desert, with an eye to maximum avoidance of the areg (singular: erg), those mountainous seas of sand which are scattered across the face of the Sahara, covering, perhaps contrary to popular belief, only about ten percent of its surface, but providing the greatest single obstacle to locomotion there. If a trail is far from the erg, even after a strong wind it will still be visible, but if it passes near to such a region, as is inevitable at certain points, the navigator's difficulties begin, for it will be covered, often for considerable distances, and he risks going astray and getting bogged down in the deep sand at some spot just far enough removed from the zone of passing vehicles so that his efforts to orientate himself or to make his presence known will be wholly futile. Then the supplementary water rations he has brought along assume an almost derisory character: what are a few extra days in the face of the infinite supply of sun and unbroken silence which the Sahara has at its disposal?

This book is a record of one man's journey southward. He went across the desolate stretches of the Algerian tell, entire regions of which are hidden beneath snow in the winter months, to Djelfa, one of the saddest places in the world – this in spite of the fact that the town is in the mountains of the Ouled Naïl and is the center from which the Berber dancing girls bearing that name set out on their travels to gladden the hearts of men, and to which they return, after having earned their dowries in the brothels of North Africa, on their way back to wed the men of their tribe who are waiting for them. South of here are the gaps in the final range of saw-tooth mountains which separate the north from the desert, and the first oasis, Laghouat.

Since the importance of an oasis is calculated by the number of female, date-bearing palms it possesses, Laghouat may be counted as one of the poorer oases. However, it is the first place where one sees the *seguiat*, or channels of running water which are so essential to the cultivation of the Saharan oases. For these palm forests which dot the face of the desert are man-made, and require unceasing work if they are to continue their existence. Wherever the subterranean sheets of water (which lie in well-nigh every part of the Sahara) were found to be close enough to the surface, men discovered ways of bringing that water out of the ground and using it to irrigate the immediate vicinity. The original Negrito population doubtless had instituted some sort of irrigation before the Arabs arrived during the centuries following the Hegira, but it was the latter who devised the amazingly complex systems of aqueducts which now operate there. The population of the *ksour* (the villages within the oases) is still largely Negro, but these are not the same Negroes who were in residence at first. The autochthonous dwellers, hostile to intruders, beat a slow retreat to the region now known as the Tibesti, and the Sudanese imported by the Arab conquerors replaced them as keepers of the oases. Without these black people, who can withstand the fierce climate, it is doubtful that there would be any towns at all in the Sahara. Tending an oasis means continuous effort to expand it; new trees must be set out and transplanted at the edges of the area of cultivation. Only this way can the depredations wrought by the shifting sand be kept pace with; in nearly every oasis there is some region which is slowly but inexorably being buried by creeping dunes.

South of Laghouat lies the *chebka*, a highly eroded region, totally devoid of vegetation, whose terrain, strewn with countless small sharp stones, is next to impossible to cross on foot. In the center of this hostile land, at a junction of several dry ravines, is the heptapolis of the M'Zab. It is a curious place, inhabited by a curious people. The Mozabites, often referred to by Europeans as the "puritans of Islam", belong to the schismatic sect of Abadites, but are designated contemptuously by orthodox Moslems as *kharedjiin*, "those who have stepped outside" (that is, of the true religion), and this in spite of the fact that they observe a fanatical meticulousness in adhering to the moral precepts of Islam.

All over North Africa it is the custom for the *tolba* (men versed in the Koran, but not yet of the status of a *fqih*) to sit in the cemeteries on Friday and for a small sum to recite appropriate *surat* from the holy book to the individual dead, the average person not being sufficiently educated to perform such a rite. The *tolba* of the M'Zab not only do this, but also frequent the graveyards at night, a custom which has led orthodox Moslems to accuse them of trafficking with black magic. Very likely it is this peculiarity more than anything else, coupled with the fact that they are the shrewdest traders of all the Algerians ("Where there is a Mozabite, the Jew must work with his hands"), which damns them in the eyes of the rest of the native population. They are a tribe of small shopkeepers with their business concentrated in Algiers and the other large cities of the Mediterranean littoral, and their custom is to leave their homes and wives behind in the desert for periods ranging from one to two years, while they make money in the big city. During this time they live penuriously, sleeping under the counters of their shops and eating as little as possible. Back in the M'Zab, their wives are under the surveillance of pitiless matrons whose responsibility it is to see to it that their virtue remains intact during their husbands' absence. The master's return is always unexpected, since he never announces his intention beforehand. One day the wife looks up, and there he is, back again for a few weeks to see his orchards, repair his house, renew his acquaintanceship with his sons, and, Allah willing, beget another. Then off he goes again for another indeterminate period, to rejoin his two eldest sons in Oran, or Constantine, or some other place, perhaps taking with him one of his younger sons who is now old enough to work in the shop. It is a serious business, being a Mozabite, and one senses the atmosphere of sobriety the moment one arrives in the place. Children are reprimanded for laughing during their play, and the women, heavily swathed in yards of white cloth so that one invisible eye peers out from within a tunnel of the material, converse in whispers and turn away their faces as one passes.

Inbreeding has gone on to such an extent since these people first emigrated here from the north that they are almost a race apart; one has the impression that everyone belongs to the same family, so pronounced are the similarities of feature between one man and the next. In general the men are short and slightly squat, with wizened yellowish faces that eternally wear an expression of seriousness, even of dissatisfaction. Doubtless this is the classical countenance of puritans; one could scarcely expect a people who disapprove so highly of pleasure to look otherwise.

Beyond the M'Zab one moves into Chaamba country. The Chaamba are Semites like the Mozabites, but unlike them they are nomads, and they made life difficult for the French soldiers during the last part of the nineteenth century when France was attempting to link Algeria with her West African colonies; now, like the rest of the Saharans, they are "pacified", but the legend of their cunning and ferocity still lives on in the market places and cafés of the towns, where tales are told.

It is in El Goléa that the traveler finds his first opportunity to explore the erg, that vast petrified sea whose unmoving waves are mountains of golden sand, fine as dust El Goléa is more ruin than actuality, more past than present. It is amusing to reflect, as one stands looking up at its decayed fortress, that the name is merely another pronunciation of the word which has finally come to grace Madrid's famous street, the Calle Alcalá. (In Morocco it is pronounced *El Qelâa.*)

Until the advent of European rule (which of course shatters all social, moral, and economic patterns, leaving in their place only inner chaos), the owners of the gardens and administrators of the town were the El Mouadhi, one of the four Chaamba tribes. It was a classical Saharan example: the El Mouadhi preferred living in tents among the dunes to dwelling in town in fixed, unmovable houses. Leaving that indignity to their Negro dependents, who worked the land and tended the palms, they never set foot inside the town until the date-harvest season, and then only for the length of time it took to pack up the dates and carry them back off into the erg. In the Sahara a town does not designate the kind of agglomeration we think of when we use the word. It is a decentralized thing, a whole region, generally coinciding with the extent of the oasis, divided into quite separate villages which may be, as in the case of oases whose form is serpentine because they follow the course of a dry river-bed, even a day's walk apart. In Salah, for instance, comprises twelve ksour, or villages; it is the political and economic center of a large region called the Tidikelt. How quickly the world changes! In 1891, according to a bulletin compiled by Commandant Bissuel (*Chef de Bataillon au 1er Régiment de Zouaves*), one went to In Salah in order to buy ivory, ostrich plumes, panther and lion skins, rhinoceros horns, gold-dust, incense, and slaves. With regard to the last-mentioned commodity, he appends an exhaustive price list as well, which gives a good idea of the relative value of slaves at that time, according to their age and sex. Costs ranged at source (Timbuktu) from fifty francs for a boy between four and ten years' old, to three hundred fifty francs for a girl not younger than eleven nor older than sixteen. Adults were evaluated at prices between these two extremes. The selling price at In Salah was double or even triple the cost. That was nine years before the beginning of this century.

Today the traveler passing through In Salah fills his gasoline tank and cools off in the municipal swimming pool. He also spends the night there, because the nearest village is three hundred kilometers in one direction and four hundred twenty in the other; that much importance is still left to the town that once was to the Sahara what Timbuktu was to the Sudan.

In Salah is an excellent place from which to study at first hand the feggaguir. These underground waterways are triumphs of primitive ingenuity. They consist of miles of gently sloping tunnels, large enough for men to go through if need be; they are fed by wells at their upper terminals, and are constructed in such a manner that each garden is assured of its share (and no more) of a steady flow of water. It is a superior system to that of surface distribution, for evaporation is kept at a minimum, and the inevitable disputes over who has been depriving whom of his rightful supply of water are obviated. In the oases where the canals are open and the flow is controlled by a series of locks which are easily tampered with, lifelong feuds with resultant bloodshed are not uncommon.

To lovers of the Sahara, its most fascinating inhabitants are the Touareg. There are obvious reasons for the interest they excite: they have chosen to live in one of the most distant and desolate regions of the world – the very center of the Sahara. There are very few of them left, and their purely medieval customs are fast disappearing. A race whose knights still engage in jousts with lance and shield can scarcely fail to attract attention. There is also the astonishing fact that out of all the people of North and West Africa they are the only ones who have devised their own alphabet, composed of twenty-four simple and thirteen compound letters, an alphabet which at the time of the French conquest was understood and used by all members of all the tribes, since all were literate. This in itself is enough to place them in a category by themselves. They are Berbers and their language is of Hamitic origin; it is generally believed that at the time of the Roman colonization of what is now Kabylia, rather than risk conquest, they began the long migration southward which finally ended in the territory whose center is the Hoggar Mountains. From this impregnable fortress they directed their systematic predatory expeditions, pillaging every caravan that came within reach, so that long centuries before the French ever heard of the Hoggar, the Touareg were known as the "pirates of the desert", and were hated and feared by everyone who had ever come within reach of their fast racing camels. In view of this, it is not surprising that when the French took it upon themselves to vanquish them, they found no difficulty in enlisting the aid of the tribes who for so long had suffered at the hands of the Touareg.

After the closed world of orthodox Islam, as exemplified in the larger cities of North Africa where a woman is a piece of property bought and hidden away in a windowless house, it is surprising to see what prestige and freedom she enjoys among the Touareg. Against all Moslem tradition she has been able to impose the unalterable obligation of monogamy: no man may have more than one wife, nor, indeed, may he take concubines or commit adultery. The children belong to and are educated by their mothers, and inherit their titles or rank from them rather than from their fathers. When a girl is of marriageable age she chooses her own husband without interference from her parents, and if she possesses any personal fortune, she is not required to contribute any part of it to the upkeep of the family. As a result of this the greater part of the property is owned by the women of the tribe. An amusing detail of this turnabout in Moslem custom is that it is the men who veil their faces heavily and fard their eyes with kohl; their explanation is that the excessive dryness of the air demands that the moisture of the breath be conserved and reabsorbed insofar as is possible, and that the kohl protects the eyelids from the dust and the sun's glare. However, the custom has come to be more than one dictated by pure practicality, since even when a man is indoors the veil is not removed, and when he eats, he turns away bashfully and pushes his food up under the veil, fearful of revealing the "nakedness" of his face.

When one has left behind the Hoggar's strange granite domes and boulder-shaped peaks (the highest of which rise up to ten thousand feet), the road continues for a long way across the rocky plateau which ends only at the frontier of the Niger Territory. It is still the center of the Sahara, but there begin to be subtle differences. There is a lower, less exalted sky, a brighter light, if possible, which at the same time somehow reduces visibility, instead of increasing it, and in the oases there is the occasional appearance of a baobab among the eternal date palms and tamarisks.

Here the air is softer, there is grass and thorny scrub vegetation which goes on for countless miles. Little by little the clothing customs change: the long, loose sleeveless garment of white cotton worn by the men is a *boubou*. Here are women walking in the open with uncovered bosoms. Once again the world seems an inhabited, inhabitable place where beasts can graze and land be cultivated. The villages are open, and the houses, built of vegetable fiber and tree trunks instead of mud, have space between them, rather then being huddled one against the other as if in fear of the hostile emptiness outside, as they were farther north. But the streets are still of sand.

The Territory of the Niger, which extends northward to a few miles beyond the Tropic of Cancer, has no particular reason to be called that. Most of it is simply the Sahara. The River Niger waters a tiny region in its south-west corner, but the greater part is no more than particularly desolate desert, complete with a huge erg which covers its central section. In the south, along the Niger itself and near the border of Nigeria, there are lions, giraffes, ostriches, boar, and other fauna typical of the savanna, while in the very south-eastern corner, which touches Lake Chad, the elephant and the hippopotamus live.

This enormous segment of Africa, with an area of five hundred thousand square miles and a population of only two million, is one of the least peopled districts in the world. Of the three principal ethnic groups, not one is, strictly speaking, Negro, although the sun naturally has long since seen to it that skins are highly pigmented. The Touareg are of course whites from the north, the Peuls (whose name seems to have as many variations as there have been anthropologists to study them) wandered down from the upper Nile and across the entire Sudan in some remote time, and the Hausa, while possessing certain Negroid characteristics, are nevertheless predominantly Hamitic, and speak a purely Hamitic tongue, which facts place them outside the category of cultures which can be considered purely Negro.

All these people practice the religion of Islam, although doubtless the *ulema* of Cairo or Fez would be scandalized at witnessing the irregularities in their observance, and still more horrified if they could probe their collective subconscious and discover the heavy residue of animism which several centuries of conversion to monotheism have not been able to eradicate. Nevertheless, they all count nominally as Moslems, and it is certain that the more educated among the city dwellers are as conversant with the faith of Mohammed as men anywhere else.

Beyond Zinder, the capital of the Niger Territory, the road turns eastward, following the northern frontier of Nigeria all the way to Lake Chad. Along the route there are herds of the magnificent long-horned cattle which have come to be the raison d'être of the Peul nation, and which, very likely, were their owners not Moslems, would have come to be objects of worship to them as they have with the Watusi. In the villages the shopkeepers are Hausa, voluble and clever. There are also the shy Bororo, whom Jean d'Esme characterizes as "effeminate" for no better reason than that their features are delicate and that they, like the Touareg, use eye make-up. The Bororo women manufacture fine pottery decorated in the Moslem style of the Sudan, with neat geometric designs.

Hausa is the most widely spoken language in West Africa, and it performs more or less the same function there as Swahili does in Central Africa, serving as a lingua franca among tribes which do not understand one another's dialects. But where the sphere of Hausa influence ends, around Lake Chad, Shuwa Arabic begins, and continues as the principal language from there eastward across to the Red Sea; in many instances this dialect sheltered from change by great distances, adheres more closely to the classical Arabic of the Koran than the languages of present day Egypt and Syria.

Those people who chance to see Lake Chad today are witnessing a geological death agony. Each year the incandescent Sahara sun drinks a little more water from its surface than the great rivers which drain into it can provide, so that the level is being constantly lowered – not very much, it is true – not quite an inch a year. But when one considers that the average depth of the lake is already less than five feet, one realizes that in a very short time indeed Lake Chad will be spoken of only in the past tense. Its disappearance will be only one more phenomenon in the history of progressive dehydration which is the Sahara's. For the time being, it is still forty times as extensive as Lake Geneva, thanks to the Komadugu which flows into it from the Nigerian side, a certain amount of water which comes down intermittently from the north via the Bahr el Ghazal, and, most important, the combined flow of the Logone and the Chari rivers which drain a vast basin of jungle land to the south. The Peuls, whom some consider to be the most beautiful people in Africa (although others claim the honor goes to the Watusi or the Masai), have been identified with such diverse groups as the Malays, the Gypsies, and the Jews. However, there would seem to be no valid reason for tracing their origins quite so far afield; it is generally conceded that they are a nomadic Nilotic tribe which has wandered considerably over the face of Africa during the past two millennia, having come to rest finally in the western Sudan. When one considers that like the Watusi and the Masai, the Peuls as well are cattle-herders, one can only conclude either that the extraordinary nobility of these three peoples is due to the occupation they all have in common, or to some as yet unproven racial link.

VIEW FROM TANGIER

THE NATION, 30 JUNE 1956

WALK DOWN into the Zoco Chico any night. In the little square lined with cafés you can see that in fact, if not officially, the integration of Tangier with the rest of Morocco has already taken place. Instead of the customary assortment of European tourists and residents, elderly Moslems in *djellabas* and native Jews from the nearby streets of the Medina, you are likely to see sitting at the tables no one but young Moslems in European dress – mostly blue jeans. From time to time a noisy cortege passes from a side street through the open space and disappears into the darkness of another alley: two or three policemen leading a protesting Moslem in torn clothing. He has been caught drinking wine or beer and is on his way to the commissariat. Tomorrow he will be given a sentence of six months in jail and a fine of 500 pesetas. If it is a woman, she will receive the same sentence plus an additional penalty: her hair and eyebrows will be shaved. It is a good law because it was made in Rabat by Moslems; there is no need to consider it further.

AND THE EUROPEANS who used to be here every night, where are they? Safe in their houses, or sitting in the fluorescent glare of the French and Italian cafés of the Boulevard Pasteur. They know better than to wander down into the part of town where they are not wanted; besides, everyone is whispering that members of the

Army of Liberation have arrived in Tangier, and that is certain to mean trouble. But the weeks succeed each other, and nothing happens. Is it possible that Tangier is going to stay like this sober and joyless, the brothels boarded up, the *camareros* of the cafés piling their chairs and pulling down their blinds at twelve-thirty or one, and after that the streets so quiet that one can hear the crickets singing and the roosters crowing from the rooftops? And great banners strung from building to building across the streets, proclaiming in Arabic characters that two Moslems of the opposite sex caught walking or talking together (unless they can prove they are married) will be prosecuted? There is, of course, no way of telling, but it is certainly a possibility that this may be a permanent state of affairs.

The *Wall Street Journal* recently ran a front-page article under the heading; "Tangier Turmoil; Tiny, Shadowy Land of Fiscal Freedoms Has the Shakes." For the moment, at least, it is quite true. Discussions of integration are ubiquitous, inexhaustible. Your Spanish barber says: "We are living in bad times. *Es una pena.*" The French waitress tells you: "It's going to be very difficult, *vous savez.* How shall we live?" The English lady sitting near you in the Café de Paris is heard to remark: "Isn't it too sad? But I do think we shall be able to stick to it, don't you?" The American bar owner stares nervously around his establishment and confides: "I don't want to be in on it. I'm getting a line on a little place in Tobago. I think that's for me." *It* means official integration; non-Moslem Tangerines are more inclined to wonder when it will come than they are to consider exactly of what it will consist. They are convinced that it won't be good for them; beyond that there is no way of being sure about anything.

The cost of living, on its way up now, is estimated to be due for a hundred per cent increase, but that is not their principal preoccupation. Will integration mean, for the first time in Tangier, property taxes, an income tax, a levy on bank holdings, the creation of a new currency – sole legal tender – whose value will be set at an arbitrary rate of exchange? Will it be all these things, plus eventual confiscation of non-Moslem businesses?

Will Europeans be forced to leave, or, worse, will they be able to get out in time if violence becomes the order of the day? The ordinary mortal is not in a position to answer, and the few political leaders who are, or who should be, prefer to give the most evasive sort of replies. An interview with Abdelhalak Torres, leader of the defunct Reformist Party (now merged with the Istiqlal) appearing in *España* on May 30, quoted him as saying, in reply to a query as to the future of Tangier: "It is not easy to answer a question which demands first of all knowing what the definitive opinion of those qualified to speak is going to be ...."

THE OUTSIDER must form his opinion regarding things to come both by reading interviews such as this, given purely for the benefit of European residents, in which there are always multiple assurances that shortly all will be well, and by reading condensations of the addresses given by the same political chiefs to the Moslem population, in which a rather different note is constantly reiterated. These speeches are earnest pleas for cooperation in the government's attempt to restore order.

Why is it that, among the Europeans, even those most sympathetic to the new regime are dubious about the immediate future? It would be absurd to expect things to run smoothly; a certain initial instability is normal in such cases, one might argue. I can trace my own doubts to the fact that I believe the whole present situation in North Africa is due to a vast series of misunderstandings. The Moslem and Western points of view are basically irreconcilable. "Independence within Interdependence," France's famous formula for Tunisia and Morocco, is so much meaningless doggerel to the man in the street, to whom independence means the power to organize an army strong enough to rid his country once and for all of the Christian invader. Everywhere Islam is emotionally committed to the principles of Bandung; nothing but the passage of time can alter that. Habib Bourghiba and Sultan Mohammed ben Youssef, on the other hand, although their ultimate aims are those of the people of their respective countries, are at the moment involved in an attempt to achieve those aims through a considerable amount of collaboration with the West. It is an untenable state of affairs, and modifications are inevitable; when and what these will be depends primarily on the outcome of the Algerian war. For it is in Kabylia, the Aurès, the Nementcha, the Medjerda, not on the Quai d'Orsay, that the fate of North Africa is being decided.

THE QUESTION OF ALGERIA continues to be the stumbling block in the road of negotiations between France and Morocco. It could scarcely be otherwise. There is not a Moroccan who is not passionately desirous of seeing the Algerian Army of Liberation victorious in its unequal war against French colonialism. Now that Morocco is independent, what France had feared might happen has become reality: the Moroccan Army of Liberation, in spite of its ritual submission to the Sultan in March, has set up recruiting stations in the cities and supply centers for the Algerian army in the waste lands of eastern Morocco along the Algerian border, activities which France is legally powerless to prevent.

For a long time the Moroccan government has hedged whenever the Army of Liberation was mentioned. First it no longer existed, having supposedly been disbanded when certain tribal chieftains journeyed to Rabat to present their arms to the Sultan. Then it did exist, but was merely maintaining order in disturbed areas. During these weeks there were constant encounters between it and French security forces in the Central Rif, the Middle Atlas and the extreme, north-western corner of Morocco. Villages and plantations were raided, French officers and Moslem dignitaries were abducted, French military convoys ambushed and an effective campaign of sabotage was carried out.

When in mid-May the new Moroccan army was formed in Rabat, the question of the Liberation Army's precise status once more became paramount. It was then announced by spokesmen of the Liberation Army that their organization was being integrated with the official army of the Sultan. The Minister of

A political demonstration against the French, calling for the reinstatement of the sultan, Mohammed V (depicted on the posters), Tangier 1956 (PB)

Defense, Si Ahmed Reda Guedira, upon being questioned as to the accuracy of this report, replied: "I have no idea."

THE PRIZE QUESTION is, of course: where is the seat of power? Who takes orders from whom? Ambiguous statements such as Guedira's are certainly instrumental in lessening one's inclination to take official declarations at their face value. There is obviously a need for an army and a police force able to cope with the widespread lawlessness which could conceivably return Morocco to its ancient condition of anarchy. But just as surely as the country at large would profit by the reestablishment of order, certain active minorities are interested in augmenting the chaos. Not only the common bandits on the highways, but also the organized colonial diehards, as well as the extreme political Left, are – to put it gently – disinclined to assist the government in its difficult task. And the new government needs all the help it can get. Being wholly dependent upon the French for guidance in administrative operations, it cannot afford to antagonize them too openly by giving voice to the political opinions of the Moslem majority, opinions whose tenor is distinctly Francophobe. In the mind of the illiterate private citizen the settling of accounts has scarcely begun.

There are still thousands of evil-doers, most of them Moslems who in the past have made a business of collaborating with or informing for the French authorities, who remain to be liquidated. The Moslem population lives in the expectation of eventual large-scale violence, and for various reasons – social, political, historical – it seems likely that it will not be disappointed.

The two men most influential in forming Morocco's political atmosphere at the moment are both in Cairo: Allal el Fassi, the religious teacher turned politician, founder of the Istiqlal Party; and the intransigent old soldier, Abd el Krim. Certain differences of opinion have recently been reported as existing between them, but the two are in disagreement only as to tactical procedure. Allal el Fassi is willing to negotiate with the French (that is, to determine the provisions of "interdependence") while the latter are still on Moroccan soil in an advisory capacity; Abd el Krim insists that no agreements can be reached so long as one French soldier remains anywhere in all North Africa. Since there are in the neighborhood of 50,000 French soldiers here at present, with more reservists arriving each week, Abd el Krim's program seems unrealistic, and if put into practice would be likely to enlarge the theater of war, which is something that responsible people on both sides hope to avoid. Both men have the classical Moslem fervor, which is to say that they are both extremists in their religious xenophobia. If you have the hardiness to frequent the little cafés in the back streets of Tangier's Medina, you can see their portraits flanking that of the Sultan. Usually on another wall, by himself, is Egypt's Gamal Abd el Nasser in full military regalia; he is the teenagers' hero, the man who succeeded in throwing out the Christians and is getting along beautifully without them.

And so it is understandable that the Europeans who live here in the still International Zone should be uneasy. More than the other cities of Morocco, Tangier, because of its lack of town planning, normally demands a constant sidewalk mingling of its population. The European city is sandwiched in between the old Medina and the big new proletarian Moslem town which in the past decade has grown up out of the fields and sand dunes. Harmony among the various elements of the population has always been taken for granted in Tangier, and the city has attained its physical form in accordance with this.

THE EUROPEANS are continuously in touch with the Moroccans whether they like it or not, and they can instantly recognize the prevailing mood of the hour. There is none of the fatal pretending to be "back home in France" in which the French used to indulge in places like Casablanca and Algiers, with the result that they quite forgot their status of guests in a foreign land. In Tangier you know what the Moslems are thinking, how they feel. They sit in the hundreds of tiny cafés, listening to the news bulletins, broadcast not in their own Moghrebi tongue but in standard Arabic (of which most of them have an imperfect understanding, but sufficient to seize what is being said). When the news is bad, the whole city seems darkened by a collective scowl, and it is not merely imagination that makes the non-Moslem passer-by feel that the scowl is directed at him. The radio is roaring to each Moroccan that Christians are killing Moslems in Algeria, that Christians still own the best land in Morocco, that Israel has not yet been destroyed, that Tangier, his native city, is still cut off from Morocco, his native land. In addition, each afternoon at four-fifteen Radio Cairo beams to North Africa a special program of vitriolic propaganda in which the French, the English, and the Americans are portrayed as monsters of evil. On the other hand, when there is a bit of good news, such as a successful ambush in which a fair number of French troops are destroyed, or a couple of helicopters shot down, everyone is jolly. There is no danger of getting out of touch with reality here. Even if like most of the residents you exercise prudence and stay out of the Moslem city you are always among Moslems.

ON THE first of June here in Tangier, Si Ahmed Balafrej, the Moroccan Minister of Foreign Affairs, made a series of declarations which one seems to have read in print innumerable times before: the Sultan was desirous that the integration of Tangier with the rest of Morocco should be effected in an atmosphere of calm; every possible precaution would be taken to safeguard foreign investments: the standard of living would rise as a result of the transfer of powers; a transitional regime was envisaged before the definitive taking over "in order not to paralyze the life of the city"; and, most important, His Majesty's subjects in Tangier must be given the impression of not being in any way separate from the "central power."

Whether or not the free money market, Tangier's principal *raison d'être*, is to be allowed to continue in existence the Minister refrained from saying. But as long as there is any kind of frontier, the Moroccans will be voluble in complaining of

Tangier's "isolation," and most Europeans find it difficult to see how a free currency market can be maintained without some sort of border control. Yet a way may be found.

So far everything is quiet. Whatever happens, we can scarcely find fault with the Moroccans' aspirations to national independence or their efforts to right some of the injustices which have for so long prevailed in their country. Nor can they, for their part, criticize our attempts to understand as clearly as possible a situation which for their own various purposes they may often prefer to leave nebulous.

All Parrots Speak   *Paul Bowles*

long-lived,
Parrots have amusing characters, are decorative, and faithful in their
affections, but obviously the quality which distinguishes them from most of God's
other inventions is their ability to imitate to perfection the sounds of human
                 cannot
speech. A parrot that can't talk or sing, is, according to our standards, an
incomplete xxxxxxx parrot. For some reason it fascinates us to see a small,
feather-covered creature with a ludicrous, senile face speaking a human lan-
            much,
guage,--so frxxxxxxxx, indeed, that the more simple-minded of us have a ten-
                                                           idea
dency to believexxxxxxxxxxxxxxxxx the take seriously the xxxxxx suggested to
us by our subconscious, which is that a parrot really is a person, in disguise,
of course, but capable of human thought and feeling. In Central America and
Mexico I have listened for hours while the Indian servants in the kitchen
held endless communion with the parrot,--a monologue xxxxxxxxxx b which the
occasional interjections from the perch miraculously transformed into a con-
            when I questioned
versation. And xxxxxxxxxxx the Indians I found a recurrent theme in their
                                                            own
replies: the parrot can be a temporary abode for a human spirit. Our rational
      unhappily gives
culturexxxxxxx us no freedom to indulge in such extravagances; nevertheless the
atavism is there, felt rather than believed.

        Companion and
        The uneducated, unsophisticated Indian, on the other hand, makes an
ideal professor for the parrot. The long colloquies about what to put in the
soup, which rebozo or trousers to wear to the fiesta, what to say to Lolita
when she comes to borrow the mango forks, are in themselves a complete education of a sort that very few of us have the time or the patience to provide.
Andxxxxxxxx It is not surprising that most of the parrots that have found their
way to the United States have been taught at some time or other by rural Latin-
Americans. As important as the spoken word in these relationships is the existence of continuous and intense association with one or two individuals.
                        usually
A parrot is not a sociable bird; it develops a strong liking for a very few
people, and either hatred for, or complete indifference toward, everyone else.
Its human relationships are after all only extensions of its strictly monogamous nature. There is not much difference between being a one-xxxx bird and a

Paul Bowles' original typescript for his *Holiday* article. He re-edited the piece for
inclusion in *Their Heads are Green* – the text reproduced in this book.

ALL PARROTS SPEAK

HOLIDAY, NOVEMBER 1956; THEIR HEADS ARE GREEN, 1963

ARROTS ARE AMUSING, decorative, long-lived, and faithful in their affections, but the quality which distinguishes them from most of God's other inventions is their ability to imitate the sounds of human speech. A parrot that cannot talk or sing is, we feel, an incomplete parrot. For some reason it fascinates us to see a small, feather-covered creature with a ludicrous, senile face speaking a human language – so much, indeed, that the more simple-minded of us tend to take seriously the idea suggested by our subconscious: that a parrot really is a person (in disguise, of course), but capable of human thought and feeling.

In Central America and Mexico I have listened for hours while the Indian servants in the kitchen held communion with the parrot – monologues which the occasional interjections from the perch miraculously transformed into conversations. And when I questioned the Indians I found a recurrent theme in their replies: the parrot can be a temporary abode for a human spirit. Our own rational system of thought unhappily forbids such extravagances; nevertheless the atavism is there, felt rather than believed.

The uneducated, unsophisticated Indian, on the other hand, makes an ideal companion and mentor for the parrot. The long colloquies about what to put into the soup, or which rebozo to wear to the fiesta, are in themselves education of a sort that few of us have the time or patience to provide. It is not surprising that most of the parrots that have found their way to the United States have been trained by rural Latin Americans. As important as the spoken word in these relationships is a continuous association with one or two individuals. A parrot is not a sociable bird; it usually develops an almost obsessive liking for a very few people, and either indifference or hatred toward everyone else. Its human relationships are simple extensions of its monogamous nature. There is not much difference between being a one-man bird and a one-bird bird.

I remember the day when I first became parrot-conscious. It was in Costa Rica; my wife and I had been riding all morning with the vaqueros and were very thirsty. At a gatehouse between ranch properties we asked a woman for water. When we had drunk our fill, rested and chatted, she motioned us into a dim corner and said "¡*Miren, qué graciosos!*" There, perched on a stick, were seven little creatures. She carried the stick out into the light, and I saw that each of the seven tiny bags of pinkish-gray skin had a perfectly shaped, hooked yellow beak, wide open. And when I looked closely, I could see miniature brilliant green feathers growing out of the wrinkles of skin. We discussed the diet and care of young parrots, and our hostess generously offered us one. Jane claimed she couldn't bear to think of breaking up the family, and so we went on our way parrotless.

But a week later, while waiting for a river boat, we had to spend the night in the "hotel" of a hamlet called Bebedero. Our room was built on stilts above a vast mud welter where enormous hogs were wallowing, and it shook perilously when they scratched their backs against the supporting piles. The boat came in fifteen hours late, and there was nothing we could do but sit in the breathlessly hot room and wait. Nothing, that is, until the proprietor appeared in the doorway with a full-grown parrot perched on his finger and asked us if we wanted to converse with it.

"Does it speak?" I asked.

"*Claro que sí.* All parrots speak." My ignorance astonished him. Then he added, "Of course it doesn't speak English. Just its own language."

He left the bird with us. It did indeed speak its own language, something that no philologist would have been able to relate to any dialect. Its favorite word, which it pronounced with the utmost tenderness, was "Budupple." When it had said that several times with increasing feeling, it would turn its head downward at an eighty-degree angle, add wistfully: "Budupple mah?" and then be quiet for a while.

Of course we bought it; the proprietor put it into a burlap sugar sack, and we set out downstream with it. The bend of the river just below Bebedero was still visible when it cut its way out of the bag and clambered triumphantly onto my lap. During the rest of the two-day trip to San José the bird was amenable enough if allowed to have its own way unconditionally. In the hotel at San José it ate a lens out of a lorgnette, a tube of toothpaste, and a good part of a Russian novel. Most parrots merely make mincemeat out of things and let the debris fall where it will, but this one actually ate whatever he destroyed. We were certain that the glass he had swallowed would bring about a catastrophe, but day after day passed, and Budupple seemed as well as ever. In Puerto Limón we had a cage made for him; unfortunately the only material available was tin, so that by the time we got off the ship at Puerto Barrios and were inside its customshouse the convict had sawed his way through the bars and got out on top of his cage. With his claws firmly grasping the cage roof, the bird could lean far out and fasten his beak into whatever presented itself. As we waited in line for the various official tortures to begin, what presented itself was a very stout French lady under whose skirt he poked his head, and up whose fleshy calf he then endeavored to climb, using beak and claw. The incident provided an engrossing intermission for the other voyagers.

The next morning, with six porters in tow, we were running through the streets to catch the train for the capital; at one point, when I set the cage down to shift burdens, Budupple slid to the ground and waddled off toward a mango tree. I threw the cage after him and we hurried on to where the train was waiting.

We got in; it had just begun to move when there was a commotion on the platform and Budupple was thrust through the open window onto the seat. The Indian who had perpetrated this enormity had just time to say, "Here's your parrot," and wave the battered cage victoriously up and down as a gesture of farewell. Tin is evidently worth more than parrot flesh in Puerto Barrios.

A few days later we arrived in Antigua, where we let Budupple get up into an avocado tree in the back patio of the pension and stay. I have often wondered if he managed to survive the resident iguana that regularly took its toll of ducks and chickens.

It might seem that after so inauspicious an introduction to parrot-keeping, I should have been content to live quietly with my memories. But I kept wondering what Budupple would have been like under happier circumstances. After all, a parrot is not supposed to travel continually. And the more I reflected, the more firmly I determined to try another bird. Two years later I found myself in Acapulco with a house whose wooded patio seemed to have ample room for whatever birds or beasts I might wish.

I started out with a Mexican *cotorro*. To a casual observer a cotorro looks like a rather small parrot. Its feathers are the same green – perhaps a shade darker – and it has the general characteristics of a parrot, save that the beak is smaller, and the head feathers, which would be yellow on a *loro real* (the Latin American's name for what we call parrot), are orange instead. Neither this cotorro, nor any other I ever had, learned to say anything intelligible. If you can imagine a tape-recording of an old-fashioned rubber-bulbed Parisian taxi horn run off at double speed, you have a fair idea of what their conversation sounds like. The only sign of intelligence this cotorro displayed was to greet me by blowing his little taxi horn immediately, over and over. After I had set him free I went out and got a true parrot.

This one came to be the darling of the servants, because, although he had no linguistic repertory to speak of, he could do a sort of Black Bottom on his perch and perform correctly, imitating the sound of a bugle, a certain military march almost to the end. The kitchen was his headquarters, where, when things got dull for Rosa, Amparo and Antonio, they could bribe him into performing with pieces of banana and tortilla. Occasionally he wandered into the patio or along the *corredor* to visit the rest of the house, but he liked best the dimness and smoke of the kitchen, where five minutes seldom passed without his being scratched or fed, or at least addressed.

The next psittacine annexation to the household (in the interim there came an armadillo, an ocelot and a tejón – a tropical version of the raccoon) was a parakeet named Hitler. He was about four inches high and no one could touch him. All day he strutted about the house scolding, in an eternal rage, sometimes pecking at the servants' bare toes. His voice was a sputter and a squeak, and his Spanish never got any further than the two words *periquito burro* (stupid parakeet), which always came at the end of one of his diatribes; trembling with emotion, he would pronounce them in a way that recalled the classical orator's "I have spoken." He was not a very interesting individual because his personality was monochromatic, but I became attached to him; his energy was incredible. When I moved away he was the only member of the menagerie that I took with me.

For some time I had had my eye on a spectacular macaw that lived up the street. She was magnificently red, with blue and yellow trimmings, and she had a voice that could have shouted orders in a foundry. I used to go in the afternoon to study her vocal abilities; after a while I decided I wanted her, although I remained convinced that the few recognizable words she was capable of screaming owed their intelligibility solely to chance. It was unlikely that anyone had ever spoken to her of the Oriental dessert known as baklava, or of the Battle of Balaklava, and even less probable that she had overheard discussions concerning Max Ernst's surrealist picture book, *La femme cent têtes*, in which the principal character is a monster called Loplop. These words, however, figured prominently in her monologues. Sometimes she threw in the Spanish word *agua*, giving equal and dire stress to each syllable, but I think

Jane Bowles with the couple's parrot, Tangier, early 1950s.

even that was luck. At all events, soon she was in my patio, driving the entire household, including the other birds, into a frenzy of irritability. At five o'clock every morning she climbed to the top of the lemon tree, the highest point in the neighborhood, flapped her clipped wings with a sound like bedsheets in the wind, and let loose that unbelievable voice. Nothing could have brought her down, save perhaps the revolver of the policeman who lived three doors away and who came early one morning to the house, weapon in hand, ready to do the deed if he could get into the patio. "I can't stand it any longer, *señor*," he explained. (He went away with two pesos to buy tequila.)

There is a certain lizardlike quality still discernible in the psittacine birds; this is particularly striking in the macaw, the most unlikely and outlandish-looking of the family. Whenever I watched Loplop closely I thought of the giant parrots whose fossils were found not so long ago in Brazil. All macaws have something antediluvian about them. In the open, when they fly in groups, making their peculiar elliptical spirals, they look like any other large bright birds; but when they are reduced by the loss of their wing tips and tail feathers to waddling, crawling, climbing and flopping, they look strangely natural, as if they might have an atavistic memory of a time when they were without those appendages and moved about as they do now in captivity.

The word "captivity" is not really apt, since in Latin America no one keeps macaws in cages; they are always loose, sometimes on perches or in nearby trees, and it seems never to occur to them to want to escape. The only macaws I have seen chained or caged belonged to Americans; they were vicious and illtempered, and the owners announced that fact with a certain pride. The parrot, too, although less fierce in its love of freedom and movement, loathes being incarcerated. It has a fondness for its cage (provided the floor is kept clean), but it wants the door left open so it can go in and out as it pleases. There is not much point in having a parrot if you are going to keep it caged.

Loplop was headstrong and incurably greedy. She had her own bowl of very sweet *café con leche* in a corner on the floor, and whatever we gave her she dipped into the bowl before devouring it. The edible contributions we made during meal-times were more like blood money than disinterested gifts, for we would have handed her practically anything on the table to keep her from climbing onto it. Once she did that, all was lost: silverware was scattered, cups were overturned, food flew. She went *through* things like a snowplow. It was not that we spoiled her, but anyone will reflect a moment before crossing a creature with a beak like a pair of hedge clippers.

The afternoon Jane left for a weekend in Taxco, Loplop decided that I was lonely. She came to tell me so while I was lying in a hammock. Reaching up from the floor and using my posterior for leverage, she climbed into the hammock. I moved quickly to another, taking care first to raise it well into the air. She gurgled. If I wanted to make things difficult, it was quite all right with her; she had plenty of time to achieve her aim. She clambered down, pushed across the floor, shinnied up one of the posts that held the hammock, and slid down the rope into my lap. By the time I realized what had happened, it was too late. I was in my bathing trunks, and she made it quite clear that if I attempted to lift her off she would show no mercy. All she wanted was to have her belly scratched, but she wanted it badly and for an indefinite period of time. For two hours I half-heartedly tickled and scratched her underside, while she lay on her back opening and closing her idiotic eyes, a prey to some mysterious, uncatalogued avian ecstasy. From that day onwards she followed me through the house, ogling me, screaming "Baklava! Loplop!" trying to use my legs as a tree trunk to climb up to my face. Absolute devotion, while admirable, tends to become tedious. I sold Loplop back to the ladies from whom I had bought her.

The following year I found the best of all my Amazons, a perfect *loro real* with a great gift for mimicry. I looked into a little garden and there it was, perched in its cage, demurely conscious of being stared at. I approached it, asked it its name, and it slowly turned itself upside down before it put its head to the bars nearest me and replied in a coquettish falsetto that was almost a whisper: "*Co-to-rri-to.*" This, although it was in truth its name, was obviously a misnomer, for the bird was not a cotorro but a parrot, and a large-sized one. We had a short conversation about the weather, after which I bought my new friend, cage and all, for six dollars and carried it home, to the delight of the Indian maids, who felt that the kitchen was not complete without a *loro* to talk to during the long hours they spent combing their hair. They wanted beauty advice. "Do you like it this way?" they would ask, and then, changing the position of the tresses, comb in mouth, "Or like this?"

Cotorrito was an intelligent bird – well-balanced emotionally, and with a passion for regularity. He wanted his cage uncovered at half past six in the morning, and bananas at seven. At about nine he had to be let out so he could perch on top of his cage, where he would stay until noon. Then he made his tour of inspection of the house, toddling from room to room, just to be sure the place was in order. After that he climbed on to an old bicycle tire, hung in a shady part of the patio, and remained perched there while we ate lunch nearby, joining in the conversation with short comments such as "*¿Verdad?*" "*¿Cómo?*" or "*¡Ay!*" and bursting into hysterical giggles if the talk became more animated than usual. During the afternoon he took his siesta along with the rest of the household. When the shadows lengthened he grew lyrical, as parrots have a way of doing toward the end of the day; and when the maids gathered in the kitchen to prepare dinner he went back there, climbed atop his cage and superintended their work for two hours or so. When he got sleepy, he stepped into the cage and softly demanded to have the door shut and the cover put over him.

His performing repertory seemed to be a matter of degree of excitement rather than of choice. Tranquillity expressed itself in a whispered monologue, quite unintelligible, punctuated with short remarks in Spanish. One step above that took him completely into Spanish. From there he went into his giggles, from that into strident song. (At some point he must have lived within hearing of a very bad soprano, because the flatted notes of a song which began "*No sé qué frio extraño se ha metido en mi corazón*," were always identical.) Beyond that there came a strange rural domestic scene which began with a baby that cried, sobbed, and choked for lack of breath, went on to a comforting mother, an effete-sounding father who shouted "*¡Cállate!*" a very nervous dog that yapped, and several varieties of poultry including a turkey. Lastly, if his emotion exceeded even this stage, which happened very seldom, he let loose a series of jungle calls. Whoever was within hearing quickly departed, in sheer self-protection. Under normal circumstances these different emotional planes were fairly widely separated, but a good loud jazz record could induce a rough synopsis of the entire gamut. The sound of the clarinet, above all, stimulated him: giggling went into wailing and wailing into barking, barking turned swiftly into jungle calls – and at that point one had to take the record off or leave the house.

Cotorrito was a good parrot: he bit me only once, and that was not his fault. It was in Mexico City. I had bought a pair of new shoes which turned out to be squeaky, and I was wearing them when I came into the apartment after dark. I neglected to turn on the light, and without speaking walked straight to where Cotorrito was perched on top of his cage. He heard the unfamiliar shoes, leaned out and attacked the stranger. When he discovered his shameful error he pretended it had been due to extreme sleepiness, but I had previously roused him from sleep innumerable times with no such deplorable result.

Two parrots live with me now. I put it thus, rather than, "I own two parrots," because there is something about them that makes them very difficult to claim as one's property. A creature that spends its entire day observing the minutiae of your habits and vocal inflections is more like a rather critical friend who comes for an indefinite stay. Both of my present birds have gone away at various times; one way or another they have been found, ransomed from their more recent friends and brought back home. Seth, the African Gray, is the greatest virtuoso performer I have ever had. But then, African Grays are all geniuses beside Amazons; it is unfair to compare them. He was born in a suburb of Leopoldville in August, 1955, and thus by parrot standards is still an infant-in-arms. If he continues to study under his present teacher, a devout Moslem lady who works in my kitchen, he ought, like any good Moslem, to know quite a bit of the Koran by the time he reaches adolescence. The other guest, who has been with me for the past fourteen years, is a yellow-headed Amazon. I bought him from a Moroccan who was hawking him around the streets of Tangier, and who insisted his name was Babarhio, which is Moghrebi for parrot. I took him to a blacksmith's to break the chains which fettered his legs. The screams which accompanied this operation drew an enormous crowd; there was great hilarity when he drew blood from the blacksmith's hand. Much more difficult was the task of finding him a cage – there was not one for sale in Tangier strong enough to hold him. I finally got wind of an English lady living far out on the Old Mountain whose parrot had died some years ago; possibly she would still have its cage. During the week it took her to find it, Babarhio made a series of interesting wire sculptures of the two cages I had bought him in the market, and wreaked general havoc in my hotel room. However much freedom one may give a parrot once it has become accustomed to its surroundings, it certainly is not feasible at the outset; only chaos can ensue.

Almost immediately I got Babarhio used to traveling. I kept him warm by wrapping around the cage two of the long woolen sashes that are worn by the men here, and putting a child's *djellaba* of white wool over everything. The little sleeves stuck out, and the cage looked vaguely like a baby with a large brass ring for a head. It was not a reassuring object, particularly when the invisible parrot coughed and chuckled as he often did when bored with the darkness of his cage.

There is no denying that in tropical and subtropical countries a parrot makes a most amusing and satisfactory companion about the house, a friend you miss very much when it is no longer with you. Doña Violeta, a middle-aged widow who sold bread in the market of Ocosingo, had hers for some thirty years, and when a dog killed it, she was so deeply affected that she closed her stall for three days. Afterward, when she resumed business, with the embalmed body of her pet lying in state in a small glass-covered coffin on her counter, she was shattered, disconsolate, and burst into tears whenever one showed signs of commiserating with her. "He was my only friend in the world," she would sob. This, of course, was quite untrue; one can forgive its exaggeration only by considering her bereavement. But when she added, "He was the only one who understood me," she was coming nearer the truth – a purely subjective one, perhaps, but still a truth. In my mind I have a picture of Doña Violeta in her little room, pouring her heart out to the bird that sat before her attentively and now and then made a senseless remark which she could interpret as she chose. The spoken word, even if devoid of reason, means a great deal to a lonely human being.

I think my susceptibility to parrots may have been partly determined by a story I heard when I was a child. One of the collection of parrots from the New World presented to King Ferdinand by Columbus escaped from the palace into the forest. A peasant saw it, and never having encountered such a bird before, picked up a stone to hit it, so he could have its brilliant feathers as a trophy. As he was taking aim, the parrot cocked its head and cried "¡Ay, Dios!" Horrified, the man dropped the stone, prostrated himself, and said, "A thousand pardons, señora! I thought you were a green bird."

How to Live on a Part-Time Island

Holiday, March 1957

TWO TYPES OF LANDSCAPE have always had the power to stimulate me, the desert and the tropical forest. These two extremes of natural terrain – one with the minimum and the other with the greatest possible amount of vegetation – are both capable of sending me into a state bordering on euphoria. Unfortunately, when you have a taste for two antithetical things, you are in danger of becoming a pendulum, moving with increasing regularity back and forth between them.

I bought a house in North Africa to be near the desert. Then, after a decent interval, I found myself thinking with nostalgia of the jungle. Since the closest rain forest to Morocco lies on the further side of both the Sahara and the Sudan, I decided to look eastward for the other extreme, and hit on the idea of trying Ceylon. There would be luxuriant vegetation, and there would also be the pleasure of contact with an unfamiliar culture.

Of course, as is almost always the case, the spot turned out to be something very different from what I had imagined it would be. Its flavor was far less "Oriental" that I had foreseen. Each successive European occupation – Portuguese, Dutch, English – had left deep marks on the culture, but there were enough

Taprobane Island, off the coast of Weligama, Sri Lanka (Ceylon)

unexpected charms to outweigh this initial disappointment. The people were unusually sympathetic and hospitable, the food was the best I had encountered in an equatorial land, the hotel service was impeccable, and, most important, the place possessed an inexhaustible supply of superb tropical scenery.

I explored Ceylon and became acquainted with its magical mornings and its incomparable sunsets. Early morning, once the mist is gone, the loveliness of the land is in full focus, and color and form are clearest; as the day progresses the increased light tends to blur both. The sunsets, particularly on the coast, are vast, breathtaking productions which last only a few minutes. The months passed. I moved from place to place, continually finding each new one better than the others, but wishing there might be some spot with which I could identify myself through ownership.

Before I had left England, I had been shown photographs of an extraordinary property off the south coast of Ceylon – a tiny dome-shaped island with a strange-looking house at its top, and, spread out along its flanks, terraces that lost themselves in the shade of giant trees. These pictures, probably more than any other one thing, provided me with the impetus to choose Ceylon rather than Thailand when I was casting about for a likely country to examine. But I returned to Europe without having caught more than a second's glimpse of the shaggy little island, from the Matara train as it rounded Weligama Bay. The memory, however, does not relinquish its images so readily; the photographs with their casuarina trees, balustrades, breaking surf and curving palm-fringed shore line remained in my head, and on my next trip to Ceylon I made a point of going to Weligama Rest House, on the shore facing the island. From here I could look straight across into the sunny verdure opposite, and I determined to explore the place.

Early the first morning I put on my bathing suit and started out. The waves were blood-warm. When I climbed up onto the long boat dock ten minutes later, there was no sound but the lapping of the sea around the piles underneath. At the far end was a padlocked gate. I called out and a dog began to bark. Soon a man appeared out of the tangle of trees, naked save for a white sarong, his lips, teeth and bristling moustache brick-red with betel nut. For a rupee he agreed to show me around the little estate.

It was far better even than I had expected – an embodiment of the innumerable fantasies and daydreams that had flitted through my mind since childhood. But when I got back to Colombo and made definite inquiries about the island, I learned without much surprise that the owner had no intention of selling it. Once again I returned to Europe laden with visions of the little island, but this time they had substance; the color of the filtered light on the wooded paths, the hot smell of the sun on the flowers, the sound of the sea breaking on the big rocks. More than ever the island represented an unfulfilled desire, an impossible wish.

One day six months later a cable arrived at my hotel in Madrid. It read: "Owner Taprobane Willing Sell X Rupees Stop If Interested Wire Money Immediately." I was suddenly downstairs at the desk, the telegram still in my hand, cabling Ceylon. The trees, the cliffs, the strange house with its Empire furniture, were all mine. I could go there and stay whenever I felt like it.

When I broke the news of the purchase to my wife, her reaction was less enthusiastic than I might have desired. "I think you're crazy!" she cried. "An island off the coast of *Ceylon*? How do you get there?" I explained that you took a ship through the Mediterranean and the Red Sea, crossed part of the Indian Ocean, landed at Colombo, and hopped on a train which let you off at the fishing village of Weligama. "And once you're on the island there's nothing between you and the South Pole," I added. She looked at me for a long moment. "You'll never get me there," she said.

But three years later she stood on a black rock under a casuarina tree and looked out across the Indian Ocean toward the South Pole.

According to the deed, the original name of the little hump rising out of the sea was Galduwa, a Sinhalese word meaning "rocky island." There seems to have been some kind of house standing on the highest point as long ago as anyone remembers. In 1925 a gentleman of leisure, the Count de Mauny-Talvande, purchased it and erected an octagonal fantasy in pseudo-Pompeiian style which, according to oral accounts, he proceeded to decorate in a manner we should now associate with mild megalomania. (He also changed the island's name to Taprobane, the word the ancient Greeks had for Ceylon.)

Right at the beginning he decided he wanted not a real house with an interior, but a pavilion which would be a continuation of the landscape outside, and from every part of which there would be multiple views. And so, blithely, he did away with walls between the rooms so that all nine rooms (including the bathrooms) would in reality be only one, and that one open to the wind. Then, having chosen as his aesthetic north a little island across the bay whose form he particularly liked, he constructed his octagonal house so that from its exact center that island would be visible – framed first by columns, then by a further doorway, the paths of the formal garden, and finally by the hand-planted jungle beyond. The result is very rational, and, like most things born of fanaticism, wildly impractical.

Since the place had been empty for several years, save for the resident guardian and his wife, a good many replacements had to be made. We had arranged before leaving Morocco to have new mattresses manufactured to fit the enormous beds, and in Colombo we had stocked up on sheets, towels, mosquito-net canopies, kitchenware, kerosene pressure lamps, a new stove and large quantities of food. I remembered that in Weligama the shops carried full lines of flashlights, sarongs, bicycles and fire-crackers, but little else. Simple things like vinegar, salt or coffee simply did not exist.

The tempo of a sojourn in an unfamiliar place is undeniably slow at the beginning, and you wonder how you will ever become accustomed to the deliberate, leaden passage of the hours. But with each successive day you find an imperceptible increase in speed, until you cease eventually to be aware of time passing at all. We settled into a life which was strange to us only because there was nothing "to do", nowhere to go, and no one to see. Perhaps it was just as well that our routine was made more difficult by an important error of judgment we committed before we arrived at Taprobane.

We had been warned that the two resident servants would not be able to prepare our food, and so on arriving in Colombo we engaged a cook, a man named Fernando who had spent a few years in the galley of a freighter. I should have heeded my initial doubts about carrying an urban Sinhalese to the country, for the friction engendered by this sophisticated outsider proved an insoluble problem. Fernando refused even to enter, much less sleep in, the cavelike servants' quarters, choosing instead to set up an army cot in the library of the main house. Though I was unversed in the rules of Ceylonese master-servant protocol, I should have had sufficient intuition to know that the resident servants would consider it scandalous behavior to permit such a thing. They showed their disapproval very soon. By that time, however, I did not need their innuendoes and grimaces to help me understand that Fernando was a distinct handicap. First of all, he screamed in his sleep. I, who had been looking forward to the luxury of long tropical nights whose only sounds would be the songs of insects and the wash of waves against the rocks, found myself being repeatedly awakened during the dark hours by hair-raising cries. Fernando's sleep was one long nightmare. Nor, to judge by his accounts, could his days have been much pleasanter. According to him not only our own servants but all the people on the south coast were dangerous thieves and cut-throats. Fights ensued at the market when he went to buy food, and the police came to complain. The only solution, they told us, was to get a cook from the region.

It proved simple enough to get rid of Fernando, but it was not so easy to find another cook. Nobody seemed to like the idea of being on the island, even one separated from the shore by only a hundred yards. Eventually friends took pity on us and bestirred themselves to find us another cook. This one, an

A view from Taprobane (PB)

inhabitant of the region, insisted on bringing his son along as assistant. We now had six servants, including the lavatory coolie.

THE SCREAMING OF the crows from the bo tree opposite the island is the alarm clock which wakens Gunadasa and prompts him to rise and make our bed tea. Each day he appears from behind the screen, chanting: "Good-morning-Master-tea-Master." Fortified with two or three cups of strong Tangana tea and a few slices of fresh white pineapple, I make my regular early-morning tour of the island, usually coming to rest on a stone bench that commands a fine view of Weligama Bay. The sun, although scarcely risen above the headlands to the east, already is giving off an intimate, powerful heat, and the distant flotilla of fishing boats slips past the white line of the reefs into the open sea, their unfurled sails like the dorsal fins of giants sharks. Scores of timorous black crabs creep out of their crevices in the rocks and sidle towards me. A sharp pain rouses me from my meditations. Big red ants make their nests in the trees that arch high above the bench, and their bite is like a minor wasp sting.

I rise quickly and go up to the house, where I work until breakfast is ready. The remainder of the morning is devoted to settling servants' disputes, keeping the marketing accounts, and jumping into the sea when the breeze suddenly dies and the air becomes like a hot damp cloth pressed against the skin. After the lunch of curry, different each day but always so hot it draws tears (a phenomenon I have grown, for some strange reason, to enjoy), there is the afternoon nap, a quick descent into oblivion while the wind, then usually at its height, ripples the mosquito nets and fills the air with the salt mist of breaking waves.

It is usually dark before the drums of the devil dancers begin. They do not drum every night; if they did, we should not get much sleep, for once they start they continue until the following noon. Not that they are so loud, but it is hard to stay home when you know what is going on. These ancient pre-Buddhist ceremonies were once of prime importance to the community, and although they have degenerated over the centuries into what is widely despised as a vestige of primitive "superstition," a really good dancer can still revive the old gods and bring shivers to the watcher.

Often we start out at night in our bathing suits, change on the opposite shore into our clothing which the servants have carried across on their heads, and go toward the drums. Sometimes the dances are held in a village home or in the market (we are always urged to enter the crowd, given ringside seats, cigarettes and soft drinks), but the most impressive rites take place in the palm forest, not far from the beach. Here in the dark, the howling masked figures leaping with their flaming torches among the trees achieve their full dramatic effect. Nominally a devil dance is a magical observance whose aim is to banish the demons of pain, psychosis and bad luck by inducing such terror in the subject that he will automatically expel them – a rudimentary shock treatment.

It is astonishing to discover how few Ceylonese have watched one of these performances, and how completely uninformed (and, alas, militantly so) most of them are about their own folklore. Among our domestics at Taprobane, the Christians are disapproving and the Buddhists mildly amused; they all prefer to spend the night fishing off the rocks for lobsters and crabs.

A GOOD MANY of the citizens of Weligama (and not a few from Colombo) have come across to the island and paid us courtesy calls. A doctor and his wife arrived one hot afternoon, very formally attired, and caught us lolling on the floor in bathing suits. Their principal interest lay in discovering why we had not yet begun attending the local Church of England. Another day the entire staff of the post office came to pay its respects. Various politicians and lawyers, the chief of police, the owners of several large rubber estates in the vicinity, reporters and photographers, and simple sightseers, all appeared unexpectedly, and all had to be entertained. One day eight young Buddhist monks came bearing a large clay figurine as a gift for the house; another day it was a delegation of Moslems who invited us to the mainland for dinner. When we hesitated, they explained that the banquet was already prepared in our honor, the food waiting to be served; obviously there was nothing to do but go. And what a banquet!

Although I should have appreciated more privacy during the first few months, because of my work, I was impressed by the people of the region, who showed an astonishing and disinterested friendliness such as you practically never find when you first settle in a foreign land. For a while I chained and padlocked the entrance gate at the landing jetty, but the keys were always getting misplaced and we kept finding ourselves imprisoned on the island. Then I put up large, carefully-lettered signs in Roman, Sinhalese, Tamil and Arabic script, announcing that admission to the domain was only by previously granted permission. This was a patent absurdity; the visitors hallooed and pounded until the gardener went down and, after arriving at some sort of financial understanding whose details were scrupulously kept from me, took them on a tour which included everything but entry into the house itself.

Perhaps owing to language difficulties, it took me about three months to convince my gardener that the extra revenue he got from tourists was not one of his inalienable rights. One visitor who had brought a delegation of schoolteachers from Colombo said to me: "This gardener is proud to be the custodian of a national monument, and you, sir, are a very lucky man to be living here."

That was a truly enlightening remark; I began to feel not only lucky but apprehensive. It is not a reassuring experience to be told by a citizen of a new and intensely nationalistic country that your home is a part of the national heritage. However, I tried to look pleased, and agreed with him.

In a densely populated, prosperous nation like Ceylon, motorists must have somewhere to go; it is a small country most of whose high points of interest lie well off the main highways, and Taprobane is listed in the guidebooks as easily accessible. Nevertheless, I was a little taken aback when I discovered that tourists arrived from as far away as Bombay. I mentioned this fact to an American lady who was spending a fortnight with us. (She had come to Asia, she confided, partly in the hope of meeting a real live maharaja; her other interest was in finding Lhasa terriers in the Himalayas.) One day while we were sitting at lunch, the gardener and his wife appeared, in a state of some disarray, to say that they had just had an altercation with a party of eight Indians down at the gate; the struggle had culminated in their pushing the one gentleman down the steps in such a way that he had knocked over two of the ladies and a little girl. We expressed polite concern, thanked them, and went on with our lunch. A little later the gardener returned and produced from his sarong a piece of paper. "From Indian master," he said. "Giving paper before fight."

I read it and handed it to my guest. Her cries were heart-rending. The gentleman requested my kind permission to allow his entourage to walk about the premises, and the note was signed "The Maharaja of Bhand."

Ceylonese law stipulates that any alien who remains in the country a day longer than the six tax-free months which are allowed him during the year will be subject to full taxation on his world income for that year. (The rates are high.) This automatically excludes the possibility of my living permanently at Taprobane.

Early one morning a parade of men advances through the waves from the island toward the shore, each with a valise on his head; bullock carts are waiting at the rest house to pull the luggage to the station, and the last pilgrimage of the season into Weligama gets under way along the narrow road past the Buddhist temple with its clean-swept vihara, past the ayurvedic pharmacy, the mango tree where the chained spider monkey capers, Abd el Azeez's Wireless and Photographic Emporium, and all the other familiar, touching landmarks. As each one moves past, I look at it hard and ask myself: "Is this the last time? Or shall I see them all again?" Nowadays it seems wiser to take nothing for granted.

Village Ceylon and Kandy Lake – two 1950s postcards from Paul Bowles' papers

LETTER FROM CEYLON

THE NATION, 13 APRIL 1957

J UST WHAT WOULD one's first impressions of Ceylon be? Mine were formed a little over seven years ago, but although the country has changed considerably since then, very likely I should notice the same details today: fireworks, flags and lanterns of festival time, thousands of clowning and chattering crows, Christmas-tree bulbs strung through the branches of the trees, catamarans like primitive wooden sculptures beached on the sand, zebus pulling enormous painted carts, umbrella-shaped shrines in the Buddhist temple precincts, the Sinhalese with their frail bodies and betel-stained lips and, more than all the rest put together, the reckless luxuriance of the vegetation. It is hard to visualize any scene here without its backdrop of trees, so completely do they dominate the landscape. They are always there, the vast rain-trees and the ancient bo-trees with their quivering sequin-like leaves, the bread-fruits and the jaks, the abnormally tall cocos (in the neighborhood of my home they grow to eighty feet) and the incredibly thin areca palms. If there were no verdure more noteworthy than the tea bushes and the rubber trees, the countryside would be rather more monotonous than most.

Ceylon has no true rain forest such as you see in South America; that is a phenomenon too forbidding to be thought of in purely aesthetic terms. Here, on the contrary, no matter how primeval the scene, you have the feeling that it has been studiously arranged to please the eye; once you leave the city, any vista looks like part of a lavish botanical garden. If you go to the Yala Game Preserve you get the same impression with regard to the animals. At sunset you can come upon a score of elephants at a water hole half a mile away, but if you want to photograph them you must do it from inside your car, since for safety's sake it is forbidden to circulate in the area without a tracker, whose principal function is to see that no one under any circumstances ever gets out of his automobile. In the final analysis you feel as though you were in a tremendous zoo whose inmates had been placed there for your amusement. The rogue elephants and buffaloes are dangerous enough; it is not uncommon for a car to be attacked and its occupants injured or even killed. But knowing this does not change the impression you get of being in a place which for some reason seems artificial. Perhaps it is because a few miles outside the sanctuary you see what look like the same buffaloes working placidly in the paddy-fields, and very similar elephants moving slowly along the roads, tinkling their bells, being led and talked to by their mahouts. As for the leopards and bears, you're lucky if you find even the footprints of one outside the kitchen of the circuit bungalow when you wake up in the morning.

Friends in Ceylon used to insist that if I liked tea I must never visit a tea factory. And it is true that the coolies walk in with cow dung on their bare feet and shuffle through the heaps of tea, and that from then on the tea is in no way sterilized before it reaches your cupboard. However, I still drink it with as much enthusiasm as ever. There is a local brand, called *Tangana*, which is quite the best I have ever tasted.

You hear a good deal of talk these days about plans to nationalize the tea industry. About ten million rupees have been spent in acquiring several estates and setting them in motion on a cooperative basis. The aim is not so much to raise the living standard of the workers as it is to keep the money in Ceylon. And it is no surprise to be told by the planters that estate land for which the government pays nine hundred rupees an acre is "really" worth three thousand.

Tea-growing used to be a highly remunerative occupation here for the man with the capital to acquire a few hundred acres of land. Let us suppose you have a small to middling estate of four hundred acres of tea; you will need five hundred laborers to work them, and you will get approximately four hundred thousand pounds of tea each year from your bushes. Yet each plant, which is picked every fifteen days throughout the year, gives only four and a half ounces per picking. This means that the picker, who is paid according to the number of pounds she can gather in a day, must move fast. It is significant that the people who perform this poorly paid work are not only Tamils, but Tamil women. No particular skill is required; the picker needs only to recognize what is called the "soap leaf" on each stem, and count upward from there in order to take exactly the right leaves. The same plant can give five different grades of tea, depending on the size of the leaves, which are put through sieves of varying mesh; the best Ceylon variety is Broken Orange Pekoe.

Tea-processing is simple; from plant to cup can take as little as twenty-four hours, although thirty hours are recommended. Tea is everyone's drink here; at each little station on a local train, vendors hand it up through the windows to the passengers. Alcoholic drinks are more difficult. There is a great deal of legislation about how, where and when arak and toddy can be sold. (These two Ceylon institutions are analogous to Mexico's tequila and pulque respectively; the difference is that they are made from the areca palm rather than from the maguey plant.) Imported drinks are for the very rich; a fifth of gin costs $8.20 in U.S. currency. Ceylon is no longer a cheap country for the tourist. On each of my five visits I have found prices higher, until this time hotel rates and meals are double what they were in 1950, although both the official and the black-market rate of the dollar have remained the same.

ON THE FRONT PAGE of this morning's *Daily News*, ("Largest Circulation in Ceylon") appears an article bewailing the fact that anti-Chou posters cropped up here and there in the streets on the eve of Chou Enlai's arrival in Colombo. "Who could have been responsible, when almost all political parties approved of this visit? Could it have been done through some foreign agency?" demands the *News*. This xenophobia is ridiculous; not native to the average man, it is being carefully manufactured, along with the rabid intolerance of non-Buddhist citizens, by the demagogues of the moment. It is, of course, mistrust directed solely at the West. According to the editors, China is the greatest Buddhist nation in the world. Says the *Times of Ceylon*, (today's edition): "Ideological differences need not stand in the way of political and economic cooperation." But the *Times* does not go on to say whether the ideological differences are religious or social; obviously they are not political. Today's *Ceylon Observer* reminds its readers that Wendell Willkie was dazzled by Chou's personal charm to the point of writing: "If this man is a Communist, I say, let's have more of them."

Everyone seems to agree that there are no Moscow-trained Ceylonese in the local Communist Party. It is an intimate, provincial affair, in which the leaders themselves will appear with their wives on the scene of a strike and give out handbills to the passers-by. A characteristic note was struck a few years ago in Matara, a Communist stronghold on the south coast, when party members, on learning of the defeat of their candidate, shaved off their eyebrows as a token of mourning. Another Ceylonese political oddity is the existence of the Lanka Sama Samaja, a Trotzkyist Party which is an active influence in the political life of the land. Since I first arrived I have been assured many times over that a wedding between the local Third and Fourth Internationals was imminent, but since the latter is still around, it would appear that the announcement was only an expression of wishful thinking by the former.

THE ORGANIZATION running the country at present, called the Mahajana Eksath Peramuna, or M.E.P., is a coalition group which at the time of its formation gathered into one pile most of the disaffected elements of Ceylon's political life, including the Sri Lanka (Bandaranaike's own Socialist group), the Sama Samaja and the Communist Parties. There was great discontent with the conservative United National Party, which had held power since the beginning of the independent regime. The very fact that its official name is in English rather than in Sinhalese is considered to indicate its orientation. By the time the U.N.P.'s Sir John Kotelawala had reached the end of, his term, he had managed to alienate just about everyone in the country (if for a variety of opposing reasons); even so, the landslide accorded to the M.E.P. with Bandaranaike as candidate came as a big surprise to everyone, perhaps most of all to the victors, who were incompletely prepared to take over the responsibilities of government.

An employee of CARE, which is administering an extensive school-lunch program here at the moment, tells me it is not an uncommon occurrence for him to arrive at an isolated country school whose master casually confides to him that his salary has not been paid for the better part of a year. "How do you live?" the American asks. "I, borrow," says the schoolmaster. "People will lend because I work for government. Presently government will pay." Each time the American has checked with the Department of Education on such a case, he has discovered that the poor schoolmasters are quite wrong; procrastination is not at all the reason why their checks have not come through. They have been teaching in schools which do not appear on any official list; the Board of Education has not even been aware that their schools existed. The CARE man adds that at the time of the switch of government a good many records were lost or destroyed, some-times by design, in order to make the incoming group's task the more onerous – a bit of spitefulness which turned out to be largely gratuitous, inasmuch as the disparity between the M.E.P.'s grandiose Utopian promises and its record of achievement is fast becoming all too clear even to M.E.P. enthusiasts. There is a widespread conviction now that the U.N.P. (not headed by Kotelawala) will take over at the time of the next elections, if not before – i.e., in the event the present government falls. But it looks as though there will be some very difficult terrain to cross before then. Those who assume that it will be possible for the country to step back peacefully into pre-M.E.P. conditions would seem to show a certain lack of imagination.

THERE IS LITTLE of the much-touted non-violence of the Indian in the Sinhalese. It would be difficult, for instance, to imagine him adopting the strategy of *satyagraha*: his emotional responses are too much like our own. Fortunately he has a natural civility and a capacity for tolerance which have not yet been totally destroyed by his politicians. But he does not take kindly to the presence of Europeans in Ceylon – a natural reaction to centuries of exploitation by outsiders. The visitor who is not an obvious tourist making the traditional tourist's pilgrimages to Anuradhapura, Polonnaruwa, Kandy and Sigiriya will find himself the object of a constantly repeated inquisition, conducted by complete strangers and in a manner not necessarily altogether friendly. "What do you want? What are you doing in Ceylon? Why have you come here?" The government's attitude is similar; it loves to play tough with visitors, particularly American ones. I may have been lucky all these years, but the fact remains that no other government has happened to slap me into a concentration camp (the local euphemism is "screening camp") for forty-eight hours because through a self-admitted technical error made by its own consular service my visa was not valid. Nor, save in Ceylon, have I ever been stripped naked by customs inspectors while their assistants fingered the seams of my garments. In the first instance they told me I was suspected of being an international spy. "But spying for whom?" I insisted "Spying for International," said the camp's temporary director (his boss was on holiday). In the second instance they were looking for sapphires and rubies. In both cases they went about their business impersonally and with deadly seriousness.

Through all the years of Portuguese and Dutch occupation the interior of the country remained independent and hostile to invaders. It was only in 1815 that the British finally managed to conquer the last King of Kandy; the tradition of independence never had time to be totally extinguished. Spirit is not lacking, but the need now is for a program of internal cohesion, a rational attempt to achieve some kind of unity. There are other dangers to the autonomy of the country besides the obvious one of Communist domination. The more literary-minded Sinhalese used to say: "Ceylon is like a tear-drop falling from the face of India." They don't say it anymore. It is too likely to become a political truth. The fierce nationalism inspired by this realization engenders religious chauvinism under which Buddhists prosper at the expense of Hindus, Moslems and Christians; it also gives rise to discriminatory laws aimed precisely at the Tamils – the minority group from whose indirect retaliation via India Ceylon has the most to fear.

Outbreaks of violence such as last year's tragic massacre at Gal Oya or this year's fatal Independence Day riots in the towns of the Tamil-inhabited northern and eastern regions thus become an inevitable concomitant of governmental policy. No one religious group is confined to any single section of the country; in each town you will find Hindu temples, Mosques, and both Catholic and Protestant churches as well as the sacred Buddhist vihara. Pilgrims to sanctuaries like Adam's Peak and the unforgettable jungle shrine of Kataragama include members of all cults. For centuries it has been the custom of the land for divergent faiths to be practiced side by side in the harmony provided by mutual tolerance. The necessity of enforcing a continuation of this custom, and enforcing it at all costs, ought to be self-evident, if, any semblance of unity within the nation is to be maintained.

LETTER FROM KENYA

THE NATION, MAY 25, 1957

MOMBASA

I DON'T REMEMBER ever hearing of Kenya until I read Baroness Blixen's stately book *Out of Africa* during the war; even after that all I remember about it was that there were people called the Masai who lived on the milk and blood of their cattle, and that lions, giraffes and zebras wandered loose over the countryside. Later, in England, I became conscious of Kenya as a place where the British consistently had themselves a rip-roaring good time; with the loss of India it had become *the* colony, the one land where British colonial tradition still existed in a relatively unaltered form. It took the recent local crisis with its sensational press reports to give me the desire to visit the country.

I landed, not at the Nairobi airport, but in classical fashion, coming from the Indian Ocean into the harbor of Mombasa. Between the north-east and the south-west monsoons Mombasa is one of the hotter cities, and the British of Kenya, unlike those left in India, Ceylon and Malaya, seem to think it more sporting to do without punkahs or fans of any sort. (The mention of air-conditioning would be *lèse-majesté*). So you sleep under mosquito canopies hung in small ovens. The city is attractive and spacious; for some indefinable reason its main streets remind

me faintly of the shopping district of Miami Beach. The population, however, is infinitely more cosmopolitan. At this season
the cafés and markets are full of groups of Arab traders from
the Hadhramaut and Socotra and Oman, fierce-faced brown
men with daggers in their belts, squatting, waiting for the wind
which will propel them homeward in their ancient-looking
dhows. They speak classical Arabic, and hopefully offer to sell
their double-edged, razor-sharp daggers for a thousand shillings. (They come without passports, and make a good deal of
money in the interior selling on credit to unsuspecting Africans,
and then applying physical intimidation to collect exorbitant
prices for their goods.) Mombasa is more Asian than African in
feeling. The shops are run by Hindus and Moslems who speak
Gujarati or Punjabi, depending on which part of India they come
from. But everyone – Africans, Asians and Europeans – speaks
Swahili. Not to know this *lingua franca* makes you feel very
much out of things; it is essential for communication between
African and European, African and Asian, and most important
of all, between Africans from different regions of Kenya itself
and from across the border of the neighboring countries. It is
phoneticized in both Roman and Arabic script; recently the government has begun to accept telegrams written in it.

The Sultan of Zanzibar claims ownership of the entire coast
of Kenya to a depth of ten miles, as well as a multitude of
islands. These claims are recognized by the British to the point
of their being willing to pay him 16,000 pounds a year rental
and interest for the land, and to use the official title "Colony and
Protectorate of Kenya." Such things may not be of much interest at the moment in Kenya, but they are in Zanzibar, and the
day when the question of autonomy for Kenya begins to be discussed, it will obviously become a matter of importance. Who
will get what, and how?

In today's local press an article headed "*Man-Eaters Kill 43*"
caught my attention. I half expected the piece to be an account
of cannibalism, but it was only about lions. Yesterday one of
them wandered into Likoni, across the harbor from Mombasa

proper. Two were surprised walking in the streets of a Nairobi suburb, where they were amusing themselves eating the residents' dogs; the police had to shoot them. If you want to shoot a lion for sport, it will cost you twenty pounds for the permit, and at least another ten pounds to have the hide cured.

NAIROBI

THERE IS ONLY ONE other city in all of Kenya besides Mombasa, and that is Nairobi, the capital. The bus trip took a little more than eleven hours, and was not uncomfortable. Most of the time the road is a ribbon of bright red earth cutting straight over the slopes and across the plains. A car a mile ahead is a small puff of red dust. Overhead is the characteristic intense sky of the tropical highlands, whose brightness emphasizes remote details at the horizon. The giraffes are for the most part unmoving; in the distance they look like enormous wooden toys. The zebras and deer are more likely to be frisky. It was in the few dreary villages where the bus stops along the way that I saw for the first and last time some shops run by Africans. Not one in Mombasa, not one in Nairobi. At the lonely spot the bus stopped and took on a few Masai passengers: the women heavy with coils of wire wound around their necks and vast wheels of it weighting down their ears, the men carrying beautifully wrought spears. They paid their fare, the bus started up. A few miles further on, in a place without a sign of habitation, they pressed the buzzer and the bus stopped. They got out in leisurely fashion, pausing in the doorway to drink casually from a bead-encrusted gourd. The language of the Masai reveals their Nilotic origin; they are generally considered to be a "backward" group, almost militantly uninterested in Western ideas and inventions. In this they differ spectacularly from their next-door neighbors, the Kikuyus, who are impressionable and desirous of assimilating a maximum of European culture. With the understanding of how the Western mind works goes political canniness: by fomenting a full-scale revolt they have managed to make themselves the focal group in this era of their country's history, for they think in national as well as in tribal terms.

THE CLIMB UP from the lowlands is so gradual as to be unnoticeable; if it were not for the coolness in the air you would refuse to believe you had climbed 5,500 feet. But the sudden emergence of a large and very modern city in the wilderness is something of a shock. All at once you are in England; amber fog-lights glare above the endless streams of traffic, and you find yourself reflecting that there is nowhere for all these cars to be going, nowhere for them to be coming from, in the middle of this desert. Nairobi covers an enormous area, and a car is considered a "necessity".

In the hotel the first thing I noticed was that my room was a cage. Every window fitted with stout iron bars. Even the door has bars running from top to bottom and the bolt is fitted to a metal frame enclosing the bars, so that even if the paneling should be broken through from the outside, the room could still not be entered. The thoughts engendered by this sight were not pleasant. It is impossible not to recall the hideous tales of tortures and slow deaths inflicted upon the Europeans by the Kikuyus, as told me by the English passengers on the ship coming to Kenya. "No one will have a Kikuyu any more as a servant," they assured me. On this score at least they obviously were misinformed. My own room boy is a Kikuyu, as are several of the waiters in the dining room.

I determined not to mention the word *Mau Mau* to anyone while I was in Kenya, and I have not. Nor have the English ever used it while talking to me. *The trouble* would appear to be the most usual way of referring to the activities of the Kikuyu nationalists which resulted in the great retaliatory campaign by the British – just *the trouble*.

I ask an Englishman: "Just what was the cause of all the trouble here?" The reply is not always the same on each occasion, but it always has the same vagueness and lack of imagination, and is expressed with uniform inarticulateness. "Russian propaganda," "free schools," "sudden upsurge of savagery within the tribe," "difficulties over ownership of land," and even "Egyptian interference" (via Radio Cairo), figure among the causes offered me. Not one answer has come near to anything like: "dissatisfaction with the policy of racial discrimination," or even: "poverty," or "hunger". These last, of course, are reasons given by the Africans. However, if the British and the Africans do not concur on causes, they seem to be in agreement as to the eventual results of the present situation. The British are generally gloomy about future prospects for their rule in Kenya; the Africans in spite of their appalling predicament, are confident of their own ultimate victory.

THE MINIMUM WAGE for Africans at present, the wage in the hope of earning which they flock to Nairobi, is 82½ shillings a month, which equals $2.75 a week. (A 20-shilling monthly rent allowance is also accorded.) Of the relatively few Africans who have jobs at all, the vast majority work for the minimum wage. (Food is not cheap in Kenya.) Members of the Kenya Federation of Labor were unanimous in assuring me that no Asian earns less than five hundred shillings a month. The English, of course, make even more than they would back in England. "Equal pay for equal work" is one of the Federation's aims, but it will not be the first to be achieved. For the "emergency" is still in force (although the British insist that Mau Mau is a thing of the past), and the emergency means that any African can be picked up at any moment and imprisoned without trial in one of the vast detention camps, or arbitrarily deported from wherever he is to the reserve. Late in March Mr. Lennox Boyd announced in the House of Commons that Africans are being arrested in Kenya this year so far at the rate of 3,000 a month.

Nairobi's residential districts for Africans, called *locations*, were already designated before the "trouble" as the only places where Africans could live; they are well outside the city in desert land, and all of them are surrounded by massive fortifications of barbed wire. No attempt is made to give them the appearance of anything but what they are: concentration camps whose gates happen at the moment to be open. If you are on some of the higher slopes of the Royal Nairobi National Park, you can see in the far distance the dismal stretches of some of these *locations*, baking in the sun of the waste land, and it is impossible to avoid having the sentimental reflection that the wild animals of Kenya fare better than its human inhabitants.

I was invited to visit some African homes, and this gave me the opportunity of inspecting several locations. In Pumwani Location, in a standard room of nine feet by seven, lived a family of five; there was not even room for a chair or table between the two sleeping-boards which filled the entire space. Next door, in an identical cubicle, lived four unmarried men. There is no point in dwelling on the hopeless dirt and squalor; under these conditions there is no alternative to filth. The rent on each room is 26 shillings a month, payable to the government. In Ziwana Location a woman was living with her twelve children in only slightly larger accommodations. Makadara Location seemed a little less crowded; my host here told me that the government provides the foundations of the huts (since Africans are not allowed to own land in the cities) after which the residents must build the rest themselves at their own expense. Notwithstanding this, they still must pay 32 shillings a month rent for the regulation one-room dwelling. The lease is for ten years, after which the constructions are pulled down, again at the builder's expense, and the property reverts to the government with no compensation paid to the builder-resident.

What must be borne in mind is that, apart from those who lost their lives in the recent hostilities and the 44,000 who still crowd the detention camps, most of the educated African citizens of Kenya are included in the 100,000 Africans who live in the Nairobi locations. To be allowed to remain there, even under these intolerable conditions, is a privilege which may at any moment be withdrawn, while to be obliged to return to the reserves is tantamount to being deprived of all means of earning a living. The Africans carry pass-books in Nairobi. It is a constant sidewalk phenomenon, the sight of a policeman examining the pass-book of a worried-looking African. It is interesting to note that the two institutions of the location and the pass-book are used in identical form and called by the same names in the Union of South African to enforce *apartheid*.

A glimmer of hope can perhaps be found in the fact that for the handful of Africans employed in the Civil Service and the High Commission services, the principle of equal pay for equal work does apply. But the request that all Africans be given the same recompense as Asians and Europeans for doing the same work is not one which is likely to be heeded as long as the authorities have absolute power over the Africans' physical movements.

IN A HOTEL BAR I asked one cynical British government employee whether the March elections for members of the Legislative Council had in his opinion been what is ordinarily called "free elections." His answer: "I suppose so, as free as in any other police state." Then he added quickly: "I really must learn to keep my mouth shut!" However, Tom Mboya, the General Secretary of the Kenya Federation of Labor, considers the elections a step in the desired direction, even though less than ten per cent of the Africans in the country were qualified to vote. On the official side of the Legislative Council the members are all British civil servants appointed to their posts. On the unofficial side the members are elected according to a "parity" system which provides sixteen posts to be filled by Europeans (who number 45,000) and sixteen by non-Europeans (who make up the rest of the 6,000,000 people in Kenya). As if this were not already derisory, there is a further breakdown of the non-European posts, eight going to Africans (nearly 6,000,000) and eight to Asians (about 150,000, of whom 25,000 are Arabs, the rest Indians).

The eight African members, having been duly elected, decided unanimously to refrain from participating in government, thus forming what amounts to an opposition. Participation, they feel, would be a tacit acceptance of things as they are. Their principal concern at the moment is to replace the Lyttleton Plan, a compromise measure passed in 1954 during the crisis, with some sort of guarantee that the country will remain under the administration of the Colonial Office in London. The Lyttleton Plan's great danger is that it leaves the door open to cabinet government (that is, home rule) in Kenya. Under present conditions self-government could result only in the establishment of a regime in which the local European colonists would be free to legislate openly in favor of total African subjection, thus ending all possibility of evolution toward democratic government.

Immediately after the March elections the eight elected African members to the Legislative Council issued a press statement defining their position. A section of this reads: "We do ... hereby declare that the most urgent and immediate need is toosecure constitutional reform in the Legislature giving everyone effective and real representation, to which end it is our intention to direct all our efforts and energies. We are firmly and unequivocally opposed to any system which serves as a device to secure for certain people permanent political and economic domination of other sections of our community in Kenya." The statement is signed by Tom Mboya (Naibori), Oginga Odinga (Central Nyanza), Masinde Muliro (Nyanza North), Bernard Mate (Central Province), Arap Moi (Rift Valley), James Nzau (Akamba Constituency), Ronald Ngala (Coast Province) and Laurence Oguda (Nyanza South).

UNLESS ONE is actually in this land of barbed wire and watch towers, it is hard to conceive that the aims expressed above should cause the man who formulated them to be consistently attacked in the local press as "Enemy Number One." In an editorial entitled "Survival" the review *New Comment* (Nairobi) of April 5 characterises Mr. Mboya's position as "ludicrous," and ends with the italicised recommendation: "*Hard work and longer hours should be the order of the day for Kenya.*"

The remarks of the more moderate *Kenya Weekly News* strike a "Now let's try to be sensible about this thing" attitude;

the argument is that government by Africans "would mean the end of civilization in Kenya and a reversion to the Dark Ages, to the countless centuries when the Africans ruled themselves and produced absolutely nothing." The Africans' answer to this line is that for a colonial power which can maintain itself only by imposing the conditions that obtain today in Kenya, it is impolitic even to mention the word "civilization". For them a "reversion to the Dark Ages" might be an improvement.

Mboya is vehement in denying one of the favorite contentions of the British in East Africa – that there is considerable tribal disunity in Kenya. I had been told again and again of how the Kikuyu were disliked by their neighbors, of how the Wakamba had offered to take charge of operations against the Mau Mau (which in the beginning was a purely Kikuyu organization), of how the Kikuyu were called "the Jews of Kenya" by the other tribes because they were more interested in education and culture than in "doing an honest day's work," of the inability of the members of any tribe to understand or agree with those of any other. Wishful thinking, says Mboya, who as a Luo is far removed ethnically from the Kikuyus. "We're all together. We have to be. Kenya is a test case for all of colonial Africa south of the Sahara."

"They call us Mau Mau," said one Kikuyu defensively. "Do you know what Mau Mau means?" I said I did not. He put his hand over his stomach. "When this is empty, a man is Mau Mau. You see?" Like most revolutionary struggles, the freedom movement in Kenya has its terrorist elements. But the number of European victims of terrorist attacks has been unbelievably small – perhaps fifty altogether since the inception of the movement. When you compare this with the number of victims of the counter-terror initiated by the British* – "100,000 would not

---

* It is not excessive to characterise the measures of British retaliation, including the expedient of setting a bounty on dead Kikuyus, as counter-terror. An additional item of interest is the number of official hangings carried out by the government during the peak period of hostilities. From October 1952 through March 1956, 1,015 were exectured, an average of one a day. [Author's original footnote]

cover the number of our dead," the secretary of one of the trade unions in Nairobi told me – you become aware of the ferocity of local European reaction to any concrete effort, however small, to change the basis of colonial society. Apart from the fact that the more easily sensationalized aspects of Mau Mau activity (its connections with animism, the ceremony of the oath and the ritual mutilation of certain victims) made it excellent copy for news correspondents, there is no justification for the enormous publicity it received at the time of its apogee. Infinitely greater numbers of French colonists, for instance, died equally horrible deaths at the hand of Moroccan terrorists during the War for Independence in 1954 and 1955, but because there was no way of camouflaging the openly anti-colonial nature of the struggle, relatively little was made of it in the world press. The inference in most of the material written on the conflict in Kenya is that Mau Mau is (the British like to say: *was*) an irrational outbreak of bloodthirstiness on the part of a group of fanatical savages. This unrealistic conception is a natural one to expect on the part of the local European population; further afield it becomes pure colonialist propaganda.

Since the industry of the country has a racial structure, the trade union movement has been obliged to organise itself in accordance with that structure. The Kenya Federation of Labor thus comprises nine unions whose membership is totally African. The most moving experience I had in East Africa was the afternoon and evening I spent going from office to office within the unions' building, talking with union directors. Their desperate faith in trade unionism came out in halting sentences, sometimes in Swahili which had to be translated for me, and sometimes in English, but all of them said the same thing: "Trade Unionism is our only hope." The office rooms were incredibly small; when night came the only illumination they had was a candle stuck on the table.

Segregation here is fairly thorough, but not complete. Thus although there are European and non-European waiting-rooms and toilets in the stations in Nairobi as in Mombasa the municipal buses merely have first- and second-class sections, and the seating depends wholly upon the class in which the passenger chooses to ride. This arrangement gives rise to some strange little scenes. An African policeman in khaki shorts was sitting alone on the wide three-passenger seat in front of me. An English woman boarded the bus, and the policeman shifted over to the end of the seat by the window, to leave space for her. She glared furiously at him for an instant, said in a voice for the whole bus to hear: "Well, *you* make a most presentable lady, I must say!" and strode indignantly to the seat behind me, where she sat down beside an Englishman, remarking: "Did you see that incredible performance?" They ended by having a good laugh together, but the meaning of the episode eluded me. I decided there must be a law providing that European women and African men shall not sit next to one another on a public conveyance. Not knowing, however, I asked about it at the first opportunity. There is no such law; it was not a question of seats at all. The English woman was angry merely because the policeman had not stood up when she came into the bus: some Africans still do, it seems, in their deference to their superiors.

MOMBASA

There was a riot in the Athi River Detention Camp two days before I left Nairobi; a British guard was stabbed. Severe disciplinary measures were urged by the press. Today there is a news story of a mass escape of Mau Mau convicts on their way back to a camp from the quarry where they had been working. Twenty prisoners are still at large. Before going up to Nairobi I should have hoped vaguely for their capture as a part of the necessary process of reestablishing order in the land. Now I find it difficult to wish them anything but the best of luck.

Tangier Diary: a
Post-Colonial Interlude

Africa South, Capetown, 1957

T HE CITY is still here, spread out along the hill-tops and overlooking the circular harbor, the strait and the mountains of Andalusia. In the late afternoon people sit along the low wall bordering a vast empty lot on the Boulevard Pasteur in the very heart of Tangier, watching the gyrating clouds of swallows in the air far above, like locusts swarming. The British still have their big villas on the Mountain, but it is harder to get workmen to keep the gardens in trim. The Americans, having given up their extra-territorial rights if not their Cadillacs, can no longer make faces at the policeman who tries to stop them from going in the wrong direction down a one-way street, or snarl "Screw you, Buster," at him as he tells them it is forbidden to park in a particular spot. To give the streets a more "European" aspect, girls are encouraged to go about "naked" – that is, without their veils. At the same time, all signs and advertisements must now be printed in Arabic as well as in Roman characters, with the result that the place looks considerably *less* European than it has in years.

If you see a new face, the chances are it belongs to a policeman; the city is overrun with police, most of them not in uniform. These are what in colonial days would have been called *chkama*, informers. They are also skilled *agents-provocateurs*, used among other things for trapping girls not averse to being followed by a young man who is making flattering remarks out of the side of his mouth as he walks along. When the right moment has come, the amorous pursuer turns back his jacket-lapel and discloses his badge, a tactic which the people of Tangier are still old-fashioned enough to find wholly offensive.

THIS IS THE SECOND anniversary of the winning of Moroccan independence. The trees along the main thoroughfares are ablaze with colored electric bulbs, and the enormous baroque kiosk in the center of the Place de France, built earlier in the year in celebration of the first visit of the Sultan to Tangier since 1947, has been cleaned up and rewired, so that its mottoes in Arabic script (as well as the four large numerals indicating the year – 1377) flash again. One waits for dusk impatiently, to walk beneath the canopies of lights strung from building to building; Tangier is such a small town in feeling, that a surfeit of light makes it seem much larger.

A segment of the Moroccan population is regretful that the celebration should come at this time, so that it could mistakenly be construed by the 50,000 or so Spanish residents as having been arranged in honor of the birthday of *Jesucristo*. Christmas has always been the great general holiday of the year in Tangier, and it was the Spanish who animated it for a fortnight beforehand, donning masks, dressing as shepherds and marching in mock-military groups through the streets playing their *zambombas* (which made a noise like a lion grunting rhythmically), clapping their hands, clicking their castanets and occasionally singing between swigs of *vino tinto* from the flasks hanging over their shoulders. Such unbridled festivities are not at all in keeping with the surge of puritanism being propagated by the younger generation of Moroccan patriots, and the fact that it was exclusively the Spanish who indulged in them (even if to the delight of the entire population of Moslems, Jews and Christians), makes their observance that much less acceptable this year. It is only two days to Christmas, and so far I've seen no sign of *zambombas*, merrymaking shepherds, or anything else indicating the advent of the December holidays. The discretion of the Spanish civilians is understandable when one considers that at the moment their armed forces are busy shooting Moroccans, their warships are bombarding the Moroccan coast south of Agadir, and that just behind Djebel Musa (Mount Moses) which I can see from my window, at the entrance to the town of Ceuta, barricades of barbed wire have been thrown up by Spanish troops to prevent possible violence between Spanish and Moroccans.

The twin cities of Ceuta and Melilla, at opposite ends of the Rif, are considered by the government in Madrid (and with the same variety of logic as that used by the French in defining the status of Algeria) to form an integral part of metropolitan Spain. One assumes that at some point in history they became detached from the mother country and floated across to Africa. Uppermost in the minds of Moroccans since independence has been the question of liberating these two key cities, which also happen to be Morocco's only Mediterranean ports. On paper, of course, there has never been any question of a change of sovereignty; officially it is understood that Melilla (Spanish since 1506) and Ceuta (since 1580) would continue to be regarded as *presidios* inseparable from the rest of Spain.

There is little doubt that the guerrilla warfare in progress at present in the south of Morocco over the relatively unimportant question of control of the Ifni enclave is merely the opening salvo in an extensive long-term military operation – a campaign led by the F.L.N. of Algeria and the Moroccan Army of Liberation with the aim of ousting both France and Spain from all Saharan territories. For the past eighteen months the Moroccans have been pointing out that there is every reason why their country should extend its hegemony southward through Rio de Oro, the Spanish Sahara and French Mauretania, to the northern borders of Senegal. The Algerians are equally determined that the area lying roughly between 20° and 30°N.L. and 0° and 10°E.L. shall not remain in French hands, regardless of what happens in Algeria proper. During a recent conversation about the "Greater Morocco" project with an official of the Moroccan government, I was interested to note that he used as justification of the policy the argument that at the time of the Saadi Dynasty, in the Sixteenth Century, Moroccan control extended to the Sudan, and I remarked lightly that in that case Andalucia and Castilla as well would have to be annexed. He smiled. "First things first", he said. "That will come later."

So far the Moroccans show surprisingly little resentment toward the Spanish when one considers that the two nations are in a sense unofficially at war with one another. A possible reason for this complacency is that in recent times anti-colonial hatred has been directed almost exclusively against the French. Generalissimo Franco made political capital out of this tradition at the time of the French-Moroccan War, between 1953 and 1955, when, in spite of French pleas, he refused to outlaw the nationalist movement in his part of the Protectorate. Then too, *relative* justice in the ex-Spanish Zone was far greater than in the ex-French; that is, the Spanish government's treatment of its colonial subjects and its treatment of Spanish subjects differed only in degree – it was all rough and authoritarian – while there was a terrifying disparity between the favoritism France showed her own nationals in Morocco and the cynical contempt with which she governed the native Moroccans. It is also true that many of the Spanish, being only slightly removed racially and culturally from the Moroccans, tended to think of the latter as human beings, whereas the French colonist's classical epithet for them was "animals". (A small illustration of the difference in attitudes: if a Moslem funeral passed through the streets of Tetuan or Larache or another of the Spanish Moroccan cities, some of the Spanish passers-by always stopped for a moment and crossed themselves respectfully; I never once saw this happen in the ex-French Zone.)

Place Amrah in the Tangier Medina – Paul Bowles bought a small traditional house close by here, when he first settled in Tangier in 1947 (PB)

Allal el Fassi, the dynamic founder-leader of the all-powerful Istiqlal party, is at the moment making a comprehensive tour of the Moroccan hinterlands, using his legendary oratorical gifts to persuade the tribesmen and peasants to defend their country by joining the ranks of the Djij Tsahrir, the army of liberation; recruiting of volunteers is going on all over Morocco. The general belief of the Europeans living here is that the Sultan is powerless to impede the activities of the Army of Liberation, and it is probably true that on occasion they have caused him embarrassment; yet there is no doubt in the mind of any Moroccan that the tactic of having an official army and another unofficial one, for whose behavior he is not necessarily to be held responsible, is definitely a part of Mohammed the Fifth's policy, as indeed there is every reason it should be. (In the Ifni hostilities the Royal Army is used purely defensively, on the "Moroccan" side of the border.)

The obvious question for the European mind to pose here is: how safe is it to have an unofficial army which is stronger than your official one? But the query does not occur to the Moroccan, because his faith in both the Sultan and the Djij Tsahrir makes their aims indistinguishable, and to him the mere postulating of such complexities and difficulties is sheer defeatism. And who can be certain that the man in the street is not correct? There is assuredly no proof that the Sultan is not in absolute control of his realm. It is true that such a supposition would necessarily alter somewhat the popular international conception of the Sultan as a staunch defender of democracy and the status quo, but is not a monarch's first responsibility to his country? When *Time* crows that Mohammed the Fifth is unconditionally with the West, it is referring only to his present foreign policy and not to what he does within his own kingdom, which is after all his own affair. In Moroccan opinion the Royal Army and the Army of Liberation are the right hand and the left hand, and each one is fully aware of what the other is doing.

TANGIER OF THE DUBIOUS BARS, the *maisons closes*, the pimps and panderers, the smugglers and refugees from Scotland Yard and the F.B.I., the old Tangier that tried valiantly if unsuccessfully to live up to its inflated reputation as a "sin city", is dead and buried. By day the place does not look very different from the way it has always looked, but its nocturnal aspect would shock a native returning home after two years' absence. "Gone! Shut!" he would murmur as he searched for the familiar landmarks in streets and alleys unexpectedly dark and deserted. For the social reformers have passed this way, and their war is waged loudly against prostitution and drunkenness and with slightly less fanfare against homosexuality and hashish-smoking. The first year was a tough one: the inhabitants of Tangier, among all Moroccans the only urbanites who had not been through at least a minimal period of terrorism and suffering, simply refused to believe that the Istiqlal was serious when it announced its clean-up campaign. Strong-arm squadrons imported in part from other cities had to be used to convince them, since the local police appeared to share the general incredulity. Street brawls were constant nightly occurrences a year ago. Now, the prisons crammed to bursting with offenders, the population is sufficiently certain of the party's seriousness of purpose for political commandos to be no longer in evidence, and for the police to be adequate to the situation.

But there is a catch: the Tangier police force had to be entirely disbanded and its members replaced by men from other parts of the country. It was inevitable that this substitution of personnel should give rise to widespread local dissatisfaction. The Tangerines were accustomed to recognizing all the faces among the officers of the law in their tiny world, and they were recognized in turn. Now personal indulgences are finished; law enforcement has become mechanical, anonymous, and with anonymity comes a certain ineptitude. As a Moroccan lawyer remarked the other day: "Every kid who ever carried a sandwich to a terrorist in hiding has been rewarded with a policeman's uniform and a revolver." The indignation of the native populace is analogous to that which would result if, say, Monaco were suddenly to be thrown open by the French and the Monegasque police replaced by French gendarmes; Tangier had become that provincial and hermetic. The only special privilege it retains is the right to buy and sell foreign currencies. From all other points of view it is just one of the Moroccan cities, still livelier than most in spite of the blue laws (Casablanca, Fez and Meknès are lugubrious), because the economic crisis gnawing at Morocco has not made as much headway here as elsewhere, but definitely no longer a place apart, operating to the advantage of get-rich-quicks from all over the world and at the expense of the poorer inhabitants, as was the case before.

Tariffs on imported goods have risen steeply, so that the European way of life costs about double what it did two years ago. The Moroccans, however, who subsist principally on Moroccan products, are a little better off than they were, since although the prices of local commodities have also increased, the higher earning capacity of most sections of the population more than compensates for the rise. It is unfortunate that along with the general improvement in living conditions has come the menace of growing unemployment. The danger at present is partially mitigated by military enlistments. The enlargement of an army, be it official or unofficial, is no true solution, obviously, but it can provide a temporary dike against the encroaching discontent, and probably for a longer period than would be thinkable in most other countries. The Sahara is a big place.

The atmosphere is that of an *entr'acte*; people are waiting for the spectacle to recommence. "What do you think will happen?" you ask them, but their replies are vague and contradictory. The only clearly expressed, heartfelt wish which emerges is the one that no responsible European wants to hear put into words, the one that highlights, albeit without clarifying, an aspect of the basic cleavage between the contemporary Moslem and "Western" viewpoints: "May there soon be another great war. Then we shall have our chance."

NOTES MAILED AT
NAGERCOIL

HARPERS, JULY 1957; THEIR HEADS ARE GREEN, 1963

CAPE COMORIN, SOUTH INDIA, MARCH, 1952

I HAVE BEEN HERE in this hotel now for a week. At no time during the night or day has the temperature been low enough for comfort; it fluctuates between ninety-five and one hundred and five degrees, and most of the time there is absolutely no breeze, which is astonishing for the seaside. Each bedroom and public room has the regulation large electric fan in its ceiling, but there is no electricity; we are obliged to use oil lamps for lighting. Today at lunch time a large Cadillac of the latest model drove up to the front door. In the back were three fat little men wearing nothing but the flimsy *dhotis* they had draped around their loins. One of them handed a bunch of keys to the chauffeur, who then got out and came into the hotel. Near the front door is the switch box. He opened it, turned on the current with one of the keys, and throughout the hotel the fans began to whir. Then the three little men got out and went into the dining room where they had their lunch. I ate quickly, so as to get upstairs and lie naked on my bed under the fan. It was an unforgettable fifteen minutes. Then the fan stopped, and I heard the visitors driving away. The hotel manager told me later that they were government employees of the State of Travancore, and that only they had a key to the switch box.*

Last night I awoke and opened my eyes. There was no moon; it was still dark, but the light of a star was shining into my face through the open window, from a point high above the Arabian Sea. I sat up, and gazed at it. The light it cast seemed as bright as that of the moon in northern countries; coming through the window, it made its rectangle on the opposite wall, broken by the shadow of my silhouetted head. I held up my hand and moved the fingers, and their shadow too was definite. There were no other stars visible in that part of the sky; this one blinded them all. It was about an hour before daybreak, which comes shortly after six, and there was not a breath of air. On such still nights the waves breaking on the nearby shore sound like great, deep explosions going on at some distant place. There is the boom, which can be felt as well as heard and which ends with a sharp rattle and hiss, then a long period of complete silence, and finally, when it seems that there will be no more sound, another sudden boom. The crows begin to scream and chatter while the darkness is still complete.

The town, like the others here in the extreme south, gives the impression of being made of dust. Dust and cow dung lie in the streets, and the huge crows hop ahead of you as you walk along. When a gust of hot wind wanders in from the sandy wastes beyond the town, the brown fans of the palmyra trees swish and bang against each other; they sound like giant sheets of heavy wrapping paper. The small black men walk quickly, the diamonds in their earlobes flashing. Because of their jewels and the gold thread woven into their *dhotis*, they all look not merely prosperous, but fantastically wealthy. When the women have diamonds, they are likely to wear them in a hole pierced through the wall of one nostril.

---

* The states of Travancore and Cochin subsequently merged to form the modern province of Kerala. [Editor's footnote]

The first time I ever saw India I entered it through Dhanush-kodi. An analogous procedure in America would be for a for-eigner to get his first glimpse of the United States by crossing the Mexican border illegally and coming out into a remote Arizona village. It was God-forsaken, uncomfortable and a little frighten-ing. Since then I have landed as a bonafide visitor should, in the impressively large and unbeautiful metropolis of Bombay. But I'm glad that my first trip did not bring me in contact with any cities. It is better to go to the villages of a strange land before trying to understand its towns, above all in a complex place like India. Now, after traveling some eight thousand miles around the country, I know approximately as little as I did on my first arrival. However, I've seen a lot of people and places, and at least I have a somewhat more detailed and precise idea of my ignorance than I did in the beginning.

If you have not taken the precaution of reserving a room in advance, you risk having considerable difficulty in find-ing one when you land in Bombay. There are very few hotels, and the two or three comfortable ones are always full. I hate being committed to a reservation because the element of adven-ture is thereby destroyed. The only place I was able to get into when I first arrived, therefore, was something less than a first-class establishment. It was all right during the day and the early hours of the evening. At night, however, every square foot of floor space in the dark corridors was occupied by sleepers who had arrived late and brought their own mats with them; the hotel was able in this way to shelter several hundred extra guests each night. Having their hands and feet kicked and trod-den on was apparently a familiar enough experience to them for them never to make any audible objection when the inevitable happened. Here in Cape Comorin, on the other hand, there are many rooms and they are vast, and at the moment I am the only one staying in the hotel.

It was raining. I was on a bus going from Alleppey to Trivan-drum, on my way down here. There were two little Indian nuns on the seat in front of mine. I wondered how they stood the heat in their heavy robes. Sitting near the driver was a man with a thick, fierce mustache who distinguished himself from the other passengers by the fact that in addition to his *dhoti* he also wore a European shirt; its scalloped tail hung down nearly to his knees. With him he had a voluminous collection of magazines and newspapers in both Tamil and English, and even from where I sat I could not help noticing that all this reading matter had been printed in the Soviet Union. (After years of practice one gets to recognize it without difficulty.)

At a certain moment, near one of the myriad villages that lie smothered in the depths of the palm forests, the motor suddenly ceased to function and the bus came to a stop. The driver, not exchanging a single glance with his passengers, let his head fall forward and remain resting on the steering wheel in a posture of despair. Expectantly the people waited a little while, and then they began to get up. One of the first out of the bus was the man with the mustache. He said a hearty good-bye to the occupants in general, although he had not been conversing with any of them, and started up the road carrying his umbrella, but not his armful of printed matter. Then I realized that at some point during the past hour, not foreseeing the failure of the motor and the mass departure which it entailed, he had left a paper or magazine on each empty seat – exactly as our American comrades used to do on subway trains three decades ago.

Almost at the moment I made this discovery, the two nuns had risen and were hurriedly collecting the "literature." They climbed down and ran along the road after the man, calling out in English, "Sir, your papers!" He turned, and they handed them to him. Without saying a word, but with an expression of fury on his face, he took the bundle and continued. But it was impossible to tell from the faces of the two nuns when they returned to gather up their belongings whether or not they were conscious of what they had done.

A few minutes later everyone had left the bus and walked to the village – everyone, that is, but the driver and me. I had too much luggage. Then I spoke to him.

"What's the matter with the bus?"

He shrugged his shoulders.

"How am I going to get to Trivandrum?"

He did not know that, either.

"Couldn't you look into the motor?" I pursued. "It sounded like the fan belt. Maybe you could repair it."

This roused him sufficiently from his apathy to make him turn and look at me.

"We have People's Government here in Travancore," he said. "Not allowed touching motor."

"But who *is* going to repair it, then?"

"Tonight making telephone call to Trivandrum. Making report. Tomorrow or other day they sending inspector to examine."

"And then what?"

"Then inspector making report. Then sending repair crew."

"I see."

"People's Government," he said again, by way of helping me to understand. "Not like other government."

"No," I said.

As if to make his meaning clearer, he indicated the seat where the man with the large mustache had sat. "That gentleman Communist."

"Oh, really?" (At least it was all in the open and the driver was under no misapprehension as to what the term "People's Government" meant.)

"Very powerful man. Member of Parliament from Travancore."

"Is he a good man, though? Do the people like him?"

"Oh, yes, sir. Powerful man."

"But is he *good*?" I insisted.

He laughed, doubtless at my ingenuousness. "Powerful man all rascals," he said.

Just before nightfall a local bus came along, and with the help of several villagers I transferred my luggage to it and continued on my way.

Most of the impressively heavy Communist vote is cast by the Hindus. The Moslems are generally in less dire economic straits, it is true, but in any case, by virtue of their strict religious views, they do not take kindly to any sort of ideological change. (A convert from Islam is unthinkable; apostasy is virtually nonexistent.) If even Christianity has retained too much of its pagan décor to be acceptable to the puritanical Moslem mind, one can imagine the loathing inspired in them by the endless proliferations of Hindu religious art with its gods, demons, metamorphoses and avatars. The two religious systems are antipodal. Fortunately the constant association with the mild and tolerant Hindus has made the Moslems of India far more understanding and tractable than their brothers in Islamic countries further west; there is much less actual friction than one might be led to expect.

During breakfast one morning at the Connemara Hotel in Madras the Moslem head waiter told me a story. He was traveling in the Province of Orissa where, in a certain town, there was a Hindu temple which was famous for having five hundred cobras on its premises. He decided he would like to see these legendary reptiles. When he had got to the town he hired a carriage and went to the temple. At the door he was met by a priest who offered to show him around. And since the Moslem looked prosperous, the priest suggested a donation of five rupees, to be paid in advance.

"Why so much?" asked the visitor.

"To buy eggs for the cobras. You know, we have five hundred of them."

The Moslem gave him the money on condition that the priest let him see the snakes. For an hour his guide dallied in the many courtyards and galleries, pointing out bas-reliefs, idols, pillars and bells. Finally the Moslem reminded him of their understanding.

"Cobras? Ah, yes. But they are dangerous. Perhaps you would rather see them another day?"

This behavior on the priest's part had delighted him, he recalled, for it had reinforced his suspicions.

"Not at all," he said. "I want to see them now."

Reluctantly the priest led him into a small alcove behind a large stone Krishna, and pointed into a very dark corner.

"Is this the place?" the visitor asked.

"This is the place."

"But where are the snakes?"

In a tiny enclosure were two sad old cobras, "almost dead from hunger," he assured me. But when his eyes had grown used to the dimness he saw that there were hundreds of egg-shells scattered around the floor outside the pen.

"You eat a lot of eggs," he told the priest.

The priest merely said, "Here. Take back your five rupees. But if you are asked about our cobras, please be so kind as to say that you saw five hundred of them here in our temple. Is that all right?"

The episode was meant to illustrate the head waiter's thesis, which was that the Hindus are abject in the practice of their religion; this is the opinion held by the Moslems. On the other hand, it must be remembered that the Hindu considers Islam an incomplete doctrine, far from satisfying. He finds its austerity singularly comfortless and deplores its lack of mystico-philosophical content, an element in which his own creed is so rich.

I was invited to lunch at one of the cinema studios in the suburbs north of Bombay. We ate our curry outdoors; our hostess was the star of the film then in production. She spoke only Marathi; her husband, who was directing the picture, spoke excellent English. During the meal he told how, as a Hindu, he had been forced to leave his job, his home, his car and his bank account in Karachi at the time of partition – when Pakistan came into existence – and emigrate empty-handed to India, where he had managed to remake his life. Another visitor to the studio, an Egyptian, was intensely interested in his story. Presently he interrupted to say, "It is unjust, of course."

"Yes," smiled our host.

"What retaliatory measures does your government plan to take against the Moslems left here in India?"

"None whatever, as far as I know."

The Egyptian was genuinely indignant. "But why not?" he demanded. "It is only right that you apply the same principle. You have plenty of Moslems here still to take action against. And I say that even though I am a Moslem."

The film director looked at him closely. "You say that *because* you are a Moslem," he told him. "But we cannot put ourselves on that level."

The conversation ended on this not entirely friendly note. A moment later packets of betel were passed around. I promptly broke a tooth, withdrew from the company and went some distance away into the garden. While I, in the interests of science, was examining the mouthful of partially chewed betel leaves and areca nut, trying to find the pieces of bicuspid, the Egyptian came up to me, his face a study in scorn.

"They are afraid of the Moslems. That's the real reason," he whispered. Whether he was right or wrong I was neither qualified nor momentarily disposed to say, but it was a classical exposition of the two opposing moral viewpoints – two concepts of behavior which cannot quickly be reconciled.

Obviously it is a gigantic task to make a nation out of a place like India, what with Hindus, Moslems, Parsees, Jainists, Jews, Catholics and Protestants, some of whom may speak the arbitrarily imposed national idiom of Hindi, but most of whom are more likely to know Gujarati, Marathi, Bengali, Urdu, Telugu, Tamil, Malayalam or some other tongue. One wonders whether any sort of unifying project can ever be undertaken, or, indeed, whether it is even desirable.

When you come to the border between two provinces you often find bars across the road, and you are obliged to undergo a thorough inspection of your luggage. As in the United States, there is a strict control of the passage of liquor between wet and dry districts, but that is not the extent of the examination.

Sample of conversation at the border on the Mercara-Cannanore highway:

Customs officer: "What is in there?"

Bowles: "Clothing."

"And in that?"

"Clothing."

"And in all those?"

"Clothing."

"Open all, please."

After eighteen suitcases have been gone through carefully: "My God, man! Close them all. I could charge duty for all of these goods, but you will never be able to do business with these things here anyway. The Moslem men are too clever."

"But I'm not intending to sell my clothes."

"Shut the luggage. It is duty-free, I tell you."

A professor from Raniket in North India arrived at the hotel here the other day, and we spent a good part of the night sitting on the window seat in my room that overlooks the sea, talking about what one always talks about here: India. Among the many questions I put to him was one concerning the reason why so many of the Hindu temples in South India prohibit entry to non-Hindus, and why they have military guards at the entrances. I imagined I knew the answer in advance: fear of Moslem disturbances. Not at all, he said. The principal purpose was to keep out certain Christian missionaries. I expressed disbelief.

"Of course," he insisted. "They come and jeer during our rituals, ridicule our sacred images."

"But even if they were stupid enough to want to do such things," I objected, "their sense of decorum would keep them from behaving like that."

He merely laughed. "Obviously you don't know them."

The post office here is a small stifling room over a shop, and it is full of boys seated on straw mats. The postmaster, a tiny old man who wears large diamond earrings and gold-rimmed spectacles, and is always naked to the waist, is also a professor; he interrupts his academic work to sell an occasional stamp. At first contact his English sounds fluent enough, but soon one discovers that it is not adapted to conversation, and that one can scarcely talk to him. Since the boys are listening, he must pretend to be omniscient; therefore he answers promptly with more or less whatever phrase comes into his head.

Yesterday I went to post a letter by airmail to Tangier. "Tanjore," he said, adjusting his spectacles. "That will be four annas." (Tanjore is in South India, near Trichinopoly.) I explained that I hoped my letter would be going to Tangier, Morocco.

"Yes, yes," he said impatiently. "There are many Tanjores." He opened the book of postal regulations and read aloud from it, quite at random, for (although it may be difficult to believe) exactly six minutes. I stood still, fascinated, and let him go on. Finally he looked up and said, "There is no mention of Tangier. No airplanes go to that place."

"Well, how much would it be to send it by sea mail?" (I thought we could then calculate the surcharge for air mail, but I had misjudged my man.)

"Yes," he replied evenly. "That is a good method, too."

I decided to keep the letter and post it in the nearby town of Nagercoil another day. In a little while I would have several to add to it, and I counted on being able to send them all together when I went. Before I left the post office I hazarded the remark that the weather was extremely hot. In that airless attic at noon it was a wild understatement. But it did not please the postmaster at all. Deliberately he removed his glasses and pointed the stems at me.

"Here we have the perfect climate," he told me. "Neither too cold nor too cool."

"That is true," I said. "Thank you."

In the past few years there have been visible quantitative changes in Indian life, all in the one direction of Europeanization. This is in the smaller towns; the cities of course have long since been westernized. The temples which before were lighted by bare electric bulbs and coconut-oil lamps now have fluorescent tubes glimmering in their ceilings. Crimson, green and amber floodlights are used to illumine bathing tanks, deities, the gateways of temples. The public-address system is the bane of the ear these days, even in the temples. And it is impossible to attend a concert or a dance recital without discovering several

The well-suited author, correcting proofs – this was probably in Ceylon or southern India, judging by the cloth behind him, in the 1950s

loudspeakers whose noise completely destroys the quality of the music. A mile before you arrive at the cinema of a small town you can hear the raucous blaring of the amplifier they have set up at its entrance.

This year in South India there are fewer men with bare torsos, *dhotis* and sandals; more shirts, trousers and shoes. There is at the same time a slow shutting-down of services which to the Western tourist make all the difference between pleasure and discomfort in traveling, such as the restaurants in the stations (there being no dining cars on the trains) and the showers in the first-class compartments. A few years ago they worked; now they have been sealed off. You can choke on the dust and soot of your compartment, or drown in your own sweat now, for all the railway cares.

At one point I was held for forty-eight hours in a concentration camp run by the Ceylon government on Indian soil. (The euphemism for this one was "screening camp.") I was told that I was under suspicion of being an international spy. My astonishment and indignation were regarded as almost convincing in their sincerity, thus proof of my guilt.

"But who am I supposed to be spying *for*?" I asked piteously.

The director shrugged. "Spying for international," he said.

More than the insects or the howling of pariah dogs outside the rolls of barbed wire, what bothered me was the fact that in the center of the camp, which at that time housed some twenty thousand people, there was a loudspeaker in a high tower which during every moment of the day roared forth Indian film music. Fortunately it was silenced at ten o'clock each evening. I got out of the hell-hole only by making such violent trouble that I was dragged before the camp doctor, who decided that I was dangerously unbalanced. The idea in letting me go was that I would be detained further along, and the responsibility would fall on other shoulders. "They will hold him at Talaimannar," I heard the doctor say. "The poor fellow is quite mad."

Here and there, in places like the bar of the Hotel Metropole at Mysore, or at the North Coorg Club of Mercara, one may still come across vestiges of the old colonial life: ghosts in the form of incredibly sunburned Englishmen in jodhpurs and boots discussing their hunting luck and prowess. But these visions are exceedingly rare in a land that wants to forget their existence.

The younger generation in India is intent on forgetting a good many things, including some that it might do better to remember. There would seem to be no good reason for getting rid of their country's most ancient heritage, the religion of Hinduism, or of its most recent acquisition, the tradition of independence. This latter, at least insofar as the illiterate masses are concerned, is inseparable not only from the religious state of mind which made political victory possible, but also from the legend which, growing up around the figure of Gandhi, has elevated him in their minds to the status of a god.

The young, politically minded intellectuals find this not at all to their liking; in their articles and addresses they have returned again and again to the attack against Gandhi as a "betrayer" of the Indian people. That they are motivated by hatred is obvious. But what do they hate?

For one thing, subconsciously they cannot accept their own inability to go on having religious beliefs. Then, belonging to the group without faith, they are thereby forced to hate the past, particularly the atavisms which are made apparent by the workings of the human mind with its irrationality, its subjective involvement in exterior phenomena. The floods of poisonous words they pour forth are directed primarily at the adolescents; this is an age group which is often likely to find demagoguery more attractive than common sense.

There are at least a few of these enlightened adolescents in every town; the ones here in Cape Comorin were horrified when by a stratagem I led them to the home of a man of their own village who claims that his brother is under a spell. (They had not imagined, they told me later, that an American would believe such nonsense.) According to the man Subramaniam, his brother was a painter who had been made art director of a major film studio in Madras. To substantiate his story he brought out a sheaf of very professional sketches for film sets.

"Then my brother had angry words with a jealous man in the studio," said Subramaniam, "and the man put a charm on him. His mind is gone. But at the end of the year it will return." The brother presently appeared in the courtyard; he was a vacant-eyed man with a beard, and he had a voluminous turkish towel draped over his head and shoulders. He walked past us and disappeared through a doorway.

"A spirit doctor is treating him . . ." The modern young men shifted their feet miserably; it was unbearable that an American should be witnessing such shameful revelations, and that they should be coming from one in their midst.

But these youths who found it so necessary to ridicule poor Subramaniam failed to understand why I laughed when, the conversation changing to the subject of cows, I watched their collective expression swiftly change to one of respect bordering on beatitude. For cow worship is one facet of popular Hinduism which has not yet been totally superseded by twentieth-century faithlessness. True, it has taken on new forms of ritual. Mass cow worship is often practiced now in vast modern concrete stadiums, with prizes being distributed to the owners of the finest bovine specimens, but the religious aspect of the celebration is still evident. The cows are decorated with garlands of jewelry, fed bananas and sugar cane by people who have waited in line for hours to be granted that rare privilege; and when the satiated animals can eat no more they simply lie down or wander about, while hundreds of young girls perform sacred dances in their honor.

In India, where the cow wishes to go she goes. She may be lying in the temple, where she may decide to get up to go and lie instead in the middle of the street. If she is annoyed by the proximity of the traffic streaming past her, she may lumber to her feet again and continue down the street to the railway station, where, should she feel like reclining in front of the ticket window, no one will disturb her. On the highways she seems to know that the drivers of trucks and buses will spot her a mile away and slow down almost to a stop before they get to her, and that therefore she need not move out from under the shade of the particular banyan tree she has chosen for her rest. Her superior position in the world is agreed upon by common consent.

The most satisfying exposition I have seen of the average Hindu's feeling about this exalted beast is a little essay composed by a candidate for a post in one of the public services, entitled simply "The Cow." The fact that it was submitted in order to show the aspirant's mastery of the English language, while touching, is of secondary importance.

The Cow

The cow is one wonderful animal, also he is quadruped and because he is female he gives milk – but he will do so only when he has got child. He is same like God, sacred to Hindu and useful to man. But he has got four legs together. Two are foreward and two are afterwards.

His whole body can be utilized for use. More so the milk. What it cannot do? Various ghee, butter, cream, curds, whey, kova and the condensed milk and so forth. Also, he is useful to cobbler, watermans and mankind generally.

His motion is slow only. That is because he is of amplitudinous species, and also his other motion is much useful to trees, plants as well as making fires. This is done by making flat cakes in hand and drying in the sun.

He is the only animal that extricates his feedings after eating. Then afterwards he eats by his teeth which are situated in the inside of his mouth. He is incessantly grazing in the meadows.

His only attacking and defending weapons are his horns, especially when he has got child. This is done by bowing his head whereby he causes the weapons to be parallel to ground of earth and instantly proceeds with great velocity forwards.

He has got tail also, but not like other similar animals. It has hairs on the end of the other side. This is done to frighten away the flies which alight on his whole body and chastises him unceasingly, whereupon he gives hit with it.

The palms of his feet are so soft unto the touch so that the grasses he eats would not get crushed. At night he reposes by going down on the ground and then he shuts his eyes like his relative the horse which does not do so. This is the cow.

The moths and night insects flutter about my single oil lamp. Occasionally, at the top of its chimney, one of them goes up in a swift, bright flame. On the concrete floor in a fairly well-defined ring around the bottom of my chair are the drops of sweat that have rolled off my body during the past two hours. The doors into both the bedroom and the bathroom are shut; I work each night in the dressing room between them, because fewer insects are attracted here. But the air is nearly unbreathable with the stale smoke of cigarettes and *bathi* sticks burned to discourage the entry of winged creatures. Today's paper announced an outbreak of bubonic plague in Bellary. I keep thinking about it, and I wonder if the almost certain eventual victory over such diseases will prove to have been worth its price: the extinction of the beliefs and rituals which gave a satisfactory meaning to the period of consciousness that goes between birth and death. I doubt it. Security is a false god; begin making sacrifices to it and you are lost.

THE PASSPORT

JOURNAL, INCLUDED IN CHERIE NUTTING'S 'YESTERDAY'S
PERFUME: AN INTIMATE PORTRAIT OF PAUL BOWLES'

AHMED AND I were invited one afternoon by the brother
of Justin Daranayafala, who was the curator of the
Dehiwala zoo. I had expressed a great desire to see the
tiger cubs. He brought them out. Of course they were beautiful,
a little larger and heavier than full grown cats, and with
enormous paws, already capable of doing damage with their
claws, which they kept politely sheathed. Indeed, their behavior
was impeccable throughout the meeting. It was hard to believe
that one was holding and caressing a real Bengal tiger. Presently
our host announced that he was willing to sell the couple, and
for a reasonable price: $800 for the two, brother and sister. I was
tempted, but quickly realized that travelling with tigers, even
in their infancy, would present insurmountable problems. And
when they grew up, what would one do with them? It would
be worse than what Sir Michael Puff was faced with, when he
purchased a young elephant and took it home to Wales. An
elephant can be managed if it has a wise mahout with it always,
but two adult tigers would present problems.

Perhaps the pleasure of holding and stroking these two
innocuous babes helped to diminish Ahmed's instinctive sense
of dread. Clearly he knew tigers were dangerous beasts, but
when we got to Mysore and had the Maharaja's tiger fields to

ourselves, he seemed to forget what he knew, and let what he felt direct his actions. He remembered the handfuls of soft fur, and since this had been his only tactile contact, the tiger became a friendly animal. At all events, he came perilously close to losing his life as a result.

I believe that the Maharaja had consulted Hagenbeck in designing the topography of his zoo. The tigers had a large tract of land at their disposal, and there was no wall to enclose them. The outside was protected from the inside by a deep dry moat, into which the animals were careful not to fall. There was a low white building which served as a bridge across the ditch. It had metal rings up the side, and Ahmed was quick to climb to the top. It was a flat roof with no railing. Three tigers became aware of his presence and came rushing down the hill. I assume it was from that roof that the attendant tossed their food down to them, for they were in a state of great excitement. They leapt and roared again and again, and their huge claws scraped the wall. When Ahmed saw how close they came to his feet as he stood at the edge he seemed to have dropped into a state of hypnosis, and might have fallen either backward or forward. I began to shout, "Don't move!" This may have brought him back to reality, as he began to move away from the edge. The roaring and leaping went on, even after he climbed down to the ground. Later he was not eager to discuss the incident.

WORLDS OF TANGIER

HOLIDAY, MARCH 1958

IN THE SUMMER of 1931, Gertrude Stein invited me to stay a fortnight in her house at Bilignin, in southern France, where she always spent the warm months of the year. At the beginning of the second week she asked me where I intended to go when I left. Not having seen much of the world, I replied that I thought Villefranche would be a good place. She was gently contemptuous. "Anybody can go to the Riviera," she declared. "You ought to go somewhere better than that. Why don't you go to Tangier?" I was hesitant, and explained that living there might cost more than my budget allowed me. "Nonsense," she said. "It's cheap. It's just the place for you."

A week later I was aboard a little ship called the *Imeréthie II* bound for various North African ports, and ever since I have been grateful to Gertrude Stein for her intelligent suggestion. Beginning with the first day and continuing through all the years I have spent in Tangier, I have loved the white city that sits astride its hills, looking out across the Strait of Gibraltar to the mountains of Andalusia.

In those days Tangier was an attractive, quiet town with about 60,000 inhabitants. The Medina looked ancient, its passageways were full of people in bright outlandish costumes, and each street leading to the outskirts was bordered by walls of cane, prickly pear and high-growing geranium. Today, where this thick vegetation grew, are the cracking façades of new apart-ment houses; the Moslems have discarded their frogged Oriental jackets and enormous trousers of turquoise, orange, pistachio or shocking pink, to don Levis, and second-hand raincoats imported by the bale from America; the population has aug-mented at least threefold, and I'm afraid the city would never strike a casual visitor as either quiet or attractive. There must be few places in the world which have altered visually to such an extent in the past quarter of a century.

A town, like a person, almost ceases to have a face once you know it intimately, and visual modifications are skin-deep; the character is determined largely by its inhabitants, and a good deal of time is required to change their attitudes and behavior. Tangier can still be a fascinating place for the outsider who has the time and inclination to get acquainted with its people. The foreigner who lives here on a long-term basis will still find most of the elements which endeared the place to him in the old days, because he knows where to look for them. Tangier is still a small town in the sense that you literally cannot walk along a principal street without meeting a dozen of your friends with whom you must stop and chat. What starts out to be a ten-minute stroll will normally take an hour or more.

You will run into a Polish refugee who arrived ten years ago without a penny, borrowed enough to become a peanut vendor, and today runs a prosperous delicatessen and liquor store; an American construction worker who came to Morocco to help build the United States air bases, and has since become a freelance journalist; a Moslem who spent who years in a Spanish jail for voicing his opinions on Generalissimo Franco, and now is a clerk in the municipal administration offices; a tailor from Rome who has not amassed the fortune he had counted on and wants to go home; an English masseuse who was passing through Tangier twenty years ago on a holiday trip and somehow has never left; a Belgian architect who also runs the principal bookshop; a Moslem who taught in the University of Prague for seventeen years and now gives private Arabic lessons;

a Swiss businessman who likes the climate and has started a restaurant and bar for his own amusement; an Indian prince who does accounting for an American firm; the Portuguese seamstress who makes your shirts; and in addition you will be hailed by a good many Spaniards, most of whom were born in Tangier and have never lived anywhere else. The Moslems account for roughly 70 percent of the population; they still sit in their tiny cafés, drinking tea and coffee, playing cards, checkers and dominoes, shouting above the din of Egyptian music on the radio. Nothing has really changed here either.

Although the people who love Tangier sometimes feel as though there were a conspiracy afoot to make it the most hideous place on earth, actually such a project would prove extremely difficult. With the exception of a few corners of the Medina, where the old Moorish architecture has not yet been improved upon, there is nothing left to spoil. And even when the veil has been removed from the face of the last woman to wear one, so she can do her shopping sporting a rayon-satin evening gown four sizes too large for her, and the final old house with a fortress-like façade and one great studded door is demolished to make room for a six-family concrete dwelling with fluorescent lighting in every room, the town will still look very much the same.

With everything old being systematically destroyed (and the new European buildings are almost without exception eyesores, while the ones the Moroccans put up are even worse), how is it that Tangier escapes becoming an aesthetic nightmare? Its topography, more than anything else, I think, saves it; the city is built along the crests and down the flanks of a series of small hills that stand between the sea on one side and a low slightly undulating plain on the other, with high mountains beyond. There are few level stretches in town; at the end of each street there is almost always a natural view, so that the eye automatically skims over that which is near at hand to dwell on a vignette of harbor with ships, or mountain ranges, or sea with distant coastline. Then, the intensity of the sky, even when cloudy, is such that wherever one happens to be, the buildings serve only as an unnoticed frame for the natural beauty beyond. You don't look at the city; you look out of it.

The back streets of the Medina, crooked, sometimes leading through short tunnels beneath the houses, sometimes up long flights of stairs, lend themselves to solitary speculative walks. With nothing more dangerous than pedestrians and an occasional burro to worry about bumping into you, you can devote part of your mind to coming to grips with your ideas. Since I returned here in 1947 I have spent a good many hours wandering through these passageways (incidentally learning to distinguish the thoroughfares from the impasses), busily trying to determine the relationship between Tangier and myself. If you don't know why you like a thing, it is usually worth your while to attempt to find out.

I have not discovered very much, but at least I am now convinced that Tangier is a place where the past and the present exist simultaneously in proportionate degree, where a very much alive today is given an added depth of reality by the presence of an equally alive yesterday. In Europe, it seems to me, the past is largely fictitious; to be aware of it one must have previous knowledge of it. In Tangier the past is a physical reality as perceptible as the sunlight.

Tangier is little more than an enormous market. Since the war it has been primarily a free-money market; and the new autonomous Moroccan government will probably take an increasingly active part in the economic life of a city without currency control. During the international years the dramatic, extra-legal facets of the city's character were much publicized, and Tangier was thought of as a place where every fourth person was a smuggler, a spy or a refugee from justice in his native land. It is true that the city was a market where diplomatic information was bought and sold; it was also a place where goods destined to pass eventually across frontiers without benefit of customs inspection were unloaded and reloaded, and, more importantly, a place where people from a variety of nations were able to exist

Paul Bowles at Gertrude Stein's house at Bilignin, 1931

without valid documents to identify them. Then, too, in the absence of all taxes, it was expedient for European exporters to maintain offices here, even though their produce might never pass within a thousand miles of the Moroccan coast. That era is over; such unregulated freedom could hardly continue indefinitely. The withdrawal of foreign business has produced a slump, and there is an unhealthy amount of unemployment. The shops are stocked with a superfluity of assorted goods from everywhere, and there are not many buyers. The city has no industry – only shopkeepers, agents, hawkers and touts.

Advertisements for watches are ever-present. They flash on and off in the shop windows and flare in neon above the sidewalks. There is an enormous watch sign on a roof at the lower end of the Zoco Chico, in the heart of the Medina's principal thoroughfare, made entirely of large sequins, ceaselessly fluttering and glittering above the crowd. All this in a place where for the great majority the smallest unit of time measurement is the *qsim*, which is equal to five of our minutes! But Tangier is very time conscious these days; the youngest children often stop you to inquire gravely what time it is, and listen with obvious relish to your mysterious answer.

Another inescapable feature of the streets is the ubiquitous *cambio*, with its slate bearing the buying and selling rates, in pesetas, of all the world's principal currencies, including the gold dollar. The rates are scribbled in chalk and are subject to change at any moment. The less elaborate *cambios* consist of a chair and a box placed on the sidewalk; the upper end of the Calle Siaghines is lined on both sides with these primitive offices. Personally I have always found that I save money by using a bank.

People here have a fondness for describing Tangier as "central," by which they mean that it is two and a half hours from Gibraltar by ferry, five hours from London by plane, seven hours from Casablanca by car (if you're a careful driver), three days from the beginning of the Sahara desert by train (assuming there is no sabotage on the line during your journey), and six days from New York by ship. Although the inhabitants of northern Europe consider it a winter resort, those who live here, no doubt having been spoiled by its excellent climate during the rest of the year, often try to escape at that time, because of the torrential rains that come blowing in, usually from the Mediterranean. It is not cold, but it is decidedly wet, and if you can find sun by going a few hundred miles southward, it seems foolish not to go. The heavy rains can come at any time from December to April; while you may have many weeks of crystalline skies in the course of that period, you can be sure of getting the rains sooner or later, just as you can count on fine weather from the beginning of July onward into November. I often wonder what the climate was like here twenty-five centuries ago, when the place was a trading port called Tingis, run by the Carthaginians up from the coast, and Morocco was a region of dense forests where herds of elephants wandered. I wonder specifically whether the winters could have been any wetter than they are now; I suppose the answer is that they were, but it's difficult to believe.

The basic character of Tangier actually has changed less definitively than its climate. From the beginnings of its known history it has always been in touch with the outside world; its affairs have been administered either directly by representatives of foreign powers or by Moroccans acting in the interests of such powers. For a long time after the fall of Carthage it was a Roman colony; then it was occupied successively by the Vandals, the Byzantines, the Visigoths, the Arabs (who fought over it almost constantly among themselves and with the Islamized Moroccans for eight long centuries), the Portuguese, the Spanish, the Moroccans themselves, eventually with French guidance, and finally the powers represented by the International Commission, of which the three favored members were France, England and Spain. (During World War II Franco, betting on an Axis victory, grabbed it, but was forced to relinquish it to the International Commission at the war's end.) At the moment it is governed by the King of Morocco and militarily occupied by troops of the Moroccan Army.

For years I have been "showing" visitors Tangier. Being an amateur guide in a town that has so many professional ones has its disadvantages, even conceivably its hazards, and in itself is not a particularly enjoyable pastime. But for the nine sight-seers who are mildly amused by the chaos and absurdity of the place, frankly repelled by its ugliness and squalor, or simply indifferent to whatever it may have to offer, there is a tenth one who straightway falls in love with it, and that is the one, of course, who makes the tedious game worthwhile. For this one, as for me, a blank wall at the end of a blind alley suggests mystery, just as being in the tiny closet-like rooms of a Moslem house in the Medina evokes the magic of early childhood games, or as the sudden call to prayer of the muezzin from his minaret is a song whose music completely transforms the moment. Such reactions, I have been told, are those of a person who refuses to grow up. If that is so, it is all right with me, to whom being childlike implies having retained the full use of the imagination. For imagination is essential for the enjoyment of a place like Tangier, where the details that meet the eye are not what they seem, but so many points of reference for a whole secret system of overlapping but wildly divergent worlds in the complex life of the city.

What do I show these visitors? Not very much, I'm afraid. Aside from the so-called Sultan's Palace, an eighteenth-century construction which now houses a small museum, there are no "points of interest" or historic monuments. In my capacity of cicerone, I have never taken anyone to the Sultan's Palace, because it is not very interesting; it is almost impossible for the visitor to escape it in any case, since every child in the Casbah has one fixed purpose in life, to guide the steps of as many tourists as possible to its entrance door.

Sometimes visitors have wanted me to see what they quaintly imagined was called "the red-light district," which consisted of a few back streets on either side of the Zoco Chico. I always let the guides take care of that; anyway, the excursions were invariably unsuccessful, the visitors being bitterly disappointed to find that the Moslem establishments were strictly closed to all but those of the Faith. I use the past tense because, since the coming of independence to Morocco, all brothels have been closed, no matter what the faith of their inmates or prospective clients.

I show visitors the Zoco Chico, whose European-style cafés close these days shortly after midnight. The era is gone when they were open all night, and you could stop by at five in the morning for coffee and watch the tired *tanguistas* from the night clubs being escorted homeward by their pomaded *chulos*. Now the Zoco Chico is a serious and early affair where the customers, mostly Moslems, sit discussing politics over soft drinks and watch, or take part in, the frequent fights that occur in the middle of the square – struggles which break out between the police and unofficial political neighborhood constables, generally over the question of who is to have custody of stray Moslems suspected of having drunk alcohol. Although it is rumored that spirits will be eventually prohibited in this part of the city, there are still plenty of *bodegas* and bars open for business; and as far as the Moslems are concerned, it is safer for them if they simply pretend these establishments don't exist.

The Zoco Chico used to be completely surrounded by sidewalk cafés; slowly these are giving way to curio shops run by members of the ever-increasing colony of Indian merchants, so that now the little square has only five left. Non-Spanish Europeans and Americans patronize the Café Central, probably because it is the largest and brightest. It is also the most consistently besieged by shoeshine boys, beggars, lottery-ticket sellers and wisecracking Moroccan youths trying to force you to buy toothbrushes, toys, fountain pens, fans, razor blades and rayon scarves; so that if you want a quiet conversation, or a half hour with your newspaper over a cup of coffee, it is better to go elsewhere.

Over the years, I have seen the most unlikely people sitting among the *djellabas* and fezzes at the Café Central, from Barbara Hutton to Somerset Maugham and Truman Capote and Cecil Beaton. The other day when I walked past, Errol Flynn was there trying to hide his face behind the pages of a newspaper while a group of Spanish girls stared from what they considered a respectful distance of three feet. Miss Hutton's presence in the Zoco Chico is accounted for by the fact that she is a sometime resident of Tangier, her house being in the Medina just around the corner from my own. An important difference between our respective dwellings should be pointed out, however. Hers, I am told, consisted originally of twenty-eight separate Moslem houses which were pulled apart and put together again to make the present structure; mine is still what it always was: a very small and uncomfortable shoe box stood on end.

The true center of Tangier is the Zoco de Fuera, an open-air market where the Moslems sell everything from parakeets to buttermilk, from Berber blankets to hot roasted chestnuts, from sofa cushions to Japanese dolls. Eighty years ago the traveler who arrived in Tangier after sunset spent the night here at the foot of the city walls, waiting for the gates to be opened the next morning at dawn. Today the Zoco is a very large square just outside the southern ramparts of the Medina – by day a sea of buses, taxis, milling pedestrians and vociferous peddlers. In the middle of this sea is an island which, over the quarter of a century during which I have known it, has grown consistently smaller and less shady as piece after piece of it has been sacrificed to make room for the increasing motor traffic. Storytellers, musicians, acrobats and assorted entertainers used to hold forth here under the trees; in recent years there has grown up a miniature village of rickety little wooden structures with narrow passageways between them. If you don't mind being caught in the crush of Moslems from the country, you can squeeze in and wander through, watching them bargain for big disks of bread and pats of goat cheese. The two wider streets of this island are given over to the display of flowers, incense and cosmetic ingredients such as lumps of alum, henna leaves, shampooing clay and sulphide of antimony for eye make-up.

There is never a moment of the day when the square and the arteries leading into it are not jammed with thousands of voluble vendors and their prospective customers. Late at night, however, a lone voice will echo across its empty darkness, and you can hear, coming from the little wooden stalls, the snores of the watchmen or of the proprietors themselves as they sleep curled up on top of their wares. Before daybreak the long caravans of Berbers and their donkeys which have been moving on their way all night along the country roads toward the city will have arrived, and the goods, mainly foodstuffs, will have been unpacked in one of the big courtyards near the Zoco. The sun will rise on the same scene on which it set the evening before; if it is a Thursday or Sunday there will be even more people from the hills roundabout, for those two days are specifically market days.

The old European residents of the town love the Zoco passionately, and have in the past fought successfully against all plans for modernizing it, cleaning it up, or making a parking lot or a public park out of it. Now that the Moroccans have the power'to decide what is to become of it, it is anyone's guess how long it will last, this lively oasis of the past in the midst of today's dreariness. I suspect that it will not disappear before the people who run it are willing to have it go, and since fortunately they are not too interested in change for change's sake – unlike the city Moslems, who have been infected with the progress virus – the din, smoke and brilliant confusion of the Zoco may remain in our midst a little longer.

(I underestimated the zeal of civic-minded Moroccans. Almost as soon as this was written the market was pulled down; gravel walks were laid and flowers planted in its stead. A few hundred feet from the old site, however, behind the Mosque of Sidi Bouabid, space is being cleared for a new Zoco de Fuera, and sometime in 1958 we shall have our new market.)

Usually I take my wards to see the beaches and the Mountain. For those who prefer company while they bathe there is the municipal beach, a fine five-mile semicircle of sand bordering the Bay of Tangier, and within walking distance of all the hotels; for lovers of solitude there is the vast Atlantic beach stretching southward from the Grottoes of Hercules in a straight white band as far as the eye can see, across the Oued Tahardatz and on into what used to be the Spanish Zone. This is utterly unspoiled and one of the most beautiful beaches I know. The Mountain, the highest point on which is about a thousand feet above the port, is heavily forested with eucalyptus, parasol pine and cypress, and is considered the pleasantest place in all Tangier to live. Three hundred years ago these forest lands served as a base of operations for the Moroccans in the unsuccessful war to liberate Tangier from the British. Today, however, the British have got a good part of them back again, for it is largely they who own land and live on the Mountain. There are also the palaces of two defunct sultans: the palace of Ben Arafa, who was not a sultan but had to play the part of one when the French exiled the present monarch in 1953; and the romantically isolated Villa Perdicaris, looking like something out of Sir Walter Scott, which was bought by the Pasha el Glaoui not long before that unpopular notable's death in 1956.

During the summer of 1957 it was announced officially that His Highness Mohammed V intends to make Tangier his summer capital. Whether this will actually happen remains to be seen, but many people here, convinced that this would provide a solution to the local economic crisis, are holding their breath in hope that the rumor will turn out to be true. My own suspicion is that the soaring prices which would result would mean the end of Tangier as one of the cheapest places for an American to live in, whatever miracles it might perform for the town's economy.

When the visitor has seen the Zocos and beaches and palaces, he still has not seen the city's most important single phenomenon, the one which gives reality to and determines the ultimate meaning of all the others: I mean the spectacle of the average Moroccan's daily life. This necessitates going into the homes, preferably those of the lower middle class, and into the small neighborhood cafés which have a strictly Moslem clientele.

The cafés are not as easily accessible as they used to be, since the recent upsurge of nationalist feeling has somewhat modified the attitude of amicable indifference which the Moslem used to show toward the anonymous foreigner. For this reason it is important for me to choose places where my face is known, where I can still get a jovial greeting from the proprietor and thus be assured a reasonably friendly reception on the part of the patrons.

In the back of practically every such establishment there is an open space covered with reed matting, generally raised above the level of the floor; entry into this part of the room demands the removal of one's shoes.

Here the men sit with their legs tucked under them and, more often than not, in spite of the unofficial prohibition, pull out their kif pipes and smoke them as they always have done. The cafés are like men's clubs. A man frequents the same one year in and year out. Often he brings his food and eats there; sometimes he stretches out on the matting and sleeps there. His café is his mail address, and rather than use his home, where there are always womenfolk about, he will use the café for keeping his social appointments. In the smaller cafés, the entrance of anyone from outside the familiar circle of daily habitués has always been regarded with a wary eye and a certain degree of suspicion. Each café has its own little legends and references which can be understood only by the initiates. It is here that the endless stories and complicated jokes which so delight the Moslem mind are told, and where the average man is at his happiest and least inhibited. If a café happens to offer any kind of native Moroccan music, which is extremely rare these days, I will force my way through any wall of hostile stares in order to get a seat and listen; I suppose not many visitors are that eager to hear Moroccan café music.

The casual outsider, however, can usually get more glimpses of café life than he can of home life. In a bourgeois household, upon the entry of any man or boy not of the immediate family, Moslem or otherwise, all the women and girls are swiftly hidden, and remain hidden until he goes out of the house. In families of lower income, on the other hand, the social strictures

Paul and Jane Bowles greeting the neighbours at their Medina house –'the small and uncomfortable shoebox stood on end' – in Tangier

have been considerably relaxed, so that I have only to suggest to my maid or chauffeur that a group of my friends would like to visit a Moslem home and meet all the members of the family, and the invitation will be willingly extended. I don't claim that the activities which we see in a Moslem house are identical with those which would be going on if we were not there. But if we stay long enough, a certain degree of relaxation is usually reached, and the household rhythm at length begins to pulse of its own accord, so that it is possible to get a pretty clear picture of what life is like in the domestic citadel.

By our standards these people are desperately poor. At present, for instance, the maid who gets our breakfast, cleans the five rooms, and does all the laundering of our clothes, earns the equivalent of $8.33 a month. Also, she gets no food from us. Even in Tangier that is a low wage for 1958. Yet if you visit her house, you find it immaculate; moreover, the manner of life that she and her family lead manages to give an impression of Oriental ease and even abundance. It is a peculiarly Moslem gift, being able to create the illusion of luxury in the midst of poverty, and it never fails to arouse my admiration when I see it displayed. But then, these people are the supreme illusionists; they can give a straightforward action the air of being a conjurer's trick or make the most tortuously devious behavior seem like naturalness itself.

I have never decided precisely why the time spent in these humble homes is so satisfying. Perhaps it is merely because both hosts and guests are playing a simple, pleasant game in which the hosts lead the way with regard to the silences to be observed as well as the conversation to be made, and the guests follow comfortably, happy to have all social responsibility taken from them. Certainly it is agreeable now and then to spend an evening reclining peaceably among piles of cushions, in effortless talk with people who are completely natural but infinitely polite. And when the end of the evening comes, and they have fully convinced you that the occasion has been even more enjoyable for them than for you, and you have pronounced the necessary formulas of farewell, it is delightful, too, to step out into the silent moonlit street, and a moment later look from a Casbah gateway down upon the thousands of white cubes which are the houses of the Medina, hearing only the waves as they break on the beach and perhaps the sleepy antiphonal crowing of two roosters on neighboring rooftops. If I ask myself occasionally whether I may not be a trifle out of my mind to have chosen to spend so many years in this crazy city, it is at such moments that I am reassured – easily able to convince myself that if it were 1931 once more, and I possessed the gift of accurately foretelling the future, I should very likely take Miss Stein's good advice and make my first journey to Tangier all over again.

THE CHALLENGE TO
IDENTITY

THE NATION, APRIL 26, 1958

WHETHER IN REVIEWS or publishers' blurbs, whether here or in England (where the genre flourishes more successfully) there would appear to be a question in the minds of those who write about travel books: who reads them, the stay-at-homes or the venturers-forth? Assuming that these categories define two kinds of temperament, and that many potential voyagers are prevented from achieving their desire to see the world only by force of circumstance, my own guess is that the travel-book public is composed almost exclusively of the venturers-forth – those who have gone and those who hope to go – but nowadays composed, unfortunately, of only a small percentage of them.

Even as recently as a century ago, travel was a specialized activity. Distant places being out-of-bounds for all but a fortunate and resistant few, it was normal that the desire for contact with the exotic should be satisfied vicariously through reading. Now that in theory anyone can go anywhere, the travel book serves a different purpose; emphasis has shifted from the place to the effect of the place upon the person. The travel book necessarily has become more subjective, more "literary." But this tends to deprive the travel writer of his natural reader. The venturer-forth is inclined to be an extrovert, to despise second-hand experience. If he is going to South America – even if he only dreams of going – he is not eager to know Isherwood's impressions of it first. He wants a concise volume of data relating to the history, climate, customs and points of interest in each republic. He is even vaguely conscious of having decided to form his own impressions, and to hell with what someone else felt when he came face to face with Aconcagua.

What is a travel book? For me it is the story of what happened to one person in a particular place, and nothing more than that; it does not contain hotel and highway information, lists of useful phrases, statistics, or hints as to what kind of clothing is needed by the intending visitor. It may be that such books form a category which is doomed to extinction. I hope not, because there is nothing I enjoy more than reading an accurate account by an intelligent writer of what happened to him away from home.

THE SUBJECT-MATTER of the best travel books is the conflict between writer and place. It is not important which of them carries the day, so long as the struggle is faithfully recorded. It takes a writer with a gift for describing a situation to do this well, which is perhaps the reason why many of the travel books that remain in the memory have been produced by writers expert at the fashioning of novels. One remembers Evelyn Waugh's indignation in Ethiopia, Graham Greene deadpanning through West Africa, Aldous Huxley letting Mexico get him down, Gide discovering his social conscience in the Congo, long after other equally accurate travel accounts have blurred and vanished. Given the novelistic skill of these particular writers it is perhaps perverse of me to prefer their few travel pieces to their novels, but I do.

The particularized travel books, those dealing with a definite quest or mission, along with records of exploration and conquest, have their own special charm, but too often the reader is made aware of the fact that they were penned by travelers who also wrote, rather than by writers who also traveled. (Michel Vieuchange's *Smara* is a distinguished exception, and for the reason that his quest was ultimately an interior one; he went in search of ecstasy, and finding only physical suffering, he was obliged to use the pages of his journal as an alembic in which to work the transformation.)

There is a category which in its approach and subject-matter comes closer to autobiography than to travel, but which because it deals with the displaced person in relatively unfamiliar surroundings is conceded to be a part of travel literature. This is the intimate account of a writer's daily life during his prolonged residence in one particular place abroad. There are several favorites of mine in this group: Flandrau's *Viva Mexico!*, Ackerley's *Hindoo Holiday*, Dinesen's *Out of Africa*, Peter Mayne's *The Alleys of Marrakesh*. They are books in which the personality of the author is the decisive element; their charm derives from this unequivocal placing of emphasis upon personal attitudes and reflections.

I am wondering: in what way, if I were now engaged in writing a travel book, would my behavior be different from what it is at this very moment? I sit here on a bench in a tiny park overlooking the city of Lisbon. Harbor sounds float up from below, to be audible between the sharp cries of small children playing on the grass nearby. The light is very strong, although the sun is covered by a veil of haze, and the smell in the air is a compound of unidentifiable suggestions of spring. Suddenly the little red rubber ball the children have been tossing back and forth bounces through the iron grillwork of the fence and over the parapet into a walled courtyard far below. There is a good deal of shouted recrimination in the wake of this event, after which the young ballplayers disperse – all but one small boy, clearly the owner of the lost plaything, who remains behind, clutching the bars of the fence, staring wistfully downward. At this point I have my answer. If I were here to write a travel book, I should call him over and talk with him, offer him the money for another ball. But since I am not, I merely sit still and continue to imagine how, if I were to attempt to write such a book, I should go about it.

FOR A TRUE travel book, I don't think a sufficiently accurate job can be done after the fact, if the writer has been living as he pleased during the time he proposes to write about, not taking notes, not conscious of his function as an instrument of reception. The ill-defined memory of his own emotional responses is always stronger than the exact memory of what caused them. Reliance upon recollection is proper to determining the substance of a novel, but not in this case, where it is too likely to alter the writing's firmness of texture.

The writer must make the decision to adhere to a scrupulous honesty in reporting. Any conscious distortion is equivalent to cheating at solitaire; the purpose of the game is nullified. The account must be as near the truth as he can get, and it seems to me the easiest way to achieve that is to aim for precision in describing his own reactions. A reader can get an idea of what a place is really like only if he knows what its effects were upon someone of whose character he has some idea, of whose preferences he is aware. Thus is seems essential that the writer place a certain insistence upon the objective presentation of his own personality; it provides an interpretative gauge with which the reader can measure for himself the relative importance of each detail, like the scale of miles in the corner of a map.

The problem of giving the travel account a linear structure is not primarily a literary one. It is more a matter involving the character and behavior of the writer. He has got to insure that the experiencing which will constitute his material comes into being. He is writing a story which he is obliged first to live out, and if the direction the story is taking appears to demand certain elements in which his life is lacking, he will need to know how to rearrange his existence so that those elements may be provided. His powers of invention must be applied to dealing, not with the question of writing, but with his own relation to the external reality around him.

It goes without saying that whatever attempts have been undertaken to make a place accessible to the tourist are just so many barricades in the way of the writer, and if he manages to make contact with the place it will be in spite of them rather than thanks to them. The purpose of official aid for the visitor is to make individual research unnecessary; in many countries there is a further, more sinister design in government-sponsored tourist bureaus: a conscious intent to discourage personal relationships between strangers and residents. Writers are particularly suspect, of course, but it is one of their routine tasks to circumvent this sort of thing. "You have no need to talk with anyone," I was assured by a policeman in an African country. "Our tourist office will supply you with guides at fixed rates and a special booklet in English free of charge that will give you all the information you require."

And again: "How do I know you're a bona fide tourist?" demanded an employee of a South American consulate in London when I applied for a visa. "Why, what would I be?" I said. "I don't know," she replied. "It says 'writer' in your passport. How do *I* know what you're going to do?" "You don't," I told her, and went to the Far East instead.

Sad for U.S., Sad for Algeria

The Nation, May 24, 1958

O NE DAY EARLY this year as I was taking the mail out of my box in the post office here in Tangier, I heard my name called softly from the door which opens into the rear part of the building where the mail is sorted. I turned and recognized a young man who works at the registry window.

"I don't want to bother you," he began, "but are you interested in Algeria?"

"Isn't everyone?" I said.

He smiled. "I should like to bring some friends one day to see you. We would stay only a few minutes."

"Of course. Whenever you like. My telephone is 14353. Call me any morning at eleven, and we can arrange the time."

"*Entendu*." He shut the door and a moment later smiled at me from the registry window as I went out.

A WEEK OR SO LATER he and two other Moslems appeared at my door. I took their raincoats and they went into the *sala*, where they remained standing until I came back into the room. The postal employee introduced himself as Monsieur Gourit; he then presented me to the other two, the Messieurs Benouar and

Youcef. The two Algerians were correctly dressed in dark suits and looked like civil servants, which is what they turned out to be – employees of the Moroccan government. My immediate feeling was that they had come to form a personal impression of me, and this did not change. We sat down. With certain deletions the conversation, in French, ran thus:

BENOUAR: I see you like Moroccan décor.

BOWLES: I like everything about Morocco. I first came to live here twenty-seven years ago, you know.

GOURIT: Before I was born.

BENOUAR: You have been here for twenty-seven years?

BOWLES: No, no. But I've been here more than half that time.

BENOUAR: You don't get tired of it?

BOWLES: No, no at all. On the contrary, I like it more all the time. I travel a good deal, and I love coming back to it.

YOUCEF: And Algeria? You have been to Algeria?

BOWLES: Yes, I've spent four winters there. Principally in the South. But I've traveled all over it, by plane, train, bus and camel. And trucks, too. I like camels the best. You don't have to ride them. You can get down and walk along beside them.

BENOUAR: I must confess I've never been on a camel.

YOUCEF: You are American, monsieur. It is for this reason that we came to see you. We have great admiration for the Americans. We thought perhaps you might be able to help us.

BOWLES: Help you? I'd like very much to help you in any way possible – except financially, which I couldn't manage – but I don't quite see what there is that I can do. I have no importance, you know, no influence, no official connections, no powerful friends, nothing.

YOUCEF: Yes, but you know America.

BOWLES: No even that any more, I'm afraid.

YOUCEF (IMPATIENTLY): Tell me, monsieur. Why does America not want to see Algeria independent? Why is she against us?

BOWLES: In the first place, I don't agree that the U.S. is against you.

YOUCEF: Come, monsieur. She finances the war being waged against us, and she has never once expressed herself in our favor. You must admit that.

BOWLES: She finances it indirectly, yes. And unfortunately France is in Europe and is still an ally of hers. I don't think she'll go on financing it much longer, though. I know she just handed France another enormous sum, but that won't last long. I think eventually she'll have had enough of France's nonsense.

YOUCEF: You're very optimistic. I wish I could be as much so.

BOWLES: On the contrary, I'm very pessimistic. I'm afraid by the time America loses her patience it will be too late.

BENOUAR: Too late? In what sense? You think the French are going to win? I can assure you that will never happen.

BOWLES: No, I don't mean that. Of course they can never win. I mean to say, by the time America decides the war has gone on long enough, the Algerians may have committed themselves to the East. Then not only wouldn't America be able to insist on negotiation, she would even feel obliged to help France continue the war, and this time in an active fashion.

YOUCEF: It's unthinkable.

BENOUAR (SIMULTANEOUSLY WITH YOUCEF): Never.

GOURIT: I see you are really pessimistic, monsieur.

YOUCEF: What you are saying there is completely hypothetical, in any case. It is a personal opinion and has no basis in fact. You have been to Algeria. You have seen the poverty and you know the causes for it.

BOWLES: Yes, of course.

YOUCEF: You know that the principal purpose of the present slaughter is to perpetuate the system which creates that poverty. And you know that is why we are fighting.

BOWLES: Yes, yes. Of course.

YOUCEF: What we want to know is, how can we bring our case to the attention of the American public? How can we convince them that they are being immoral and short-sighted in supporting France? How can we gain their sympathy?

BOWLES: I'm sure you already have the sympathy of most of the Americans who are conscious of the fact that there is a war going on in Algeria.

YOUCEF: Who are conscious of it? What do you mean? How could anyone not be conscious of it?

BOWLES: Easily. Americans are indifferent, you know, to events that don't touch them directly. But as I say, practically everyone who knows anything at all about the war sympathizes with you, not with the French. You can be sure of that.

GOURIT: But then – the American government does not represent the American people.

BOWLES (LAUGHING): Are you serious? (Pause.) I mean, the government functions like all democratic governments, more or less in accordance with the desires of the majority, yes. But I'm afraid most Americans have no interest in Algeria one way or the other. It's sad, but that's the way it is. That's America.

BENOUAR: *C'est triste, en effet.* Sad for us, and sad for the Americans.

YOUCEF: Yes. You were saying, monsieur, that you feared an alignment on our part with what you call "the East." You know, I suppose, that we have consistently rejected all overtures made to us by the Communist Party of Algeria?

BOWLES: And yet members of the French Communist Party have been repeatedly identified among the bodies of dead *fellagha.*

YOUCEF: That means nothing. After all, we have soldiers from many nations fighting in our ranks. The French are careful not to mention that. But they never miss an opportunity to make propaganda if they find a Communist somewhere around. You realize that all the news you read here or in America is from official French sources. You are not so naive as to believe it implicitly.

BOWLES: Naturally, I only wish it were possible to get news occasionally from other sources.

Paul Bowles flew back from Adrar to Algiers on this 'Trans-Saharienne' plane (PB)

GOURIT: I'll see that our organ, *El Moudjahid*, is put into your mailbox every week. You'll find different news in it.

BOWLES: That's very kind. Are you sure it won't be a bother?

GOURIT: You can pay me each week at the registry window.

(Gourit and Benouar briefly discuss, in Arabic, the question of whether it would not be better for me to buy *El Moudjahid* at one of the several newsstands which carry it, but decide in favor of Gourit's suggestion.)

YOUCEF: You say you spent four winters in Algeria. You must have formed some friendships while you were there. With Algerians, I mean.

BOWLES: Yes, I had casual acquaintances in various places. But most of them disappeared suddenly. For instance, I was in Adrar in January, 1948. I don't know whether you consider that Algeria or not –

YOUCEF: Of course it's Algeria.

BENOUAR: Not Algeria proper. It's the Sahara.

YOUCEF: Algeria is bounded on the South by French West Africa, my friend. That's what the French have always said, so it must be true, no?

BOWLES: Well, I had friends there. (Turning to GOURIT) In fact, one of them worked in the post office. He sent me a box of dates later, to New York. But he also wrote me a letter begging me not to write to thank him. The next year when I went back he was gone. The French had arrested him and ten or twelve others and sent them to prison in France. No one seemed to know precisely why. (Seeing that YOUCEF was about to speak) I know, they were Nationalists, but then, so was everyone else. The same thing happened to other friends in Béni Abbès. In this case, I was told their offense. They had whistled a Nationalist song one night under the commandant's window.

BENOUAR: You mean Sidi-bel-Abbès?

BOWLES: No, Béni Abbès. South of Colomb-Béchar. It was the first time I had realized the trouble really existed. Of course, I'd read of the bombardments by the French in 1945, but that was disconnected from –

YOUCEF: Really? Where did you read about them?

BOWLES: In *Les Temps Modernes*. Incidentally, in that article the number of Moslems killed during those three days was put at forty-six thousand. Do you think that was an exaggeration?

YOUCEF: No. I should think the true figure was probably higher. It's very difficult to arrive at an exact number in such circumstances.

BOWLES: Anyway, since the night of October thirty-first, 1954, I've followed events with the greatest interest. For a long time I've been waiting for the pleasure of seeing France commit suicide, and it's possible that this is one occasion when America won't be able to stop her from doing it.

YOUCEF: Yes. To get back to what I was saying a while ago. I should be interested to know whether in your opinion there is in your country a general conviction or, let us say, a tendency to believe, that we are sympathetic to what you call "the East."

BOWLES: But I never meant to imply that you were! I only said I was afraid that by the time the United States came to the realization that she had enough of France's misbehavior in Algeria, it would be too late to build a new country upon any semblance of friendship with the West.

YOUCEF: Because we should be committed to the other side, no?

BOWLES: I'm not saying I'd attach any blame to you for that. After all, what reasons would you have for maintaining loyalty to those who had refused to help you?

YOUCEF: You will pardon me, monsieur, if I say that you do not seem to have understood the situation very clearly. For us it is not a question of loyalty or disloyalty. It is a question rather of being practical. First, we want independence. Most of the arms we have been using to fight for it, we captured with our own hands from the French in Algeria. We also have arms and ammunition from Egypt and Syria, yes, and if that is due indirectly to the Soviet Union's assistance to these two countries, that is all the same to us. The Soviet Union already upholds our cause in the United Nations. As long as these conditions continued, we have no need to mortgage our future independence by asking for help from that direction. What would we have to gain by exposing ourselves to Communist domination? Surely that should be clear to you. The F.L.N. has no intention of allying itself with Communists, now or later.

BOWLES: I'm very glad to hear you say all this. I've read two or three of your brochures: one on the members of the Foreign Legion in the Army of Liberation, one on the history of Algeria, one on how the F.L.N. works. It seems to me it would be very useful if you were to publish one in which you make clear your position regarding communism. I think it would help a great deal, in the United States, at least. It's about the only concrete suggestion I can think of at the moment. Can't I give you some whiskey? (They all declined, and I served them three glasses of water. Before leaving Youcef asked for copies of my novels in French translation, which I gave him. I have not seen either Youcef or Benouar since.)

Author's note: Somewhat later there appeared in the newspaper *Die Welt* the account of an interview, by a journalist named Wirsing, with Ferhat Abbas at his Geneva residence, during the course of which the Algerian leader was quoted as saying that a three-man commission representing the F.L.N. had visited Moscow and Prague in quest of heavy arms. According to the article, the members of the commission were told that such aid could be granted only if the F.L.N. broadened its political base to include the interests of "all sectors of the Algerian people." It was suggested to the commission that its request would receive serious attention if a certain Ali bou Hali, an old-time member of the Algerian Communist Party, now resident in the Albanian capital of Tirana, were to be included on the executive committee of the F.L.N.

The F.L.N. quickly denied that such an interview had taken place, and denounced the article in *Die Welt* as a journalistic invention.

AFRICA MINOR

HOLIDAY, APRIL 1959; THEIR HEADS ARE GREEN, 1963

I T HAD TAKEN the truck fourteen hours to get from Kerzaz to Adrar and, except for the lunch stop in the oasis of El Aougherout, the old man had sat the whole time on the floor without moving, his legs tucked up beneath him, the hood of his burnoose pulled up over his turban to protect his face from the fine dust that sifted up through the floor. First-class passage on vehicles of the Compagnie Générale Transsaharienne entitled the voyager to travel in the glassed-in compartment with the driver, and that was where I sat, occasionally turning to look through the smeared panes at the solitary figure sitting sedately in the midst of the tornado of dust behind. At lunch, when I had seen his face with its burning brown eyes and magnificent white beard, it had occurred to me that he looked like a handsome and very serious Santa Claus.

The dust grew worse during the afternoon, so that by sunset, when we finally pulled into Adrar, even the driver and I were covered. I got out and shook myself, and the little old man clambered out of the back, cascades of dust spilling from his garments. Then he came around to the front of the truck to speak to the driver, who, being a good Moslem, wanted to get a shower and wash himself. Unfortunately he was a city Moslem as well as being a good one, so that he was impatient with the measured cadence of his countryman's speech and suddenly slammed the door, unaware that the old man's hand was in the way.

Calmly the old man opened the door with his other hand. The tip of his middle finger dangled by a bit of skin. He looked at it an instant, then quietly scooped up a handful of that ubiquitous dust, put the two parts of the finger together and poured the dust over it, saying softly, "Thanks be to Allah." With that, the expression on his face never having changed, he picked up his bundle and staff and walked away. I stood looking after him, full of wonder, and reflecting upon the difference between his behavior and what mine would have been under the same circumstances. To show no outward sign of pain is unusual enough, but to express no resentment against the person who has hurt you seems very strange, and to give thanks to God at such a moment is the strangest touch of all.

Clearly, examples of such stoical behavior are not met every day, or I should not have remembered this one; my experience since then, however, has shown me that it is not untypical, and it has remained with me and become a symbol of that which is admirable in the people of North Africa. "This world we see is unimportant and ephemeral as a dream," they say. "To take it seriously would be an absurdity. Let us think rather of the heavens that surround us." And the landscape is conducive to reflections upon the nature of the infinite. In other parts of Africa you are aware of the earth beneath your feet, of the vegetation and the animals; all power seems concentrated in the earth. In North Africa the earth becomes the less important part of the landscape because you find yourself constantly raising your eyes to look at the sky. In the arid landscape the sky is the final arbiter. When you have understood that, not intellectually but emotionally, you have also understood why it is that the great trinity of monotheistic religions – Judaism, Christianity and Islam – which removed the source of power from the earth itself to the spaces outside the earth – were evolved in desert regions. And of the three, Islam, perhaps because it is the most recently evolved, operates the most directly and with the greatest strength upon the daily actions of those who embrace it.

For a person born into a culture where religion has long ago become a thing quite separate from daily life, it is a startling experience to find himself suddenly in the midst of a culture where there is a minimum of discrepancy between dogma and natural behavior, and this is one of the great fascinations of being in North Africa. I am not speaking of Egypt, where the old harmony is gone, decayed from within. My own impressions of Egypt before Nasser are those of a great panorama of sun-dried disintegration. In any case, she has had a different history from the rest of Mediterranean Africa; she is ethnically and linguistically distinct and is more a part of the Levant than of the region we ordinarily mean when we speak of North Africa. But in Tunisia, Algeria and Morocco there are still people whose lives proceed according to the ancient pattern of concord between God and man, agreement between theory and practice, identity of word and flesh (or however one prefers to conceive and define that pristine state of existence we intuitively feel we once enjoyed and now have lost).

I don't claim that the Moslems of North Africa are a group of mystics, heedless of bodily comfort, interested only in the welfare of the spirit. If you have ever bought so much as an egg from one of them, you have learned that they are quite able to fend for themselves when it comes to money matters. The spoiled strawberries are at the bottom of the basket, the pebbles inextricably mixed with the lentils and the water with the milk, the same as in many other parts of the world, with the difference that if you ask the price of an object in a rural market, they will reply, all in one breath, "Fifty, how much will you give?" I should say that in the realm of *beah o chra* (selling and buying; note that in their minds selling comes first), they are surpassed only by the Hindus, who are less emotional about it and therefore more successful, and by the Chinese, acknowledged masters of the Oriental branch of the science of commerce.

In Morocco you go into a bazaar to buy a wallet and some-how find yourself being propelled toward the back room to look at antique brass and rugs. In an instant you are seated with a glass of mint tea in your hand and a platter of pastries in your lap, while smiling gentlemen modeling ancient caftans and mar-riage robes parade in front of you, the salesman who greeted you at the door having completely vanished. Later on you may once again ask timidly to see the wallets, which you noticed on display near the entrance. Likely as not, you will be told that the man in charge of wallets is at the moment saying his prayers, but that he will soon be back, and in the meantime would you not be pleased to see some magnificent jewelry from the court of Moulay Ismail? Business is business and prayers are prayers, and both are a part of the day's work.

When I meet fellow Americans traveling about here in North Africa, I ask them, "What did you expect to find here?" Almost without exception, regardless of the way they express it, the answer, reduced to its simplest terms, is: a sense of mystery. They expect mystery, and they find it, since fortunately it is a quality difficult to extinguish all in a moment. They find it in the pat-terns of sunlight filtering through the latticework that covers the souks, in the unexpected turnings and tunnels of the narrow streets, in the women whose features still go hidden beneath the *litham*, in the secretiveness of the architecture, which is such that even if the front door of a house is open it is impossible to see inside. If they listen as well as look, they find it too in the song the lone camel driver sings by his fire before dawn, in the calling of the muezzins at night, when their voices are like bright beams of sound piercing the silence, and, most often, in the dry beat of the *darbouka*, the hand drum played by the women everywhere, in the great city houses and in the humblest country hut.

It is a strange sensation, when you are walking alone in a still, dark street late at night, to come upon a pile of cardboard boxes soaked with rain, and, as you pass by it, to find yourself staring into the eyes of a man sitting upright behind it. A thief? A beggar? The night watchman of the quarter? A spy for the secret police?

You just keep walking, looking at the ground, hearing your footsteps echo between the walls of the deserted street. Into your head comes the idea that you may suddenly hear the sound of a conspiratorial whistle and that something unpleasant may be about to happen. A little farther along you see, deep in the recess of an arcade of shops, another man reclining in a deck chair, asleep. Then you realize that all along the street there are men both sleeping and sitting quietly awake, and that even in the hours of its most intense silence the place is never empty of people.

It is only since the end of 1955 that Morocco has had its independence, but already there is a nucleus of younger Moslems who fraternize freely with the writers and painters (most of whom are American girls and youths) who have wandered into this part of the world and found it to their liking. Together they give very staid, quiet parties which show a curious blend of Eastern and Western etiquette. Usually no Moslem girls are present. Everyone is either stretched out on mattresses or seated on the floor, and kif and hashish are on hand, but half the foreigners content themselves with highballs. A good many paintings are looked at, and there is a lot of uninformed conversation about art and expression and religion. When food is passed around, the Moslems, for all their passionate devotion to European manners, not only adhere to their own custom of using chunks of bread to sop up the oily *mruq* at the bottom of their plates, but manage to impose the system on the others as well, so that everybody is busy rubbing pieces of bread over his plate. Why not? The food is cooked to be eaten in that fashion, and is less tasty if eaten in any other way.

Many of the Moslems paint, too; after so many centuries of religious taboo with regard to the making of representational images, abstraction is their natural mode of expression. You can see in their canvases the elaboration of design worked out by the Berbers in their crafts: patterns that show constant avoidance of representation but manage all the same to suggest recognizable things. Naturally, their paintings are a great success with the visiting artists, who carry their admiration to the point of imitation. The beat-generation North Africans are music-mad, but they get their music via radio, phonograph and tape-recorder. They are enthusiastic about the music of their own country, but unlike their fathers, they don't sing or play it. They are also fond of such exotic items as Congo drumming, the music of India, and particularly the more recent American jazz (Art Blakey, Horace Silver, Cannonball Adderley).

At the moment, writing about any part of Africa is a little like trying to draw a picture of a roller coaster in motion. You can say: It *was* thus and so, or, it is *becoming* this or that, but you risk making a misstatement if you say categorically that any-thing *is*, because likely as not you will open tomorrow's news-paper to discover that it has changed. On the whole the new governments of Tunisia and Morocco wish to further tourism in their respective countries; they are learning that the average tourist is more interested in native dancing than in the new bus terminal, that he is more willing to spend money in the Casbah than to inspect new housing projects. For a while, after the demise of the violently unpopular Pasha of Marrakesh, Thami el Glaoui, the great public square of Marrakesh, the Djemâa el Fna, was used solely as a parking lot. Anyone will tell you that the biggest single attraction for tourists in all North Africa was the Djemâa el Fna in Marrakesh. It was hard to find a moment of the day or night when tourists could not be found prowling around among its acrobats, singers, storytellers, snake charmers, dancers and medicine men. Without it Marrakesh became just another Moroccan city. And so the Djemâa el Fna was reinstated, and now goes on more or less as before.

North Africa is inhabited, like Malaya and Pakistan, by Moslems who are not Arabs. The *Encyclopaedia Britannica's* esti-mate of the percentage of Arab stock in the population of Morocco dates from two decades ago, but there has been no influx of Arabs since, so we can accept its figure of ten percent as being still valid. The remaining ninety percent of the people are Berbers, who anthropologically have nothing to do with the Arabs. They are

Paul Bowles with his Jaguar and long-term driver, Mohammed Temsamany, outside the casbah of Aït Benhaddou, near Ouarzazate, southern Morocco, 1950s

not of Semitic origin, and were right where they are now long before the Arab conquerors ever suspected their existence.

Even after thirteen hundred years, the Berbers' conception of how to observe the Moslem religion is by no means identical with that of the descendants of the men who brought it to them. And the city Moslems complain that they do not observe the fast of Ramadan properly, they neither veil nor segregate their women and, most objectionable of all, they have a passion for forming cults dedicated to the worship of local saints. In this their religious practices show a serious deviation from orthodoxy, inasmuch as during the *moussems*, the gigantic pilgrimages which are held periodically at the many shrines where these holy men are buried, men and women can be seen dancing *together*, working themselves into a prolonged frenzy. This is the height of immorality, the young puritans tell you. But it is not the extent, they add, of the Berbers' reprehensible behavior at these manifestations. Self-torture, the inducing of trances, ordeal by fire and the sword, and the eating of broken glass and scorpions are also not unusual on such occasions.

The traveler who has been present at one of these indescribable gatherings will never forget it, although if he dislikes the sight of blood and physical suffering he may try hard to put it out of his mind. To me these spectacles are filled with great beauty, because their obvious purpose is to prove the power of the spirit over the flesh. The sight of ten or twenty thousand people actively declaring their faith, demonstrating en masse the power of that faith, can scarcely be anything but inspiring. You lie in the fire, I gash my legs and arms with a knife, he pounds a sharpened bone into his thigh with a rock – then, together, covered with ashes and blood, we sing and dance in joyous praise of the saint and the god who make it possible for us to triumph over pain, and by extension, over death itself. For the participants exhaustion and ecstasy are inseparable.

This saint-worship, based on vestiges of an earlier religion, has long been frowned upon by the devout urban Moslems; as early as the mid-thirties restrictions were placed on its practice.

For a time, public manifestations of it were effectively suppressed. There were several reasons why the educated Moslems objected to the brotherhoods. During the periods of the protectorates in Tunisia and Morocco, the colonial administrations did not hesitate to use them for their own political ends, to ensure more complete domination. Also, it has always been felt that visitors who happened to witness the members of a cult in action were given an unfortunate impression of cultural backwardness. Most important was the fact that the rituals were unorthodox and thus unacceptable to true Moslems. If you mentioned such cults as the Derqaoua, the Aissaoua, the Haddaoua, the Hamatcha, the Jilala or the Guennaoua to a city man, he cried, "They're all criminals! They should be put in jail!" without stopping to reflect that it would be difficult to incarcerate more than half the population of any country. I think one reason why the city folk are so violent in their denunciation of the cults is that most of them are only one generation removed from them themselves; knowing the official attitude toward such things, they feel a certain guilt at being even that much involved with them. Having been born into a family of adepts is not a circumstance which anyone can quickly forget. Each brotherhood has its own songs and drum rhythms, immediately recognizable as such by persons both within and outside the group. In early childhood rhythmical patterns and sequences of tones become a part of an adept's subconscious, and in later life it is not difficult to attain the trance state when one hears them again.

A variation on this phenomenon is the story of Farid. Not long ago he called by to see me. I made tea, and since there was a fire in the fireplace, I took some embers out and put them into a brazier. Over them I sprinkled some *mska*, a translucent yellow resin which makes a sweet, clean-smelling smoke. Moroccans appreciate pleasant odors; Farid is no exception. A little later, before the embers had cooled off, I added some *djaoui*, a compound resinous substance of uncertain ingredients.

Farid jumped up. "What have you put into the *mijmah*?" he cried.

As soon as I had pronounced the word *djaoui*, he ran into the next room and slammed the door. "Let air into the room!" he shouted. "I can't smell *djaoui*! It's very bad for me!"

When all trace of the scent released by the *djaoui* was gone from the room, I opened the door and Farid came back in, still looking fearful.

"What's the matter with you?" I asked him. "What makes you think a little *djaoui* could hurt you? I've smelled it a hundred times and it's never done me any harm."

He snorted. "You! Of course it couldn't hurt you. You're not a Jilali, but I am. I don't want to be, but I still am. Last year I hurt myself and had to go to the clinic, all because of *djaoui*."

He had been walking in a street of Emsallah and had stopped in front of a café to talk to a friend. Without warning he had collapsed on the sidewalk; when he came to, he was at home and a drum was being beaten over him. Then he recalled the smoke that had been issuing from the café, and knew what had happened.

Farid had passed his childhood in a mountain village where all the members of his family were practicing Jilala. His earliest memories were of being strapped to his mother's back while she, dancing with the others, attained a state of trance. The two indispensable exterior agents they always used to assure the desired alteration of consciousness were drums and *djaoui*. By the time the boy was four or five years old, he already had a built-in mechanism, an infallible guarantee of being able to reach the trance state very swiftly in the presence of the proper stimulus. When he moved to the city he ceased to be an adept and, in fact, abandoned all religious practice. The conditioned reflex remained, as might be expected, with the result that now as a man in his mid-twenties, although he is at liberty to accept or refuse the effect of the specific drum rhythms, he is entirely at the mercy of a pinch of burning *djaoui*.

His exposition of the therapeutic process by which he is "brought back" each time there is an accident involves a good many other details, such as the necessity for the presence of a member of the paternal side of his family who will agree to eat a piece of the offending *djaoui*, the pronouncing of certain key phrases, and the playing on the *bendir* the proper rhythms necessary to break the spell. But the indisputable fact remains that when Farid breathes in *djaoui* smoke, whether or not he is aware of doing so, straightway he loses consciousness.

One of my acquaintances, who has always been vociferous in his condemnation of the brotherhoods, eventually admitted to me that all the older members of his family were adherents to the Jilala cult, citing immediately afterward, as an example of their perniciousness, an experience of his grandmother some three years before. Like the rest of the family, she was brought up as a Jilalia but had grown too old to take part in the observances, which nowadays are held secretly. (Prohibition, as usual, does not mean abolition, but merely being driven underground.) One evening the old lady was alone in the house, her children and grandchildren having all gone to the cinema, and since she had nothing else to do she went to bed. Somewhere nearby, on the outskirts of town, there was a meeting of Jilala going on. In her sleep she rose and, dressed just as she was, began to make her way toward the sounds. She was found next morning unconscious in a vegetable garden near the house where the meeting had taken place, having fallen into an ant colony and been badly bitten. The reason she fell, the family assured me, was that at a certain moment the drumming had stopped; if it had gone on she would have arrived. The drummers always continue until everyone present has been brought out of his trance.

"But they did not know she was coming," they said, "and so the next morning, after we had carried her home, we had to send for the drummers to bring her to her senses." The younger generation of French-educated Moslems is infuriated when this sort of story is told to foreigners. And that the latter are interested in such things upsets them even more. "Are all the people in your country Holy Rollers?" they demand. "Why don't you write about the civilized people here instead of the most backward?"

I suppose it is natural for them to want to see themselves presented to the outside world in the most "advanced" light possible. They find it perverse of a Westerner to be interested only in the dissimilarities between their culture and his. However, that's the way some of us Westerners are.

Not long ago I wrote on the character of the North Africa Moslem. An illiterate Moroccan friend wanted to know what was in it, and so, in a running translation into Moghrebi, I read him certain passages. His comment was terse: "That's shameful."

"Why?" I demanded.

"Because you've written about people just as they are."

"For us that's not shameful."

"For us it is. You've made us like animals. You've said that only a few of us can read or write."

"Isn't that true?"

"Of course not! We can all read and write, just like you. And we would, if only we'd had lessons."

I thought this interesting and told it to a Moslem lawyer, assuming it would amuse him. It did not. "He's quite right," he announced. "Truth is not what you perceive with your senses, but what you feel in your heart."

"But there is such a thing as objective truth!" I cried. "Or don't you attach importance to that?"

He smiled tolerantly. "Not in the way you do, for its own sake. That is statistical truth. We are interested in that, yes, but only as a means of getting to the real truth underneath. For us there is very little visible truth in the world these days." However specious this kind of talk may seem, it is still clear to me that the lawyer was voicing a feeling common to the great mass of city dwellers here, educated or not.

With an estimated adult illiteracy rate of eighty to ninety percent, perhaps the greatest need of all for North Africa is universal education. So far there has been a very small amount, and as we ourselves say, a little learning is a dangerous thing. The Europeans always have been guilty of massive neglect with regard to schools for Moslems in their North African possessions. In time, their short-sighted policy is likely to prove the heaviest handicap of all in the desperate attempt of the present rulers to keep the region within the Western sphere of influence. The task of educating these people is not made easier by the fact that Moghrebi, the language of the majority, is purely a spoken tongue, and that for reading and writing they must resort to standard Arabic, which is as far from their idiom as Latin is from Italian. But slowly the transition is taking place. If you sit in a Moroccan café at the hour of a news broadcast, the boy fanning the fire will pause with the bellows in his hand, the card players lay down their cards, the talkers cease to argue as the announcer begins to speak, and an expression of ferocious intensity appears on every countenance. Certainly they are vitally interested in what is being said (even the women have taken up discussing politics lately), for they are aware of their own increasing importance in the world pattern, but the almost painful expressions are due to each man's effort to understand the words of standard Arabic as they come over the air. Afterward, there is often an argument as to exactly what the news contained.

"The British are at war with Yemen for being friendly to Gamal Abd el Nasser."

"You're crazy. He said Gamal Abd el Nasser is making war against Yemen because the British are there."

"No. He said Gamal Abd el Nasser *will* make war against Yemen if they let the British in."

"No, no! Against the *British* if they send guns to Yemen."

This state of affairs, if it does not keep all members of the populace accurately informed, at least has the advantage of increasing their familiarity with the language their children are learning at school.

There is a word which non-Moslems invariably use to describe Moslems in general: fanatical. As though the word could not be applied equally well to any group of people who care deeply about anything! Just now, the North African Moslems are passionately involved in proving to themselves that they are of the same stature as Europeans. The attainment of political independence is only one facet of their problem. The North African knows that when it comes to appreciating his culture, the average tourist cannot go much closer toward understanding it than a certain condescending curiosity. He realizes that, at best, to the European he is merely picturesque. Therefore, he reasons, to be taken seriously he must cease being picturesque. Traditional customs, clothing and behavior must be replaced by something unequivocally European. In this he is fanatical. It does not occur to him that what he is rejecting is authentic and valid, and that what he is taking on is meaningless imitation. And if it did occur to him, it would not matter in the least. This total indifference to cultural heritage appears to be a necessary adjunct to the early stages of nationalism.

Hospitality in North Africa knows no limits. You are taken in and treated as a member of the family. If you don't enjoy yourself, it is not your host's fault, but rather the result of your own inadaptability, for every attempt is made to see that you are happy and comfortable. Some time ago I was the guest of two brothers who had an enormous house in the Medina of Fez. So that I should feel truly at home, I was given an entire wing of the establishment, a tiled patio with a room on either side and a fountain in the center. There were great numbers of servants to bring me food and drink, and also to inquire, before my hosts came to call, whether I was disposed to receive them. When they came they often brought singers and musicians to entertain me. The only hitch was that they went to such lengths to treat me as one of them that they also assumed I was not interested in going out into the city. During the entire fortnight I spent with them I never once found my way out of the house, or even out of my own section of it, since all doors were kept locked and bolted, and only the guard, an old Sudanese slave, had the keys. For long hours I sat in the patio listening to the sounds of the city outside, sometimes hearing faint strains of music that I would have given anything really to hear, watching the square of deep-blue sky above my head slowly become a softer and lighter blue as twilight approached, waiting for the swallows that wheeled above the patio when the day was finally over and the muezzins began their calls to evening prayer, and merely existing in the hope that someone would come, something would happen before too many more hours had gone past. But as I say, if I was bored, that was my own fault and not theirs. They were doing everything they could to please me.

Just as in that twelfth-century fortress in Fez I had been provided with a small hand-wound phonograph and one record (Josephine Baker singing "*J'ai deux amours*," a song hit of that year), so all over North Africa you are confronted with a mélange of the very old and the most recent, with no hint of anything from the intervening centuries. It is one of the great charms of the place, the fact that your today carries with it no memories of yesterday or the day before; everything that is not medieval is completely new. The younger generation of French and Jews, born and raised in the cities of North Africa, for the most part have no contact with that which is ancient in their countries. A Moroccan girl whose family moved from Rabat to New York, upon being asked what she thought of her new home, replied: "Well, of course, coming from a new country as I do, it's very hard to get used to all these old houses here in New York. I had no idea New York was so *old*." One is inclined to forget that the French began to settle in Morocco only at the time of World War I, and that the mushroom cities of Casablanca, Agadir and Tangier grew up in the thirties. Xauen, whose mountains are visible from the terrace of my apartment in Tangier, was entered by European troops for the first time in 1920. Even in southern Algeria, where one is likely to think of the French as having been stationed for a much longer time, there are war monuments bearing battle dates as recent as 1912. Throughout the whole first quarter of the century the North African frontier was continuously being pushed southward by means of warfare, and south of the Grand Atlas it was 1936 before "pacification" came to an end and European civilians were allowed, albeit on the strict terms laid down by the military, to look for the first time into the magic valleys of the Draa, the Dadès and the Todra.

Appearing unexpectedly in out-of-the-way regions of North Africa has never been without its difficulties. I remember making an impossible journey before the last world war in a produce

Paul Bowles outside an abandoned brothel, southern Morocco

truck over the Grand Atlas to Ouarzazat, full of excitement at the prospect of seeing the Casbah there with its strange painted towers, only to be forced to remain three days inside the shack that passed for a hotel, and then sent on another truck straight back to Marrakesh, having seen nothing but Foreign Legionnaires, and having heard no music other than the bugle calls that issued every so often from the nearby camp. Another time I entered Tunisia on camelback from across the Great Eastern Erg. I had two camels and one hard-working camel driver, whose job it was to run all day long from one beast to the other and try, by whacking their hind legs, to keep them walking in something resembling a straight line. This was a much more difficult task than it sounds; although our course was generally due east, one of the animals had an inexplicable desire to walk southward, while the other was possessed by an equally mysterious urge to go north. The poor man passed his time screaming: "Hut! Aïda!" and trying to run both ways at once. His turban was continually coming unwound, and he had no time to attend to the scarf he was knitting, in spite of the fact that he kept the yarn and needles dangling around his neck, ready to work on at any moment.

We did finally cross the border and amble into Tunisia, where we were immediately apprehended by the police. The camel driver and his beasts were sent back to Algeria where they belonged, and I started on my painful way up through Tunisia, where the French authorities evidently had made a concerted decision to make my stay in the country as wretched as possible. In the oasis at Nefta, in the hotel at Tozeur, even in the mosque of Sidi Oqba at Kairouan, I was arrested and lugged off to the commissariat, carefully questioned and told that I need not imagine I could make a move of which they would not be fully aware.

The explanation was that in spite of my American passport they were convinced I was a German; in those days anybody wandering around *l'Afrique Mineure* (as one of the more erudite officers called this corner of the continent), if he did not satisfy the French idea of what a tourist should look like, was immediately suspect. Even the Moslems would look at me closely and say: "*Toi pas Français. Toi Allemand,*" to which I never replied, for fear of having to pay the prices that would have been demanded if my true status had been revealed to them.

Algeria is a country where it is better to keep moving around than to stay long in one place. Its towns are not very interesting, but its landscapes are impressive. In the winter, traveling by train across the western steppes, you can go all day and see nothing but flat stretches of snow on all sides, unrelieved by trees in the foreground or by mountains in the distance. In the summer these same desolate lands are cruelly hot, and the wind swirls the dust into tall yellow pillars that move deliberately from one side of the empty horizon to the other. When you come upon a town in such regions, lying like the remains of a picnic lunch in the middle of an endless parking lot, you know it was the French who put it there. The Algerians prefer to live along the wild and beautiful sea coast, in the palm gardens of the south, atop the cliffs bordering the dry rivers, or on the crests of the high mountains in the center of the country. Up there above the slopes dotted with almond trees, the Berber villages sit astride the long spines of the lesser ranges. The men and women file down the zigzagging paths to cultivate the rich valleys below, here and there in full view of the snowfields where the French formerly had their skiing resorts. Far to the south lie the parallel chains of red sawtooth mountains which run northeast to southwest across the entire country and divide the plains from the desert.

No part of North Africa will again be the same sort of paradise for Europeans that it has been for them these last fifty years. The place has been thrown open to the twentieth century. With Europeanization and nationalism have come a consciousness of identity and the awareness of that identity's commercial possibilities. From now on the North Africans, like the Mexicans, will control and exploit their own charms, rather than being placed on exhibit for us by their managers, and the result will be a very different thing from what it has been in the past. Tourist land it still is, and doubtless will continue to be for a while; and it is on that basis only that we as residents or intending visitors are now obliged to consider it. We now come here as paying guests of the inhabitants themselves rather than of their exploiters. Travel here is certain not to be so easy or so comfortable as before, and prices are many times higher than they were, but at least we meet the people on terms of equality, which is a healthier situation.

If you live long enough in a place where the question of colonialism versus self-government is constantly being discussed, you are bound to find yourself having a very definite opinion on the subject. The difficulty is that some of your co-residents feel one way and some the other, but all feel strongly. Those in favor of colonialism argue that you can't "give" (quotes mine) an almost totally illiterate people political power and expect them to create a democracy, and that is doubtless true; but the point is that since they are inevitably going to take the power sooner or later, it is only reasonable to help them take it while they still have at least some measure of good will toward their erstwhile masters. The die-hard French attitude is summed up in a remark made to me by a friendly immigration officer at the Algiers airport. "Our great mistake," he said sadly, "was ever to allow these savages to learn to read and write." I said I supposed that was a logical thing to say if one expected to rule forever, which I knew, given the intelligence of the French, that they did not intend to try, since it was impossible. The official ceased looking sad and became much less friendly.

At a dinner in Marrakesh during the French occupation, the Frenchman sitting beside me became engaged in an amicable discussion with a Moroccan across the table. "But look at the facts, *mon cher ami*. Before our arrival, there was constant warfare between the tribes. Since we came the population has doubled. Is that true or not?"

The Moroccan leaned forward. "We can take care of our own births and deaths," he said, smiling. "If we must be killed, just let other Moroccans attend to it. We really prefer that."

THE RIF, TO MUSIC

KULCHUR, SPRING 1960; THEIR HEADS ARE GREEN, 1963

T
HE MOST IMPORTANT single element in Morocco's folk culture is its music. In a land like this, where almost total illiteracy has been the rule, the production of written literature is of course negligible. On the other hand, like the Negroes of West Africa the Moroccans have a magnificent and highly evolved sense of rhythm which manifests itself in the twin arts of music and the dance. Islam, however, does not look with favor upon any sort of dancing, and thus the art of the dance, while being the natural mode of religious expression of the native population, has not been encouraged here since the arrival of the Moslem conquerors. At the same time, the very illiteracy which through the centuries has precluded the possibility of literature has abetted the development of music; the entire history and mythology of the people is clothed in song. Instrumentalists and singers have come into being in lieu of chroniclers and poets, and even during the most recent chapter in the country's evolution – the war for independence and the setting up of the present pre-democratic regime – each phase of the struggle has been celebrated in countless songs.

The neolithic Berbers have always had their own music, and they still have it. It is a highly percussive art with complicated juxtapositions of rhythms, limited scalar range (often of no more than three adjacent tones) and a unique manner of vocalizing.

Like most Africans, the Berbers developed a music of mass participation, one whose psychological effects were aimed more often than not at causing hypnosis. When the Arabs invaded the land they brought with them music of a very different sort, addressed to the individual, seeking by sensory means to induce a state of philosophical speculativeness. In the middle of Morocco's hostile landscape they built their great walled cities, where they entrenched themselves and from which they sent out soldiers to continue the conquest, southward into the Sudan, northward into Europe. With the importation of large numbers of Negro slaves the urban culture ceased being a purely Arabic one. (The child of a union between a female slave and her master was considered legitimate.) On the central plains and in the foothills of the mountains of the north the Berber music took on many elements of Arabic music; while in the pre-Sahara it borrowed from the Negroes, remaining a hybrid product in both cases. Only in the regions which remained generally inaccessible to non-Berbers – roughly speaking, the mountains themselves and the high plateaux – was Berber music left intact, a purely autochthonous art.

My stint, in attempting to record the music of Morocco, was to capture in the space of the six months which the Rockefeller Foundation allotted to me for the project, examples of every major musical genre to be found within the boundaries of the country. This required the close cooperation of the Moroccan government, everyone agreed. But with which branch of it? No one knew. Because the material was to belong to the archives of the Library of Congress in Washington, the American Embassy in Rabat agreed to help me in my efforts to locate an official who might be empowered to grant the necessary permission, for I needed a guarantee that I would be allowed to move freely about the untraveled parts of the country, and once in those parts, I needed the power to persuade the local authorities to find the musicians in each tribe and round them up for me.

We approached several ministries, some of which claimed to be in a position to grant such permission, but none of which was willing to give formal approval to the project. Probably there was no precedent for such an undertaking, and no one wanted to assume the responsibility of creating such a precedent. In desperation, working through personal channels, I managed eventually to evolve a document to which was stapled my photograph, with official stamps and signatures; this paper made it possible to start work. By this time it was early July. In October, when I had been at work for more than three months, I received a communication from the ministry of foreign affairs which informed me that since my project was ill-timed I would not be allowed to undertake it. The American Embassy advised me to continue my work. By December the Moroccan government had become aware of what was going on; they informed me summarily that no recordings could be made in Morocco save by special permission from the Ministry of the Interior. By then I had practically completed the project, and the snow was beginning to block the mountain passes, so this blow was not too bitter. However, from then on it was no longer possible to make any recordings which required the cooperation of the government; this deprived the collection of certain tribal musics of southeastern Morocco. But I already had more than two hundred and fifty selections from the rest of the country, as diversified a body of music as one could find in any land west of India.

Christopher is a level-headed Canadian with a Volkswagen and all the time in the world. Mohammed Larbi, a good contact man and assistant, as a youth had spent a year accompanying an expedition across the Sahara to Nigeria. The three of us set out together from Tangier following four roughly circular itineraries of five weeks' duration each: southwestern Morocco, northern Morocco, the Atlas, and the pre-Sahara. Between trips we recuperated in Tangier. The pages which follow were written from day to day during the course of the second journey, most of whose days were spent in the mountains of the Rif, in what used to be the Spanish protectorate.

ALHUCEMAS, AUGUST 29, 1959

THE ROAD TO KETAMA goes along the backbone of the western
Rif. You can see for miles, both to the Mediterranean side and
to the southern side, big mountains and more big mountains –
mountains covered with olive trees, with oak trees, with bushes,
and finally with giant cedars. For two or three hours before getting up to Ketama we had been passing large gangs of workmen
repairing the road; it needed it badly. We had been going to cook
lunch in a little pine grove just above a village between Bab Taza
and Bab Berret, but when we got in among the trees, wherever
we looked there were workmen lying on the dry pine needles
in the shade, sleeping or smoking kif, so we set up our equipment in the sun and wind, a little below the crest where the
pine grove was. The wind kept blowing out the butagaz flame,
but in the end we managed to eat. Christopher drank his usual
Chaudsoleil *rosé*, and Mohammed Larbi and I drank piping hot
Pepsi-Cola, since there was no water left in the thermos we had
filled in Xauen. That one thermosful proved to be the last good
water we were to have for three weeks.

During lunch Mohammed Larbi insisted on amusing himself
with the radio; he was trying to get Damascus on the nineteen-
meter band in order to hear the news. When eventually he did
get it he could not understand it, of course, because it was in
Syrian Arabic, but that made no difference to him. It was news,
and they were talking about Kassem and excoriating the French,
which was easy enough for even me to understand. Mohammed
Larbi had been smoking kif constantly all morning and was a bit
exalted. We packed up and started on our way again.

It was about half past four when we came in sight of the
wide plain of Ketama they call Llano Amarillo. It is aptly named,
at least in summer, for then it is dry and yellow. Here and there,
scattered over a distance which went toward infinity, was a herd
of cattle or a flock of sheep. They looked as though they had
been put there purposely to give the place scale. At first you saw
nothing but the yellow flatness with the great cedar trees along

the sides. Then you saw the dots that were the nearest sheep, then to the right the pinpoints that were cows, but smaller than the sheep, then far over to the left almost invisible specks that were another herd.

The *parador* of Bab Berret, which has about twenty rooms, looked completely abandoned, but there was a chair on the wide front terrace, and the door was open. I went in to inquire about sleeping quarters. The inside seemed deserted too. The dining room had furniture in it; the other rooms had been stripped. In the town of Bab Berret, the Spanish, when they relinquished their protectorate, took the generator with them; the vicinity has been without electricity ever since. There was no sign of life at the reception desk, no piece of paper or ledger in sight – nothing but the keys hung in three rows on the wall. I called out, "*¿Hay alguien?*" and got no answer. Finally, behind the big door of what had been the bar, I saw a pair of legs lying on a decayed divan and peered around the door. A young man lay there with his eyes open, but he wasn't looking at me; he was staring at the ceiling. When he did see me, he slowly sat up and stretched a little, never answering my "excuse me's" and "good afternoons." I decided he must be a guest and went out again into the main hall, but in a minute he was there behind me, and then he did not ask me what he could do for me, but what was the matter.

When he heard I wanted rooms he turned away with disgust. "There are no rooms," he said.

"None at all?"

"None at all."

"Is the hotel open?"

"The hotel's open and there are no rooms. Tomorrow you can have some if you want."

"And tonight where am I going to sleep?"

He turned around again and looked at me blankly. Too much kif, I could see that. He was scratching his crotch voluptuously all this time. He yawned and began to walk around toward the bar. "You couldn't put up a cot somewhere?" I called after him.

Paul Bowles with Mohammed Larbi on their recording trip to the Rif

But he continued to move away. I went out to the car to report. Christopher and Mohammed Larbi came back in with me; they didn't believe any of it.

The scratcher was already back on his broken-down couch, getting himself into a comfortable position. This time he looked really hostile. I decided to go back out onto the terrace. I didn't want to see him any more. Mohammed Larbi was examining the main entrance hall and the staircase. When Christopher came out he said there were plenty of rooms, that the young man was finally awake, and that we could stay after all. The foremen of the various road construction gangs had requisitioned several rooms (for which they were not paying), but there were a dozen or more vacant ones.

The scratcher was manager, bellboy, waiter, dishwasher and accountant. Besides him there was a crazy-looking cook and an old Riffian woman who made the beds and scrubbed the floors, but that was the entire personnel. The cook also ran a small generator in the garage; he took us out to admire it later on.

Someone had removed the doorknobs from the bedroom doors, so that if the door of your room happened to blow shut, you had to pound on it until the manager heard you and came upstairs with a piece of metal of his own fashioning which he stuck through the hole where the knob had been and turned the lock to let you either in or out, depending on where you happened to be. This was true of the hotel's one toilet, too, but that was of no importance because the place was so filthy that you didn't go into it anyway. The toilet bowl had been filled up and so people had begun using the floor. In 1950 I had spent a night in that one bathroom. They put a cot beside the tub and hung a scribbled sign on the door saying the bathroom was out of order, but that didn't prevent a steady stream of French tourists from pounding indignantly on the door throughout the long night. Some of them tried to break the door in, but the bolt was strong. Now that I stuck my head into the stinking room, I remembered that endless night and the noise of the unloading bus beneath my window at five in the morning, the bugle calls from the barracks back in the cedar forest and the gobbling of the turkeys in crates out on the terrace.

We wanted to get down to Laazib Ketama as quickly as possible, in order to see the caid or the *khalifa* before the government offices closed, so after leaving our luggage in our rooms we started out, bumping down the crazy, wide Tirak d'l Ouahada. Hundreds of Riffians on horseback, muleback and donkeyback, the women walking, were on their way up. We covered them all with layers of white dust; there was no help for it. They were in a fine humor, however, laughing and waving.

At one point you could look directly down from the road into a deep ravine whose sides were planted wholly with kif. Ketama is the kif center of all North Africa, and very likely of the world now. It is the only region where it is legal to grow it, and that is because the Sultan has agreed to allow the cultivation of it to continue until the land has been made feasible for other crops. At present the only crop that will grow is kif, and although any Moroccan can plant a few stalks in his garden, the only really good kif is the Ketami. So you have miles and miles of it growing out of the stony soil on the edges of the steep slopes, and under the present ruling this will go on until some other means of livelihood has been found for the inhabitants.

At present the kif situation is ridiculous. Tons of the drug are grown each year and shipped out of Ketama in all directions. That is legal. But if anyone is caught selling it he is immediately given a heavy fine and/or a prison sentence. No penalties are attached to the possession of it, but the official attitude toward the smoking of it in public places differs according to the way the local authorities of each town feel about it. I was in Marrakesh in August and found it wide open. In Fez I saw only one old man holding a *sebsi*. In Tangier and Tetuan clouds of kif smoke pour out of the cafés. In Rabat, Essaouira, Oujda, nothing. In some towns it's easy to get and cheap and good; in others, you almost might as well not even try. These conditions are of course far from static. The city in which two months ago you could run around the corner for a paper of kif is suddenly closed tight, whereas in another town where previously there was strict vigilance, men are observed puffing on their pipes in the street, in full view of police headquarters. Generally speaking, when you get to the southern side of the Grand Atlas, kif is a luxury and greatly prized, whereas in the extreme north, among the Djebala, for instance, the average village male over fourteen has his little mottoui full of it and his *sebsi* in his pocket.

We stopped the car and climbed down a way to examine the phenomenon. None of us had ever before seen so much kif. We could have filled the back of the car with it and no one would have known. Mohammed Larbi stroked a stalk lovingly and murmured, "Like green diamonds everywhere. *Fijate.*" An old man ambled by and sat down beside the road to look at us with curiosity. Mohammed Larbi shouted to him in Moghrebi: "Is this kif yours?" It was clear that next he was going to ask to be given some. But the old man did not understand. He merely stared at us. "Like donkeys!" snorted Mohammed Larbi. He never fails to be annoyed with the Riffians when they speak only Tarifcht; if a Moroccan does not understand at least some Moghrebi he takes it as a personal affront. When we got back to the car he pulled out his enormous sheep's bladder, packed with three pounds of the powerful greasy green kif he prepares himself, and filled a cigarette paper with it. "I've got to smoke!" he cried in great excitement. "I can't see all that kif and not feel some of it in me." He continued to smoke until we got down to Laazib Ketama.

The main body of the tribesmen had already left (it was market day), but there were still several hundred men lying around on rugs and sacks under the cedars in the three big courtyards where the souk had been taking place. The merchants were winding bolts of cloth and packing sugar and toys and cutlery away into big bundles. The dust that hung in the air, where it came in contact with the last rays of the sun, made blinding golden streamers across the scene. We sneezed repeatedly as we picked our way through the emptying market. There were the customary blank faces when we inquired after the *khalifa's* office, but we found it, and eventually managed to get into it. I had forgotten about the short war of 1958 between the Riffians and the forces of the Rabat government, but the memory of it came back soon enough. They told me that since we were in a military zone we would have to consult the comandante if we expected to be allowed to record. Yes, the *comandante* had been down here in Laazib Ketama all day, but now he had left, and who knew where he was now? However, they were building a bridge just below the village, and perhaps he was down there watching. We went further down the trail. It looked a hopeless task to find anyone in the midst of such chaos. In any case, it was already twilight and we had about fifteen miles of rough trail to climb in order to get back to the parador. So we backed up, nearly went over a small cliff, and headed toward Llano Amarillo.

Because the *khalifa* had also suggested that we stop off at the barracks on the way back to the parador, we turned in toward a three-story log cabin that looked like an expensive hotel in a skiing resort, and were met by a dozen wide-eyed Moroccan youths in uniform who immediately trained their submachine guns on us, just in case it turned out that we needed to be captured. A sergeant made them back up and told us that the comandante would be coming in about eight o'clock.

The *khalifa* in Laazib Ketama had mentioned a village some thirty kilometers further on where there were some *rhaita* players. His news did not stimulate me particularly, because I already had taped a good many sequences of *rhaita* music, including some excellent ones from Beni Aros, the capital of Djebala musicians. The *rhaita* among the Djebala is not notice-ably different from the *rhaita* in the Rif, save perhaps that the Riffians' playing shows a more accurate rhythmical sense. What I was looking for was the *zamar*, a double-reed instrument fit-ted with a pair of bull's horns. The *khalifa* had assured me that the Beni Uriaghel in the Central Rif would supply that; for lack of anything better I had shown polite interest in his offer of *rhaitas*, and I was ready to devote a day to recording them. It would depend upon whether the comandante proved willing to collect the musicians for me; I did not want to waste any energy or time having to persuade him, even if it meant no recording in the Ketama region. I was eager to get on eastward to where the true Riffian music is.

We drove back to the hotel. The mountain night had settled over the valley. The wind was whistling through the rooms; doors were squeaking and banging all by themselves. Each minute I was becoming less interested in finding the comandante. We went to my room and turned on the shivering little electric light bulb over the bed. Christopher and Mohammed Larbi make a habit of meeting in my room because I have the equipment with me: the two tape-recorders, the radio, the food and drink, and the fire. There is seldom a reason for either of them ever to go to his own room save to sleep. On our twilight visit to the generator in the garage we had learned that it supplied two-hundred-and-twenty-volt direct current to the parador, and so I already knew that it was not going to be possible to work the tape-recorders, either for studying tapes already recorded or for our amusement. This was bad news. The night would be cold and uncomfortable, once we were in those forbidding beds. We needed a reason to stay up late.

Ketama is fairly high for the Rif: about six thousand feet up. With the setting of the sun a mountain chill had crept down through the forest from the heights. The road menders were eating sardines in their rooms. It was cold in the empty *comedor* at dinner time. As soon as we had eaten we went upstairs and made coffee. Mohammed Larbi brought out the bottle of Budapest kümmel, and Christopher handed us the half-kilo bag of *majoun* someone had sold him in Xauen. We all drank kümmel, but only Mohammed Larbi ate any *majoun*. If someone is entirely comfortable and contented, *majoun* can enhance his pleasure, but there is no point in italicizing an unsatisfactory experience.

It suddenly occurred to me that the lights might be turned off and that we had no candles. I went down to look for the manager. He was drying dishes in the kitchen with the cook, who was smoking kif in a very long *sebsi*. I was right, he said; the lights would be going off within twenty minutes, at ten o'clock, and there were no candles in the parador. That I did not believe. I objected that there must be at least one, somewhere.

"No candles," he said, firmly.

"Haven't you got a piece of one?"

"No pieces of candles," he replied, drying dishes, not looking up. "Nothing."

It was clearly a provocation. I had seen what had happened when I had tried to get the rooms. Christopher had been able to get them out of him, I had not, and he was aware of this. He was playing his inexplicable little game again. I stood there. Finally I said: "I don't understand this hotel."

Now he set down his dish and turned to face me. "*Señor*," he said deliberately, "don't you know this is the worst hotel in the world?"

"What?"

He repeated the words slowly, "It's the worst hotel in the world."

"No, I didn't know," I said. "Who owns it?"

"A poor slob who lives around here." He and the cook exchanged mysterious, amused glances. I could think of nothing to retort save that I had been under the impression that it was run by the government. Formerly it was the family or religion that one criticized, if in the course of one's personal relations one found it expedient to infuriate a Moroccan; nowadays one gets the same reaction by ridiculing the government, since at last it is Moroccans who are responsible for it. But neither one of them understood my remark as the insult I had intended. "No, no, no!" they laughed. "Just a *pobre desgraciado*."

I went back upstairs and reported all this; it was greeted with loud laughter. Christopher got up and left the room. A minute or two later he was back with three new candles and two half-burned ones. The lights stayed on until half past ten. We went to bed. In the morning there was a blinding fog and it was still cold. I had a hacking cough and decided that I must be about to come down with something. Christopher and Mohammed Larbi came in and made coffee. I told them I wanted no music from Ketama; we were leaving immediately for Alhucemas. When I went down to pay the bill, for the first time the manager looked nearly awake. I got back my change, and out of curiosity I handed him two hundred francs as a tip, determined, if he threw the coins on the floor, merely to pick them up and leave. But his face suddenly came alive.

"I'm going crazy here," he confided. "How can I do anything? There's nothing here, nothing works, everything's broken, there's no money, nobody comes but road workers. Anybody would go crazy."

I nodded in sympathy.

"I'll be leaving soon, of course," he continued. "I'm not used to places like this. I'm from Tetuan."

"Is that so?"

"I've been here two months almost, but next week I'm getting out."

"I'd say that's lucky for you." I did not believe he would really be leaving, although at the moment he looked passionate enough to walk out the door and down the highway and never return. Some Moroccans can work themselves into a state of emotional imbalance with astonishing speed.

"I'm going, all right. You've got to be crazy to live up here. *Ma hadou.*"

I said good-bye and he wished me good luck.

The road east of Ketama was extremely bad: a rough surface sprinkled with small sharp stones, and unbanked curves every few yards. At times the fog was so thick that nothing at all was visible but the dirt bed of the road three feet ahead of the car. We crawled along. The fog dissolved. There were villages down in the valleys at our feet. The earth was whitish gray, and so were the enormous, square earthen houses. Traditional Riffian architecture, untouched. The landscape was timeless.

We bought gasoline in Targuist. The place was the last refuge of poor old Abd el Krim; the French captured him here in 1926.

There are many Jews, speaking Spanish; and the modern town is a monstrous excrescence with long dirty streets, the wind blowing along them, whipping clouds of dust and filth against the face, stinging the skin. The Moslem village across the highway was of a more attractive aspect, but proved to be unreachable in the car. Beyond Targuist were a dark sky and a high wind and a countryside which grew more arid and forlorn by the mile. Finally it was raining, but the storm passed in time for us to have our lunch beside a culvert where the dirt in the wind cut less (for in this valley it had not rained), and where we could keep the flame of the butagaz alive.

We drove into Alhucemas at about half past four. The sea looked like lead. The town itself has a certain paranoid quality: the classic Spanish fishing village seen as in a bad dream. There is a vague atmosphere of impending disaster, of being cut off from the world, as in a penal colony. A penal colony, yes. It is in the faces of the few Spaniards sitting in the shabby cafés. Most of the Spanioline have gone away. The ones who remain are not likely to admit that the only reason they are still here is that it is impossible for them to go anywhere else.

The Moroccans have taken over Alhucemas – all of it except the Hotel España. I am in a luxurious room with a tile shower; there is hot water in the pipes, which is unbelievable; it is the first since Tangier. The weather remains lowering, and suddenly it is dark. At dinner the fat Spanish waiter is the principal source of amusement: he is definitely drunk and even staggers classically as he brings in the food. Mohammed Larbi makes fairly brutal fun of him all through the meal.

This morning we went to see the governor. He is friendly, speaks in Tarifcht to his assistants; in the government offices of the south they are likely to use French. He says that tomorrow evening we are to report to the fort at Ajdir. There the Caid of Einzoren will meet us and take over. We have agreed. The sky is still dark and the air heavy.

AUGUST 31, 4 A.M.

THE CAID OF EINZOREN proved to be a jolly young man from Rabat, not much more than twenty years old. He is enjoying himself enormously up here in the Rif, he confided, because he has a girl in Einzoren, a "hundred percent Española," named Josefina. In the middle of our recording session he invited us to have dinner with him and Josefina. We accepted, but were given a table where we sat alone eating the food he had ordered for us, while he sat with Josefina and her family.

We had set up the recording equipment in an empty municipal building which stood in the middle of the main plaza. It gave the impression of being a school which was no longer in use. When we arrived, we found one of the rooms already filled with women and girls, three dozen or so of them, singing and tapping lightly on their drums. They sat in straight-backed chairs, their heads and shoulders entirely hidden under the bath towels they wore. A great hushed crowd of men and boys stood outside in the plaza, pressing against the building, trying to peer over the high window sills. Now and then someone whispered; I was grateful for their silence.

The tribe was the Beni Uriaghel, but in spite of that there was no *zamar*. It was a great disappointment. I questioned the caid about the possibilities of finding one. He knew even less than I about it; he had never suspected the existence of such an instrument. The musicians themselves shook their heads; the Beni Uriaghel did not use it, they said. Not even in the country, I pursued, outside Einzoren? They laughed, because they were all rustics from the mountains roundabout and had been summoned to the village to take part in the "festival."

No one had told me that the girls were going to sing in competitive teams, or that each village would be represented by two rival sets of duo-vocalists, so that I was not prepared for the strange aspect of the room. They sat in pairs, their heads close enough together so that each couple could be wholly covered by the one large turkish towel. The voices were directed floorward through the folds of cloth, and since no gesture, no movement of the head, accompanied the singing, it was literally impossible to know who was performing and who was merely sitting. The song was surprisingly repetitious even for Berber music; nevertheless I was annoyed to have it marred by the constant sound of murmurs and whispers and sotto-voce remarks during the performance, an interference the microphone would inevitably register. But there was no way of catching anyone's eye, since no eyes were visible. Even the matrons, who were supplying the drumming, were covered. The first selection went on and on, strophe after strophe, the older women tapping the membranes of their disc-shaped *bendirs* almost inaudibly on arbitrary offbeats. I took advantage of the piece's length to leave the controls and go over to whisper a question to the caid, who sat beaming in an honorific arm-chair, flanked by his subordinates who were crouching on the floor around him. "Why are they all talking so much?" I asked him.

He smiled. "They're making up the words they're going to sing next," he told me. I was pleased to hear that the texts were improvised and went back to my Ampex and earphones to wait for the song to end. When the girls had gone on for thirty-five minutes more, and the tape had run out, I tiptoed across the room once again to the caid. "Are all the pieces going to be this long?" I inquired.

"Oh, they'll go on until I stop them," he said. "All night, if you like."

"The same song?"

"Oh, yes. It's about me. Do you want them to sing a different one?"

I explained that it was no longer being recorded, and he called a halt. After that I was able to control the length of the selections.

Presently word arrived that the *rhaita* group was sitting in a café somewhere at the edge of town, waiting for transportation; and so, accompanied by a cicerone, Christopher drove out to fetch them. The café proved to be in a village about twenty kilometers distant. The men were playing when he arrived; when he told them to get into the car they did so without ceasing to play. They played all the way to Einzoren and walked into the building where I was without ever having interrupted the piece. I let them finish it, and then had them taken back outside into the public square. Mohammed Larbi carried the microphone out and set it up in the middle of the great circle formed by the male onlookers. The *rhaita*, a super-oboe whose jagged, strident sound has been developed precisely for long-distance listening, is not an indoor instrument.

While we were away in the restaurant, the men and the women in the public square somehow got together and put on a *fraja*. This would not have happened in the regions of Morocco where Arab culture has been imposed on the population, but in the Rif it is not considered improper for the two sexes to take part in the same entertainment. Even here the men did not dance; they played, sang and shouted while the women danced. I heard the racket from the restaurant and hurried back to try and tape it, but as soon as they saw what I was doing they became quiet. There was a group of excellent musicians from a village called Tazourakht; their music was both more primitive and more precise rhythmically than that of the others, and I showed open favoritism in asking for more of it. This proved to be not too good an idea, for they were the only men to belong to another tribe, the Beni Bouayache. The recording session, which had been in progress since dusk, gave signs of being about to degenerate into a wild party somewhere around two o'clock in the morning. I suggested to the caid that we stop, but he saw no reason for that. At twenty to three we disconnected the machines and packed them up. "We're going on with this until tomorrow," said the caid, declining our offer of a ride to Alhucemas. The sounds of revelry were definitely growing louder as we drove away.

LAST NIGHT was really enough; we ought to go on eastward. But the governor has gone out of his way to be helpful and has arranged another session in Ismoren, a village in the hills to the west, for tomorrow evening. Today I succeeded in enticing the two Riffian maids at the hotel here into my room to help me identify sixteen pieces on a tape I recorded in 1956. I knew it was all music from the Rif, but I wanted to find out which pieces were from which tribes, in order to have a clearer idea of what each genre was worth in terms of the effort required to capture it. The girls refused to come into the room without a chaperone; they found a thirteen-year-old boy and brought him with them. This was fortunate, because the boy spoke some Moghrebi, while they knew only Tarifcht and a few words of Spanish. I would play a piece and they would listen for a moment before identifying its source. Only two pieces caused them any hesitation, and they soon agreed on those. I still need examples of the Beni Bouifrour, the Beni Touzine, the Ait Ulixxek, the Gzennaia and the Temsaman. The girls were delighted with the small sum I gave them; upon leaving the room they insisted on taking some soiled laundry with them to wash for me.

NADOR, SEPTEMBER 6

WE WENT UP to Ismoren as scheduled, at twilight on the following day. The landscape reminded me of central Mexico. The trail from the highway up to the village was a constant slow climb along a wide, tilting plain. The caid was not at home; there had been a misunderstanding and he was in Alhucemas. The villagers invited us into his home, saying that the musicians were ready to play when we wanted to begin. It was a Spanish house with large rooms, dimly lit and sparsely furnished. There were great piles of almonds lying about in the corners; they reached almost up to the ceiling. The dank odor they gave off made the place smell like an abandoned farmhouse. The feeble electricity trembled and wavered. I had Mohammed Larbi test the current because I suspected it of being direct. Unhappily, that was what it proved to be, and I had to announce that in spite of all the preparations it was not going to be possible to record in Ismoren. There was incredulity and then disappointment on all faces. "Stay the night," they told us, "and tomorrow perhaps the electric force will be better." I thanked them and said we could not do that, but Mohammed Larbi, exasperated by their ignorance, launched into an expository monologue on electricity. Nobody listened. Men were beginning to bang drums outside on the terrace, and someone who looked like the local schoolteacher was delegated to serve tea. He invited me to preside at the caid's big desk. When they saw me sitting there, they laughed. An elderly man remarked, "He makes a good caid," and they all agreed. I opened three packs of cigarettes and passed them around. Everyone was looking longingly at the equipment, wanting very much to see it set up. We had tea, more tea, and still more tea, and finally got off for Alhucemas to a noisy accompaniment of benadir, with two men running ahead of us along the cactus-bordered lanes to show us the way out of the village.

And so each morning I continued to go down to the government offices to study their detailed wall maps and try to locate the tribes with which I hoped to make contact. The first day I had spotted an official surreptitiously looking up our police records; apparently they were satisfactory. The governor and his aides had begun with a maximum of cordiality; but as the novelty of seeing us wore off, their attitude underwent a metamorphosis. It seemed to them that we were being arbitrary and difficult in our insistence upon certain tribes instead of others, and they had had enough of telephoning and making abortive arrangements. It involved about two hours' work for them each day. It was the electricity which frustrated us every time; we had been supplied with a transformer but not with a generator, and Einzoren appeared to be the only village in the region with alternating current.

One night when we went in to have dinner in the *comedor* of the Hotel España there was a murderous-looking soldier sitting at the table with Mohammed Larbi. We sat down; he was drunk and wanted to deliver a political lecture. He and Mohammed Larbi went out together. At three in the morning there was a great racket in the corridors. Mohammed Larbi was finding the way to his room with the help of various recruits from the street and with the voluble hindrance of the hotel's night watchman. The next day, which had been set as the day of departure, he was moaning sick. He managed to pack the car for us, and then fell into the back with the luggage, to say no more. The weather had gone on being dramatic and threatening. South of Temsaman the mountains, even in normal weather, look like imaginary sketches of another planet. Under the black sky and with the outrageous lighting effects that poured through unexpected valleys, they were a disquieting sight. Mohammed Larbi moaned occasionally.

The trail was execrable, but fortunately we did not meet another car all day – at least, not until late afternoon when we had got down into the plain to Laazib Midar, where a real road is suddenly born. My idea was to find some sort of place thereabouts where we could stay when we returned after seeing the Governor at Nador (since we were now in the Province of Nador and had to go all the way to the capital to get permission to work). But, Laazib Midar being only a frontierlike agglomeration of small adobe houses strung along the road, we went on through.

From the back seat Mohammed Larbi began once more to wail. "Ay, *yimma habiba*! Ay, what bad luck!" I told him that nobody had forced him to drink whatever he had drunk. "But they did!" he lamented. "That's just what happened. I was forced." I laughed unsympathetically. No one can smoke as much kif as Mohammed Larbi does and be able to drink, too. I thought it was time he knew it, inasmuch as he has been smoking regularly since he was eleven and he is now twenty-five.

"But it was at the barracks, and there were eight soldiers, and they said if I didn't drink I must be a woman. Is that *b'd drah* or not?"

"It's very sad," I said, and he was quiet.

It was black night and raining quietly when we got into Nador. After driving up and down the muddy streets we stopped at a grocery store to ask about a hotel. A Spaniard in the doorway said there was no hotel and that we should go on to Melilla. That was completely out of the question, since Melilla, although in Morocco, has been Spanish for the past four hundred and fifty years, and still is; even if Christopher and Mohammed Larbi had been in possession of Spanish visas, which they were not, we could never have got the equipment across the border. I said we had to stay in Nador no matter what. The Spaniard said: "Try Paco Gonzalez at the gasoline pump. He might put you up. He's a European, at least."

A small Moroccan boy who was listening shouted: "Hotel Mokhtar is good!" The word "hotel" interested me, and we set out in search of it. Less than an hour later we came across it; it was over a Moslem café. Above the door someone had printed in crooked letters: H. MOKHTAR. The place reminds me somewhat of the Turkish baths that used to exist in the Casbah of Algiers thirty years ago. It is run by a bevy of inquisitive Riffian women; I know there are a great many of them, but I haven't yet been able to distinguish one from the others. After assigning us three uniformly melancholy rooms, they all came, one at a time, to examine our luggage and equipment; then apparently they held a conference, after which they put a "kitchen" at our disposal. This room was strewn with garbage, but it had two grids where charcoal fires could be built if you had charcoal. It also had a sink which was stopped up and full, I should guess, of last year's dishwater. We threw the garbage out the window onto the flowers in the patio, (there was nowhere else to put it) and installed ourselves. By now we are used to inhaling the stench of the latrines at each breath, but that first night it bothered us considerably. I flung my window open and discovered that the air outside was worse. The interior odor was of ancient urine, but the breeze that entered through the window brought a heavy scent of fresh human excrement. Just how that could be was unascertainable for the moment. However, I shut the window and lighted several bathi sticks, and then we settled down to prepare some food.

The next morning when I looked out into the sunlight I understood. The Hotel Mokhtar is built at the edge of town; for about five hundred yards beyond it the earth is crisscrossed by trenches three feet deep. These are the town's lavatories; at any moment during the day you can see a dozen or more men, women and children squatting in the trenches. Until 1955 Nador was just another poor Moroccan village with a few Spaniards in it; suddenly it was made the capital of a newly designated province. The Spanish still have several thousand troops stationed here to "protect" Melilla – which Rabat more or less openly claims and will undoubtedly sooner or later recover. And so, naturally enough, the Moroccans have that many thousand soldiers, plus several thousand more, quartered here in order to protect Nador.

There are many more people here than there should be. Water has to be got in pails and oil tins from pumps in the street; food is at a premium and all commodities are scarce. Dust hangs over the town and refuse surrounds it, except on the east, where the shallow waters of the Mar Chica lap against the mud, disturbing the dead fish that unaccountably float there in large numbers. The Mar Chica is a useless inland sea with an average depth of about six feet – just enough to drown a man. At the horizon, glistening and white, is the sandbar where the Mediterranean begins, and toward which one gazes wistfully, imagining the clean-smelling breeze that must sometimes blow out there. Nador is a prison. The presence of a wide, palm-and-flower-planted boulevard leading down the half-mile from the administration building to the dead shore of the Mar Chica only makes the place more revolting. At the lower end of the thoroughfare is a monstrous edifice built to look like a huge juke box, and supported by piles that raise it above the water. This is the town's principal restaurant, where we eat each noon. The *paseo* is lined with sidewalk cafés and concrete benches. When the benches are full of the hundreds of desperate-looking Spanish and Moroccan soldiers who roam the streets, the only place for new arrivals to sit is in the chairs put out under the palms by the café-keepers. They sit there, but they stare down the boulevard and order nothing. At night it's a little less depressing because the thoroughfare is not at all well lighted and the intense shabbiness doesn't show. Besides, after dark the two military populations are shut into their respective barracks.

Late this morning we went to the governor's office; he was in Meknès with the Sultan, but his voluble *katib* had stayed behind, and it was he who took charge of us. "Let's see. You want the Beni Bouifrour tribe. You will have them tomorrow without fail. Go now to Segangan."

That sounded too easy. He saw my hesitation. "You can still catch the *khalifa* before he goes out for his aperitif. Wait. I shall telephone him. He will wait." And when I looked dubious, "By my order he will wait. Go."

To get us out of the way, I thought. When we come back, this one will be gone, and I'll lose the whole day. Maybe two days. My doubt must have made itself even more noticeable, for he became dramatic. "I am telephoning. Now. Look. My hand is on the telephone. As soon as you go out that door I shall speak with the *khalifa*. You can go with the certainty that I shall keep my word." I understood that the longer I listened to him go on in this vein, the less I was going to believe anything that he said. There seemed to be nothing to do but start out for Segangan immediately.

But the katib had telephoned, after all, and the *khalifa* of Segangan, once we found the military headquarters where he had his office, proved to be pleasant and unreserved. He closed his office and walked with us into the street. As we strolled under the acacias he said, "We have many charming gardens here in Segangan." (He pronounced it Az-rheung-ng'n, in the Riffian fashion.) "It only remains for you to choose the garden of your preference for the recording."

"Haven't you a room somewhere?" I suggested. "It would be quieter, and besides, I need to plug my equipment into the electric current."

"Gardens are better than rooms," he said. "And we have our own electrician who will do whatever you ask him."

We examined bowers and arbors and fountains and nooks. I explained that I did not care where we did it, if outside noises were kept at a minimum, and that bearing this in mind, it seemed that indoors would perhaps be preferable.

"Not at all!" cried the *khalifa*. "I shall have all traffic deflected during the recording."

"But then the people of the town will know something is going on, and they'll come to find out what it is, and there will be more noise than ever!"

"No, no," he said reassuringly. "Foot traffic will not be allowed to circulate."

It was clear that any such measures would call attention to us straightway, because they never would be fully enforced. But his excessive proposals were a part of his desire to appear friendly, and so I ceased objecting, and resolved to speak to the katib about it when I got back here to Nador. We found a place in which to record, a remote corner of one of the parks, as shady as a thicket and quiet save for the crowing of roosters in the distance. The session was arranged for tomorrow morning. Back here in Nador I went to find the katib, but he had left his office for the day; we shall be at the mercy of the well-meaning *khalifa*.

SEPTEMBER 7

MY ANXIETY was unnecessary. When we got to Segangan this morning, we were taken to a completely different garden, quite outside the town. The *khalifa's* electrician had already installed the cable, and everything went with beautiful smoothness.

Among the Berbers, not only in the Rif, but much further south in the Grand Atlas, the professional troubadour still exists; the social category allotted him is not exactly that of an accepted member of the community, but neither is he a pariah. As an entertainer he is respected; as an itinerant worker he is naturally open to some suspicion. The Riffians are fond of drawing an analogy between the *imdyazen* (as the minstrels are called both here and in the Atlas) and the *gitanos* of Spain – only, as they point out, the *imdyazen* live in houses like other people, and not in camps outside the towns like the gypsies. If you ask them why that is, they will usually reply: "Because they are of the same blood as we." In Segangan I had my first encounter with the imdyazen. Their *chikh* looked like a well-chosen extra in a pirate film – an enormous, rough, good-natured man with a bandana around his head instead of a turban. He, at last, had a *zamar* with him. Even Mohammed Larbi had never seen one before. We examined it at some length and photographed it from various angles. It consists of two separate reed pipes wired together, each with its own mouthpiece and perforations; fitted to the end of each reed is a large bull's horn. The instrument can be played with or without the horns, which are easily detached.

Yesterday the effusive *khalifa* promised me two *zamars*, and even this morning he let me go on believing, for the first half-hour or so, that a second player would be forthcoming. But when I began to seem anxious about his arrival and made inquiries among some of the officials, meaningful glances were exchanged, and the language abruptly shifted from Moghrebi into Tarifcht. I realized then that I was being boorish; one does not bring a lie out into the open. For some personal reason the *chikh* did not want another *zamar*, and that was that. He was an expert on his instrument, and he played it in every conceivable manner: standing, seated, while dancing, with horns, without, in company with drums and vocal chorus, and as a solo. He insisted on playing it even when I asked him not to. Within two hours my principal problem was to make him stop playing it, because its sound covered that of the other instruments to such an extent that there was a danger of monotony in sonorous effect. I finally seated him ten or twelve yards away from the other musicians. He went on playing, his cheeks puffed out like balloons, sitting all alone under an orange tree, happily unaware that his music was not being recorded.

One very good reason why I wanted to cut out the *zamar* was the presence among the players of an admirable musician named Boujemaa ben Mimoun, one of the few North African instrumentalists I have seen who had an understanding of the concept of personal expression in interpretation. His instrument was the *qsbah*, the long reed flute with the low register, common in the Sahara of southern Algeria but not generally used in most parts of Morocco. I had been trying to get a *qsbah* solo ever since I had found a group of Rhmara musicians in Tetuan. The Rhmara had agreed to do it, but their technique was indifferent and their sound was not at all what I had hoped for. Again I tried at Einzoren, and got good results musically, but once more not in the deep octave, which because of the demands it makes on breath control is the most difficult register to manage.

When I drew ben Mimoun aside and asked him if he would be willing to play a solo, he was perplexed. He wanted to please me, but as he said, "How is anybody going to know what the qsbah is saying all by itself, unless there is somebody to sing the words?" The *chikh* saw us conferring together and came over to investigate. When he heard my request, he immediately proclaimed that the thing was impossible. Ben Mimoun hastily agreed with him. I continued to record, but clandestinely carried my problem to the caid of the village from which the *imdyazen* had been recruited. He was sitting, smoking kif with some other notables in a small pergola nearby. He seemed to think that a *qsbah* could play alone if it were really necessary. I assured him that it was, that the American government wished it. After a certain length of time spent in discussion, during which Mohammed Larbi passed out large quantities of kif to everyone, the experiment was made. The *chikh* saved face by insisting that two versions of each number be made – one for *qsbah* solo and one with sung text. I was delighted with the results. The solos are among the very best things in the collection. One called "Reh dial Beni Bouhiya" is particularly beautiful. In a landscape of immensity and desolation it is a moving thing to come upon a lone camel driver, sitting beside his fire at night while the camels sleep, and listen for a long time to the querulous, hesitant cadences of the qsbah. The music, more than any other I know, most completely expresses the essence of solitude. "Reh dial Beni Bouhiya" is a perfect example of the genre. Ben Mimoun looked unhappy while he played, because there was a tension in the air caused by general disapproval of my procedure. Everyone sat quietly, however, until he had finished.

After that they went back to ensemble playing and dancing. The kif had sharpened not only their sense of rhythm but their appetites as well, and I could see that we had come to the end of the session. As the drummers frantically leapt about, nearly tripping over the microphone cable, a tall man in a fat turban approached the microphone and began to shout directly into it. "It's a dedication," explained the caid. First there was praise of the Sultan, Mohammed Khamiss, as well as of his two sons, Prince Moulay Hassan and Prince Moulay Abdallah. After that came our friend the Governor of Alhucemas Province (because in the 1958 Riffian war of dissidence he found a solution which pleased nearly everybody), and finally, with the highest enthusiasm, came a glorification of the Algerian fighters who are being slaughtered by the French next door, may Allah help them. (Drums and shouting, and the bull's horns pointing toward the sky, spouting wild sound.) We drank far too much tea and got back here to Nador too late to eat in the juke box restaurant on stilts, so we opened some baked beans and ate them in the filth and squalor of my room.

SEPTEMBER 10

MOHAMMED LARBI is still fairly ill as a result of his experience in Alhucemas; his liver is not functioning properly, and he is trying to remedy it by doubling the amount of kif he smokes. The device is not working. It does, however, have one advantage: the stink of urine in the corridor is somewhat tempered by the overpowering but cleaner smell of burning kif, particularly if he leaves his door open, a habit I am trying to encourage. He

lies in his room all day on the bed in an intense stupor, somewhere above the stratosphere, with the radio tuned constantly
into either Cairo or Damascus. We cook breakfast and supper in
my room, which gradually has come to look like a stall in any
Moroccan joteya, with the most diverse objects covering every
square foot of floor space. The only way I can get out of bed is
to climb over the footboard and land in front of the *lavabo*. Each
day several of the bright-eyed Riffian proprietresses come and
look in happily, saying: "We don't have to make up the room
today, either?" The bed has never yet been made, and the floor
never swept; I don't want anyone in the room.

This morning Mohammed Larbi's sickness put him in mind
of the time his stepmother tried to poison him. This is a favorite
story of his which he recounts often and graphically. It seems to
have been a traumatic experience for him, and this is scarcely
surprising. As a result of it he walked out the door of his home
and remained in hiding from his family for more than five years.
It is merely incidental that during that time he married two former prostitutes; they were the only girls he knew personally. All
others were potential poisoners. To him they still are; his fulmi-
nations against human females are hair-raising.

It appears that his mother left his father when the latter took
a fourth wife, because although she had put up with the other
two, she did not want to live in the house with the latest addition. So she packed up and went back to Tcharhanem where
she had a little mud hut with nothing in it but a straw pallet
and some earthenware pots. Mohammed Larbi stayed on with
his father and the other wives. The new one, being the youngest, tried to get him into bed with her while his father was away
from the house, and being a normally moral young man he
indignantly refused. The girl was then overcome by fear that he
might talk, and so she decided to get rid of him. Soon after,
she pretended that something had gone wrong with the lunch,
and that she would have to cook it again. It was half past four
in the afternoon before she appeared with Mohammed Larbi's
food. She was counting, and correctly, on his being more than

ordinarily hungry. However, while he was wolfing his meal he caught sight of a bit of thread sticking out of the meat in the middle of the tajine. He pulled on it to no avail, and finally bit into the meat. It was only then that it occurred to him what the string might mean, and he ripped open the meat with his fingers, to find that a small inner pocket of meat enclosing various powders and other things had been sewn into the larger piece. He also discovered that he had eaten a certain amount of that pocket and its contents. He said nothing, scrambled up off the floor and ran out of the house, and to this day he has never been back there, although subsequently he did manage to persuade his father to get rid of that particular wife.

The "other things" in the food, in addition to the assorted drugs, were, by his reluctant admission, powdered fingernails and finely cut hair – pubic hair, he maintains – along with bits of excrement from various small creatures. "Like what?" I wanted to know. "Like bats, mice, lizards, owls . . . how should I know what women find to feed to men?" he cried aggrievedly. At the end of a month his skin began to slough off, and one arm turned bluish purple. That is usual; I have seen it on occasion. It is also considered a good sign; it means that the poison is "coming out." The consensus of opinion is that if it stays in, there is not much that anyone can do in the way of finding an antidote. The poisons are provided by professionals; Larache is said to be a good place to go if you are interested in working magic on somebody. You are certain to come back with something efficacious.

Every Moroccan male has a horror of *tseuheur*. Many of them, like Mohammed Larbi, will not eat any food to which a Moslem woman has had access beforehand, unless it be his mother or sister, or, if he really trusts her, his wife. But too often it is the wife of whom he must be the most careful. She uses *tseuheur* to make him malleable and suggestible. It may take many months, or even several years, but the drugs are reliable. Often it is the central nervous system which is attacked. Blindness, paralysis, imbecility or dementia may occur, although by that time the wife probably has gone off to another part of the country. If the husband dies, there is no investigation. His hour has come, nothing more. Even though the practice of magic is a punishable offense, in the unlikely event that it can be proven, hundreds of thousands of men live in daily dread of it. Fortunately Mohammed Larbi is sure of his present wife; he beats her up regularly and she is terrified of him. "She'll never try to give me *tseuheur*," he boasts. "I'd kill her before she had it half made." This story is always essentially the same, but at each telling I gather a few more descriptive details.

"That's why I can't drink any more," he laments. "It's the *tseuheur* still in there somewhere, and it turns the drink to poison."

"It's the kif," I tell him.

SEPTEMBER 13

THE COUGH that began at Ketama is still with me. The dry air at Alhucemas helped to keep it somewhat in abeyance; the conditions here in the Hotel Mokhtar seem to aggravate it. But now it's too late. We've stayed too long and I feel feverish.

SEPTEMBER 15

TWO DAYS LATER. Still in bed but much better. Christopher is disgusted with the situation and Mohammed Larbi is in a state of advanced disintegration. The idea of going back to Midar does not bother me so much as knowing that after that we shall have to return here to Nador once again. The pail of dark water provided for us by the women, out of which I have been filling empty wine bottles and adding Halazone tablets to them so we could have some kind of water to drink, proved to have a large, indescribably filthy cleaning rag buried in the silt at the bottom. I discovered it only this morning when all the water had been drunk. At that moment I wanted more than anything merely to escape from here. During lunch I said tentatively, "What do you think of going east, soon?" Christopher thought well of the idea, and so did Mohammed Larbi. I have renounced Temsaman, the Beni Touzine and the Ait Ulixxek.

OUJDA, SEPTEMBER 17

EVEN THE WEATHER seemed brighter when we had left Nador behind and were hurrying toward the Algerian border. We crossed the chastened, dry-weather Oued Moulouya and the flat rich farmlands north of the Zegzel country where the Beni Snassen live. It was getting dark as we went through Berkane, new and resplendent. The town was full of people, palms and fluorescent lights. After Nador it looked like Hong Kong; but we decided not to stop, because we wanted to get to Oujda in time to have dinner at the hotel – that is, if the hotel was still functioning.

About seven o'clock we saw the lights of Martimprey spread out ahead, perhaps twenty miles away, slightly below us. While we were still looking out across the plain, three flares exploded overhead and sailed slowly earthward. Very strong searchlight beams began to revolve, projected from behind the mountains in Algeria. There was a turn-off before Martimprey; we got onto the Saidia road just south of the town. That avoided possible difficulties with the authorities, for Martimprey is literally on the frontier, and is little more than a military headquarters these days. On this road there was a certain small amount of traffic. About every ten minutes we met a car coming toward us. Ahead there was a nervous driver who steadfastly refused to let us pass him. But when Christopher slowed down, in order to let him get well ahead of us, he slowed down too; there was no way of not being directly behind him. In exasperation Christopher finally drew up beside the road and stopped, saying, "I want to see a little of this war, anyway. Let's watch awhile." The red flares illumined the mountainsides to the east, and the sharp beams of blue light intersected each other at varying angles. It was completely silent; there were not even any crickets. But the other car had stopped too, perhaps five hundred feet ahead of us, and soon we saw a figure approaching. Mohammed Larbi whispered: "If he asks questions, just answer them. He has a pistol." "How do you know?" I countered, but he did not reply. Christopher had turned off the headlights and the road was very dark, so we were not able to see the man's face until he had come right up to us.

"*Vous êtes en panne?*" he inquired, looking in through the front window like a customs inspector. In the reflection from the dashboard light I could see that he was young and well-dressed. He made a swift examination of the interior by turning his head slowly from one side to the other. The searchlights continued to move across the sky. We said we were only watching, as though we were in a shop where we didn't want to buy anything. "I see," he said presently. "I thought maybe you were in trouble." We thanked him. "Not at all," he said lightly, and he went back into the darkness. A minute or two later we heard the door of his car shut, but the motor did not start up. We waited another ten minutes or so; then Christopher turned on the headlights and the motor. The other car did likewise, started up and kept ahead of us all the way to Oujda. Before we got to the center it turned down a side street and disappeared.

I had been afraid that with the Algerian border closed, the *raison d'être* of the Hotel Terminus would be gone, and it might no longer exist. It is open as usual, but its prices are much higher and the food has deteriorated. What the food now lacks in quality the service compensates for in pretentiousness. Dinner was served outdoors under the palms, around a large circular basin of water. The popping of corks punctuated the sequences of French conversation. Suddenly there was a very loud explosion; the ground under my feet shuddered a little with the force of it. No one seemed to have noticed; the relaxed monotone of words and laughter continued as before. Within the minute there was another boom, somewhat less strong but still powerful. When the waiter came up I questioned him.

"It's the bombardments in the Tlemcen sector," he said. "*Un engagement.* It's been going on for the past two nights.

Sometimes it's quiet for a week or so, sometimes it's very active." During dessert there was a long string of machine-gun fire not more than half a mile distant – in Oujda itself. "What's that?" I demanded. The waiter's face did not change. "I didn't hear anything," he said. All kinds of things happen in Oujda nowadays, and no one asks any questions.

This was the night De Gaulle was to make his long-awaited "peace" offer to the F.L.N. via the radio. Out of idle curiosity, we went immediately upstairs after eating to listen to it. While the General intoned his pious-sounding syllables the deep-toned explosions continued outside, sometimes like nearby thunder and sometimes quite recognizably bombs. Mohammed Larbi sat quietly, filling empty cigarette papers with kif and tamping them down before closing the ends. Now and then he demanded: "What's he saying?" (for he has never learned French), and each time he made the query I quickly said: "*Reh.*" (Wind.) Christopher was annoyed with both of us. He has never been violently partisan in the Algerian dispute, because he is willing to credit the French with a modicum of good will. In order not to disturb his listening, I went to stand on the balcony, where I could hear the bombs instead of the words. There was no hypocrisy in their sound, no difference between what they meant and what they said, which was: death to Algerians.

I wondered how many millions of Moslems in North Africa were hearing the radio words at that instant, and imagined the epithets of contempt and hatred coming from their lips as they listened. "*Zbil!*" "*Jiffa!*" "*Kharra!*" "*Ouild d'l qhaba!*" "*Inaal dinou!*" "*El khannez!*" When the General had finished his monologue, Christopher said sadly: "I only hope they believe him." I didn't think there was much danger of that, so I said nothing. The noise from the front kept going until a little after midnight. I felt feverish again, and I had to hunt for my clinical thermometer. It registered a little over 39 degrees. "Multiply by one point eight and add thirty-two. A hundred and two point two. My God! I'm sick."

"I've got to go to bed," I announced.

I STAYED IN BED yesterday morning. About three in the afternoon I got up long enough to drive to the governor's office. He too was in Meknès with the Sultan, and his katib was politely uncooperative. His jurisdiction extended to the Beni Snassen, he agreed, but the truth was that the Beni Snassen had absolutely no music; in fact, he declared, they hire their musicians from the Beni Uriaghel when they need music. Nothing. And Figuig? I suggested. "There is no music in Figuig," he said flatly. "You can go. But you will get no music. I guarantee you that." I understood that he meant he would see to it that we got none. The anger was beginning to boil up inside me, and I thought it more prudent to get out of his office quickly. I thanked him and went back to bed.

He is not an unusual type, the partially educated young Moroccan for whom material progress has become such an important symbol that he would be willing to sacrifice the religion, culture, happiness, and even the lives of his compatriots in order to achieve even a modicum of it. Few of them are as frank about their convictions as the official in Fez who told me, "I detest all folk music, and particularly ours here in Morocco. It sounds like the noises made by savages. Why should I help you to export a thing which we are trying to destroy? You are looking for tribal music. There are no more tribes. We have dissolved them. So the word means nothing. And there never was any tribal music anyway – only noise. *Non, monsieur*, I am not in accord with your project." In reality, the present government's policy is far less extreme than this man's opinion. The music itself has not been much tampered with – only the lyrics, which are now indoctrinated with patriotic sentiments. Practically all large official celebrations are attended by groups of folk musicians from all over the country; their travel and living expenses are paid by the government, and they perform before large audiences. As a result the performing style is becoming slick, and the extended forms are disappearing in favor of truncated versions which are devoid of musical sense.

OUJDA, SEPTEMBER 20

I HAVE LAIN in bed for the past three days, feverish and depressed, having lost the Beni Snassen as well as the others. Now all that remains open to me in the way of Riffian music is that of the Gzennaia. They live in the Province of Taza, and it will probably be difficult to get to them because of the roads.

During the day there seems to be no sound from the front, but at night the bombardments begin, shortly after dark, and continue for three or four hours. Mohammed Larbi refuses to go out of the hotel; he claims Oujda is a dangerous place these days. According to him, there are ambushes and executions daily. I suspect that most of the explosions we hear during the day are fireworks celebrating the beginning of Mouloud, but I agree that some of the sounds are hard to explain away in that manner. In any case, the city is too close to the border to be restful. All I want is to be well enough to leave for Taza.

TAZA, SEPTEMBER 22

YESTERDAY MORNING I had no fever at all, so in spite of feeling a little shaky, I got up and packed, and we set out on the road once more. It was a cool, sunny morning when we left. As we got into the desert beyond El Ayoun, however, the heat waves began to dance on the horizon. We ate in a wheatfield outside Taourirt. Passers-by stopped under the tamarisk trees and sat down to watch us. When we got back into the car there was a struggle going on among several of them for possession of the empty tins and bottles we had left.

By the time we arrived in Taza it was nearly sunset, and I was ready again for bed. But since the government buildings had not yet shut for the night I decided to try and see the governor while I was still up and walking around. I had a feeling that the fever had returned. I went straight to the hotel from there to get into bed, and I have not yet got out of it, so it is just as well that I stayed up an extra hour and saw the *katib*. The governor, not surprisingly, was in Meknès with the Sultan.

This *katib* was a young intellectual with thick-lensed glasses. He made it clear that he thought my project an absurdity, but he did not openly express disapproval. He even went through the motions of telephoning all the way to Aknoul to a subordinate up there in the mountains.

"I see, I see," he said presently. "He died last year. Ah, yes. Too bad. And Tizi Ouzli?" he added, as I gestured and stage-whispered to him. "Nothing there, either. I see." He listened awhile, commenting in monosyllables from time to time, then finally thanked his informant and hung up.

"The last *chikh* in Aknoul died last summer. He was an old man. There is no music in the region. In Tizi Ouzli the people won't come out. When the Sultan went through, the women refused to leave their houses to sing for him. So you see" – he smiled, spreading his hands out, palms up – "it will not be possible with the Gzennaia."

I sat looking at him while he spoke, already aware of what he was going to report, letting fragments of thoughts flit through my tired head. How they mistrust and fear the Riffians! But how naive this one is to admit openly that the alienation is so great! Were the women punished? And I remembered a remark a Riffian had once made to me, "You have your Negroes in America, and Morocco has us."

"End of the Rif," I said sadly to Christopher.

The young *katib* pointed to the wall map behind his desk. "In the Middle Atlas, on the other hand, I can arrange something for you. Within a very few days, if you like. The Ait Ouaraine."

"Yes, I should like it very much," I told him.

"Come, please, tomorrow morning at ten o'clock."

"Thank you," we said.

I came back here to the Hôtel Guillaume Tell and got into bed. The room is not made up here, either, but there is plenty of space in it and my meals are brought up on a tray, so it is not important. Yesterday Christopher and Mohammed Larbi made contact in the street with a group of professional musicians who agreed to record today. Their ensemble consisted of three *rhaitas*, four *tbola* (beaten with sticks) and eight rifles. The first price asked was high; then it was explained that if the rifles were not to be fired during the playing the cost would be cut in half. The agreement reached provided that only the *rhaitas* and tbola would perform.

Mohammed Larbi's excessive consumption of kif has given him a serious chronic liver disorder; he feels ill most of the time. Last night he went out for a walk after dinner. At the end of an hour he came in, his expression more determined than usual, and announced to us: "I'm finished with kif." Christopher laughed derisively. To implement his words, Mohammed Larbi tossed both his *naboula*, bulging with kif, and his cherished pipe, on my bed, saying, "Keep all this. You can have it. I don't want to see any of it again." But this morning before breakfast he went out and bought a fifth of Scotch, which he sampled before his morning coffee. When he came into my room later to pack up the recording equipment, he had the bottle with him, and Christopher made loud fun of him.

"*O chnou brhitsi?*" he cried indignantly. "I'm not smoking kif any more. Do you expect me to leave my poor head empty?" This amused Christopher and depressed me. I foresee difficulties with a belligerent Mohammed Larbi. Kif keeps men quiet and vegetative; alcohol sends them out to break shop windows. In Mohammed Larbi's case it often means a fight with a policeman. I watched with misgivings as he prepared to go out.

This was the first time any recording had been done in my absence. But it all went smoothly, said Christopher on their return. There was a slight altercation at the moment of payment, because in spite of the agreement by which the men were not to discharge their rifles, they had not been able to resist participating, so that at three separate points in the music they fired them off, all eight of them, and simultaneously. At the end they presented a bill for twenty-four cartridges, which Mohammed Larbi, by then well fortified with White Label, steadfastly refused to pay. "All right. Good-bye," they said, and they went happily off to play at a wedding in a nearby village.

SEPTEMBER 22

THE WHISKEY HAS done its work, but in a fashion I had not expected. This evening, when the bottle was nearly empty, Mohammed Larbi spent two hours trying to telephone his wife in Tangier. Finally he got the proprietor of a grocery near his house to go and fetch her, and had a stormy conversation with her for five minutes. I could hear him bellowing from where I lay, at the other end of the hotel. When he came into my room he looked maniacal.

"I've heard my wife's voice!" he shouted. "Now I've got to see her. She may have somebody else. I'm going tonight. I'll get there by tomorrow night."

"You're walking out on your job?"

"I'm going to see my wife!" he cried, even louder, as though I had not understood. "I have to do that, don't I?"

"You're going to leave me here, sick in bed?"

He hesitated only an instant. "Christopher knows how to take care of you. Besides, you're not sick. You just have a fever. I'll give you the grocer's number, and you telephone me when you get to Fez. I'll see you in a week or ten days. In Fez."

"All right," I said, without any intention of calling him. If he is going to be on whiskey, it would be better not to have him along, in any case.

And so now I have at least a pound of very strong kif among my possessions. In another two or three days I should be well enough to go up to Tahala and capture the Ait Ouaraine. The Rif is finished, and I managed to record only in two places.

MADEIRA

HOLIDAY, SEPTEMBER 1960

W HEN I FIRST thought of visiting Madeira I was advised by my English friends to reconsider. "You'll loathe it," they told me. "No character whatever."

"Dreary, stuffy little place."

"Nobody goes there but *very* elderly ladies."

"Madeira! Whatever for?"

"I had a great aunt who used to go religiously. I believe the poor old thing eventually died out there."

"It's the absolute end!"

This unanimity of adverse opinion might have dissuaded me had I not already made up my mind that I was going there no matter what; besides, it turned out each time that my informant had not actually been there, but was expressing an opinion prevalent nowadays in literary London.

I had always felt I should like Madeira, and so I came, and was glad I did. Their descriptions now strike me as completely unreal; by assessing the place in terms of British tourists, it was as if they had insisted that New York's streets are empty save for Chinese, or that California consisted solely of film studios. Madeira has plenty of character, even though it is not precisely the character ascribed to it by the tourist brochures. "Ideal year-round climate." "Madeira rises out of the Atlantic like some fantastic emerald out of an incredible waste of lapis lazuli."

(I believe similar visions are not uncommon with the peculiar narcotic mescaline, but I doubt there is a pill which can make the winter climate seem ideal.)

It's true that the cliffs rise spectacularly from the depths of the Atlantic. Madeira is a country of about 285 square miles which is literally one huge volcanic rock surrounded by the sea. The sea air is all-pervasive; even in the quiet valleys of the interior there is often the unmistakable smell of the salt water. You cannot reach the island except by ship; it lies 570 miles southwest of Lisbon, and 320 miles due west of the coast of Morocco. There is no airstrip, and the seaplane service was discontinued in 1958.

Four hundred years ago Camoëns, the Portuguese poet, described the place as being "*do mundo a derradeira*" (at the end of the world), and there are occasions now when it gives the same impression, particularly on a sunless day when the rough Atlantic pounds against it and the tops of the perpendicular cliffs are smothered in low-flying clouds. It is a rough, uncomfortable country with a relatively mild climate and a strong hybrid people. The original Portuguese stock was soon reinforced by Italian, Spanish and Dutch settlers; later came Moslem and Jewish refugees from Christian Spain, and finally Negroes from the African mainland, who were brought in as slaves to work the sugar plantations. The present population is an undifferentiated amalgam of these various strains. A hardy race of men, accustomed to dealing with wind and waves, but not capable of understanding the twentieth-century mentality of visitors who find such a race an admirable phenomenon. They see no advantage in their own extraordinary sturdiness – only misfortune in the conditions that made it necessary for them to develop it.

A small conversation I had during my first visit has remained in my mind. I was enthusing to a Madeiran about the charm of the country. I remarked that he didn't know how lucky he was to live in such a delightful spot, and he said quietly: "Yes. A bird can light in the courtyard of a prison and fly away again without ever knowing where it has been."

In the park of Funchal's Quinta Vigia there are little signs that read: RESPECT THE PLANTS. It would be hard not to. Madeira is a land where you are very conscious of the vegetable world around you. Plants grow quickly in the mild, humid air. As you drive through the countryside you feel that every acre at some point in the past must have been laboriously landscaped; it is hard to believe that such a vast rock garden could have come into existence without human planning.

Where the land is worked, whole mountain slopes have been transformed by terracing. Often each level has its tiny channel of water, fed by the nearest *levada*. The *levadas* are a complicated network of irrigation canals that guide the valuable rainwater down from the peaks to the sea. The average *levada* is not more than three feet wide and two feet deep, but the water in it is so clear and cold that you are tempted to drink it. The canal project was begun in 1836 and is still going on; at present there are 435 miles of it, every stone hewn and laid by hand.

But when the day is finished and the laborer goes home, instead of reading the paper he scratches around in his garden. There is no dwelling too miserable to have its little flower plots, its trellises and arbors. Every window has its flower box, the smallest courtyard is crowded with palms and philodendron, the most wretched shack stands in the midst of blossoming vines and banana plants. Often the edges of the road in the remote country have been planted with ivy, or lilies, or fern. Sometimes grapevines are trained in arbors across the highway so that wayfarers may walk comfortably in the shade. In the center of Funchal there are three deep ravines where, in the rainy season, wild torrents roar down from above, on their way to the ocean. These have been transformed into tunnels by planting bougain-villaeas and other flowering shrubs and stretching them from bank to bank, so that from the bridges, as you look up or down a ravine, nothing is visible of it, but the roof of the tunnel – a long prospect of solid flowers. Twenty feet below, the water rushes by.

When the Portuguese first discovered Madeira more than 600 years ago its slopes were entirely covered with virgin forest.

There was no sign that a human being had ever set foot on it. The density of the vegetation was such that the colonists decided to burn everything. This proved to be a poor idea, since the resulting holocaust forced them to put to sea again. It is said to have been seven years before the fire finally burned itself out, and the primeval forest was almost completely destroyed (a few patches of it still exist in the northern part of the island). But during the ensuing centuries the fertile soil and the peculiar climatic conditions have managed to make an impressive second growth.

Although the original flora of the island was not specifically tropical, a great many exotic trees and flowers from Portugal's African colonies grow well here, not because the temperature ever rises very high, but because it never sinks very low.

Where the virgin forest was not razed, there are such native juxtapositions as tree ferns and maples, or chestnut trees and bamboo; in the towns there are the imported champac, jacaranda and kapok trees.

In one respect my London friends were right: most of the visitors to the island are British. They arrive in Funchal on British ships and go directly to the big British-run hotels in the suburbs, where they remain a week or two – possibly three – but rarely longer, and where, in theory, they pass their time playing tennis or golf, and swimming in one of the big pools (since beaches are nonexistent). But only if they are lucky with the weather, which they generally are not, since most of them come in the winter when it rains. My advice to Americans is to visit Madeira in the dry season, which is the summer, or they will be bitterly disappointed.

However, people who live in the British Isles are appreciative of an occasional half hour of sun or even of a cloudy day when no rain falls and this explains why they continue to use the island as a winter resort.

The first time I landed in Funchal not having been able to get previous information about any other kind of establishment, I went along with the British to one of these enormous institutions. It was quiet, comfortable and depressing like a sanatorium. I had to wear my coat in the bedroom because there was no heat, it is true. (But then, Americans have to wear extra clothing indoors during the winter in England too, if they want to be warm enough.) Through the tiny meshes of the screens in my windows I had a dim panorama of terraced gardens with palms, bananas and papayas rising above occasional villas with red tile roofs and beyond, the gigantic gray backdrop of nearby mountains whose peaks were permanently hidden by clouds. Several times each day a thin curtain of rain would unroll from the sky above the mountains and softly advance toward me. By the time it had reached the hotel a shaft of pale sunlight would already be illuminating some distant cliff up on the heights, and the English guests in their wet mackintoshes would be atwitter down in the drenched garden.

"I really think we shall have some sun."

"Isn't it lovely?"

"*Much* nicer than yesterday." I never ceased to marvel at their pleasure in what seemed a show of unmitigatedly foul weather.

It was the monotony of the "English" meals which finally decided me to change living quarters. I moved into town to a Portuguese hotel with a brazenly Portuguese bill-of-fare, and never looked back with longing on the roast beef and Yorkshire pudding. There was no heat here, either, but then, if you are getting a room and three good meals for two dollars and a half a day, you don't expect *grand luxe*.

Fashions in drink come and go like fashions in everything else; for the past few decades sweet wines have not been much in favor. I, for instance, had drunk very little port before living in Portugal; and had scarcely tasted Madeira until I came here. Surprisingly enough, good Sercial, which can be had in any can-tina of Funchal, is almost as dry as dry sherry. I don't remember ever having had Sercial in the United States, but I should think it could have considerable popularity there. Its texture gives an indefinable impression of luxury.

All the Madeira wines have this quality to some extent, but the Malmsey, Boal and even the Verdelho are too sweet to suit my American taste. Sercial became my password in the cafés and cantinas of Funchal. Later in Lisbon I was indignant when I couldn't get it in an ordinary bar and was forced to settle for *vinho verde*. Now I am back in Funchal once again, and this time I appreciate the luxury of finding it at the humblest wine counter.

The simplest way for the visitor to get an exact idea of the range of bouquet and body in Madeira wines is for him to visit the *armazem* of one of the large export firms in Funchal. There he can spend a pleasant hour sitting at a bar in a roomful of old casks, sampling century-old vintages and having the technique of preparing each variety described to him by a barman who keeps no tab since all drinks are on the house.

It was mid-afternoon, and I was leaning against a haystack looking westward. No matter in which direction you look, the landscape at Santana is hard to believe. It is as if a nineteenth century painter with a taste for the baroque had invented a countryside to suit his own personal fantasy. Worked into the canvas are pictorial details of a "poetic" variety, which such a man would have felt belonged there: an Alpine background with a high waterfall, meadows of an unlikely green, carpeted in patches with unnecessarily bright flowers and coquettish little thatched cottages, their steep roofs reaching to the ground, smothered in masses of rambler roses. It is the sort of picture that used to adorn the grocer's calendar. I accepted it because I stood in the middle of it.

To my right stretched an unending expanse of poster-blue sea, silent and motionless because it was some thirteen hundred feet below. From the map I had gathered that Santana was on the coast, and so it is, but at the top of a cliff that nobody ever seems to climb up and down. The cobbled road leading back to the village was about two feet wide, with moss and tiny flowers growing between its stones. Soon a barefoot peasant appeared wearing the hand-made, archaic-looking costume fitting to the general décor, and I called down to him for a match. He looked up, smiled, and said: "I have none, but I'll go back and get you some." Then he turned and went back the way he had just come.

It happened so quickly that my reaction was a second late. "No, no, no! Don't bother!" I shouted. He continued on his way up to the village.

In ten or fifteen minutes he reappeared at the top of the hill, running. I went to meet him. Breathless and still smiling, he held out the box of matches he had just bought and, with a curious mixture of pride and reserve, presented it to me as if it were a valuable gift. I accepted it in the same spirit. We lighted cigarettes, and I looked at him. He was probably in his thirties, with unruly hair and wide-apart eyes. There was a definite difference between this face and the kind of faces I was used to seeing. It was as if this one had been made by hand, the others mass-produced. Even as this thought occurred to me I was aware of my own weakness for romanticizing about unevolved people. But this time I quickly decided I was right: here was the first Madeiran peasant I had spoken with, and even before meeting me he had gone far out of his way to be friendly. It seemed a good beginning.

Funchal, where I had lived for a month, was four hours away by bus. I inquired if he knew the city, and regretted my question. I might as well have asked if he had been to New York. Funchal was a long way off, he explained, and he had never had the occasion to make the trip. However, he added, there were many people in the village who had been there. Then he wanted to know if I was from Lisbon. No, I said: America. Ah, he sighed, smoking thoughtfully. He had a cousin who had sought refuge in America – Venezuela, to be exact. (There is a good deal of emigration from Madeira to Brazil, Venezuela and Mexico, as well as a smaller amount to the United States, and this change of homeland is often referred to as "seeking refuge". The refuge is purely economic, but they don't specify that. It seemed there was also a lady from America who had been in Santana earlier in the year. She had come back to visit, and of course had brought a great deal of money.

"Oh?" I said.

"Of course. If she hadn't got the money she couldn't have come all the way back to Madeira." He stood with his legs far apart, digging his bare toes into the soft black earth beside the path. "Tell me," he said suddenly. "How does it happen that it's so easy to make money in America?"

"It isn't," I assured him. "It's very difficult."

He shook his head. "But if you put aside a certain amount of money each year, you have enough to pay for the ship. And in Madeira, even if you save up two thousand, five thousand, even ten thousand escudos, it still isn't enough to pay for a trip to America and back. Why is that?"

In the air was the sound of many songbirds: an invisible brook murmured nearby. It was impossible to give him a satisfactory explanation. I shrugged, and said: "The exchange," doubting that this would satisfy him.

His expression became even more serious. "The exchange. Of course." We had begun to walk slowly down the road, and we stopped in front of the first cottage. I asked him how long the thatch lasted. Three or four years, he told me, adding that when it began to leak the owner called in his neighbors to help him repair it. "And do they always come?" I inquired.

His eyes grew large with surprise. "Of course they always come!" he exclaimed.

A refusal to help in such work is obviously unthinkable. There was the lowing of a cow nearby, but no cow was visible. I held out my box of State Express to him, and he took another cigarette.

"These are not made in Madeira. They're from Portugal, aren't they?"

"No, from England. I got them on the ship from Lisbon."

"Is your father in Lisbon?"

"No, no. My father is in America."

"But it was your father who taught you to speak Portuguese."

It was too much work to explain that not only was my father not Portuguese but that in any case I was not speaking Portuguese. So I said, "Yes". (I had been through this language routine before. I had discovered that most Portuguese-speaking people understood Spanish perfectly well; I had also found that if I listened carefully I understood Portuguese. Our dialogues, then, had always been in two distinct languages, with no difficulties on either side. The educated people were aware of this, but the rustics, often illiterate, believed I was speaking a dialectal Portuguese.)

The cow lowed again; she seemed practically beside us, but there was still no sign of her. "Where *is* that cow?" I demanded. He laughed. "In her house," he replied, indicating a small cottage across the road. And she was there, and it was one of the curiosities of the country – the fact that the Madeirans keep their cattle in individual animal-sized dwellings rather than allowing them to graze the dangerous mountain-side pastures. Each animal spends its life in its own house which fits over it like the cover on a dish. You can hear and smell them, but you are not likely to see them.

"You're right," I said, retrieving a subject of conversation which had been discarded, but which I felt still might prove to have life in it. "No one can save enough money for the round-trip voyage to America." This, if not quite true, was near enough, since among those who leave Madeira behind, the majority either have their passage paid for by the company about to employ them, or are assisted by relatives already established in the New World.

"No, it is not possible," he sighed. Then he stopped and stood very straight.

"Welcome to Santana," he told me.

"Good-by." We shook hands and he went on his way down the cobbled lane.

IN WINTER Funchal has many rainy nights. Even in good weather the town is deserted by midnight. This means that you can stand for an hour on the main street and not see a single car go by. When the fine rain sweeps in from the sea and the wet wind rushes around corners, outdoor activity is reduced to a minimum. I like to walk through the streets about twelve o'clock. It is like pacing round the deck of a ship during a storm after all the passengers have gone to bed. No one stands on the arched bridges over the *ribeiras*, even the Avenida Arriaga is empty save for the jacaranda trees that line its central walk, and to left and right up the crooked side streets the vistas are only of cobblestones glistening where the street lamps hit them. Everyone is at home with the blinds shut.

In a small city on a small island people behave. It would be hard to find a less criminal group than the Funchalenses. The size of the police force may have something to do with it; there is an army of them loose in the town at night. They loom up in the recessed doorways, solemn-faced figures in black, just standing, looking at the dead street. I come upon them conscientiously making their rounds along dark lanes in suburban valleys high up the face of the mountain. I see them standing in front of neighborhood chapels or sitting on stone benches in the dark, staring out over the rooftops. No delinquents roam the streets of Funchal. Apart from the police, there is no one at all.

I arrange my itinerary so that I can come out at least once upon the Praça do Municipio. Empty and lighted only by its own lamps, it is surely one of the most elegant little public squares in the world. The splendid asymmetrical building are whitewashed, trimmed with black stone, and the paving of the center is an abstract mosaic of black and white lava. Late at night, shining in the rain, the square has a dramatic and unorthodox beauty. I cross it slowly and plunge into the gloom of a side street. The clock in the cathedral rings an elaborate chime pattern every fifteen minutes. Sometimes, if I am walking along beside one of the *ribeiras*, the rushing of the water over the rocks down below will partially, but never completely, cover the sound of the chimes.

Or I go down to the Cais, the town's one pier, that is built out into very deep water. The Cais is where the passenger ship tenders tie up when they bring the visitors ashore, and it is a favorite strolling spot. Not so, of course, on rainy nights, when I have with me only the angry sound of the mid-ocean waves pounding on the steep beach of black stones that roll and strike against each other. Even out at the end of the long Cais I can hear the sullen rumble of the heavy stones rubbing together each time a wave hits the shore.

The land goes down steeply along this coast. A short distance out from the harbor the water is thirteen thousand feet deep. As one guidebook puts it: "The island is really the summit of a steep mountain." This unreassuring thought has sometimes occurred to me just as I was dropping off to sleep (leaving me with what I remember about the fate of Port Royal in Jamaica, when one night an earthquake knocked part of it into the sea). Then the crowing of a rooster would bring comforting images of farm life, or the familiar chime would ring out and remind me that the cathedral was begun in the late fifteenth century and that, after all, if the island of Madeira had not moved during all the intervening years it was not likely to do so now.

THIS MORNING in the office of the Delegação de Turismo a middle-aged Englishman with a very red face turned to me. "I say," he began, "do you speak English?" When I said I did, he went on, "I wish you'd explain to this charming young lady that we British don't come here to gad about the island. We come for sports. Now, I'm interested in bowling, myself, and I'm told there's a club here with facilities. Would you mind asking her about it? Thanks so much." The young lady's English was excellent but he was not trusting it. I got them together on the desired subject and quickly went out.

FEW ENGLISH visiting Madeira have any interest in the place itself. The inhabitants, except for servants and vendors, might as well not be there. The British sojourners are as external to the life of the place as the flower maids in "native" costume who sell orchids in front of the cathedral. Beyond certain material benefits their continued presence has brought the country, they have had little effect on the Madeirans.

How different the island would be today if all this time its tourists had been Americans! For Americans ask questions: How much? Why this? What's that? The ideas set in motion by their constant interrogations would probably have set in motion a social revolution long ago.

As it is, the old habitués find the island as it always was. Even the various antiquated means of transport have been retained for them: decorated oxsledges that drag along the streets of Funchal, hand-guided toboggans that slide down the face of the mountain, even hammocks from which the tourist can survey the country-side in comfort while his two husky bearers navigate the rough terrain. Go up to Monte and hire one of the toboggans at the top of the long, steep cobbled lane. The two men will run rapidly along beside you, exerting all their strength to hold the contrap-tion back as it gathers momentum, and straining like dray horses to pull it ahead along the flatter portions of the course.

When they are both streaming with sweat, ask them how they like their work. Probably they will be astonished that a for-eigner should be concerned; the ones I interrogated were, but they merely answered, "It's work like any other which is true, save that it is more strenuous than most, and no better paid. However, there is always the possibility of a one and six pence tip if the *senhor* is pleased."

As an "adjacent province" of Portugal, Madeira has been spared, along with the motherland, the accelerated life that so changed European countries which participated in World War II. Nor has there been any social ferment inside Portugal to upset the calm continuation of a nineteenth-century mode of life: there is only the desire of the populace to share what it con-siders to be the normal existence of its contemporaries. There is consequently a slight dissatisfaction with the status quo.

The other day during lunch at the Hotel Voga I looked up and recognized a man I had known ten years ago in Ceylon, not long after he had given up tea planting. "What are you doing here?" I demanded: had I run into him in Singapore or Hong Kong, or even Nairobi, I should have been so surprised, but here, I was, and I said so.

"I'm living here," he said, "and I expect to stay. Just a ques-tion of finding the right house. I'm seventy now and I want a quiet place." Certainly Madeira is a quiet place. It is too remote to feel the emotional impact of the world events, and too small to create much agitation of its own. Life on such an island is necessarily tranquil. But the Madeirans somehow manage to get a great deal of pleasure out of that life, in spite of the isolation of which they complain.

There came a holiday and all Funchal went to the mountain-side to celebrate. Here and there on the forested slopes, two or three thousand feet above the city, are several parks. One of these is a former private estate which is thrown open to the public on certain days. Here the largest crowd gathered. At noon there a procession of packed buses passes through the main street of Funchal. I got on one and joined the pilgrimage up and around the curves toward the heights. The last mile, being too steep, we had to walk. The roadside was lined with stalls offering food, drink and flowers. The crowd straggled upward, purchasing a little of everything, some playing tambourines and accordions. The park itself was splendid – a great bright cape of stairways and gardens and balustrades spread out across the lap of the mountain. I had the feeling that there were flowers everywhere: on the ground, in the trees, in the arms of the passers-by. Some thirty thousand people were in the park; it was a crowd bent on enjoying itself, full of high spirits. Each face looked entirely happy, and all of them, including the small children and those who had stopped too often at the rustic wine counters along the way, behaved in an exemplary fashion.

Obviously, there is no point in having a car in Madeira. The roads are few, narrow and tortuous, and you are content to leave the driving to men who have spent their lives navigating them. Most of the taxis are small modern sedans, but hedonists will spot a few old Packard touring cars, vintage of the mid-twenties, which, tops down, are ideal for mountain driving. At first I had intended to use one of these to take me to Santana, but then, having used buses for several short trips, I decided that buses were what I really wanted. They are comfortable and they run regularly to all corners of the island. Every vehicle is adorned with fresh flowers, usually roses and jasmine, all over the bus. When a lady of Madeira goes on a trip, it is practically inevitable that she will be handed at least one bouquet (often it is a spray of several dozen orchids) at the moment of departure; upon arriving she presents the flowers to those who meet her.

The Madeirans are fresh-air fiends. The only fault they ever have to find with the temperature is that it is too hot: this critical observation is forthcoming at all times, including mid-winter when no place could be considered hot. But being children of nature, they want to feel the air stirring around them, and so they open all the windows and the winds blow through the bus.

You are going across the island to the northern coast, to Faial or Santana. Within three minutes of leaving the bus station you begin a climb withich does not cease for almost two hours. Except for the heart of the city, Funchal is one vast mountain-side of terraced gardens, each with its little house. The few roads snake up the steep slope, and at each curve there is the brief vista upwards along an endless stairway for pedestrians, leading to the next curve above. At first, from certain bends in the road, you can look back down upon Funchal spread out along the water: its buildings are a little smaller at each glance, and the passenger ships in the harbor look increasingly like yachts as the Atlantic grows more vast, calm and blue.

The air has been getting constantly cooler; already it is weighted with the somber odor of the forests above – forests whose high trees, blocking the daylight, imprison a dank nocturnal chill. All at once the color goes out of the landscape. The bus has entered the shadow of that great bank of clouds that normally hides the mountaintops. You want to close the window beside you, but the others are taking such evident pleasure in the cold air and wet vegetable smells coming in that you resist.

As the bus swings around one of the hairpin curves, you look up ahead and see skeins of white mist entangled in the branches of the trees. Thick gusts of fog sweep past; the bus is pushing up the lower fringes of the cloud. You try to peer into the forest that you know is brushing past the window, but all you can see is the stone ditch full of swiftly running water and the lilies and ferns that skirt it. Whatever is beyond that is far away. And suddenly you are in the blind gray world of cloud. The crawling bus has its headlights on, but they do no good. The conversation, which has been desultory, now dies altogether, and for a moment there is only the sound of the old motor straining in low gear. Then, as if by common agreement, everyone begins to talk. It is too sad to be silent, moving through this dark place where everything is invisible. And on and on the bus goes, around and upward, as the air grows colder, until even a few of the Madeirans decide to close their windows.

It is only when you are above the tree line and the wind is roaring over the bare tops of the mountains that suddenly there is blinding sunlight overhead. Uncanny clouds are rising up from behind rocks, swiftly taking form before your eyes, and rushing down the mountainside into the abyss behind you. For a moment it looks like a very expensive production of *Götterdämmerung*. From here on the voyage is down and up, across valleys and along the edges of cliffs. You swing around a curve and are poised above a village some two thousand feet below. A half hour later the bus rocks through its main street; the church bell is clanging in the steeple as you bump across the sunlit *praça*. There are stops where it is so quiet that from your seat you hear the water gurgling in the *levada* beside the road. And when you finally arrive, you have a very clear sensation of being somewhere else, not so much in place as in time. For your sixty-two American cents you have traveled a long way back into the past. The birds are singing, people sit in groups beside the brooks weaving baskets out of willow branches, cows call from inside their little houses, and you realize that beyond a doubt you are there, a part of the picture on the calendar.

Soon, probably, you will be returning to Funchal, but that does not matter. You know now that such a place exists and that you can get back to it someday if you want to, and it is satisfying to have that certainty.

THE BALL AT SIDI HOSNI

KULCHUR #2, 1961

SIDI HOSNI, EL KASBAH, TANGIER

MRS. BARBARA WOOLWORTH HUTTON REQUESTS THE PLEASURE OF YOUR COMPANY FOR A BALL ON THE ROOF OF HER HOUSE IN THE KASBAH (WEATHER PERMITTING) AT 10:30 ON THE NIGHT OF THE TWENTY NINTH OF AUGUST. BLACK TIE. R.V.S.P. IN CASE OF WIND, YOUR HOSTESS REQUESTS YOU TO INDULGE HER BY COMING ANOTHER NIGHT.

INSTEAD OF WIND, the Strait of Gibraltar has provided a thick, cold fog for the evening. We have been invited for dinner on the Old Mountain. Some of the guests are served outdoors by the pool and are soaked by the condensing moisture that drips down on them from the trees above. A little before midnight about twenty of us start out, in a convoy of six cars, to drive down the mountain through the fog into Tangier. I am in my hostess' car and suggest a shortcut through Hasnona into the Casbah, so that we arrive before the others and have less difficulty finding space in the Plaza in front of the Sultan's palace, already jammed with scores of erratically parked cars and worried police. Our progress on foot through the ill-smelling alleys and down the broken stairways is slow, because it is difficult terrain for the ladies to navigate. Moroccans stand in the doorways of their tiny houses and shops and watch us file past, as if we were part of a parade.

As long as Tangier was international – that is, until 1955, when it was integrated with the rest of Morocco – there was no question of whether or not it was safe for Europeans to wander in the native quarter at night. Everyone went where he pleased at any hour, with no thought of danger. The reason for this utopian state of affairs was that it was impossible to get into or out of the city without thorough police and customs inspection, and this discouraged whatever criminal elements there were among the Moroccans (almost all of whom were members of the new French-created proletariat in Casablanca) from attempting to invade Tangier, the city of idle rich.

With the arrival of independence the local golden age was abruptly terminated. At the same time that servants began to grumble about working for seven or eight dollars a month, and started to ask for ten, or even fifteen, muggers appeared in the alleys of the Medina, intent upon relieving unwary Europeans of their wallets and handbags. Equally undesirable from the viewpoint of foreign residents was the emergence of a hitherto non-existent kind of Moroccan: the politically conscious, Marxist-orientated man in the street, in whose eyes those who live on their incomes are evildoers, and to whom all European residents in Morocco, with or without money, are by definition undesirables.

With this phenomenon in mind, many of those who planned to attend the Hutton ball have been concerned lest the police protection provided for prospective guests might prove insufficient, and lest "hoodlums" thus manage to molest them before they ever arrived at the house. But the police don't have the opportunity to earn this much extra money every night, so they are being very conscientious. This includes smiling now and then at the foreigners distastefully picking their way down the none-too-clean passageways. The address given in the invitation is erroneous: Derb Sidi Hosni is not in the Casbah, but well outside it, below the ramparts.

When we get down to Sidi Hosni, there is a crowd of Moroccans standing along the railing by the saint's tomb, watching what goes on below in front of the entrance to the house. We pass through a further cordon of police, have our names checked by a row of men at the door, and go in. Immediately we are presented to our hostess, who stands in a doorway at the top of a short flight of stairs. Beyond here, inside, are some two hundred guests amusing themselves, but the house is so designed that there are surprisingly few people in any one spot. This impression is confirmed when we begin to wander through the rooms. Some are completely empty; others have ten or fifteen people in them. There is a certain amount of movement en masse; groups of guests speaking Italian or French hurry by, in search of other groups. On a partially uncovered terrace overlooking a dark, well-lit patio there are thirty or forty people sitting at tables eating. Waiters rush in all directions.

We are greeted by a Spanish friend who has just got off the plane from Madrid. He has been up there seeing Sam Spiegel, for whom he has written a filmscript. I want to talk about the script, but Emilio is more interested in showing us a piece of red velvet which hangs on the wall of an inner room, and which is insured for a million dollars, so we go to look at that. When we get there I understand the detail about the insurance, for the cloth, originally the property of a certain maharajah, is decorated with a border about a foot wide which is embroidered with large pearls, rubies and emeralds. I examine it closely and announce that the center of one of the designs, a particularly large emerald, is missing. Jane, who has sat down at the base of the cloth among some pillows also sewn with pearls and sapphires, jumps up nervously and says: "Let's sit somewhere else." I have already recognized members of Tangier's secret police mingling with the guests.

Strains of Djibli music are coming from a nearby room. We go in that direction. On our way we meet an old Tangier resident who stops us and remarks: "It's a fine house, isn't it?" We agree. "It's the last of the great Moroccan houses. There'll never be another." (Every square inch of plaster in the house is hand-incized with lacelike arabesques.) "The plaster work alone," explains the old gentleman, "took a gang of workmen more than ten years to do. I used to come and watch them work. The old maalem was from

Jane Bowles (right) at a Tangier ball, with the Comtesse de Faille and Jay Haselwood, owner of the Parade Bar, an 'international Tangier' landmark

Fez. He's dead now, of course. They all are. Have you noticed the angle of the incisions? It changes gradually according to the height. Below eye-level they slant one way. At eye-level they're horizontal. At ten feet they slant a little the other way. Up there," he pointed to the top of the wall twenty-five feet above us, "the slant is very much accentuated. Nobody knows how to do it now." I say that is interesting, and that I had not known it. "Oh, yes," he says. "Otherwise you don't get the same illusion of depth all the way up. It's a beautiful house." Again we agree, and go into the room from which the native music is coming.

Among the mountains of cushions on the floor recline a dozen or so Moroccans in turbans and bdeyas. They are playing hand drums, tambourines, lutes and *guinbris*. There are two youths dressed in the traditional costume of Djibli boy-dancers (always semi-disguised as girls) doing somewhat prim belly-dances. In a corner of this room is an old Moroccan servant in scarlet *serrouelles*, squatting on the floor beside a large American flag built of flowers. The stripes are alternate rows of jasmine and hibiscus. The square for the stars, in the darkest part of the corner, is of some blue flower I'm not able to identify. The old man is afraid someone is going to step on the flag, which someone tells me is his creation. He has bordered the whole thing with candles, but they are not yet lighted. An English lady comes by and says: "The Ameddican flag. How sweet!" The old man looks up at her distrustfully.

There are bars here and there. Since neither of us drinks, we don't stop at them. In one room there is an almost invisible balcony halfway up the wall; from behind its *moucharabia* comes the sound of a piano playing a Mozart sonata. I try to find a spot from where I can see the performer, and finally get a glimpse of a man in tails sitting up there. One of the belly-dancers slithers into the room and circulates briefly among the guests, doing a neck and shoulder dance, but he has lost touch with headquarters; the Nazarene music disturbs him, and he hurries back to his own music. Jane suddenly sees someone from Rabat from whom she wants some political information; she ditches me and goes off with him. I stray out onto a small terrace and look at the view.

The fog has lifted and the moon is bright over the city. It is a fine night, after all, if perhaps a little cool for ladies in décolleté attire. A White Russian woman comes up to me and tells me that more than thirty people have had to be turned away from the door. Some had invitations with them which they had ingenuously bought from Moroccans who are presumed to have stolen them, (they have been fetching up to 20,000 francs each during the past few days) and some had no invitations at all. An American woman, the wife of a local banker, arrived fully bedecked, and on being refused admission became hysterical. As the police hurried her away, she screamed; "You'll hear from me about this!" "Fantastic," I say to the Russian woman, and then I decide to go and eat something.

The food all looks extremely rich. I notice several huge lobsters waiting to be dissected. I sit with a Britisher and his wife who apparently know me, although I'm not able to identify them. Suddenly the woman stares at her arm incredulously and cries to her husband: "It's gone!" The man registers dismay, says: "Which one?" "The platinum grapes," she says, rising and looking helplessly around her. "Do excuse us," says the husband, and they leave the table and disappear.

Soon Jane comes along with some friends. "Did you find out what you wanted to know?" I ask her. "Yes," she replies; she is obviously in good humor. We climb a long stairway and come out onto a broad terrace where at least a hundred people are standing; it is here that everyone is concentrated. Another flight of stairs leads us to the top terrace. Here a big dance floor has been built. Moroccans in slave costumes are sprinkling wax over it, taking care to make little designs of the powder as they work. A pavilion has been constructed to house the orchestra, which is playing Latin-American dance music. The combined façades of fifteen or twenty native houses just above and facing the Hutton house have been freshly whitewashed and their woodwork painted, and the whole mass is brilliantly floodlighted. There are Moroccans in all the windows and along the edges of the roofs, watching the show. But if the party is entertainment for them, the floodlighting of their dwellings makes it clear that these are meant to be a dramatic backdrop for the party, and indeed nothing in the house itself strikes me as being nearly so theatrical in effect as this unexpected view of the quarter of Amrah with its unmoving rows of shrouded women, merely sitting and looking. On the other side of the terrace, the native houses go down steeply toward the harbor, their flat white roofs making a kind of stairway in the moonlight. And now, as I examine the nearby roofs and my eyes grow used to the relative darkness of the night, I see that we are surrounded by staring Moroccans on all sides. Some are rolled in blankets, lying on mats, some are leaning out the tiny windows, some are just sitting cross-legged on their terraces under the moon. They don't seem to be talking to one another, and it is obvious that in order to miss nothing they are going to stay where they are until the party is over. I mention to Jane, the English lady who lost her bracelet. "It's all right," she says. "Each guest is insured for a million francs." While I am trying to understand the reason for this arbitrary figure, she says she is cold, and so we go back down into the house.

Now there are a few more guests in the room with the Moroccan musicians, and the air is full of kif smoke. They are all puffing on their *sebsis* at the moment, stretched out among the cushions in attitudes of extreme comfort. Someone is singing as if to himself, and someone is beating a drum in a desultory fashion. Soon the old man begins to light the candles around his flag of flowers, and the dancing boys rise, tighten their sashes, straighten their turbans, and once again go into their ancient routines. It is apparent that they have been smoking a good deal; their expressions and gestures are more obsessive. The state of trance is not distant. The music is better, too, particular in its rhythm. One dancer moves like a sleep-walker afflicted with chorea in the direction of a divan where two American couples, a European lady, and her Moroccan lover are sitting. When he arrives opposite the Moroccan, he makes the customary obeisance before him and rises to his feet with his arms outstretched. The Moroccan hands his glass to the woman beside him and gets to his feet, and the two begin a long, serious mutual belly-dance facing each other, exactly as if they were in a tent-café at an amara in the mountains. No one pays them much attention. The other dancer singles out the son of a British peer and invites him to dance, which he does, but he seems to think it is amusing, and he does not know the steps. As far as I can make out, he is doing an exhibition rumba. After a long five minutes he stops, executes a mock bow to the boy, and leaves the room. The Moroccan guest, one of the very few Moslems present in a capacity other than that of servant (apart from the secret police) continues to dance until the end of the piece, and then takes a thousand-franc note from his pockets, runs his tongue over it, and plasters it against the youth's forehead. The next dance finds the boy still wearing the money.

It seems that some Gypsies have been imported from Granada for our pleasure. Everyone is on his way to a large patio where they are about to perform. We go in that direction, find it impossible to get into the patio because there are so many people already installed there, and decided to go to the upper terrace and look down. On our way up we meet our hostess coming down. "Come and see the Gypsies," she says. "There's no room," I tell her. "We're really going to try and see them from above." She shrugs. "Really? I was told to go down." She continues on her way and we on ours. Once on the terrace we kneel on cushions and look down. I see the motionless Moslems up there on their roofs, and I wonder if they are able to see the fandango going on in the patio. On a remote and less brightly lighted part of the terrace a few people are lying on the pillows that cover the floor, talking and looking up at the moon. The dancers are directly below us, but they are not always visible. They are extremely professional, and so is the guitarist, – all of them very precise, as flamenco performers must be. On the western side of our terrace there is a throne of brocades, feathers and spears; it is a nook where the hostess can receive her particular friends during the party. I have not seen her use it, but a photo in the London *Daily Mail* of two days later will show her there, surrounded by intimates, some time shortly before dawn.

It is after three o'clock and we are sleepy. We are worried, too, that we will have to walk all the way down through the Medina to the Zoco Chico in order to get a cab, since there is no way for any vehicle to get anywhere near the house, nor is there a parade de taxis in the neighborhood. No one else is leaving so early, but with the help of a guest who knows someone in the police, we are finally presented to a taxi-driver standing in the crowd on the street above, and he takes us up to the Place de la Casbah where his cab is waiting. When I get home I am not sleepy any more, so I decide to record the muezzins calling the *fjer*. At this time of year the pre-dawn call to prayer lasts roughly from four fifteen to four forty-five. A little past five I get into bed and listen to the play-back. I have recorded the *fjer* from my window innumerable times before; each night it is a different arrangement of many voices chanting from many minarets, always against a rich background of cockcrow, dogbark and assbray. But tonight there are faint strains of Nazarene music floating from time to time across the auditory landscape: it is the dance orchestra atop the Hutton house, a good mile and a half to the east. I go to sleep. The next day I hear that by nine o'clock in the morning the ball was definitely over.

(On August 27th, two days before the party, the Moroccan authorities closed down both the local newspapers published for the foreign colony of Tangier: the daily *Dépêche Marocaine* and the weekly *Tangier Gazette*, the oldest paper in Morocco. The suppression of the English-language paper, which has been appearing since 1883, caused consternation, because it was preceded by a savage campaign in the Moroccan press; the editor, an American, was denounced as a stooge for the foreign colony in general, a group consisting, it alleged, of "thieves and smugglers" who should be deported. The violence of the attack shocked a good many people. It's not unlikely that more substantial shocks than this are in store for Tangier's foreign residents in the not-too-distant future. The question is how spectacular can the disparity between the very well-fed and the nearly starving segments of the population be, without the danger of incidents tending to reduce that disparity?)

THE ROUTE TO TASSEMSIT

HOLIDAY, FEBRUARY 1963; THEIR HEADS ARE GREEN, 1963

WHENEVER I LEAVE Tangier to go south, my home takes on the look of a place where serious disaster has just struck. The night before I set out on this particular trip the usual disorder prevailed. There were crates of canned foodstuffs and bundles of blankets and pillows in the living room. The recording equipment was scattered over an unnecessarily large area, so that coils of extra cable hid the portable butane-gas stove and boxes of tape covered the road maps. The servants had induced me to write down the specifications of the things they hoped I would remember to buy for them while I was away. Fatima wanted a white woolen blanket at least eight meters long, and Mina a silver-plated circular tray with three detachable legs. Following tradition, they had scrupulously insisted that these things were to be paid for out of their wages after I returned, and I had agreed, although each of us was aware that such deductions would never be made. Moroccan etiquette demands that when the master of the house goes on a journey he bring back souvenirs for everyone. The farther he goes and the longer he stays, the more substantial these gifts are expected to be.

In this country, departure is often a pre-dawn activity. After the half-hour of early morning prayer-calling is finished and the muezzins have extinguished the lights at the tops of the minarets, there is still about an hour of dark left. The choir of roosters trails on in the air above the rooftops of the city until daybreak. It is a good moment to leave, just as the sky is growing white in the east and objects are black and sharp against it. By the time the sun was up Christopher and I were far out in the country, rolling along at a speed determined only by the curves and the occasional livestock in the road. The empty highway, visible far ahead, measured off the miles of grandiose countryside, and along the way no billboards came between us and the land.

During the last six months of 1959 I traveled some twenty-five thousand miles around Morocco, recording music for the Library of Congress on a grant from the Rockefeller Foundation. The quality of the material was uniformly splendid; nevertheless, one always has preferences. After a great deal of listening, the tapes which interested me most were the ones I had recorded in Tafraout, a region in the western Anti-Atlas. Since I had managed to get only six selections there, I wanted now to go back and try to find some more, although this time it would have to be without the assistance of the Moroccan government. By my inland itinerary there was a distance of 1,370 kilometers (855 miles) to be covered between Tangier and Tafraout, and the roads would be fairly good all the way. The direct route to Marrakesh via Rabat runs over flat terrain and has a certain amount of traffic along it. The unfrequented interior route we used, which leads through the western foothills of the Rif Mountains and over the Middle Atlas, takes an extra day, but is beautiful at every point.

Beyond Xauen we followed the River Loukos for a while, here a clear, swift stream at the bottom of a narrow valley. Christopher, who was driving, suggested that it was time for lunch. We stopped, spread a rug under an old olive tree and ate, listening to the sound of the water skipping over the stones beside us. The hills rose steeply on both sides of the river; there was not a person or a dwelling in sight. We started out again. A half-hour further on, we rounded a corner and came upon a man lying face down on the paved surface of the road, his *djellaba* covering his head. Immediately I thought: he's dead. We stopped, got out, prodded him a bit, and he sat up, rubbing his eyes, mumbling, annoyed at being awakened. He explained that the clean, smooth road was a better place to sleep than the stony ground beside it. When we objected that he might easily be killed, he replied with fine peasant logic that no one had killed him yet. Nevertheless, he got up and walked a few yards off the highway, where he slumped down again all in one motion, wrapped the hood of his *djellaba* around his head, and went back into the comfortable world of sleep.

The next day was hotter. We climbed up along the slowly rising ramp of the Middle Atlas, a gray, glistening landscape. The shiny leaves of the scrub live oaks, and even the exposed bedrock beneath, reflected the hot light of the overhead sun. Further along, on the southern slope of the mountains, we passed the mangled body of a large ape that had not got out of the road fast enough – an unusual sight here, since the monkeys generally stay far from the highways.

All afternoon we had been speeding along the gradually descending valley between the Middle Atlas and the Grand Atlas. The sun went down ahead of us and the moon rose behind us. We drank coffee from the Thermos and hoped we would get into Marrakesh in time to find some food. The new Moroccan regime has brought early closing hours to a land where heretofore night was merely a continuation of day.

After the lunar brightness of the empty waste land, the oasis seemed dark. The highway went for miles between high mud walls and canebrakes; the black tracery of date palms rose above them, against the brilliant night sky. Suddenly the walls and the oasis came to an end, and ahead, standing in the rubble of the desert, was a big new cinema trimmed with tubes of colored neon, the tin and straw shacks of a *bidonville* clustering around it like the cottages of a village around the church. In Morocco the very poor live neither in the country nor in the city; they come as far as the outer walls of the town, build these desperate-looking squatters' colonies out of whatever materials they can find, and there they stay.

Marrakesh is a city of great distances, flat as a table. When the wind blows, the pink dust of the plain sweeps into the sky, obscuring the sun, and the whole city, painted with a wash made of the pink earth on which it rests, glows red in the cataclysmic light. At night, from a car window, it looks not unlike one of our own Western cities: long miles of street lights stretching in straight lines across the plain. Only by day does one see that most of these lights illumine nothing more than empty reaches of palm garden and desert. Over the years, the outer fringes of the Medina have been made navigable to automobiles and horse-drawn carriages, of which there are still a great many, but it takes a brave man to drive his car into the maze of serpentine alleys full of porters, bicycles, carts, donkeys and ordinary pedestrians. Besides, the only way to see anything in the Medina is to walk. In order to be really present, you must have your feet in the dust, and be aware of the hot, dusty smell of the mud walls beside your face.

The night we arrived in Marrakesh, Christopher and I went to a café in the heart of the Medina. On the roof, under the stars, they spread matting, blankets and cushions for us, and we sat there drinking mint tea, savoring the cool air that begins to stir above the city after midnight, when the stored heat of the sun is finally dissipated. At a certain moment, out of the silence of the street below, there came a succession of strange, explosive cries. I leaned over the edge and peered down into the dim passageway three floors beneath. Among the few late strollers an impossible, phantom-like figure was dancing. It galloped, it stopped, it made great gravitation-defying leaps into the air as if the earth under its feet were helping. At each leap it yelled. No one paid any attention. As the figure came along below the café, I was able to identify it as a powerfully built young man; he was almost naked. I watched him disappear into the dark. Almost immediately he returned, doing the same inspired dance, occasionally rushing savagely toward other pedestrians, but always stopping himself in time to avoid touching them. He passed back and forth through the alley in this way for a quarter of an hour or so before the qa-houaji climbed the ladder again to the roof where we sat. When he came I said casually, "What's going on down there?" Although in most places it would have been clear enough that a madman was loose in the streets, in Morocco there are subtle distinctions to be made. Sometimes the person turns out to be merely holy, or indisposed.

"Ah, poor man," said the *qahaouaji*. "He's a friend of mine. We were in school together. He got high marks and played good soccer."

"What happened?"

"What do you think? A woman, of course."

This had not occurred to me. "You mean she worked magic on him?"

"What else? At first he was like this – " He let his jaw drop and his mouth hang open; his eyes became fixed and vacant. "Then after a few weeks he tore off his clothes and began to run. And ever since, he runs like that, in the summer and in the winter. The woman was rich. Her husband had died and she wanted Allal. But he's of a good family and they didn't like her. So she said in her head: 'No other woman is going to have him either.' And she gave him what she gave him."

"And his family?"

"He doesn't know his family. He lives in the street."

"And the woman? What happened to her?"

He shrugged. "She's not here any more. She moved somewhere else." At that moment the cries came up again.

"But why do they let him run in the street like that? Can't they do anything for him?"

"Oh, he never hurts anybody. He's just playful. He likes to scare people, that's all."

I decided to ask my question. "Is he crazy?"

"No, just playful."

"Ah, yes. I see."

At twilight one day we were the tea guests of Moulay Brahim, one of the Moroccans who previously had helped me make contacts with musicians. He lived in a rooming house near the dyers' souk. The establishment, on the second floor, consisted of a dozen or more cubicles situated around an open central court with a dead fountain in the middle. No women were allowed in the building; it was a place for men who have left home and family behind. Not an object was visible that could even remind one of the existence of traditional Moroccan life.

Moulay Brahim is militantly of his epoch; his life is almost wholly abstract. He spends his hours in an attitude of prostration on his mattress, his head touching a large short-wave radio. He knows what time it is in Jakarta, just where the Nigerian representative to the United Nations is at this moment, and what Sékou Touré said to Nkrumah about Nasser. The radio is never silent save for a useless five minutes now and then while he waits impatiently for a program in Cairo or Damascus or Baghdad to begin. He follows the moves of the cold war like an onlooker at a chess match, making searing comments on what he considers the blunders of both sides. Only the neutralist powers have his sympathy. We sat in the dusk around the dimly illumined radio and listened to it hiss and crackle. Moulay Brahim dispensed kif silently, intent on the panel of the instrument, weighing each gradation of static with the expression of a connoisseur certain of his ground. Fifteen minutes might go by without a trace of any sort of program coming out – only the unvarying noise of interference. His face did not change; he knows how to wait. At any moment he may hear something more, something identifiable. Then he can relax for a bit, while the tea-concession man from across the courtyard brings in the big tray, sets up the glasses and rolls the mint between his hands before stuffing it into the pot. But soon it is not enough for Moulay Brahim to know that he is in touch with the BBC service to the Middle East, and he begins once again the painful search for the unfindable.

Inhabitants of the other rooms came in and squatted, but it was difficult to engage them in anything more than desultory conversation. They had learned from experience that in Moulay Brahim's room it was better to be quiet. At one point, when a particularly confused noise had for some time been issuing from

Musicians in Essaouira, southern Morocco, on the recording trip Bowles made for his
Library of Congress project (PB)

the loudspeaker, I rashly suggested that he adjust the dial. "No, no!" he cried. "This is what I want. I've got five stations here now. Sometimes others come in. It's a place where they all like to get together and talk at once. Like in a café." For a young and deracinated Moroccan like Moulay Brahim, radio is primarily neither a form of entertainment nor a medium of information. It is a sort of metaphysical umbilical cord – a whole manner of existence, an essential adjunct to feeling that he is in contact with life.

When we had finally persuaded him that it was time for us to leave, he reluctantly rose from the radio and took us out into the streets to the apothecary market, where I had expressed a desire to go. It is the place you visit if you want the ingredients for making black magic. There were six stalls in a row, all bristling with the dried parts of birds, reptiles and mammals. We wandered slowly by, examining the horns, quills, hair, eggs, bones, feathers, feet and bills that were strung on wires in the doorways. I was put in mind of the unfortunate Allal and the rich widow, and I described Allal to Moulay Brahim. He knew him; everybody in Marrakesh knew him, he declared, adding as he pointed to the rows of glass containers in front of us, "You can get everything for that sort of business here. But you've got to know how to blend them. That takes an expert." He raised his eyebrows significantly, and approached the nearest merchant to mutter a few words to him. A packet containing tiny seeds was brought out. Moulay Brahim examined them at some length, and bought fifty grams. "What is it?" I asked him. But he was enjoying his brief role as mystery man, and merely rattled the seeds in their paper, saying, "Something very special, very special."

TAROUDANT, OCTOBER 6, 1961

Brilliant day. Sky like a blue enamel bowl overhead. Left Marrakesh at noon, driving straight up to Ouirgane, in a valley only about three thousand feet above the plain. Lunch outside in the sun at Le Sanglier Qui Fume. Our table midway between a chained eagle and a chained monkey, both of which watched us distrustfully while we ate. Below, hidden, somewhere nearby, the little river roared over its rocks. The Grand Atlas sun fiery. Monsieur gave us drooping old straw sombreros to wear while we ate. A tame stork, very proprietary, strutted around, poking its beak into everything. It was wary, however, of the monkey, which had a long bamboo pole in its hand and patiently tried to trip it up each time it came past. Everything excellent: hors d'oeuvre, frogs' legs and chicken paprika. Madame is Hungarian, said she lives in the hope that people coming through Ouirgane will prove to speak her language, "Or at least know Budapest," she added. Obviously disappointed in us. On up to the pass at Tizi n'Test and over the top. The valley of the Souss thick with a mist that looked like smoke. Only the long sloping rim of the Anti-Atlas showed in the sky to the south, fifty miles across. Below, a gulf of vapor. Got into Taroudant at seven. The heat was still everywhere inside the walls. While I was unpacking, a procession of Guennaoua shuffled by in the street. Tried to get out through a door into the patio, but it was padlocked. I peeked through a crack and saw them going past slowly, carrying candle lanterns. The pounding of the drums shook the air.

After Taroudant – Tiznit, Tanout, Tirmi, Tiffermit. Great hot dust-colored valleys among the naked mountains, dotted with leafless argan trees as gray as puffs of smoke. Sometimes a dry stream twists among the boulders at the bottom of a valley, and there is a peppering of locust-ravaged date palms whose branches look like the ribs of a broken umbrella. Or hanging to the flank of a mountain a thousand feet below the road is a terraced village, visible only as an abstract design of flat roofs, some the color of the earth of which they are built, and some bright yellow with the corn that is spread out to dry in the sun.

The argan trees are everywhere, thousands of them, squat and thorny, anchored to the rocks that lie beneath in their dubious shade. They flourish where nothing else can live, not even weeds or cacti. Their scaly bark looks like crocodile hide and feels like iron. Where the argan grows the goats have a good life. The trunk is short and the branches begin to proliferate only a few feet from the ground. This suits the goats perfectly; they climb from branch to branch eating both the leaves and the greasy, bitter, olive-like fruit. Subsequently their excrement is collected, and the argan pits in it are pressed to make a thick cooking oil.

Tafraout is rough country – the Bad Lands of South Dakota on a grand scale, with Death Valley in the background. The mountains are vast humps of solid granite, their sides strewn with gigantic boulders; at sunset the black line of their crests is deckle-edged in silhouette against the flaming sky. Seen from a height, the troughs between the humps are like long gray lakes, the only places in the landscape where there is at least a covering of what might pass for loose earth. Above the level surface of this detritus in the valleys rise the smooth expanses of solid rock.

The locusts have fed well here, too. Tafraout could never subsist on its dates. But the bourgeois Berbers who live here learned long ago that organized commerce could provide greater security than either the pastoral or the agricultural life. They inaugurated a successful campaign to create a virtual monopoly on grocery and hardware stores all over Morocco. Taking his male children with him, a man goes to a city in the north where he has a shop, or several shops, and remains there for two or three years at a stretch, living usually in conditions of extreme discomfort on the floor behind the counter. Being industrious, thrifty and invariably successful, he is naturally open to a good deal of adverse criticism from those of his compatriots who are less so, and who despise his frugal manner of living and deride his custom of leaving small boys of eight in charge of his shops. But the children run the establishments quite as well as their elders; they know the price of every object and are equally difficult to deal with in the national pastime of persuading the seller to lower his asking price. The boys merely refuse to talk; often they do not even look at the customer. They quote the price, and if it is accepted, hand over the article and return the change. It is a very serious matter to be in charge of a store, and the boys behave accordingly.

As you come up from Tiznit over the pass, the first Tafraout settlements on the trail occur at the neck of a narrow valley; built in among, underneath, and on top of the great fallen lumps of granite, the fortress-houses dominate the countryside. It is hard to reconcile the architectural sophistication of these pink and white castles with the unassuming aspect of their owners back in the north, just as it is difficult to believe that the splendid women, shrouded in black and carrying copper amphoras or calfskin-covered baskets on their shoulders, can be these inconspicuous little men's wives and sisters. But then, no one would expect a tribe of shopkeepers to have originated in the fortresses of this savage landscape.

TAFRAOUT, OCTOBER 9

Arrived yesterday about five, after having a puncture ten miles up the trail. Hotel completely empty, save for a handful of ragged children and one old gentleman in a *djellaba* who has been left in charge of the premises while the regular guardian is down in Tiznit. He helped with luggage, hung up our clothes, prepared the beds, brought pails of washing water and bottles of drinking water, and filled the lamps with kerosene. Slept heavily and late for the first time since Meknès. Woke once in the night to hear a great chorus of howling and barking below in the village. Lunch better than dinner last night, but everything was drowned in an inch of hot oil. Tajine of beef, almonds, grapes, olives and onions. Came back up to the hotel to make Nescafé on the terrace afterward. The old man who received us last night was sitting in a corner, buried under his *djellaba*. He saw we were looking at magazines, got up and came over. Soon he said timidly, "Is that an American book you are reading?" I said it was. He pointed to a color photograph and asked, "And are the mountains in America really all green like that?" I told him many of them were. He stood a while studying the picture. Then he said bitterly, "It's not pretty here. The locusts eat the trees and all the rest of the plants. Here we're poor."

During the next few days I discovered how unrealistic my recording project had been. We visited at least two dozen villages in the region, and made no progress toward uncovering an occasion where there might prove to be music. The previous year even the government had needed thirty-six hours' notice for sending its directives via a network of caids and messengers up into the heights before the musicians had put in their appearance in Tafraout. When Friday morning arrived, Christopher said to me at breakfast, "What do you think? Do we leave tomorrow for Essaouira?" I said I supposed there was nothing else to do. Then I suggested we go down to the hospital to see if they had any Rovamycine.

A bearded Moroccan intern stood under a pepper tree in the hospital's patio, a syringe in his hand; he said the doctor had gone to Agadir for the weekend, but that if I wished I could speak with the French pharmacist, who in the absence of his chief was in charge of the institution.

The pharmacist arrived rubbing his eyes. He had been working all night, he told us. There was no Rovamycine. "It's an expensive drug. They don't supply us with that sort of thing here."

Christopher invited him to come up to the hotel for a whiskey. "*Avec plaisir*," he said. Alcoholic drinks are not on sale in Tafraout, since Moslems cannot drink legally. The only two Europeans in the region were the doctor and the pharmacist, and they got by with the occasional bottle of wine or cognac they brought up from Tiznit.

The pharmacist had with him a young Moroccan medical student who had just arrived from Rabat the day before; he thought Tafraout the strangest place he had ever seen. We sat on the terrace in the scalding sun and watched the crows flying in a slowly revolving circle high above the valley. I was disappointed in my sojourn this time, I told Monsieur Rousselot, because I hadn't got into the life of the people and because there was no edible food. The second reason touched the Frenchman. "I shall do my best to fill these unfortunate lacunae," he said. "First let us go to my house for lunch. I have a good chef."

The house behind the hospital was comfortable. There were several servants. Walls were lined with books, particularly art books, for like many French men of medicine, Monsieur Rousselot loved painting, and had a hankering to try his hand at it himself one day.

During lunch he announced, "I have a little excursion in mind for this afternoon. Have you ever drunk *mahia*?" I said I had, many years ago, with Jewish friends in Fez. "Ah!" he exclaimed happily. "Then you are acquainted with its virtues. You will have an opportunity to drink *mahia* again later this afternoon." I smiled politely, having already determined that when the moment arrived I should decline the offer. I am not fond of *eau de vie*, even when it is made of figs, as it is in Fez. In the Anti-Atlas they use dates, said Monsieur Rousselot; this didn't seem an improvement.

After coffee and cognac, we started out down the Tiznit trail. Some thirty miles to the south, in a parched lower valley, we came to a poor-looking village called Tahala, which, besides its Moslem population, contains a Jewish colony of considerable size. The air was breathless as we got out of the car in front of the primitive little mosque. Five or six Moslem elders sat on the dusty rocks in the shade, talking quietly. "The Israelites add to their modest revenue by selling us the ambrosia they distill," explained Monsieur Rousselot. Seddiq, the medical student, now expressed himself on the subject for the first time. "It's terrible!" he said with feeling. "*Bien sûr*," agreed Monsieur Rousselot, "but you'll drink it."

House near Tafraout in the Ammeln Valley. 'The houses were wonderful colors ... rose-pink and orange and gray. It's what they had handy, it's made of earth, that's the color of the earth ... This was the main door.' (PB)

Several children who had seen us arrive and park the car had run ahead into the village to announce our advent; now as we went along the oven-hot alleys, on all sides doors were being unceremoniously slammed shut and bolted. There was no one visible. But Monsieur Rousselot knew where he was going. He sent us ahead around a corner to wait out of sight while he pounded on one of the doors. It was a quarter of an hour before he reappeared and called to us. In the doorway where he had been standing talking stood an exceptionally pretty girl. The baby she held had an infected arm. Its forehead and nose were decorated in simple designs applied with kohl; one would have said that its face had been inexpertly tattooed. The room we went into was as dark and cool as a farmhouse cellar; the dirt floor slanted in various directions. A short flight of mud steps led up into an open patio with a well in its center. Seven or eight very white-skinned women sat there on a bench around the well; they wore medieval headdresses like those Tenniel gave the duchess in his illustrations for *Alice in Wonderland*. But they were all exceptionally handsome – even the old ones. No pictures could be taken, Monsieur Rousselot warned. The excuse they gave was that it was Friday afternoon.

We were beckoned on into a further patio, this one full of men and boys, all wearing *yamakas* on their heads. From there we went into a small room with a brass bed at one end and a straw mat on the floor at the other. Asleep in the bed was a baby, naked and besieged by flies. We sat down on the mat in the sunlight, disturbing several hundred groggy flies; the men and boys came in from the patio one by one and solemnly shook hands with us. The big tray they put on the mat in front of us was piled high with almonds, dates, and flies – both alive and dead. Then the patriarch of the house was helped into the room by a younger man and eased into a sprawling position on the floor. His face was drawn and sad, and his replies to Monsieur Rousselot's questions were apathetic. "You must come to the hospital and let us examine you," urged Monsieur Rousselot. The old man frowned and shook his head slowly. "They're all afraid,"

Monsieur Rousselot explained to me in French. "They consider the hospital a place where one goes to die, nothing more."

"Do you know what's wrong with him?" I asked.

"I'm almost certain it's the scourge."

"The scourge?"

"Cancer," snapped Monsieur Rousselot, as if the word itself were evil. "It carries them off, *whsht, whsht*." He clicked his fingers twice.

Someone came and carried the baby away, still asleep. The flies remained behind. A small bottle of *mahia* was produced, and miniature glasses of it were passed around. Surreptitiously I poured mine into Monsieur Rousselot's glass. Only the old man and I went without.

"He can't eat anything," explained one of the sons to Monsieur Rousselot. "Haven't you any pills for him?"

"Yes, yes, yes," said Monsieur Rousselot jovially, opening his doctor's bag. He took out two large jars, one filled with aspirin tablets, the other with Vitamin-C pills, and poured a pile of them onto the mat. A murmur went around the patio, started by those who were crowding the doorway watching. "This is the only medicament I ever carry with me. It's all I have to give them. *Mais vous allez voir.* The pills will all stay behind here in Tahala." The flies crawled on our faces, trying to drink from the corners of our eyes. Monsieur Rousselot conferred quietly with one of the younger members of the family; presently two liter-bottles of *mahia* appeared and were packed into the medical bag. When we got up to leave, Monsieur Rousselot said to the old man, "Then it's agreed. You'll bring your grandson on Tuesday." To me he muttered, "Perhaps for the baby he'll come, and I can get him to stay for an examination. But it's doubtful."

Outside the front door a crowd of people had gathered. Word had got around that the *toubib* was there with his medicine. Monsieur Rousselot's prediction was accurate; there were not enough pills to go around.

On the way back up to Tafraout I said to him; "This has been an unforgettable day. Without it our trip to Tafraout would have been a failure." And I thanked him and said we would be leaving in the morning.

"Oh, no! You can't go!" he cried. "I have something much better for you tomorrow."

I said we had to start moving northward.

"But this is something special. Something I discovered. I've never shown it to anyone before."

"It's not possible. No, no."

He pleaded. "Tomorrow is Saturday. Leave on Monday morning. We can spend tomorrow night in the palace and have Sunday morning for exploring the oases."

"Two days!" I cried. But the curiosity he had counted on awakening must have shown through my protestations. Before we left his house, I had agreed to go to Tassemsit. I could scarcely have resisted after his description of the place. According to him, Tassemsit was a feudal town at the bottom of a narrow canyon, which by virtue of being the seat of an influential religious brotherhood had so far escaped coming under governmental jurisdiction and was still functioning in a wholly traditional fashion. Absolute power was nominally in the hands of a nineteen-year-old girl, the present hereditary saint whose palace was inside the walls. In reality, however, said Monsieur Rousselot, lowering his voice to a whisper, it was the family chauffeur who held the power of life and death over the citizens of Tassemsit. The old Cherif, father of the girl-saint, for many years had run the *zaouia* where religious pilgrims came to pray and leave offerings. Not long ago he had bought a car to get up to Tafraout now and then, and had hired a young Marrakchi to drive it. The old Cherif's somewhat younger wife had found the chauffeur interesting, as wives sometimes do, and *l'inévitable* had happened: the old Cherif had suddenly died and the wife had married the young Marrakchi, who had taken charge of everything: the woman, the holy daughter, the car, the palace and the administration of the shrine and the town around it. "It's an equivocal situation," said Monsieur Rousselot with relish. "You'll see."

TASSEMSIT, OCTOBER 16

Early morning. Others still asleep. Big grilled window right beside my head. A world of dappled sunlight and shadow on the other side of the wrought-iron filigree, an orchard of fig trees where small birds dart and chirp. Then the mud wall, and beyond, the stony floor of the canyon. A few pools of water in the river bed. The women are out there, getting water, bringing it back in jugs. Background to all views: the orange sidewall of the canyon, perpendicular and high enough to block out the sky from where I sit on the mattress.

More lurid details about the place from Rousselot yesterday during lunch. When the chauffeur took over, he instituted a novelty in Tassemsit: it seems he conceived the idea of providing girls to keep the pilgrims occupied at night, when the *zaouia* is closed. A great boost to the local economy. "A holy city of sin," said Rousselot with enthusiasm. Merely speak to the chauffeur, and you get any woman in town, even if she happens to be married. He had hardly finished telling us all this when a little fat man came in. Rousselot's face was a study in chagrin, dropped jaw and all. He rallied then, introduced the little man around as Monsieur Omar, and made him sit down with us for coffee. Some sort of government employee. When he heard that we were about to leave for Tassemsit, Monsieur Omar said very simply that he would go with us. It was clear enough that he wasn't wanted, but since nobody said anything to the contrary, he came along, sitting in back with Monsieur Rousselot and Seddiq.

Trail rough in spots on the way up over the peaks just south of Tafraout. Going down the other side it was narrower, but the surface was no worse. Had we met another car, one of us would have had to back up for a half-hour. The landscape became constantly more dramatic. For two hours the trail followed a valley that cut itself deeper and deeper into the rock walls as it went downward. Sometimes we drove along the bed of the stream for a half-mile or so. At the date-palm level we came across small oases, cool and green, that filled the canyon floor from cliff to cliff. The lower we went, the higher the mountain walls rose above, and the sunlight seemed to be coming from further away. When I was a child I used to imagine Persephone going along a similar road each year on her way down to Hades. A little like having found a back way out of the world. No house, no car, no human being all afternoon. Later, after we had been driving in shadow a good while, the canyon widened, and there on a promontory above a bend in the dry river bed, was Tassemsit, compact, orange-gold like the naked rock of the countryside around it, still in the sunlight. A small, rich oasis just below it to the south. The *zaouia* with its mosque and other buildings seemed to occupy a large part of the town's space. A big, tall minaret in northern style, well-preserved. We stopped and got out. Complete silence throughout the valley.

Monsieur Rousselot had seemed pensive and nervous all during the afternoon, and now I understood why. He got me aside on some pretext, and we walked together down the trail a way, he talking urgently the whole time. It worried him very much that Monsieur Omar should be with us; he felt that his presence represented a very real danger to the status quo of the place. "One false move, and the story of Tassemsit can be finished forever," he said. "*C'est très délicat.* Above all, not a word about what I told you. Any of it." I said he could count on me, and promised to warn Christopher. It came to me as we walked back up toward the car that there was probably another reason, besides the fact that he wanted to keep the place as his private playground, why Monsieur Rousselot was worried. A Frenchman's job in Morocco, if he works for the government, is never too secure in any case; it is easy to find a pretext which will dispose of him and replace him with a Moroccan.

When we got to the car I spoke to Christopher, but he had already guessed the situation. At Monsieur Rousselot's insistence we waited another half-hour; then we drove down a side trail to the right, to within two hundred feet of the town gate. A mist of sweet-smelling wood smoke hung over the canyon. Several tall black men in white cotton robes appeared at the top of the rocks above us, came down to the car, and recognized Monsieur Rousselot. Smiling, they led us through a short alley into the palace itself, which was small, primitive and elegant. The big room where they left us was a conscious synthesis of luxury and wild fantasy; with its irresponsible color juxtapositions it was like something Matisse would have produced had he been asked to design a Moorish salon.

"This is our room," said Monsieur Rousselot. "Here we are going to eat and sleep, the five of us." While we were unpacking, our host, the late Cherif's chauffeur, came in and sat down in our midst for a while. He was pleasant-mannered, quick-witted, and he spoke a little French. A man in his late twenties, born in the country, one would guess, but used to living in the city. At one point I became aware of the conversation he was having with Monsieur Rousselot, who had sat down beside him on the mattress. It concerned the possibility of an *ahouache*, performed by the citizens of Tassemsit later on in the evening.

Afterward, when the host had left, Monsieur Rousselot announced that not only would we have the entertainment, but that there would be a certain number of women taking part in it. "Very unusual," he commented, looking owlishly at Monsieur Omar. Monsieur Omar grinned. "We are fortunate," he said; he was from Casablanca and might as well have been visiting Bali for all he knew about local customs. "You understand, of course," Monsieur Rousselot went on to say to me with some embarrassment, "this *ahouache* will have to be paid for."

"Of course," I said.

"If you and Monsieur Christopher can give three thousand, I should be glad to contribute two."

I protested that we should be delighted to pay the whole five thousand francs, if that was the price, but he wouldn't consider it.

Through the windows, from the silence in the canyon outside, came the thin sound of the muezzin's voice calling from the mosque, and as we listened, two light bulbs near the ceiling began to glow feebly. "It's not possible!" cried Christopher. "Electricity *here*?" "*Tiens*," murmured Monsieur Rousselot. "He's got his generator going at last." I looked wistfully up at the trembling filaments above my head, wondering whether the current and voltage might conceivably be right for recording. A tall servant came in and announced that the Cherif was expecting us on the floor above. We filed out under the arcade and up a long flight of stairs. There at the top, on an open terrace, surrounded by roaring pressure-lamps, sat our host with two women. We were presented to the mother first. She would have been considered elegant anywhere in the world, with her handsome head, her regal white garments and her massive gold jewelry. The daughter, present titular ruler of Tassemsit, was something else; it was difficult to believe that the two had anything in common, or even that they inhabited the same town. The girl wore a pleated woolen skirt and a yellow sweater. She had had her front teeth capped with gold, and noisily snapped her chewing gum from time to time as she chatted with us. Presently our host rose and conducted us back down the stairs into our room, where servants had begun to arrive with trays and small tables.

It was an old-fashioned Moroccan dinner, beginning with soap, towels, and a big ewer of hot water. When everyone had washed and dried himself, an earthenware dish at least a foot and a half across was brought in and set in our midst; it held a mountain of couscous surrounded by a sea of sauce. We ate in the traditional manner, using our fingers, a process which demands a certain minimum of technique. The sauce was bubbling hot, and the tiny grains of semolina (since the cook knew his business) did not adhere to each other. Some of the food we extracted from the mound in front of us got to our mouths, but a good deal of it did not. I decided to wait a bit until someone had uncovered some of the meat buried in the center of the mass, and when my opportunity came I seized a small piece of lamb which was still too hot to touch with comfort, but which I managed nevertheless to eat.

"I see that even the rudiments of local etiquette remain unknown to you," remarked Monsieur Rousselot to me in a voice which carried overtones of triumph rather than the friendly concern it might have expressed. I said I didn't know what he meant.

"Have I committed an infraction?" I asked him.

"Of the gravest," he said solemnly. "You ate a piece of meat. One is constrained to try some of every other element in the dish first, and even then one may not try the meat until one's host has offered one a piece of it with his own fingers."

I said this was the first time I had eaten in a home of the region. Seddiq, the medical student, observed that in Rabat such behavior as Monsieur described would be considered absurd. But Monsieur Rousselot was determined to be an old Moroccan hand. "*Quelle décadence!*" he snorted. "The younger generation knows nothing." A few minutes later he upset a full glass of tea on the rug.

"In Rabat we don't do that, either," murmured Seddiq.

Shortly after tea had been served for the third time, the electricity began to fail, and eventually it died. There was a pause in the talking. From where he sat, the head of the house shouted an order. Five white-dustered black men brought in candle lanterns; they were still placing them in strategic positions around the room when the lights came on again, brighter than before. The lanterns were quickly blown out. Candles are shameful. Twenty minutes later, in the midst of a lion story (stories about lions are inevitable whenever city people gather in the country in South Morocco, although according to reliable sources the beasts have been extinct in the region for several generations), the current failed again, abruptly. In the silence of sudden dark-

ness we heard a jackal yapping; the high sharp sound came from
the direction of the river bed.

"Very near," I remarked, partly in order to seem unaware of
the host's probable embarrassment at having us witness the failure of his power system.

"Yes, isn't it?" He seemed to want to talk. "I have recorded
them many times. Not one jackal – whole packs of them."

"You've recorded them? You have a tape-recorder here?"

"From Marrakesh. It doesn't work very well. At least, not
always."

Monsieur Rousselot had been busy scrabbling around his
portion of the rug; now he suddenly lit a match and put it to
the candle of the lantern near him. Then he stood up and went
the length of the big room, lighting the others. As the patterns
painted on the high ceiling became visible again, there was the
sound of hand drums approaching from the town.

"The entertainers are coming," said our host.

Monsieur Rousselot stepped out into the courtyard. There
was the increasing sound of voices; servants had appeared and
were moving about beyond the doorway in the gloom. By the
time we all went to look out, the courtyard had some fifty or
sixty men in it, with more arriving. Someone was building a
fire over in a corner under the far arcade. A drum banged now
and then as its owner tested the membrane. Again the electricity came on. The master of the palace smiled at Monsieur
Rousselot, disappeared, and returned almost immediately with a
servant who carried a tape-recorder. It was a small model made
by Philips of Holland. He set it up on a chair outside the doorway and had great difficulty connecting it because none of the
wall plugs appeared to work. Eventually he found a live one. By
that time there were more than a hundred men massed under
the arches around the open center of the courtyard, and in the
middle were thirty or more musicians standing in an irregu-
lar circle. The host had propped the microphone against the
machine itself, thus dooming his recording from the outset.
"Why not hang it up there on the wall?" I suggested.

"I want to talk into it once in a while," he said. When he turned the volume up the machine howled, of course, and there was laughter from the spectators, who until then had been very quiet, just standing and watching. The host had another chair brought, and he sat down in it, holding the microphone in his hand – a position not likely to produce much better results than the first one. Christopher caught my eye and shook his head sadly. More chairs were provided from out of the darkness, and someone arrived bringing a pressure-lantern, which was set inside the musicians' circle. That was where the fire ought to have been, but there was not enough space in the courtyard to put it there.

The performers, all Negroes, wore loose white tunics, and each carried a *poignard* in a silver scabbard at his waist. Their drums were the regulation *bendir* – a skin stretched over a wooden hoop about a foot and a half in diameter. This simple instrument is capable of great sonorous variety, depending on the kind of blow and the exact spot on the membrane struck by the fingertips or palm. The men of South Morocco do not stand still when they play the drums; they dance, but the purpose of their choreography is to facilitate the production of rhythm. No matter how involved or frenzied the body movements of the players (who also sing in chorus and as soloists), the dancing is subordinate to the sound. It is very difficult to hear the music if one is watching the performance; I often keep my eyes shut during an entire number. The particular interest of the Anti-Atlas *ahouache* is that drummers divide themselves into complementary groups, each of which provides only certain regularly recurring notes in the complex total of the rhythmical pattern.

The men began to play; the tempo was exaggeratedly slow. As they increased it imperceptibly, the subtle syncopations became more apparent. A man brandishing a *gannega*, a smaller drum with a higher pitch and an almost metallic sonority, moved into the center of the circle and started an electrifying counter-rhythmic solo. His virtuoso drumbeats showered out over the continuing basic design like machine-gun fire. There was no singing in this prelude. The drummers, shuffling their feet, began to lope forward as they played, and the circle's counter-clockwise movement gathered momentum. The laughter and comments from our side of the courtyard ceased, and even the master of the palace, sitting there with his microphone in his hand, surrendered to the general hypnosis the drummers were striving to create.

When the opening number was over, there was a noisy rearranging of chairs. These were straight-backed and completely uncomfortable, no matter how one sat in them, and it seemed clear that no one ever used them save when Europeans were present. Few chairs are as comfortable as the Moroccan *m'tarrba* with its piles of cushions.

"Art Blakey'd enjoy this," said Christopher. "There's a lot of material here for him."

Our host leaned sideways, holding the microphone in front of his mouth, and said, "*Comment?*" Then he held it closer to Christopher for his reply.

"I was talking about a great Negro drummer in America."

He shifted it again. "Ah, yes. The Negroes are always the strongest."

Out in the open part of the courtyard, groups of three or four men were going across into the far corner to tune their drums over the fire. Almost at once they began again to per-form; a long, querulous vocal solo was the prelude. One might have thought it was coming from the silence of the town, from somewhere outside the palace, it was so thin and distant in sound. This was the leader, creating his effect by standing in the darkness under the arches, with his face turned to the wall, as far away as he could get from the other performers. Between each strophe of his chant there was a long, profound silence. I became more aware of the night outside, and of the superb remoteness of the town between the invisible canyon walls, whose only connection with the world was the unlikely trail we had rattled down a few hours earlier. There was nothing to listen for in the spaces between the plaintive cries, but everyone listened just the same. Finally, the chorus answered the far-away soloist, and a new rhythm got under way. This time the circle remained stationary, and the men danced into and out of the center in pairs and groups, facing one another.

About halfway through the piece there was whispering and commotion in the darkness by the entrance door. It was the women arriving en masse. By the time the number was finished, sixty or seventy of them had crowded into the courtyard. During the intermission they squeezed through the ranks of standing men and seated themselves on the floor, around the center – bundles without form or face, wrapped in great dark lengths of cloth. Still, one could hear their jewelry clinking. One of them on my left suddenly rearranged her outer covering, revealing a magnificent turquoise robe embroidered in gold; then swiftly she became a sack of laundry once more. Several set pieces by the men followed, during which the women kept up a constant whispering among themselves; they watched politely, but it was evident that their minds were on the performance they themselves were about to give.

When the men had finished and had retired from the center, half the women present stood up and set about removing their outer garments. As they moved into the light they created a fine theatrical effect; the beauty of the scene, however, came solely from the variety of color in the splendid robes and the flash of heavy gold adornments. There were no girls at all among them – which is another way of saying that they were all very fat. A curious phenomenon among female musicians in Morocco is that at the beginning of their performance they seldom give much evidence of rhythmic sense. This has to be worked up by the men playing the drums. At the outset they seem distraught, they talk and fidget, smooth their clothing, and seem interested in everything but the business at hand. It took a good deal of insistent drumming to capture the women on this occasion, but after two numbers the men had them completely. From then on the music grew consistently more inspired. "*N'est-ce pas qu'elles sont magnifiques?*" whispered Monsieur Rousselot. I agreed that they were wonderful; at the same time I found it difficult to reconcile what I was seeing with his earlier description of Tassemsit as a holy city of sin. Still, doubtless he knew best.

As the shrill voices and the drumming grew in force and excitement, I became convinced that what was going on was indeed extraordinarily good, something I would have given a good deal to be able to record and listen to later at my leisure. Watching my host in the act of idly ruining what might have been a valuable tape was scarcely a pleasure. Throughout their performance, the women never stirred from where they stood, limiting their movements to a slight swaying of the body and occasional fantastic outbursts of antiphonal hand-clapping that would have silenced the Gypsies of Granada. With all that excess flesh, it was just as well they had no dance steps to execute. When the final cadence had died away, and while we applauded, they filed back to the shadows of the arcade and modestly wrapped their great cloths around them, to sit and listen to the *ahouache's* purely percussive coda. This was vigorous and brief; then a great crash of drums announced the end of the entertainment. We all stood up quickly, in considerable discomfort for having sat so long in the impossible chairs, and went back into the big room.

Five inviting beds had been made up along the mattresses at intervals of perhaps twenty feet. I chose one in a corner by a window and sat down, feeling that I should probably sleep very well. The courtyard emptied in no time, and the servants carried away the chairs, the lantern and the tape-recorder. Monsieur Rousselot stood in the middle of the room, yawning as he took off his shirt. The host was shaking hands with each one of us in turn and wishing us elaborate good-nights. When he came to me, he held out the flat box containing the tape he had just recorded. "A souvenir of Tassemsit," he said, and he bowed as he handed it to me.

The final irony, I thought. Of course, the spoiled tape has to be given to me, so that I can know in detail just what I failed to get. But my words to him were even more florid than his to me;

I told him that it had been an unforgettable occasion, and that I was eternally indebted to him for this undeserved favor, and I wished him a pleasant night. Monsieur Omar was lying in his bed smoking, clad only in his shorts, a delighted and indestructible Humpty Dumpty. He was blowing smoke rings toward the ceiling. I did not feel that the future of Tassemsit was in immediate danger. Our host went out, and the door into the courtyard was shut behind him.

After everyone had gone to sleep, I lay there in the dark, listening to the jackals and considering my bad luck. Yet the original objective of the trip had been attained, a fact I discovered only when I got to the next place that had electricity. When I tried the tape in the hotel at Essaouira, fourteen out of its eighteen pieces proved to be flawless. There was no point in wondering why, since logically the thing was impossible; it had to be accepted as a joyful mystery. It is always satisfying to succeed in a quest, even when success is due entirely to outside factors. We bought blankets, trays, rugs and teapots, and set out again for the north.

TANGIER

GENTLEMEN'S QUARTERLY, OCTOBER 1963

THE LEAST CONFUSING introduction to Tangier would be to make a low, leisurely flight, preferably by helicopter, over the very tip of northwestern Morocco. The jagged southern coast of the Strait of Gibraltar ends suddenly at Cape Malabata and becomes a wide white semicircle of sand, the shore of the Bay of Tangier. The European quarter, most of it build since World War II, includes the beach and covers more space than all the various native quarters put together. The Medina, a chaos of whitewashed cubes, begins at the port's edge and climbs up a steep hill to the walls of the Casbah, the fort built on the conveniently flat top of the hill. York Castle is at the northeast corner; it is astonishing to think that there is a tunnel leading from its dungeons all the way down to the port. Beyond the Casbah is the Marshan, a continuation of the tableland overlooking the Strait's cliffs. Here are big, Spanish-style villas, built at the turn of the century. The high trees that shaded them have been cut down, as they have in many parts of the city, to the fury of the British and Americans. (The average Moroccan thinks of a tree as potential firewood, nothing more.) And everywhere, in the interstices of open country between the various European settlements, are the thousands of permanently unfinished box-like houses that represent the new architecture of Morocco! No more blank walls pierced by one grilled peephole – instead, large European-style windows with glass in them, through which the women can watch the world outside without fear of being beaten by their husbands for having shown a momentary interest in the life of the street. This excrescence of haphazard constructions is beginning to grow up even along the base of the heavily forested hill behind the city, known simply as "The Mountain," a territory which has long been a bastion of foreign (largely British) property owners. The thick vegetation up here isolates each estate and gives it a degree of privacy no longer easy to come by in most places. High cliffs drop off into the widening Strait of Gibraltar; to the south and east there is a vast panorama of rolling countryside, with the foothills of the Rif Mountains in the background. Ahead is the open Atlantic.

Tangier seems to call forth a different reaction from each observer. Over the years, a great deal of disparate material about the place has been written – for, neutral and against – labeling it everything from a paradise to a hellhole, so that by now practically everybody knows that the little Moslem city at the northwest corner of Africa is not exactly like other cities, that it is a place of unlikely people and unexpected occurrences. It also seems that Tangier has become a kind of legend. I was not aware of this until three or four years ago, and I am still uncertain as to what the legend is and where it came from. When a man from N.B.C paid me a visit earlier this year, I put the question to him. "It's the name," he murmured. "Timbuctoo, Tangier, Samarkand ... You know." I nodded assent, but I was not clear as to why Tangier was being listed along with the other two admittedly legendary names. It goes without saying that I like living here, or else I should not still be doing so after these many years. At the same time, I can only speculate as to the reasons for the legend.

There is no visible civilized elegance of the sort found in European resorts; nor, on the other hand, has any effort been made to conserve the town's original "exotic" flavor, with the result that the latter has been largely lost. (The Chamber of Commerce of Biskra in Algeria, for instance, used to hire a bevy of local girls to spend their days carrying empty water jars on their shoulders up and down the streets so the tourists would have proper subjects for their snapshots.) To the uninitiated, the greater part of Tangier looks like either slum or suburb. In the Medina and the Casbah there are no streets. The alleys are narrow, often piled with garbage, and most of the houses have no water. Yet outside the walls, where there are streets and traffic, one has the recurring impression that one is on the outskirts of a larger city whose center is not far away. But the city never appears.

Certainly there is no great architecture in Tangier. Apart from the old Treasury in the Casbah and the tiny Sultan's Palace behind it, there is not an edifice worth inspecting. It is true that for visual charm the town does not have to depend on its buildings. It has its own special light and is fortunate topographical situation; the two combined go a long way to making an essentially ugly city into a reasonably attractive one. Painters arriving here for the first time always remark on the power and quality of the light. Not being a painter myself, I am unable to isolate and analyze its characteristics; I only know that it enhances whatever it illuminates, above all at a distance. And since Tangier ranges up and down over a series of hills, in such a way that at the end of every street there is a view of open countryside, sea or distant mountains, the eye naturally seeks out the bright vignette ahead of it, and remains relatively unaware of the building beside it.

There is the climate: the perfect summers that continue into November, the winters which, if often tempestuous, are still far better than those of Europe. There are the miles of magnificent beaches both on the Atlantic and on the Strait. These are assets, obviously, but they are scarcely sufficient to explain the city's renown. I suspect the legend of being nothing more than a residue of the lurid publicity Tangier was accorded in its international days. What most people expect to find is neither the place I knew when I first came thirty-two years ago, nor yet the one which actually exists today. They are looking for the boom city of fifteen years back, with its easy life and its crowd of free spenders; they also hope vaguely to unearth signs of the natural concomitants of such a phenomenon: organized vice and crime. The era is long since past; visible reminders of it are few.

The town is still the confused, heterogeneous and polyglot little center, but it will never again look as it used to. During even the years that I have known it, there have been three distinct phases in its succession of metamorphoses: the colonial era, the boom period and the not-so-rosy days being lived through at present, now that the city has lost its international status and has been integrated into the body of independent Morocco.

Colonial Tangier consisted of the Medina, with its winding alleys, its mosques and its thousands of cube-shaped houses. Outside the walls was a leisurely, unassuming European town that straggled upward over the several hills. There were horse-drawn carriages to ride in; the streets were shaded by high eucalyptus trees and protected from the ubiquitous wind by jungles of canebrake. The good life was cheap if you were a European. It did not occur to many people to wonder how the Moroccans got along; the common belief was that they could live on nothing. They did almost that, and managed never to project an image of poverty.

With the boom, Tangier ceased being a sleepy port somewhere in North Africa. Empty reaches of sand became city blocks of office buildings; olive groves suddenly grew hotels and apartment houses. Streets were indefinitely extended, across distant wheat fields and through inaccessible meadows where shepherds sat playing their flutes while they watched the flocks. Wealthy Europeans, intent on becoming more wealthy, declared themselves residents of the International Zone and built impressive homes on choice parcels of land commanding vistas of forest, mountain and sea. (No taxes, no restrictions, no labor unions. Madame wants twenty servants? Why not?) The shops were crammed with products from all over the world, often at prices below those of the country of origin. These were the good days; everyone knew they were, and made the most of them while they lasted. Parties were elaborate: you hired a whole village to come and amuse your guests for a half-hour of music, dancing, snake-charming and acrobatics. The end came on March 30, 1952, in the form of riots sparked by French-Spanish rivalry in the Zone. Tangier was dead long before the French precipitated the war by kidnapping the Sultan and carrying him off to Corsica. It is noteworthy that throughout the entire course of the war for independence it was the only city in Morocco without a program of systematic terrorism, and this in spite of the fact that many of the political leaders wanted by the French had sought refuge there; not one death due to political violence was reported.

Tangier's present, more prosaic state is that of a minor Moroccan city; when it was stripped of its privileges it was at the same time largely emptied of its European population. (They are beginning to come back, however.) Banks have been turned into bazaars and barbershops, the stock exchange has become the headquarters of the municipal lottery, the tiny offices from which dubious import-export transactions were conducted have had beds put into them and are being rented out by the week or day (and often, I might add, by the hour); and there is a whole new generation for whose members the wearing of exclusively European clothes serves as reassuring proof that they are a part of the civilized world.

Living in Tangier, however, has still meant being witness to an array of strange episodes in the lives of a whole series of bizarre characters. Nowhere have I seen such a concentration of eccentrics. You have been invited to Sir Malcolm's for dinner. When the meal is over, and the cook comes to carry out the coffee cups, Sir Malcolm mutters to her in Arabic: "Bring in the girls." She returns at the head of a procession of seven teenage maids in mountain garb, with their hair hanging loose down their backs. "Get the drums!" shouts Sir Malcolm, and they obligingly fetch a collection of large and small African drums covered with zebra hide. "Got 'em in Zanzibar one winter," he explains. Then, after a certain amount of chin-chucking and cheek-pinching, he adopts a more serious mien, and brings out a long black horsewhip, which he holds at his side while the girls begin to work up a rhythm on the skins. The drumming has a startling effect on Sir Malcolm: his nostrils dilate and he shouts exhortations. Then he commences a flourishing of the whip above their heads, making it crack in sharp explosions. They scream, but one feels that they are not really afraid, even when Sir Malcolm advances upon them and seizes one of them by the hair. He drags her to her feet in an effort to make her dance, but she covers her face with her hands and merely stands there. Sir Malcolm goes into English. "Dance, damn you!" he cries, striking her lightly with the handle of the whip. After a few listless wriggles, she pretends to trip and fall, landing in the midst of the drummers. A kind of circus ensues, in which the drums are sent rolling across the room as all seven girls pile on top of one another, shrieking, pulling whatever tresses are within reach, pinching whatever flesh is at hand. For a moment the guests are concerned: someone is bound to be hurt. But Sir Malcolm rushes in with his whip, not hesitating to use it as he pries them apart and shoves them one by one through the door-way where the cook is waiting to lock them into their quarters. When they are all gone, he tosses the whip on the floor and turns back to his guests, panting and red-faced. "Sorry," he says. "Wild little things." (But no one feels that the evening has been a failure.) "Take a bit of training. Of course they never stay more than two weeks, and that makes it difficult. They go back to the hills and spread the word. Sometimes one of them will come back after a while. Most of them are new." (Sir Malcolm is gone now; I wonder what country he has found to live in, now that such shenanigans are no longer practicable.)

There was the somewhat sinister Mr. Black, whom I never met, but who, I am told, kept an outsize electric refrigerator in his sitting room, in which there was a collection of half-pint glass jars. Occasionally he would open the refrigerator door, inspect the labels on the bottles and select one. Then in front of his guests he would pour its contents into a glass and drink. A lady I know, who was present one day when he did this, inno-cently inquired if what he had in the glass were a combination of beet and tomato juice. "This is blood," he said. "Will you have some? It's delicious chilled, you know." The lady, who had lived in Tangier for many years and was thus determined to show no astonishment at anything, replied: "I don't think I will right now, thank you. But may I see the jar?" Mr. Black handed it to her. The label read: *Mohammed*. "He's a Riffian boy," explained Mr. Black. "I see," she said, "and the other jars?" "Each one is from a different boy," her host explained. "I never take more than a half-pint at a time from any one of them. That wouldn't do. Too debilitating for them."

Not at all sinister is Miss Higginbotham, who, like so many of the older residents, came to Tangier for a short vacation and never again managed to leave. Since it was all of forty years ago that she arrived, one can assume that she will be staying on a while longer. She calls everyone "Ducks," including the members of the large company of animals and fowls that have come her way over the years. You go into her kitchen and find it bustling with hens and roosters. You pass by the door of her bedroom and hear the fierce barking of many dogs. The screams that issue from her dining room are only some cockatoos and a macaw conversing, but the door from there into the sitting room must be kept shut, or the spider monkey will get in and tease the birds. And if you are unfortunate enough to go into her bathroom you will be met by an irate goat that resents even Miss Higginbotham's intrusions. "I tried to tether the poor dear in the garden," she explains. "But those beastly Spaniards who live downstairs tormented him night and day. Sooner or later they'd have eaten him. They're Communists, you know."

Not all the peculiar people in Tangier are outsiders. Si Mokhtar, who wears rags, spends his days hurrying from bazaar to bazaar demanding money from the proprietors. He always gets what he asks for, and immediately distributes his loot to the small children in the street. When he is tired, he climbs into the nearest taxi and commands the driver to take him somewhere well out of town – to the top of The Mountain or the lighthouse at Malabata. Since he never has a franc on his person, these excursions are necessarily gratis. For Si Mokhtar is *mejdoub*, which means that he has every right and no responsibility. According to popular belief, the feebler the individual consciousness, the better equipped it is to serve as an instrument through which God can speak.

There was an extraordinary young man who stood for several years in the Zoco Chico, looking into the sky for a portent that would herald the return of the English lady with whom he had had a liaison. It was a full-time occupation for his waking hours; no matter what went on in the crowd moving past him, his attention was never diverted from its object: the patch of sky above the Spanish telegraph office.

You are bound to run into offbeat characters like these, no matter how and where you live. And there are various ways of living in Tangier. The most satisfactory is probably to buy a Moroccan house or two (or an entire neighborhood of Moroccan houses, as was done by Miss Barbara Hutton) and rebuild according to your own fantasy. Or you can rent an American-style bungalow in the Barrio California and pretend you are back home. I lived in hotels for years before I finally bought a house. The younger Americans do exactly what the younger Americans did thirty years ago, although then they were not called Beats for doing it. They rent spacious old houses in the Medina or the Casbah and occupy them in groups, so that each one comes out paying two or three dollars a month for his room. Food is a minor consideration: there are tiny Moroccan restaurants where they eat lunch for twenty-five cents. Dinner is usually a cooperative undertaking: you all get the meat and salad and we'll get the bread and wine. It's a pleasant enough way to live until winter comes along and the houses begin filling up with rainwater. Then leases are broken and pleasure-palaces evacuated, and the younger Americans disappear into anonymous little hotels in a futile effort to escape their landlords. Settlements are generally reached; sometimes, if the house is not too wet, the hardier tenants remain in it and shiver until spring. There is always the chance of their being invited to The Mountain, where they can

The Beats, famously, sought out Bowles in Tangier. This group, photographed by Allen Ginsberg in the Villa Muniria hotel garden, is, from left: Gregory Corso, Paul Bowles, Ian Sommerville, Michael Portman and William Burroughs.

thaw out in front of a blazing fireplace while the butler prepares a fresh supply of vodka martinis. When I was young, everyone went down to the desert in the winter. But with the expanding economy, the pleasures of the poor have become the privileges of the rich; it costs money now to winter in the Sahara, and so the younger Americans do without that luxury. But as they tell you, the Tangier scene is worth making, and they are making it.

Zany Costa del Sol

Holiday, April 1965

I WAS JUBILANT at my luck in La Línea. The Spanish are conducting a program of official harassment of motorists here, at the border between Gibraltar and Spain. By holding each car arbitrarily at the gate for fifteen minutes they can create an impressive bottleneck; the purpose is to discourage people with cars from passing between the two territories. If there is any traffic at all, the wait can be interminable. Six or seven hours of sitting at La Línea is not unusual. On the advice of my driver, we left very early in the morning and had only two cars ahead of us. In thirty-five minutes we were through the gate.

It was very fine to be moving along through the precise countryside of Andalusia in the bright morning sunlight. The Mediterranean was spread out on my right like a great sheet of glass, without a ripple on its surface, and along the curving coast ahead, the tiny white towns were just visible at the base of the bare brown and violet mountains.

The first time I saw this region, now known as the Costa del Sol, was in 1934. At that time it was nameless, and no one seemed to think of it as an entity. I drove from Granada straight down to Motril on the sea, and then along the coast to Gibraltar. There were no striking features in the landscape. Large barren mountains on the north; between their base and the Mediterranean, a slightly sloping plain where figs, olives, sugar cane, cork oaks and small parasol pines grew. An occasional long alley, bordered by date palms, led to an isolated farm. Here and there a camel, hitched to a mule, pulled a plow. What was impressive about the ride was the fact that here were a hundred and forty miles of Mediterranean shore whose dun-colored sand had never been used for anything more than drying nets and beaching fishing boats. The villages were very white, like all the villages of Andalusia; possibly they were a little poorer than most.

Since then the strip of shore has become the site of Europe's most spectacular land boom. When a region is growing as fast as this, it can have a different aspect every few months; and it was more than three years since I had paid a visit to the Costa. Already in 1961 the donkey's bray had been overpowered by the roar of traffic, and the sound of the guitar replaced by that of the jukebox. Today the transformation has gone much farther; at certain focal points of activity there is a small chaos of trucks, derricks, cement mixers and sewer pipes. Hillsides are being leveled, depressions filled, roads extended. And everywhere concrete boxes are going up. The small ones are "authentic Andalusian villas," the large ones "blocks of superb luxury flats." The twentieth century has taken roots.

That which is new is good. In the center of Torremolinos, outside of Málaga, I got into a cab and asked to be taken to the Hotel Carihuela Palace, adding: "That's the best one, isn't it?"

"No, *señor!*" the driver announced, relishing my ignorance. "The Carihuela's been running since 1960. They've built several here since then." He began to list the newer and therefore better hotels, detailing their advantages, eager to have me see any one of them for myself. Condescending when I declined, he agreed that the Carihuela was a very good hotel, but there was no getting around the fact that it was already four years old. He had thought the señor might be happier at one of the better ones.

On my first walk around Torremolinos I had the impression that a series of blockbusters had fallen on the region. It used to be a quiet little town at the top of a not very high cliff above the sea, where in the early decades of the century a few urban

Spaniards had built some hideous villas. It had much in common with Praia da Rocha on Portugal's Algarve coast, but it did have some high shade trees. (It does not have them anymore.) There were two *pensiónes* atop the cliff overlooking the sea. I had stayed at both for weeks at a time, but now I could not even find the original site of either. From the Pensión Santa Clara you used to look down on La Carihuela, a string of fishing shacks along the beach where the nets were spread out to dry and the children ran naked. La Carihuela is still there; it has become a tough little nucleus full of bars and rooming houses, where the original inhabitants in their partially remodelled huts live side by side with vacationing party girls from Stockholm and Hamburg.

The foreigners who have been in the region for ten years or more consider themselves old residents; they are indignant that Torremolinos should have become more like Las Vegas than like Santa Barbara. And then Torremolinos has set the style for the whole coast; it is where the boom started, and where the haphazard construction, having been longer in process, has reached monstrous proportions. "Look what they've done to it! It used to be so charming, and now look at it!"

It certainly does not look Spanish, if that is what they mean. But it is a much more serious matter that the great Andalusian cities of Seville, Cordova and Granada should have come down with the same disease and been disfigured by it. In the face of that, how can we care what has happened to a tacky little suburb of Málaga? I am inclined to hope the fever in Torremolinos rages even more furiously. Perhaps if it reaches an extreme whose absurdity is manifest to the Spanish themselves, they will take steps to protect other parts of their country from being attacked by a similar architectural blight. It seems likely that one day the entire Costa del Sol will offer the same anarchic aspect as the present two-mile strip of Torremolinos; planning could scarcely rescue any of it now.

I AM TOLD that this is too lugubrious a view, that there is a recently formed association of property owners which stresses as one of its

The cover of *Holiday* magazine, for which Paul Bowles wrote this piece. The magazine, published in Philadelphia, commissioned most of Bowles' travel writing, alongside contributions from John Steinbeck, Ernest Hemingway and Lawrence Durrell.

objectives the encouragement of legislation restricting the height of buildings constructed outside the town limits of a given community. Should such a law be enacted, and then Señor Contreras takes it into his head to put up a hotel in the form of a battleship or Señor Peralta decides to erect a row of apartment houses that look like igloos or pagodas, these errors at least will not be visible from ten miles away. If they can do even this much, they reason, it will be a beginning.

What is Torremolinos like? A short letter from a resident, printed in the pages of *Lookout*, the English-language magazine published on the main street of the town, provides us with a concise portrait of its soul: "This morning when I looked out the window I saw two large objects bobbing up and down in the water. On closer inspection they proved to be enormous plastic replicas of a Pepsi Cola and a Mirinda bottle anchored there as advertisements." Torremolinos is pop art in the flesh. Its residents defend it fiercely. As a riposte to Kenneth Tynan's *Esquire* article entitled "Eclipse of the Fun", *Lookout* came up with an issue called "Terrible, Terrible Torremolinos". Here, expressing the local point of view, the editor opines: "A small, provocative, sinful, razzle-dazzle seaside resort such as Torremolinos is just what was needed to complete the picture."

IN A 238-page report called "The Costa del Sol and its Problems", recently issued by Málaga's Technical Office of Coordination and Development, there is a large folding graph showing the motor accidents, fatal and otherwise, which occurred during the past year along the single highway that links the towns of the coast. To see the Ferraris, Mercedes 300's, Jaguars and Aston Martins in orbit on the congested fifteen-foot-wide road is to wonder how it is that so many people are still alive. But precisely where the road has been widened, as at Torremolinos, the accident incidence is far higher.

I take a taxi into Málaga. Sure enough, I am nearly killed. As usual, a quarter of the vehicles in the road are ten-ton trucks transporting crushed stone and building materials. Without warning, one of them applies all its brakes and stops. There are three cars between us and the truck; we are all going along at a good clip. Each driver swerves to the left, and we all end up almost touching one another; at that moment there happens to be no oncoming traffic, so we remain alive.

An American of Torremolinos tells me, "The accidents here are famous."

"Yes. I've heard about them all along the coast."

"But the ones here are spectacular. A man's head will land on one side of the road and his body on the other."

Wherever the pieces may land, Torremolinos is definitely not a place for anyone who likes to walk. Each time I wanted to go into the town I had to walk part of the distance in the highway; there was nowhere else to put my feet. Later they may build sidewalks where hillocks of dirt are now.

Miss Honor Tracy, the novelist, appears to have suffered a traumatic shock when she returned to Torremolinos after several years' absence. "To look at it now," she wrote, "is like looking at the face of a friend struck with not one but every affliction of the skin: warts, wens, carbuncles, pox, leprosy and lupus." Naturally I sympathize with her, but the vehemence of her language bewilders me, because the face of her friend was 'nothing remarkable in the beginning.'

Lookout warns its readers against journalists, because they are "dangerous." It takes umbrage at any reference in the foreign press to drunkenness, the using of drugs, or unusual sexual behavior among the inhabitants of the coast. This is natural and desirable. Everyone knows that journalistic reports of large-scale misconduct, whether they be date-lined Torremolinos, Tangier, Naples or Macao, are necessarily invented or, at their most objective, very much inflated.

The local authorities show an admirable tolerance of extravagant behavior, but only on the part of outsiders. A local Bohemian put it succinctly: "Foreigners never get busted here. Only the Spanish." There is no doubt that the citizens of the land are closely supervised. I doubt, however, that this is the reason for the low incidence of crime in Spain. It seems much more likely that the causes are in the actual fabric of Spanish culture: more than anything, I should think, in the stress put upon family loyalty, which presupposes love. There are few neurotics among the Spanish, few who feel themselves unwanted and thus outside.

THE RED NEON tubes spell out BAR, *Bar*, *B*A*R*S, and the noise rolls out into the narrow streets. Everyone is playing at being Spanish, handclapping and screaming "*Olé!*" In the naming of establishments the tropical motif has been emphasized: Tahiti, Aloha, Tabú, Acapulco, Las Antillas, Ecuador, La Tropicana. A waiter remarks proudly, "Now we have the Miami Beach in Espain."

If Torremolinos is Miami, then Marbella, down the coast to the west, is Palm Beach. Its roster of property owners glistens with titles and fortunes, includes such names as Los Duques de Alba, Prince and Princess Bismarck, Los Marqueses de Villaverde, the Duke and Duchess of Windsor. It boasts the best winter climate of Europe, and at the moment is considered the most elegant place to live on the Costa del Sol. This is reflected in the prices; even in the supermarket they are 10 to 20 percent higher than in other towns of the region. The visitor should feel that he is paying a luxury tax for the privilege of being in a place that has retained some of its Andalusian flavor.

Perfect weather, but the sun sets early in November. Afternoons I sit in a café opposite the plaza. There is a sharp edge to the wind; the leaves are coming down and covering the walks around the kiosks and benches. I sit until I am too cold to sit any longer, and then I walk down toward the beach. The wind is bitter here. A large Swede is just beginning to wade out into the darkening water for his late-afternoon dip.

It is difficult to get anything done in Marbella in the afternoon. Some shops shut at one, others at two, and still others at two-thirty; they open again approximately three hours afterward. Franco's campaign to persuade the people to adopt an earlier living schedule seems to have had no success on the Costa del Sol. One evening there was a performance of de Falla's *La Vida Breve* by the Teatro de la Zarzuela, at Málaga's Teatro Cervantes, a gala affair at which I felt conspicuous, being in neither white tie nor black. At precisely midnight the first notes of the opera filled the hall, and at ten minutes to two we came out of the theater. Everything was just as it always has been.

PRINCE ALFONSO HOHENLOHE, who built and owns the Marbella Club Hotel, tells of a wager he made with a visiting Swiss banker; he bet him a thousand pesetas that, given three tries, he would not be able to guess the rate of profit he had realized on a piece of land. The banker must have known he would lose, but being a guest at the hotel he accepted the wager. "I warn you it's exceptionally high," the prince told him.

"Two thousand percent," suggested the banker.

"Much higher."

"Well, five thousand percent."

"Far, far higher. I warned you."

"Twenty-five thousand percent?"

"You've lost," said the Prince. "I bought the land when it was going at fifty centimos a square meter and sold it for two thousand pesetas a square meter. Four hundred thousand percent."

There are placards in the shop windows and bars announcing a Thanksgiving Dinner and Dance. (Three hundred tickets only, five dollars per person, including full Turkey Dinner, Champagne, Dancing, Floor Show.) But you must have your American passport with you. I am told that there are not three hundred American residents in the entire region. The directors of the tourist bureau in Málaga claim that no records are kept of the nationality of either residents or visitors; they doubt that even the police have such a list. The assumption is, however, that the Germans would top it numerically, with the Swedes coming next, and after that the Danes and the English.

The Costa del Sol is no wider than a bit of thread dropped onto the map of Spain; behind it is the vast beautiful land of

Andalusia. Any road leading from the main highway takes you directly into the mountains, where the villages, straddling their hilltops planted with pomegranates and almond trees, still look as they have looked for centuries. Three or four of these, too near the shore, have been gobbled up by foreigners. The pleasantest of the occupied villages is Churriana, up above Torremolinos, about two miles away, where Hemingway used to come and stay with Bill Davis. Down the road from the Davises live the Brenans. If there is a visiting literary or artistic celebrity in the vicinity, he is likely to be found sitting in the Brenans' garden in the shade of the bamboo brake.

When I first went into Gerald Brenan's house it occurred to me that every architect, decorator and landscape gardener working in the region ought to be required to inspect the property thoroughly before being allowed to exercise his profession. I suggested to my hosts that it must be an ideal state of affairs, living like this in a fine old rambling house crammed with books, the magnificent garden outside full of fruit and flowers, and the same quiet, happy servants always there to make life pleasant. Not exactly, they said, and then they told me a strange story.

During the Spanish Civil War the Brenans left Churriana and went to England. Not unexpectedly, the authorities requisitioned the house and placed several Spanish families in it. The gardener, being used to working for English people, found the new conditions intolerable, and when he heard of an eccentric Englishman nearby who was looking for a place to live, sought him out and suggested the Brenan house. Eventually the squatters were dispossessed and the Englishman and his French wife took over the house at a monthly rental of 135 pesetas. When the Brenans finally were able to return to Churriana, the new tenants had for some time been happily installed on the ground floor in the principal rooms of the house – so happily that they had no desire to leave.

"But of course we must have our house back – the whole house," the Brenans told them.

"Try and get it," the Englishman replied.

Lawyers were retained by both parties, the tenant having either the luck or the astuteness to hire a very young man just about to hang out his shingle. There is a Spanish precedent which specifies that a lawyer trying his first case has the right to approach the judge before the hearing and present a personal appeal for his client; it is usual for the judge to rule in his favor. All this happened, and the tenants stayed on. Then Brenan sent them an offer of £1,000 to clear out. They were not interested.

"Look!" He pointed over the banisters to the bottom of a staircase, where a barricade of old screens and furniture had been piled up against the doors.

I was incredulous. "You mean they're *still* in there?"

"Still in our best rooms, still using our best furniture." (And, I learned, still paying 135 pesetas a month, which is equal to about $2.25.)

"What sort of man is he, anyway?" I asked indignantly.

"Oh, I've never spoken to him since the first day. I've only caught sight of him twice," he said.

"You mean *ever*? In all these years? In twenty-seven years?"

"Yes, it must be about twenty seven years," he agreed.

SPANISH HOTEL ROOMS often leave a good deal to be desired regarding temperature and lighting. In the summer your bedroom, when you got back to it at night, was on occasion so incredibly hot that you elected to lie out flat on the tile floor rather than go near the bed; in the winter it was better to wear an overcoat during your waking hours. Today, for a hotel to be listed officially in the luxury category, it must be air-conditioned, so that hazard has been got around. The lighting, however, is still strictly for the owls. I have been informed that night is not the time, nor bed the place, for reading and writing.

The Andalusians, like their Moroccan forebears, are an excessively gregarious people, and they look upon the desire for solitude and privacy as an abnormality, if not downright suspect. For them, to be aware of being alone is to be lonely. It is almost impossible to find a single room on the Costa del Sol, and usually no reduction is made in the price if there is to be only one occupant. The lone traveler is penalized.

In discussing what constitutes a good hotel there is, of course, ample room for disagreement. Since to me a hotel means primarily sleep, my own criterion is comfort pure and simple, which I translate as meaning maximum quiet and a good bed. Heating, plumbing and service come afterward. The public rooms, shops, grounds, pools, tennis courts and golf courses don't come into my consideration at all. Hotel food the world over being notoriously negative, an edible meal is a delightful if unexpected bonus, and by no means a *sine qua non*.

Service in Spanish hotels has always been more a matter of good will than anything else. I suppose this is because the Spanish do not really demand or expect service; what they like is a good show. If there is at their disposition a standing army of men and small boys in smartly tailored uniforms, perfectly trained in the art of bowing, smiling and saying, "*Si, señor*," they seem well satisfied.

There is a lot of talk along the Costa del Sol about the newest big hotel, the Don Pepe. (Why anyone should want to build a vast luxury establishment and call it the Mister Joe Hotel is a matter for conjecture, although around here they find it perfectly natural; they say it is the owner's name.) The hotel stands in the middle of the country at the edge of the sea, a mile west of Marbella, and boasts "three lighted swimming pools and sauna." It is the most expensive place on the coast, but alas, not the best. Contemporary building techniques may be acceptable for urban living, where the myriad sounds in the air help to disguise those being made in the rooms above, below and beside yours, but in silent surroundings they are clearly counter-indicated.

I was in the bathroom shaving for dinner. Suddenly there was a man's voice in my bedroom, calling "Hey, Anna!" It called again, louder. I hurried out, razor in hand. It was a surprise, but not a consolation, to find that the voice came from the other side of the wall in the adjoining room. "I'm gonna wear a sports shirt," it declared.

There was a wait. "What's the matter with a sports shirt?" the voice then wanted to know.

Unintelligible mutterings issued from the bathroom.

"Oh." The voice was dead now, all hope gone.

The voice did not pass a restful night. I shouldn't think Anna could have, either, but very likely she was used to the fully orchestrated snoring. I put some wax plugs in my ears, and what with the whir of the air-conditioning got through the night fairly well. The first thing I heard in the morning was Anna saying, "You're wrong, Harry, and I'll tell you why." At that moment someone dropped a coin into the nickelodeon that stood in the bar at the end of the garden under the balcony, and it began to gurgle and tinkle. (Apparently they had tested jukeboxes and found their volume insufficient for outdoor use.)

I ordered breakfast. On the balcony sometime later, above the cries of the sea gulls and the swish of the water on the sand (the nickelodeon having stopped for the moment), I drank my tepid coffee. "Hello, dear," said Anna to a woman on a balcony farther along the deck. (They both must have been leaning over the railing in order to see each other.) "You know what Harry did last night? He went right to bed and slept like a baby for ten hours."

It is a mark of distinction in Spanish hotels to have a chain by the bathtub, to be pulled to summon help in case the ordeal proves too much for the bather. The Don Pepe supplements the chain with a telephone. One evening before dinner I was in the bathtub; the phone began to ring furiously beside my ear. I hesitated, reflected that electrocution is at least a rapid death, and seized the apparatus.

"Hola!" said a musical female voice.

"Manolo?"

"No. No soy Manolo." I imagined that would be sufficient. But she went right on.

"Ah, Manolo's gone out?"

"What room do you want?" The soap was getting into my eyes.

"Six-fifteen."

"This is room six-fifteen all right, but there's no Manolo here. There's some mistake."

She just laughed. "We're down in the lobby. Paco and Antonio are with us. We're coming up."

It seemed imperative to switch to English; I did so, and in a somewhat louder voice. She apologized.

Notwithstanding minor contretemps like the Don Pepe, coming to the Costa del Sol could seem almost like a rest cure to the person who has been moving around other parts of Europe, where palms are permanently upturned and the service charge is not to be confused with the gratuity. When you ask for your bill at the desk, it turns out to be exactly right; there is no list of charges at the bottom to bring it up an extra 20 or 30 percent. The classical dissatisfied expression that goes with pocketing a tip is not to be found. It is almost like the years of the Republic, when there was a sign on every café table announcing that it was forbidden to tip, and when, if you made a misstep, your coins were courteously but firmly returned to you.

The swiftly rising standard of living has already transformed the inhabitants of the coast; the younger generation is taller, and not even recognizably "Spanish" in appearance. One begins to understand that much of what was originally considered the character of the country was due only to excessive poverty. The hunched shoulders, bowed head and dusty black garments which were the mark of Andalusia are gone. Prosperity has made the old French wisecrack, about Europe being bounded on the south by the Mediterranean and the Pyrenees, no longer apposite. Unending change is the essence of life, and whether things go right or wrong, the people in these parts have a stoical but succinct little phrase that says it all:

Arriba la vida!

CASABLANCA

HOLIDAY, SEPTEMBER 1966

WHEN THE AMERICAN visitor arrives in Morocco for the first time, often the one city of whose name he is absolutely sure, and which he is determined to see, is Casablanca. For a resident of the country such a desire demands an explanation. He says: "Why Casablanca?" It appears that the very name suggests a mysterious and exciting place. Continuing the inquisition, the resident can usually trace the other's interest back to the fact that there was once a film bearing that title, and that since then the city has enjoyed the reputation of being a glamorously sinister Oriental labyrinth. (*Casablanca*, made in the United States during World War II, might just as well have been called *Cairo* or *Damascus*, for all the resemblance its scenes had to the Atlantic port in question. But that is irrelevant; the glamor is embedded in the place name.) So the visitor comes, finds no twisting alleys, no turbaned sheiks conducting international intrigues. Instead, he is confronted with a modern metropolis that looks like a somewhat newer Havana, whose wide boulevards go on for miles, and it is only by chance that he will come upon either an alley or a turban. The place has its share of intrigue and crime, but none of all this is particularly mysterious or Eastern. Casablanca is not Morocco; it is a foreign enclave, an alien nail piercing Morocco's flank, If the resident can't dissuade the visitor from his project altogether, he can at least advise him to visit other parts of the country first.

The city is like a vast shell, above all at night, when under their fluorescent arc lamps the long thoroughfares are absolutely empty, and one gets the impression of a town just evacuated by retreating forces. In the daytime the place is still haunted by a shadowy *présence francaise*, a ghost that refuses to be exorcised. Indeed, we shall be increasingly aware of it as time passes, until there ceases to be any appreciable difference between French and Moroccan culture. The Moroccans were understandably eager to get rid of the colonizing French, but it was not immediately apparent that one of their principal objectives was to usurp their place here by becoming more French than the French.

It is a bit frightening, this European city peopled by Moslems. For the foreign residents of other cities in the land, Casablanca is a kind of scapegoat. Things are always worse there; one enjoys reminding oneself that all the elements he dislikes in Morocco are to be found there in greater concentration. So often it has been the place one has been the most thankful to be away from. Beginning with the first morning in 1931 when I awoke in a hotel there and heard the racket outside in the street, I have felt a strong antipathy toward it. I know Morocco, but not Casablanca, and this is because I have consistently avoided it when it was possible to do so; often I have taken an extra day or two and driven through the mountains rather than have even a brief contact with the big city. During the years of the French Protectorate it was a common saying that Casablanca offered the worst of both worlds: its French were the most arrogant and disagreeable, and its Moroccans the most decadent, which is to say the most Europeanized.

Of course, the day eventually came when I had to go there for one reason or another; I went more often, and in the course of my visits found that it was not without what the French call *agréments*. The implicit hybridization of the town still bothers me; the Japanese and even the Indians have managed viable patterns of cultural amalgamation, and perhaps in time there will emerge here some sort of selectivity with regard to which facets of European life are to be accepted and which rejected as hazards to the existing culture.

You go out of your hotel in the morning and hail one of the toy-sized taxis that race along the boulevards, and likely as not, you are straightway projected into Lewis Carroll Land. Practically any conversation with a taxi driver can accomplish it. Precise antilogic, studied non sequiturs, shameless self-contradiction, the sly introduction of wholly unexpected subject matter, plus an implicit air of general disapproval – the elements are all there to give you the sudden illusion of having fallen down the rabbit hole or slipped through the mirror. At first you work to convince yourself that it is merely a well-rehearsed spiel the driver is giving you, under the mistaken impression that it will help squeeze a few extra francs from you at the end of the ride, but after a few more such experiments you reluctantly set aside the theory, for it does not explain the general air of belligerency mixed with condescension that the drivers show you, nor the apparently uniformly insane course of their thoughts.

One day I took a cab out to the Aquarium. As soon as I had given the address, the driver turned and remarked: "I know why you want to go there."

"Do you?" I said, not paying much attention.

"Yes. I've been there. I've seen what they've got there, and it's a fake. I've seen that cat there that wants everybody to think he's a dog. But I've seen him eat, too, and he eats nothing but fish. Did you ever see a dog do that?" At this I began to suspect that he was drunk, and I watched the traffic coming in from the side streets. However, we arrived without mishap. I bought my ticket and went in. Immediately I saw his cat: in the tank just inside the entrance, barking and playing the clown, was a brown seal.

Another driver, as he waited for a red light to change to green, turned to face me and, as though continuing a conversation, said: "The gloves you're wearing. How much did they cost?" I was taken unawares. It was clear that he was set on having the gloves – preferably as a gift, but failing that, as a purchase. They were several years old, and I had no idea of their price. Nothing marks one for a fool so immediately in the mind of a Moroccan as not to know how much one has paid for something.

I invented. "Two thousand francs."

He waited for the next red light. "I'll give you one thousand."

I laughed. We drove on. Presently he said: "Or tomorrow I'll drive you to Ain Diab and wait while you swim. That's worth more than a thousand francs."

"I don't want to go to Ain Diab tomorrow."

He said no more until I got out and paid him. Then he looked reproachfully at me. "I thought you were a friendly man," he said sadly.

There is a meter on every cab, but the drivers do not bother to use them, preferring to make an arbitrary price at the end of the ride. One day I determined to attempt to get one of them to set the meter going. As I got into the cab I said:

"How does it happen that you taxi chauffeurs never turn on your meters?"

"The meters don't work," he said.

"You mean *all* the meters are broken?"

"They don't work fast enough. Besides, everybody knows how much it costs to go from one place to another. If you put the meter on, people get mixed up and don't know how much to pay."

"They'd pay what the meter reads, wouldn't they?"

He seemed briefly scandalized; then he laughed. "That wouldn't be any good. Everything's too expensive these days for that." He began to recite a list of food items, giving their recent and their present prices. I interrupted him.

"How much are you going to charge *me*?"

"Oh, everybody knows the price is two hundred and fifty francs," he answered airily, and went on with his food market quotations until we arrived. Then he stopped, turned in his seat, and said: "That will be three hundred francs."

"You just told me two hundred and fifty."

"Yes, monsieur," he agreed. "The price is two hundred and fifty. But that's the thing about prices." Now he pretended to laugh uproariously, his eyes watching me very closely from the middle of the grimace. "You never know when they're going up."

It is true that the constant rise in the cost of living is felt more intensely in Casablanca than in the small towns and rural areas. The working class here is first of all displaced, therefore deculturized; it is an island, cut off from the mainland of the mother culture. Semi-literate and oriented toward Europe, its members literally do not know how to function in the manner of their forebears, or even like the provincial Moroccans of today. The food suffers; the girls grow up without knowing how to prepare the customary dishes made with native grown staples. They are thus obliged to fall back upon packaged and semi-processed foods, which they flavor with prepared sauces and wash down with Coca-Cola and Orange Crush. It is precisely these manufactured products, often imported, thus highly taxed, that cost the most, and their regular consumption is ruinous to the average worker's budget.

The city has not yet recovered from the economic blow dealt it by the establishment of Moroccan independence, when it was severed from France. The resulting exodus of European capital and personnel created a state of depression and unemployment that has not been alleviated during the intervening years by any initiative on the part of Moroccan businessmen. In the past five years even the population has decreased. (The *Guide Bleu*, published in Paris in 1952, confidently predicted a population of a million and a half for the city in 1960. If the compilers had been politically more astute they would have refrained from making such a rash forecast, since the misunderstanding had already arisen between the French and the sultan which led the following year to the latter's exile, and thence directly to independence.) The total 1965 population, 947,000, of whom 817,000 are Moslems, 76,000 are Europeans and 54,000 are Moroccan Jews, is literally smaller now than it was in 1960; the drop in the last two categories is not compensated for by the increase in the first.

In keeping with the present fashion of minimizing European guilt in the country's economic difficulties, there is a tendency on the part of Moroccan businessmen to blame their own lack of initiative. Yet for things to have been otherwise, history would have had to be totally different. Under French rule the area left for exploitation by Moroccans was extremely limited, consisting solely of textiles, sugar, tea and real estate, none of which necessitated a departure from the traditional business methods. It is hard to see how blame can be attached to such a group, which by its very nature was one to resist evolution and remain militantly unequipped to function in twentieth-century terms. "In spite of appearances," says M. Driss Charaf, one of Casablanca's younger, more analytical economic observers, "the Moroccan businessman has remained an ordinary shopkeeper. He is still ignorant of long-term investments, of the spirit of enterprise and the sense of calculated risk. In a word, he lacks basic economic education."

This is doubtless true, but to provide the necessary training is a long-term venture, and the situation demands quick action. *Étatisation* (an acceptable euphemism for socialization) is the solution. Thus, as a penalty for not having taken their business affairs into their own hands while they had the opportunity, Moroccan citizens may shortly lose the possibility of ever doing so.

What with the passage of time and the worsened economic situation, a temporary truce seems to have been reached between Moroccans and Europeans. There are no visible signs of unfriendliness on either side. During the city's most recent riots, in March, 1965, as a result of which there were many deaths and much damage to property, the astonishing detail emerged that not one European was even injured, and not one European- owned shop was touched. The really nasty French, the hard-core, racist-minded colonials, are gone, and have been replaced by fellow Moslems to serve as the target of popular dissatisfaction.

Normally the Moroccan, even if he is wearing only one ancient tattered garment, retains an air of indestructible self-sufficiency, even of nobility. It does not occur to one to attribute a financial status to him, nor does the word *poverty* suggest itself in connection with his life. Simplicity, austerity, even stoicism, but not poverty. These days, however, in Casablanca, to look Moroccan means to look poor. It is not surprising that the great majority of the inhabitants do not come into the center of the city at all, preferring to remain outside in the vast sordid quarters reserved for the poor. To wander out there is a little like being in India: there are the same endless crowds of disparate and ill-clad people passing constantly through the long sad streets. At night the destitute do not hesitate to invade the center; not being allowed to sleep in the parks, they lie in doorways and passages along the main thoroughfares. All one can say is that there are fewer of them than in the days of the French occupation. Where are the others? Dead, or in jail.

The poverty, for all its impressiveness, is nevertheless only the second topic of conversation aboard a cruise ship the night the tourists come back aboard after a day's liberty in Casablanca. First place is accorded to the convoluted financial adventures everyone has had while ashore. Each tourist has a small picaresque novel to relate; tales range from outright and dramatic defeat to imagined victory. (I say *imagined* because I suspect that no one ever brought off a truly victorious coup in dealing with Casablanca bazaar keepers; however, I may have an exaggerated respect for the business acumen and powers of salesmanship of the latter.)

But it is not only tourists buying rugs and hassocks and trays who meet with difficulties; it can be anyone buying anything at all. Two entirely ordinary examples, dating from yesterday and this morning, indicate the kind of complications inherent in any transaction.

I go into a small stationery shop that sells second-hand books, and begin compulsively to look through the titles on the shelf. To my astonishment I find a volume by Borges that has been out of print for several years, its pages still uncut. As with all the books, the price is marked on the end papers. I hand the volume to the shopkeeper with 500 francs, only to be told that there is a 1,000-franc deposit to be made in addition to the price marked, which he insists is really only the rental price. "Some books are for sale and others for rent," he explains.

"But how can I tell which are which?" I want to know.

"Only I can tell you that," he says. So I go out, buying nothing.

Today, on the way back to the hotel, I stop in a large self-service grocery store. The Dubonnet is marked 1,050 francs and the Vichy Celestins 125 francs. I take a bottle of Dubonnet and three bottles of Vichy. The bill is for 1,625 francs; I discover that they have charged me 1,250 for the Dubonnet. We argue about that and I show them the shelf where the price is exhibited. They make out a new bill, adding a thirty-five franc deposit for the Dubonnet bottle – an on-the-spot invention – and changing the price of the Vichy to 130. Unable to put through Operation 200 Francs, they have contented themselves with a quickly devised fifty franc supplement. I pay, smiling conspiratorially at the bill and then at them. This troubles them; I am not supposed to know what they have done. Christians like me are not expected to itemize a bill; they are assumed to be perpetually unaware of both value and price. And since I have made it clear that I am conscious of their overcharging, my being willing to pay makes me into an unfriendly and suspicious character. They glare at me and mutter as I go out.

The police are courteous and charming, and would like to be helpful. If you ask for directions, they are willing to give you a good deal of their time and attention, but it is unlikely that they will be able to produce the information you want. Their connection with the city around them seems very tenuous; one would say they were busy leading intense inner lives. An English resident of Tangier was stopped in a Casablanca street and told to pull over to the curb. "Your lights are not in order, monsieur," said the young officer, sauntering up. Since it was broad daylight, the Englishman was astonished. "They have white glass," the young man informed him, "and they should have yellow glass. You'll have to get new headlights."

"Can you give me one good reason why I should go to the expense and trouble of ordering new headlights?

The policeman shrugged. "I don't know," he said. "It's the fashion."

Saturday is sad in the center of town, with the shops all shut and the long, arcaded streets deserted. Weekdays there are echoes of Paris in the working-class restaurants near the central market; it is a pre-war Paris, with sawdust on the floor, big sheets of paper that cover the tables, the drone of conversation in the smoky air, and the *patronne* watching everything from her little box in the corner, forsaking her knitting from time to time in order to prepare a café espresso or to hand a waiter a bottle of wine. These are good places to sit during the middle of the day, but alas, on Saturday and Sunday they are shut. Thus I get the idea of going out to Ain Diab and eating by the sea. While I am waiting for a taxi I smell the moist breath of the ocean coming up the boulevard from the port, and I recall the familiar complaint about Casablanca's eternal humidity. In winter the wind that blows through the city is wet; in summer it is only damp, and the weather is not unduly hot. But the moss on the ground under the palms in the Pare Lyautey remains bright green the year around.

THE COAST ON the way to Ain Diab alternates between sand and rocks; there is a rough sea, and a misty white spray blows inland across the flat earth dotted with vast new housing projects. A certain number of people seem to have had the same idea as I: some of the restaurants are full. I choose one whose terrace is empty, which probably means that the food is indifferent, and sit down. The wind keeps flipping the tablecloth over the carafe of water. The waiter brings the menu. I study it a moment, and begin to laugh. It is a folded card, typewritten in French on the left and in English on the right. The first item, *Pâté Maison*, is presented to English-speaking guests as *House Paste*. I am sure then that the food is going to be terrible. However, aided by a bottle of Gris de Boulaouane, Morocco's good *vin rosé*, the meal turns out to be adequate if not exactly tasty, and I sit for a long time over it, watching the people go past.

When I am almost finished, a large Moroccan group arrives in two cars and deploys on the terrace near me; its members are engaged in playing the well-known game of the new upper class, which consists in uttering the louder sentences and phrases in French, all the while continuing the conversation *sotto voce* in Arabic. I say "in French" because that is what it is meant to be, though in reality it is only an unsuccessful attempt to reproduce the accent of the former Corsican and Marseillais colonials, who spoke a lamentable French at best. The vowel sounds are unrecognizable, and the vocal inflection distorted, with syllabic emphasis displaced and consonants given Arabic equivalents. The greater the fluency of the speaker, the further metamorphosed are the sounds of his French. One of the men cries excitedly: "*Chpépalvoikhkh, chpépalvoikhkh!*" and I know this means: "I can't stand him!" ("*Je ne peux pas le voir.*") But would I know this if I hadn't lived here for years? I doubt it. This neo-French is another language.

Alter a quarter of an hour or so they settle down into their own tongue, and I decide to see what Hachette's *Guide Bleu du Maroc* has to say about the history of Casablanca. A guidebook is like a telephone book: to be consulted rather than read. But sometimes in the welter of factual material one can pick out and bring to the fore some hitherto unnoticed pattern that justifies taking the trouble. In this case, however, all that happens is that I read the text, took out at the traffic and at the big waves breaking down the coast, and mentally shrug.

THE ORIGINAL SITE of the city is a low hill beside the ocean, about a mile from the restaurant where I am sitting, and it was called Anfa. It is still called Anfa, and there are a lot of expensive houses there. But nobody knows whether it was the Phoenicians, the Romans or the Berbers themselves who first built the town. There is no uncertainty, however, about the activities of the Arabs after they arrived from the Middle East and took the place in hand. They made it the home of a well-organized band of pirates whose habit it was to sail up to Portugal and lie in wait at the mouth of the Tagus for ships going in or out. When the Portuguese had had enough of this, they followed the marauders back to Anfa and sacked the place. Later, in the sixteenth century, they occupied the site and rebuilt it, calling it Casa Branca. It took two hundred years for the Moroccans to get back into their town, and by this time everyone was so used to hearing the place spoken of as White House that the name was not changed, but merely translated, to Dar el Beida, which is what it is called today by the entire Arab-speaking world.

I suppose the ancient history of Casablanca is dull because the place itself had no importance until the French arrived. They planned their blow meticulously, having taken care beforehand to create a condition that could serve as a pretext for attack. (Europeans need to have a moral justification for doing evil.) They sent General Drude down with a force of 3,000 men. There is an evocative inscription in the garden of Place Lyautey; it begins with these words:

IT WAS ON THIS SPOT, THE SEVENTH OF AUGUST NINETEEN HUN-
DRED SEVEN, THE OCCASION OF THE FIRST FRENCH LANDING ON
MOROCCAN TERRITORY, THAT GENERAL DRUDE ESTABLISHED HIS
POST OF COMMAND, PLANTED HIS FLAG, AND SET UP HIS TENT.

I pour out the last half glass of Gris de Boulaouane and think of the general standing there that night under the wide sky of the new land, listening to the barking of the dogs, and noting perhaps, as did Camus, that the sound carries ten times as far in North Africa as in Europe. Did it occur to him that the place would never again be as it had been, now that he had arrived? No, I decide. He was worrying about his liver, and wondering fretfully if enough cases of Vittel and Vichy had been brought along.

I turn to a folding map of the region, idly glance at it, and all at once am astonished. The coast at Casablanca runs due east and west, and I had always thought of it as going from southwest to north-east. I have learned something from the *Guide Bleu* after all. Then I study the map of the city and discover that its plan looks something like the plan of a theater, with the port like a curved proscenium and the principal avenues leading upward from it like aisles.

Someone clicks on a transistor radio; I pay the bill and leave, directing my steps downward to the park that lies halfway between the boulevard above and the beach below. The air is damp and the park is deserted. No – there is one man in a gray business suit, who could be either European or Moroccan, pacing about restlessly. I have the impression that he is looking for something. Suddenly he steps over a low fence that borders the path, and walks a short distance across the turf toward a palm tree. A second later he is kissing the grass, beginning his ritual obeisance, his tie blowing in the wind. Why is there an element of the absurd here where there should be none? I have seen Moslems praying in the streets for the better part of my life. If the place looked like Morocco, if the man wore even one piece of clothing that could identify him as a Moslem, everything would be different. It is simply that the gestures of Moslem life are at variance with the commonplace European décor of Casablanca, and are thus unexpected and very noticeable. There is a permanent contradiction between the way the city looks and what goes on in its streets.

I take a cab back to the Place de France, the heart of the city, where the two civilizations confront each other across the big sun-flooded square; on one side the tall banks and life insurance buildings with their vault-like cafés at street level where men sit in rows watching television, and on the other side, like the façade of a shabby small-town fair, the crowded and untidy portals of the Ancienne Medina. A few small streets near the entrance are devoted exclusively to restaurants. I wander about here for a while, sniffing the cinnamon and the cumin. The *plat du jour* is the same in several of the larger establishments: calf's-foot-and-artichoke stew. Then I go back into the main alley and let the mob push me through the maze. It is supposed to be a bad place for a European to go alone, but no one has ever paid me the slightest attention there. Sartorial anarchy is the norm. Tablecloths, blue jeans, *djellabas*, business suits, pajamas, strips of plastic oilcloth, sheets, sports jackets, *burnouses*, towels, haiks and bedspreads are all called into service to cover the human form.

EACH MORNING the shopkeepers here bring their wares out into the alleys, where they stack, range and hang them; the passages are decorated as if for a fiesta, but the banners are all garments and household articles for sale. The bicycles slicing through the crowd at all angles, from all directions, manage finally to induce a mild chronic anguish. While I am sidestepping one coming from the front, I tangle with two coming from the sides. I step into a cul-de-sac and turn around. The top ten or twelve stories of a white office building rise into the sky above the formless jumble of nearby structures. In the crowd is an occasional Hindu; there are also surprisingly many Jews and Spaniards. The Ancienne Medina does not cover a very great area; it makes me think of a water hole, a puddle of old Morocco surrounded by concrete, inexorably drying up, becoming always smaller and shallower. Contiguous to it on the south is a spacious *joteya*, or flea market, where, if anything worth having in the way of Moroccan articles is still available in the region, one will find it, rather than in the bazaars run for the tourist trade. Moroccans no longer make many things worth acquiring. With the exception of rugs, there is not much point in buying objects made recently. Workmanship has deteriorated, and taste in styling, which remained intact so long as tradition was strictly adhered to, has vanished utterly. However, second-hand artifacts dating from ten or fifteen years ago can often be found for next to nothing in the *joteya*.

Watch a Moroccan on a busy boulevard, completely unaffected by the traffic roaring past. He does not move along as one is supposed to do in a modem street. He always has time to lend a hand to the anonymous passer-by. He will hold the baby for a woman, help reload a donkey whose burden has slipped, rescue a child's ball from under a truck, push a stalled car, help gather up an overturned basket of fruit, all without the expectation of being thanked, or even noticed, since it is taken for granted that anyone will do such things for anyone else.

As a resident of Tangier I envy Casablancans two things: their public gardens and their restaurants. There are enough French still living in the city to make possible the existence of good eating places in all price categories; it is the only place left in all North Africa where there is gastronomic excellence and variety.

I AM TOLD that the following Saturday, if I want, I can hear some interesting music in a small synagogue near the Boulevard d'Anfa. The tip, given me by a Jewish friend, includes the information that a particularly good cantor from Marrakesh will be present. There are eighty synagogues in Casablanca, of which fifty are currently in use. The Jews of Morocco, all Sephardim, while on the whole no better off financially than their Moslem compatriots, have a highly organized and culturally rich community life. Thanks to their own initiative, as well as to the aid provided by certain charitable organizations in the United States, they have improved their lot considerably. There is no such thing as a Jewish beggar or a Jewish illiterate, for instance.

I set out early and eventually find the place. There is a courtyard where a large dog is chained beside a dry fountain. Three small boys are playing under a tree. I go over to them and ask them if they know where I can get hold of a skullcap like the ones they are wearing, so that I will be able to go into the synagogue. They confer for a moment. "Wait here," says the biggest. "We'll be right back." I stand there looking at the dog, as the sound of chanting begins to issue from the building.

After about fifteen minutes the boys return, flushed and out of breath. "You have no luck," they tell me. "We can't find any *toques*. And you can't even buy one because it's Saturday." A fourth boy comes along; they consult with him and he goes inside. "His father's the rabbi," they explain. Immediately the boy returns and hands me a tiny black *yarmulke*.

I place it on the back of my head. "It's very small," I say uncertainly.

The boy, who is a complete adult in miniature, says severely: "It's not important. Go in." I step inside the door and sit down at the back.

The attractive white and gold auditorium is empty save for a group of perhaps twenty men and youths sitting in two rows face to face across the central aisle. Most of them are dressed in business suits; a few of the older men have flowing white beards and wear caftans, and are straight out of a Chagall canvas. They are all leaning forward in their seats, their faces gleeful, and I have the impression that they are singing at one another. Each man holds a book in his left hand; some are continually bending forward and backward vigorously, while others merely emphasize certain cadences by raising the index finger, or tap out the rhythm with their feet. The principal singer occasionally makes spoken asides. More than anything else the scene reminds me of an old-fashioned *cuadro flamenco*, such as one used to see in the provinces of Spain in the days before the civil war. Furthermore, they swing. The beat is always accurate, as are the body and neck movements. From time to time, two or three men hold a low-pitched discussion under the singing.

Presently a middle-aged man wearing glasses turns and notices me. He holds up his book expectantly, then indicates that I should come and sit beside him. When I am there seated by his side, he leans over and raises the book in front of me, whispering: "So you can follow the poetry." There is no musical notation on the page, merely a text in Hebrew characters. I whisper back that unfortunately I am unable to read Hebrew. There is pity in his glance, but he is not deterred by my confession. Assuming that at the very least I can read the characters, he runs his forefinger slowly across the page from right to left, underlining each word for me as it is being sung. Now and then he whispers: "These are extra syllables not in the text," and I nod. This goes on for a little more than an hour. Someone brings in a tray laden with glasses of tea. The smell of mint fills the air. I have been in synagogues in Morocco where the men have brought out hip flasks of rum and *mahia*, but apparently this congregation contents itself with tea.

I have been glancing surreptitiously every few minutes in the direction of the balcony. A large blond woman is sitting in the front row, following the music apparently with intense interest, even though she has not once stopped eating something out of a bag in her lap. While the tea is being drunk the music goes on. Tea continues to arrive; I drink three glasses and eat a large cupcake. The fourth glass I decline. I look up at the balcony: the woman has been given a glass of tea.

For an hour and a half the music has remained in a stolid four-four meter; suddenly it goes into an increasingly rapid three-eight. "It is becoming more animated," says my mentor.

"Yes, I noticed that."

"You have a musical ear," he remarks. Then he adds: "All these poems are in preparation for Purim."

"Aren't they what you call *pyotim*?" I whisper.

"That's correct." He looks pleased. "You know the story of Esther, of course?"

"Yes," I lie.

"Mordecai, Mordecai" – he stabs the page with his finger, so that I will begin again to follow the text ". . . and my faith in God is like a fine girdle about my waist." He translates freely, between strophes of singing.

"You are not from here?" he suggests softly, after a few minutes.

"No, from New York."

This appears to interest him. After a moment he says: "You are free to come and live at my house."

I thank him profusely and explain that I am staying in a hotel. He asks if I am satisfied with it, and I say I am. "Good. Then tomorrow you will come to lunch with me. Is that all right? Be in the street outside the synagogue at two. *Sans faute*." I agree. Presently I get up, bow and go out.

THE NEXT DAY I arrive in the forlorn little street at the appointed time. As I am paying my cab driver a chic, very attractive girl steps up to me and says: "I am Madame Castiel. Monsieur Castiel has gone to look for you in a café on the boulevard. Here he comes now!"

We greet one another and get into a car parked at the curb. My hosts sit in front and apologetically indicate a place on the back seat in among piles of vegetables, fruit and canned goods. "We've been to market," Monsieur Castiel explains. "I am a schoolteacher. On Sundays we have nothing to do, so we spend the morning buying food."

The Castiels live alone, but there are constant arrivals and departures of members of the family. They are all warm, friendly and intelligent. Monsieur Castiel plays Andalusian records on the phonograph; a Moslem servant girl brings six kinds of sweet wine. I have a pleasant and unreasoning conviction that if a frustration or the beginning of a neurosis arises in one of these people, it will be gently and effectively dispelled by the group; it is as if they were all interconnected by invisible wires.

When at last everyone is gone, my two hosts and I sit down to lunch. "We are very strict in my family, from a religious point of view. It is the only way to live," Monsieur Castiel tells me. I remark that in America it is not like that, that most Jews there do not adhere to orthodoxy, and that many people who are partly Jewish are not at all interested in Judaism, and indeed tend to want to forget the whole subject. Monsieur Castiel looks pained.

The meal is complicated and lengthy; the maid keeps appearing with more dishes from the kitchen. "You must come to Casablanca and let me teach you Hebrew," says Monsieur Castiel. "I am a good teacher, I can teach you very quickly. It is a beautiful language. You ought to know it."

"It is very kind of you. I shall consider it seriously when I return from America," I tell him.

"Perhaps at that time, too," he adds drily, referring to an earlier conversation, "I shall be able to persuade you that Judaism is superior to atheist existentialism."

I say that it is erroneous to imagine that anyone is at liberty to believe what he wishes to believe.

"That is just the pride of the intellect speaking," he says sadly. I look at him, marveling a bit: it is so difficult to identify this man sitting at the head of the table with the tentative, slightly gauche individual of yesterday. Before I leave, I tell the Castiels that I had not realized it was possible for the city of Casablanca to provide three such delightful hours. "We hope there will be many more," they say. Then Monsieur Castiel insists on driving me back to the hotel, and before I go inside we sit in the car for another hour discussing religion.

A FEW DAYS LATER I decide to pay a visit to the cathedral, a very large concrete structure near the Pare Lyautey. As I am about to go through the entrance door, several Moslems lying under a tree nearby spring up and come running toward me, crying: "Wait! We work here! We'll show you the inside!" The onslaught so disgusts me that I quickly turn around and walk away through the garden; their cries follow me for a moment. I am a bit disappointed not to have seen whether the interior is as hideous as the outside. The French are responsible for some excellent modern buildings in Casablanca, but these are grouped around the Place Lyautey and the Palais du Sultan in the Nouvelle Medina, and are neo-Mauresque, a generally successful adaptation of the Portuguese Moorish style that characterizes the architecture of the Atlantic coast from Rabat to Essaouira. The cathedral looks like something invented by a clever child using a set of expensive German building blocks; it has no style whatever.

Two idiotic little scenes remain in my mind with suspicious clarity. A country youth in tattered clothing lies asleep in the sun on one of the benches in the garden near the Palais de Justice. Along comes a group of modern young Moslem men and girls, dressed in their European best. They have seen scores of such derelicts every day of their lives, but at the moment they feel the need of amusing themselves. The men begin to shout: "Get up! Come on! Up!" The girls bend double with shrieks of merriment. Luckily, the rustic goes on sleeping. Still shaken by spasms of laughter, the strollers continue on their way. I watch them disappear, too astonished to do anything more than stare after them. There is something grotesque in the whole-heartedness with which they display their ugliness of spirit; it is an unsavory and dangerous thing, the unthinking laughter of the secure.

The other vignette strikes me as more mysterious, but equally significant. It is the end of the lunch hour, and several hundred Moslem girls are waiting in the street to go back into the school building. At least, that is my impression when I arrive at the intersection where they are all gathered. But then I see that they are standing in a huge unmoving circle, staring impassively down at the pavement. In the center is an overturned motor-cycle, with a great pool of congealing blood beside it. Nothing happens, no one arrives, no one speaks. They clutch their books and gape, unable to raise their eyes from the big red spot shining there in the sunlight.

It is hard enough to know what Casablanca is like now, while one is looking at it, without trying to imagine what it will be like in five, ten or twenty years. So much of what one sees is tragic, but it is at the same time ludicrous; there is undirected hostility in the air, but to offset it there is also a seemingly inexhaustible store of patience. The present inert quality of the populace is bound to change, but regardless of the means through which the change comes about, the country will still have to reckon with a powerful popular philosophy whose credo holds that destiny is stronger than causation. How can anyone make predictions about a city in ebullition? He might as well hold up a baby and announce what it is going to look like when (and if) it grows into a man.

KIF – PROLOGUE AND
COMPENDIUM OF TERMS

THE BOOK OF GRASS, 1967

ONE OF THE GREAT phenomena of the century is the unquestioning world-wide acceptance of the accessories of Judeo-Christian civilization, regardless of whether or not these trappings have any relevance to the peoples adopting them. The United Nations, like a philanthropical society devoted to reclaiming and educating young delinquents, points the way grandly for the little nations just recruited, assuring them that they too one day may be important and respected members of world society. Political schisms do not really exist. Whether the new ones study Marx or Jefferson, the destructive impact on the original culture is identical. It would seem that the important task is to get them into the parade, now that they have been convinced that there is only the one direction in which they can go. Once they are marching too, they will appreciate more fully how far ahead of them we are. These are *faits accomplis*; in the future it will be fascinating to watch the annihilation of the entire structure of Judeo-Christian culture by these 'underprivileged' groups which, having had only the most superficial contacts with that culture, nevertheless will have learned enough thereby to do a thorough job of destroying it.

If you are going to sit at table with the grown-ups, you have to be willing to give up certain childish habits that the grown-ups don't like: cannibalism, magic, and all the other facets of 'irrational' religious observances. You must eat, drink, relax and make love the way the grown-ups do, otherwise your heart won't really be in it; you won't truly be disciplining yourself to become like them. One of the first things you must accept when you join the grown-ups' club is the fact that the Judeo-Christians approve of only one out of all the substances capable of effecting a quick psychic change in the human organism – and that one is alcohol. The liquid is sacred in the ceremonies of both branches of the Judeo-Christian religion. Therefore all other such substances are taboo. But since you are forsaking your own culture in any case, you won't mind giving up the traditional prescriptions for relaxation it provided for you; enthusiastically you will accept alcohol along with democratic (or communist) ideology and the gadgets that go with it, since the sooner you learn to use these things, the sooner you can expect to be patted on the head, granted special privileges, and told that you are growing up – fulfilling your destiny, I think they sometimes call it. This news, presumably, you find particularly exciting.

And so the last strongholds fashioned around the use of substances other than alcohol are being flushed out, to make everything clean and in readiness for the great alcoholic future. In Africa particularly, the dagga, the ganja, the bangui, the kif, as well as the dawamesk, the sammit, the *majoun* and the hashish, are all on their way to the bonfires of progressivism. They just don't go with pretending to be European. The young fanatics of the four corners of the continent are furiously aware of that. They are, incidentally, also aware that a population of satisfied smokers or eaters offers no foothold to an ambitious demagogue. The crowd pleasantly heated by alcohol behaves in a classical and foreseeable fashion, but you can't even get together a crowd of smokers: each man is alone and happy to stay that way. (Then, too, there is the fact to be considered that once one gets power, one can regulate the revenue on alcohol, and sit back to count one's take. The other substances don't lend themselves so easily to efficient governmental racketeering.)

Cannabis, the only serious world-wide rival to alcohol, reckoned in millions of users, is always described in alcoholic countries as a 'social menace'. And the grown-ups mean just that. They don't infer that it's detrimental to the health or welfare of the individual who uses it, since for them the individual separated from his social context is an irregularity to be remedied, in any case. No, they mean that the user of cannabis is all too likely to see the truth where it exists, and to fail to see it where it does not. Obviously few things are potentially more dangerous to those interested in prolonging the status quo of organized society. If people refuse to play the game of society at all, of what use are they? How can they be enticed or threatened, save by the ultimately unsatisfactory device of brute force? No, no, there are no two ways about it: society has got to go on being played (and quietly directed); alcohol is the only safe substance to allow human beings, and everything else must go.

In spite of the Madison Avenue techniques being applied to the launching of campaigns in praise of the new millennium, old cultures do not lie down and die merely because they are told to. They have to be methodically killed, and that takes a certain time. Deculturizing programmes have to be arranged, resettlement projects undertaken, rehabilitation camps set up and filled, and all this in each place before the party in power is superseded by an enemy party, which in Africa often means very soon indeed. It is not astonishing, then, that the drive to standardization should have proven to be a bumpy one and that, now, there should be geographical pockets on the continent where all kinds of anachronisms are the temporary norm. There is still bangui in the Congo precisely because the region has not yet been successfully unified and steam-rollered by the grown-ups' pets; the hillsides of South Africa are still covered with dagga because no organized group has had the time to uproot it; kif is still widely smoked in Morocco because the forces which would otherwise be being used to suppress the practice are too busy tracking

Kif pipe with *mottoul* – the traditional storage bag of camel leather.
Paul Bowles photographed this for the cover of his four kif-inspired tales,
A Hundred Camels in the Courtyard (City Lights, 1962).

down illicit arms and blackmarket currency. There is so much the African progressives find themselves unable to do that this complaint might almost seem premature, were it not for the fact that their eventual success is guaranteed: they are implemented by all the technology of the Judeo-Christian world.

The terms expounded below have nothing esoteric about them; they are as much a part of the everyday vocabulary in North Africa as words like chaser, neat or soda are in the United States, with the difference that over the centuries cannabis has played a far more important part in shaping the local culture than alcohol has with us. The music, the literature, and even certain aspects of the architecture, have evolved with cannabis -directed appreciation in mind.

In the wintertime a family will often have a 'hashish evening': father, mother, children and relatives shut themselves in, eat the jam prepared by the womenfolk of the household, and enjoy several hours of stories, song, dance and laughter in complete intimacy. 'To hear this music you must have kif first', you are sometimes told, or: 'This is a kif room. Everything in it is meant to be looked at through kif.' The typical kif story is an endless, proliferated tale of intrigue and fantasy in which the unexpected turns of the narrative line play a far more decisive role than the development of character or plot

Quite apart from the intimate relationship that exists between cannabis and the cultural and religious manifestations of both Moslem and animist Africa, there exists also the explicit proscription of alcohol in the Koran's accompanying Hadith. The moral (and often the legal) codes of Moslem countries are based solely upon Koranic law. The advocated switch to alcohol can cause only moral confusion in the mind of the average Moslem citizen, and further lower his respect for the authorities responsible for it.

CHQAF (plural CHQOTA) The L-shaped bowl, generally made of baked clay, which fits the end of the pipe-stem and holds the kif. The diameter of the bowl's opening is about a quarter of an inch. In the throat, at the angle, is a tiny uvula upon which the chqaf's efficacy depends. In order to avoid damaging this, smokers never clean their chqofa when they get clogged with tar, but put them into the fire until they are burned out. The chqaf breaks with great ease, usually as it is being fitted on to the stem. Attempts have been made to obviate this by fashioning chqofa of metal (a failure, since no one will use them) and of stone. In Taroudant there are artisans who carve excellent ones out of a translucent soapstone; these have the advantage of enabling the smoker to see just how far down his ash has burned in the bowl. The only objection to these is that they cost roughly twenty times as much as the clay ones.

CORREDOR (northern Morocco) A small-time kif retailer who sells to cafés and acquaintances. Never has a large quantity on hand.

DJIBLI Third-grade kif, grown in the lowlands. The plant attains a great height, but is short on cannabin. There are two categories of djibli kif: hameimoun, considered slightly better because it is at least able to cause hunger, and the ordinary – the harsh, cheap kif sold to tourists.

HACHICH The word has various meanings. First, it is a blanket term for all parts of the kif plant save the small top leaves. In the preparation of good smoking kif, these small leaves are the only part used. At least two-thirds of the plant is discarded. Large, dried or damaged leaves, flowers, seeds and stalks are all rejected. The term is also used to refer to candy made by boiling these unusable parts with water and sugar. This is the poor man's *majoun*. You can buy two pounds of it for a quarter of a dollar. (Xauen, 1960.) True hashish, made with the pollen of the flower, is not commercially available in North Africa. The word M'HACHIYICH indicates the state of mind induced by having eaten the candy.

JDUQ JMEL (known in northern Morocco as QOQA) Tiny snail-shaped seeds, available at the magic stalls of Marrakesh and other cities, which are sometimes used to intensify the active properties of edible kif preparations, and even on occasion in kif for smoking. Popular belief holds that too many seeds can cause permanent mental derangement.

KETAMI Adjective derived from the place-name Ketama, a town in the western Rif, center of a large kif-growing district. It is still legal to grow the plant here, since it is the only crop that can be grown on the steep mountainsides. In other words, it can be grown but not transported. As soon as it leaves the vicinity of Ketama the chase is on; if the shipment gets through the block-ade, it reaches the consumer directly, by the normal channels. If it is captured by the authorities, the route to the consumer is of necessity more circuitous. Fines are levied according to quan-tity seized. Several thousand people of the area depend for their livelihood upon its cultivation. Ketama, at an altitude of about five thousand feet, supplies all of Morocco with its first-grade kif; and the word ketami is a synonym of the best.

KHALDI Second-grade kif, grown in the mountains around Beni Khaled, which although in the Rif lies at a lower altitude and thus produces a somewhat inferior smoking leaf.

KIF The *Cannabis saliva* plant of northern Africa and the Middle East. (The cannabis of east Africa, south east Asia and the Americas is of a stronger and less subtle flavor.) Also the small leaves of the plant, chopped to a coarse, slightly greasy, grayish green powder for smoking.

KSESS The cutting of the kif. No matter how good the quality of the raw material, if the cutter does not know his business, the result cannot be the desired one. It takes roughly eight hours of steady hard work for a professional to cut a pound of finished kif properly. The cutter has the marks of his trade emblazoned in callouses on his fingers.

MAJOUN Literally, jam, but universally understood to be jam con-taining cannabis. There are almost as many procedures for mak-ing majoun as there are people who make it, but the ingredients are more or less standard: kif, honey, nuts, fruit and spices in varying proportions.

MKIYIF The state of the individual who has smoked enough kif to feel its effect clearly. (Usually followed by the phrase *ma ras* plus the proper pronominal suffix.)

MOTTOU Leather pouch for kif. There are always at least two compartments in a mottoui, and sometimes as many as four. A different grade goes into each compartment. If you know A well and watch him offer kif to B, you can tell the degree of his esteem for B by the kif he gives him to smoke. The ceremonial facets of kif smoking are fast disappearing as persecution of the custom increases. Good mottouis are no longer made, and the average worker now carries his kif in a small tin box, or, even more abject, in the paper in which he purchased it.

MSOUSS Kif which has not a sufficient quantity of tobacco blended with it is described by this adjective (as are unsweetened or partially sweetened tea or coffee). Kif is never smoked neat, the popular belief being that kif msouss is bound to give the smoker a headache.

NABOULA A cured sheep's bladder for storing kif. Glass and metal are not considered as efficacious for preserving the highly volatile preparation. The naboula, tightly tied at the neck, is truly hermetic, and the kif kept in it remains as fresh as the day it was packed.

NCHAIOUI A man whose entire life is devoted to the preparation, smoking and appreciation of kif.

RHAITA The datura flower. A square inch of the petal dropped into the teapot is enough to paralyse five or six people, particularly in combination with kif. (Generally added by the host without the knowledge of his guests.)

SBOULA The unit by which kif is sold wholesale. A sboula comprises a dozen or more stalks tightly tied together. Stalks are about eight inches long.

SEBSI (plural SBASSA) The stem of the kif pipe. A few decades ago the *sebsi* was commonly, anywhere, from sixteen to twenty-four inches long, and usually came in two parts that could be coupled to make the pipe. The recent tendency has been to make them increasingly shorter, so that they can be pocketed as swiftly as possible under adverse conditions. The elaborately carved *sebsi* is becoming a thing of the past; nowadays they are often simple wooden tubes. The variety of wood determines the quality of the *sebsi*. Olive and walnut are considered good, run-of-the-mill materials, although there are still numerous recherché varieties to be found by the connoisseur in the interior of Morocco. There are *sebsi* stalls in the public markets of most towns.

SMINN Rancid butter, preferably aged for a year or longer, which when mixed with kif makes an unpleasant-tasting but powerful and cheap substitute for majoun.

ZBIL The residue of stalks, leaves, seeds and flowers which is thrown out after the small leaves have been extracted. The foreigner is always appalled the first time he sees this great quantity of what elsewhere would be considered perfectly good material being tossed into the fire. In cafés it is chopped up and used by unscrupulous *corredores* to hoodwink the ingenuous foreigner. Moslems refuse to smoke it.

ZREYA The uncrushed seeds of the kif plant, sold until recently in pharmacies and apothecary shops as a culinary adjunct.

CAFÉ IN MOROCCO

HOLIDAY, SEPTEMBER, 1966

THE BEACH, very wide along this coast, is protected by a crumbling breakwater a few hundred feet offshore, so that from here in the garden the waves make only a distant murmur, a somnolent backdrop for the nearer sounds of bees buzzing and the occasional low voices of the men inside the café. I came into the garden a few minutes ago and sat down on a large woven-grass mat near the well. The mat has been provided with piles of bottle tops to be used as counters in whatever game I may be going to play.

The garden spreads out along the foot of the town's ramparts, hidden behind a jungle of fig trees and cactus, buried in total shade beneath a ceiling of grape leaves. At this season the heavy bunches of grapes hang down between the meshes of cane trellis above, and bump against my forehead as I come through on my way to the well. Facing me, in a corner, like a Chinese lantern big enough to hold a man, is a wicker fish trap left to dry: this is a fisherman's café. At night, after it is shut and the beach is deserted, the customers often return with their own teapots and invade the garden, lying on the mats talking and smoking, and when the grapes and figs are ripe, eating the fruit. Mrhait, who runs the establishment, find this as it should be. "The fruit is here for our friends to eat," he declares. There are a few tables and chairs around for those who want them, and even these are left out all night for the customers' convenience. They represent the major part of his capital, and they could easily be carried away. But this is a small town; no one has ever stolen anything from him.

The traditional café in this part of the world is conceived of as a club where, in addition to enjoying the usual amenities of a café, a man may, if he wishes, eat, sleep, bathe and store his personal effects. The fact that the nearest café may be five or ten minutes' walk from where he lives (it is seldom farther, for the establishments are numerous) does not prevent him from considering it an extension of his home. Each café has its regular clientele whose members know one another; the habitués form a limited little community in which the appearance of an unfamiliar local face is as much an intrusion as that of a complete foreigner. It is difficult to induce a Muslim to go into a café where he is not known: he does not enjoy being stared at.

Upper-class Muslims generally refuse to be seen in cafés at all, their contention being that one sits and drinks tea in a crowded public place only if one cannot do so in one's own house. But for these good bourgeois, as for us Europeans, the taking of tea is thought of as a relaxing pause, a respite from the affairs of the day. The hour or two spent on the terrace of a café counts as time off from the involvements of daily routine; one sits and watches life go past. The average Muslim here, on the contrary, goes into a café in order to participate as intensely as possible in the collective existence of his friends and neighbors. In a land whose social life is predicated on the separation of the sexes, the home is indisputably the woman's precinct; the man must seek his life outside. And the generally prevalent uproar in even the middle-class Muslim household makes the all-male café a necessity. Only there does the man feel free to talk, smoke his kif pipe, play or listen to music, and even, if the spirit moves him, to dance a little in front of his friends.

And it is in the café that the foreign visitor, too, can feel the pulse of the country. Nowhere else can he manage to observe a group of individuals repeatedly and at length in their daily contacts with one another, or succeed in existing at their tempo, achieving in occasional unguarded moments a state of empathy with their very different sense of the passage of time. And to experience time from the vantage point of these people is essential to understanding their attitudes and behavior. Today, when even in the farthest reaches of the bush there is beginning to be established a relationship between the number of hours a man works and the amount of wages he collects, any human institution where the awareness of time has not yet penetrated is a phenomenon to be cherished.

With its luxury of unmeasured time the Moroccan café is out of harmony with present-day concepts, and thus it is doomed to extinction. Ask any café owner. It takes approximately three minutes to prepare each glass of tea. The customer may then sit for as many hours as he wishes over the one glass. Since the maximum profit per order is equivalent to about one cent, it seems clear that economically there is no future in the café business. There are other factors, too, that militate against the continued life of the traditional "Moorish" café. It is claimed by the authorities that cafés cause men to waste time that might be used to better advantage. Whatever places are shut down in periods of civic reform (and latter-day puritanism has made these campaigns fairly frequent) are thereby permanently destroyed, since if and when they are reopened, it is invariably as European-style establishments. The change-over in clothing also has its effect. As long as the clientele was composed exclusively of men wearing the customary garments, it was sufficient to cover the floor with grass matting. The increasing number of those who sport European apparel, however, induces the owners to provide chairs, since the Moroccans like their trousers to be so tight-fitting that to sit in their normal position on the floor while wearing them would be an impossibility.

The traditional floor-café is a result of natural processes; one might say it is strictly functional, in that the intent is merely to make as comfortable and pleasant a place as possible for the greatest number of people, and at minimum cost. The cheapest materials – cane, bamboo, palm, thatch, woven reeds and grass – are not only the most attractive visually, but also provide the most satisfactory acoustics for the music. The modern table-and-chair café, on the other hand, is an abstraction: its primary aim has come to be the showing off of the expensive foreign objects that have been acquired (including, in the cities, electric refrigerator and television) and that distinguish the place from its humbler rivals. Practical considerations fade before the determination to make this all-important display. Thus it is that the new-style cafés achieve only a sordid uniformity in their discomfort and metallic noisiness, while the old-fashioned places are as diverse as the individuals who created them.

This garden here by the sea with its ceiling of grapes; the flat roofs of the Marrakesh cafés where men sit at midnight waiting for a breath of cool air; the cave-like rooms in the mountain markets of the High Atlas, to which the customers must bring their own tea, sugar and mint, the establishment furnishing only the fire, water and teapot; in Fez the baroque wooden palaces among the weeping willows of the Djenane es Sebir, whose deck chairs line the river's wandering channels; the cafés where the tea drinkers bring their prayer mats and retire into a small carpeted room to perform their sundown prostrations; the countless little niches in the alleys of every town, where a plank along the wall and bottle crates turned on end are the only furnishings; and then the cafés with dancing boys, like the Stah in Tangier; the sanctuary cafés whose shadiest customers remain unmolested by the authorities, like the one opposite the gardens of the Koutoubia in Marrakesh; the superb improvised tent cafés at the great religious pilgrimages in the wilderness; the range is vast. Few countries can supply such a variety of décor and atmosphere.

And what goes on in these places? The men converse, tell interminable stories, eat, smoke kif, sleep and play games: cards, checkers, dominoes, parchisi and, during Ramadan, bingo, whose prize used to be a glass of tea for each winner, but which nowadays often mysteriously turns out to be a bottle of cooking oil. In cold weather they sit as near as they can to the bed of burning charcoal under the water boiler. At night late-comers anxiously ask as they enter: "Is there still fire?" Once the embers have been allowed to die there is no more tea until the next day. The water boiler is an improvised samovar made of copper with a tap on the side; once in a while it proves to be the real article, with Cyrillic characters incised on its flank. Being the most important item in the place, it is put in the spot where there is the most light.

The elaboration of niches and shelves around the fire and water is the living heart of the café – rather like the altar of a church. In the cities it is a complicated tile-covered construction that serves as sink, stove and cabinet. One compartment contains the fire and the samovar, another the water tap or pail; smaller cubicles are for storing sugar, tea and mint. In the lesser cafés the single table is put beside this unlikely looking installation. Close friends of the proprietor and the kif concessionaire generally sit here. Nowadays, what with official frowns being directed at the smoking of the herb, the kif seller is not likely to be in evidence; nevertheless, he is a very important factor in the functioning of the café. He not only brings his own raw material, which traditionally he cleans and cuts in full view of the clients before selling it to them, thus forestalling doubts about is purity, but also processes (for a price) the kif that others have brought with them, blending the tobacco with it to suit each man's individual taste. How much of this must go on clandestinely depends on local circumstances; the ban on kif is being enforced with increasing firmness.

Unless he has been at the pipe for many hours, it is impossible to tell from a North African's behavior whether or not he has smoked kif. The same observation cannot be made, I am afraid, if alcohol has been taken instead. In the bars, loosened inhibitions send tempers up in flames, but I have never seen anything more serious than an argument in a café full of men smoking kif; the prevailing atmosphere is calm and jovial.

When the tea maker gets an order, he takes a long-handled tin canister and puts in a heaping teaspoonful of green China tea (usually Formosan chun mee). Next he adds four or five tea-spoonfuls of sugar. Another little canister filled with hot water from the samovar is already embedded in the coals. As soon as it is boiling, he pours the water over the mixed tea and sugar. While it is steeping he crushes as many stalks of fresh spear-mint as he can into a glass. Then he strains the tea into the glass, often garnishing it with a sprig of verbena, two or three unopened orange blossoms, or a few leaves of rosemary, *chiba* or some other locally available herb. The result, hot, sweet and strongly aromatic, bears very little resemblance to tea as it is drunk anywhere else in the world; it is *até*, a refresher in its own right, not unlike maté in Argentina but a good deal more tasty. Usually when newcomers try their first glass, they are appalled by the concentrated sweetness and get into the habit of ordering it with less sugar. The results are catastrophic. Indeed, the cafés that cater to the tourist trade now serve an unpalatable hybrid concoction, neither *até* nor tea. The Moroccans were quick to heed the foreigner's preferences; what with the constantly rising cost of sugar, the new preparation saves them money.

ALL CAFÉS PROVIDE neighborhood delivery service. A boy carries racks holding six glasses, back and forth, full and empty, all day long between the samovar and the nearby offices, banks and shops. Boiling-hot mint tea is still the favorite drink in the land, notwithstanding the increasing sales of colas and other bottled gaseous beverages. Even the customs officials in the port may be sipping tea offhandedly while they go through the luggage: the traveler who is automatically unnerved by the prospect of cus-toms inspection often finds this reassuring.

A part of each café is occupied by the *soudda*, a wooden platform raised a foot or so above the floor, usually with a low railing around it, and always with a covering of woven grass or reed matting. If there are any musicians they sit here, as do the establishment's most regular and esteemed habitués. After hours at night, this space may be used as a dormitory for transients. Ten or twelve years ago in the Calle Ben Charki of Tangier there

Paul Bowles at the Café Hafa – his habitual favourite in Tangier – with the Rif-born storyteller Mohammed Mrabet, with whom he produced a dozen books.

was a large café with an unusual clientele. It made no difference whether you went at midnight or at three in the morning: scores of boys between the ages of eight and fourteen sat at the tables in the center of the sparsely lighted room, fiercely playing cards. A wide platform extended along three of the walls, where there was even less light. The boys lying here tossed and scratched in their sleep; even so, they were the lucky ones, for when the card players began to yawn and look around for a place to stretch out, the platform was often full, and they had to be content to move to a table where others were already asleep, leaning forward from the little straight-backed chairs, their heads and arms lying flat on the boards. Month in, month out, the ragged horde filled the café. They were the *boleros* of Tangier, children who had strayed into the city from the hills beyond, and having managed to acquire a wooden box, a tin or two of polish, an old toothbrush and a rag, had set themselves up in business as shoeshine boys. As an old resident, I found the place a natural concomitant of North African life; however, the foreign visitors I took there thought it offensive. Children ought not to live that way. Apparently, the authorities shared these prejudices, for the establishment has long since ceased to function, nor are there any others similar to it.

Like all the African countries, Morocco has been thrown open to the forces of rapid modernization. The fact that its indigenous culture is so much more highly evolved than that of most other places on the continent tends, however, to retard the process. In a primitive land where the disparity between the old and the new worlds is total, the conversion conceivably can be effected in one generation, but where there is a perfectly viable, if archaic, tradition of civilization already in existence, as there is in Morocco, it will naturally take more time. This spirit of resistance to arbitrary, senseless change is a stock subject of the humorous anecdotes exchanged among café sitters, particularly in small towns.

A story I heard here in Mrhait's café the other day delighted me. This was a factual account of something that happened in a little country market up in the hill behind Larache. It was the day of the week when all the peasants of the region come on foot and on donkeyback to the village and sit in the market selling the things they have brought in with them. Swaggering through the throng of rustics came a young man who, if he was not really from the city, at least was doing everything he could to create that impression, his most blatant claim to urban refinement being a brand-new pair of locally made Levis, so skin-tight that he had a little difficulty in walking. He came up to an old woman, one among many others like her, who sat in the dust with a few figs, a half-dozen green peppers and some tomatoes, each being arranged according to custom in a neat little pyramid in front of her. Indicating the figs with the toe of his shoe, and thus upsetting the pile, the youth asked their price in an offhand manner calculated to widen the social difference he felt existed between him and the old woman.

"Don't kick the fruit, my son," she said evenly. She had taken his measure as he came, but now she did not even look up at him. Then she added: "If you'll sit down here beside me, I'll give you a good price."

The prospect of a bargain proved too much for the young man. He squatted down, and that was the end of him. With an explosive sound the seams of his trousers split wide open. ("His face was red, red!" the raconteur recalled with relish.) To the accompaniment of loud peasant laughter the young man made his way back through the crowd and out of the market.

One night I went to Mrhait's café with the idea of telling him that what I had been writing there at the end of his garden was a piece about cafés, to see if he had anything to say on the subject. But I intended to wait until everyone had gone, in order to avoid interruptions. It was fairly late, and there was a hot east wind roaring overhead. Even there behind the ramparts I recognized the dry spicy smell of parched hillsides that is borne on the *cherqi* at this time of year. The waves rolled in across the dark beach with mechanical regularity. I sat until there was no one in the garden and I could hear no voices inside the café.

Eventually Mrhait came out of the doorway and peered through the tangle of vines toward my dim corner. He finally saw me and came over.

After he had sat down opposite me and lighted a cigarette, I began. "You know, I've been writing about cafés here in Morocco so that Americans will know what they're like. I thought maybe you might have something to say about your own café, something you'd like them to know."

The cigarette end flared; his voice betrayed a surprising degree of feeling. "For sixteen years, ever since I was twelve and my father put me in this café, I've worked here and lived here and slept here. I made all this with my own hands. Why are those roses growing there? Because I planted the bushes. Why do we have these figs and grapes? Because I take care of the trees and vines. Why is there good sweet water in the well? Because I keep it clean. This morning, this very day, I went down inside and scooped out eight wheelbarrows full of sand and mud. That's what it means to run a café – not making one glass or a thousand glasses of tea."

Failing to see just where his rhetoric was leading him, I interrupted cautiously: "But you do like your work, don't you?"

"My work is in the garden, and that's only in the summer. In the winter I stay inside the café, and the wind blows, and some days nobody comes at all. Just the empty café and outside the rain and the waves. That's not work. That's prison. There's nobody left in this town. Everybody's gone. And that's why I'm going to go to the city myself and get a job in a café where they pay you every week."

HE ROSE to his feet. I was silent, considering again the transitoriness of everything in this land. In my imagination the café had long ago assumed the character of a landmark; it seemed impossible that Mrhait should be willing to walk out and leave it. I got up, too, and followed him slowly across the garden.

"But it's your café!" I was saying. "It belongs to you! After all these years you want to begin working for wages? At your age?"

In front of the doorway onto the beach he stopped and turned to face me. "Look. If you can't make a living by working for yourself, then you go to work for somebody else, don't you?"

"I suppose so."

"It's better to carry glasses in a busy café than own an empty one. Better to eat than starve, no?"

As we shook hands, he added reassuringly: "I'll be back. I'm sure to come back, later on. Just as soon as I get a little money together."

Fortunately it was dark and he did not see my smile, which he would have recognized as cynical. The familiar refrain: *There is money in the city! I'm going to get it.* Whether or not Mrhait gets it, once he has lived in the city he will not return here.

What's So Different About Marrakesh?

Travel & Leisure, June July 1971

MARRAKESH, with its encircling oasis, was the idea of Yusuf ibn Tashfin, a Saharan chieftain of the eleventh century. The site was a treeless plain, flat as a table, some 35 miles from the northern flanks of the High Atlas. It was natural that he should have imported the date palm, which any Saharan considers the only true tree, and used it to transform the empty wasteland into a vast palm grove. The miles of enclosing ramparts were built, the mosques and markets established, and Yusuf ibn Tashfin went on to glorify the name of Allah in Spain. He had left behind a work of art a city of noble proportions and spectacular beauty. What is astonishing is the fact that after 900 hard years (for life in Morocco has seldom proceeded smoothly) the beauty should still be so evident and so dazzling. Part of the reason is that, as they worked, the builders of the city saw each garden, terrace and pool in relation to the long chain of snowy peaks behind it.

In Marrakesh more than in other cities, the eye is continually being encouraged to contemplate that which is far away. Automatically it follows the line of the ramparts to the empty plain, coming to rest on the most distant vista. The mountains are so much a part of the scene that on the days when they are invisible the city seems incomplete.

Contemporary Moroccans feel much the same about the peaks of the Atlas as their forebears. In my drives around the city, each time my chauffeur looks up and sees them shining and white against the sky, he sighs and says, "Look at the works of God!"

When I first came here, camels ambled through the back alleys of the Medina, and 12,000 girls lived inside the walls of the Quartier Réservé, ready to provide amusement for their prospective clients. The camels are restricted to the country now, and the Quartier has long since been razed. Otherwise the character of Marrakesh is little changed.

What is different is the tempo of life. The era of the automobile has finally arrived, and the aim of every Marrakchi is to own one. Thousands already do; the rest use motorcycles and bicycles and live in hope. Bicycle riders are in the great majority. They are the natural enemy of the pedestrian. He who dares walk finds that there is no safe place for him; in the narrowest alley he can suddenly be run down by someone coming along silently from behind. Since it is impossible to see the Medina save on foot, visitors find themselves obliged to be constantly on the lookout.

Being in Marrakesh in winter, if there is sun, is a little like standing in front of a fireplace: you are hot on one side and cold on the other. If there is no sun, you are cold on both sides. The changes in temperature between day and night are impressive.

Winter is the high season, but spring and autumn are far more pleasant. As for the summer, it is the favorite season of many foreign residents, in spite of the temperature, which goes above 120 degrees in the shade during an east wind. But to be comfortable under such conditions one must be living at home, not in hotels. Not having a house in Marrakesh, I generally stay away from it between June and September.

Surprisingly, when the French arrived in 1912 their take-over did not cause any great changes in the aspect of the Medina. Following the pattern established by Marshal Lyautey, they left it intact and built their own town, El Gueliz, two miles away to the west. Now that the two nuclei have more or less grown together without, however, confusing their respective identities – it is clear that here is by far the most successful example of French city-planning in Morocco. The landscape gardening throughout the city is superb, and while one may have reservations about the extensive use of floodlighting, there is no denying that the ramparts are dramatic when bathed in their gold light.

One of the great touristic pleasures of Marrakesh is to take a horse-drawn carriage at sunset and drive the seven and a half miles around the periphery of the Medina, following the line of the ramparts and watching the bisque-pink walls and bastions as their color is modified by the changing light.

The Djemâa el Fna is probably the most fascinating open square in the world. Every afternoon all Marrakesh comes here as to a fair. On a sample afternoon one can watch some expert Sudanese dancing by a troupe of Gnaoua, a troupe of acrobats, Jilala drinking boiling water, Aissaoua charming cobras and vipers, trained monkeys, and a Surrealist act by two Haddaoua seated on carpets surrounded by plastic flowers and live pigeons.

At a certain point in the Haddaoua's routine one of the men beckons to a pigeon, which comes to him and perches on his shoulder. Then he orders the bird to go across the square to the Banque du Maroc and steal some banknotes. The pigeon flies over to the bank and alights above the entrance door, looking warily down at the armed guards standing there. Soon it returns to the man's shoulder, where it appears to be whispering into his ear. "What? No money?" cries the man. "How are we going to eat?" Meanwhile his partner has been intoning pious phrases, preparatory to going around the circle of watchers and taking up a collection.

During recent decades, as the population has grown and property values have increased, the Djemâa el Fna has constantly been reduced in size.

A police station has been built, space has been allotted for carriage and taxi stands, and long rows of stalls have been set up on two sides of the square. This year a sizable section of the east end has been cut off, to be used as a parking space for several thousand bicycles, and still another row of stalls constructed. Were it not for the fact that the Djemâa el Fna is the number one tourist attraction of Morocco, the authorities undoubtedly would have done away with it.

In the late-fifties, Eleanor Roosevelt was in Marrakesh as the guest of His Majesty Mohammed V. At dinner the first night, Mrs. Roosevelt confided to her host that the one place she always visited when she came to Marrakesh was the Djemâa el Fna; she could hardly wait to see it again, she added. Regretfully the king told her that the square had been converted into a parking lot. When she heard this, her disappointment was so intense that the king promised to reinstate the institution at the earliest opportunity. He did so, and it has functioned in its traditional fashion ever since.

Behind the Djemâa el Fna is a quarter generally referred to as "the bazaars". Until 1961 the streets here were covered with cane lattice work, an attractive architectural formula, but one which caused the destruction of the entire section. About 500 shops were gutted that summer by a fire which started in a chickpea-roasting stall. Rebuilding has been done in metal – less picturesque but more likely to preserve the few valuable objects that survived the holocaust. Beyond the bazaars are the souks. Each souk consists of many stalls selling the same kind of merchandise, which is often being made on the premises in full view of the buyer. Here prices are lower and there is more variety to choose from, but purchasing takes correspondingly longer.

There is generally considered to be only one *hôtel de grand luxe* in Morocco, and that is the Mamounia of Marrakesh. I think of luxury in terms of comfort, service and privacy, while those who run today's hotels would appear to conceive it in terms of swimming pools, saunas and air-conditioning units. Perhaps that is why the Mamounia's luxury now seems largely vestigial, a nostalgic reminder of the era not too long ago when Winston Churchill came each winter to sit painting in the garden.

The Mamounia is still the biggest and best – there is no doubt of that and if you are fortunate enough to get a room with a southern exposure you have an unparalleled view of the famous olive grove and the Atlas. Among the more recently built hotels are the Es Saadi, by the Casino, the Almoravides, just inside Bab Doukkala, and the Menara, about halfway between the Medina and the modern quarter of El Gueliz. These are all first-class establishments. There are also two new American-style motels, both on the Avenue de la Menara, outside the city. Several more hotels are under construction at the moment, including an enormous Club Méditerranée directly on the Djemâa el Fna. However, the more room they make for visitors, the more visitors there are. Residents speak glumly of a saturation point, but so far there is no sign of such a thing.

Night life as we conceive it is not a part of the mores of the land; what little is provided has been arranged specifically for tourists, and is therefore not of much interest. Entertainment with dinner, however, is another matter. Often one can find some of the best Moroccan musicians and dancers at the large tourist restaurants of the Medina that specialize in local dishes. The Gharnatta, the Ksar-el-Hamra, and the Dar-es-Salaam are spacious, elaborate establishments where the accent is on atmosphere and entertainment rather than food.

Moroccan cooking is at last beginning to be known and appreciated by Americans. Every gastronome who comes to Morocco should learn during his stay how to make at least one Moroccan dish. In any case he will want the experience of tasting the most delectable samples of *cuisine marocaine* to be had anywhere, and he will find them at La Maison Arabe just inside the huge arched gate of Bab Doukkala. He must remember to make his reservation at least a day in advance, and he must be so devoted to the art of eating that he is not disturbed by the severity of the *patronne* and the almost monastic atmosphere.

The resident expatriate colony is smaller than reports might lead one to believe. The Comtesse de Breteuil lives in the famous Villa Taylor which housed Roosevelt and Churchill

The Djemâa el Fna in 1963 (PB)

during World War II; this is the hub of what social life exists in Marrakesh. The Getty house is a brilliant example of the glamor that can be created by stringing together a number of old houses. Arndt von Bohlen (heir to the Krupp empire) has a large estate just to the west of El Gueliz, outside the city. Yves Saint Laurent a few years ago bought a beautiful little house which he uses strictly as a retreat from the rigors of life in Paris. The house was designed by its original owner, whose brother Prince Doan Vinh na Champassak recently gave up his quiet life as a painter here in Marrakesh to marry Barbara Hutton. Ira Belline, costume designer for Diaghileff and Jouvet, the niece of Igor Stravinsky, has lived for a good many years in the oasis, several miles out of town. The American writer John Hopkins has an adobe house among the palm trees on this property.

The most recent addition to the colony of homeowners is Pierre Balmain. There are American and European residents in hidden corners throughout the Medina, living quietly in their rebuilt Moroccan houses. The architectural transformations seldom affect the outer wall of a house, so that it is impossible to tell from the street whether Moroccans or foreigners live there.

The only Americans visible to the naked eye are the temporary visitors, who can be subdivided into tourists and those whom the Moroccans call the *hippiya*, (feminine singular with the accent on the second syllable). As might be expected, the natives here find the hippie phenomenon very difficult to understand. Their reactions, which initially were favorable, have been modified by several years of contact with members of the movement and are now at best ambivalent, and often frankly fearful. The authorities are worried that the attitude of disrespect for the law shown by some hippies may infect young Moroccans who fraternize with them. A good number of local youths now carefully cultivate the hippie look. There have been public campaigns against long hair and eccentric clothing with mobile guards roaming the cities, but these tactics have not had an appreciable effect.

Last year the large Café du Glacier on the Djemâa el Fna teemed with young travelers wearing beards, chains, parkas, tchamiras, *djellabas*, Reguibat *rezzas*, and a whole assortment of African accouterments. This year it is frequented only by Moroccans and stray tourists. The Friends of the World have opted for secrecy and have abandoned the big public places in favor of tiny, hidden stalls in the back alleys where the tourists are unable to find them. For, in the past years, the hippies have become a principal tourist attraction of Marrakesh.

At the age of 20, I was here in Marrakesh, without drugs and fancy dress, it is true, but living in very much the same fashion as the hippies live here today, showing scorn for that which was familiar and boundless enthusiasm for everything Moroccan. The principal difference between us is that they, traveling in numbers and having no self-consciousness, are not satisfied with being spectators; they want to participate. It is as if they thought that if they try hard and long enough, they will become Moroccans themselves.

Sometimes at night as you walk through the Djemâa el Fna you come upon a circle of seated, *burnouse*-clad figures. In the center there will be two or three Moroccans playing on drums. Upon examination one circle turns out to be composed of Americans, sitting in religious silence while their heads respond in spastic movements to the rhythm of the drums. Participation at such a basic level, while not likely to lead to further understanding between the two cultures, is a harmless enough activity, and certainly a more meaningful one than the tourist custom of sitting in a nightclub whose every detail has been planned in anticipation of Western tastes. Now Moroccan girls are being trained to become belly dancers – a hitherto unheard-of thing in Morocco. But since that is what tourists are said to want, that is what they get.

Inaccurate information is responsible for the disappointments of most travelers. I have known people to return from their first visit to Marrakesh and express surprise, if not chagrin, at finding the city so open and accessible. It had no mystery. But no one ever claimed that Marrakesh was mysterious, I tell them. During the time of the Protectorate, in their touristic propaganda the French were quite explicit about it. Assuming that "mystery" was furnished by such conventional items as winding tunnels, narrow alleys and eyes peering from behind latticed peep-holes, they reserved the word for descriptions of Fez. It was "*Fès la mystérieuse*"; Marrakesh was strictly "*la Rouge*."

If one stays in a city for any length of time, one discovers that its general atmosphere depends largely upon the attitude of its inhabitants. The Marrakchis themselves can be quite as baffling to the visitor as any succession of tunnels and alleys. They love to engage in strange little games with foreigners – games in which often they have nothing whatever to gain, unless it be the expressions of bewilderment and frustration they can call forth on the foreigners' faces. For the visitor, Marrakesh is a constant confrontation with the unlikely, outlandish and absurd.

For example, I enter a restaurant not far from the Djemâa el Fna, sit down and ask for the *carte* and the *menu*. There are no prices mentioned on either. I call the attention of the waiter to the oversight. He says airily: "You order what you like and I'll charge what I like."

I am sitting in a café in Gueliz. A taxi drives up, and a little man gets out. He is about three feet high, with a huge head and practically no legs. He pays the driver and comes tottering directly to the *terrasse* of the café, where he begins to go from table to table asking for alms. I am wondering why he took no pains to hide his mode of arrival, and I ask him about it. "I always take taxis," he says proudly. "I have plenty of money." Perhaps he sees incredulity in my face, for he goes on. "I have three houses and a store in the Medina." It takes me a moment to digest this information. "But then," I begin hesitantly, "why don't you just sit at a table like everyone else?" His hand is still out. "That's no good," he says. "I want to know what's going on. I go to *all* the cafés." I give him the coin I have been holding in my hand, and he waddles on.

For those spending the season in Marrakesh, the two most popular places to visit nearby are Essaouira and Oukaimeden, where the activities are respectively sea-bathing and skiing. Essaouira, 125 miles due west of Marrakesh, is on a spit of land jutting out into the Atlantic. It is one of the most attractive small towns in all North Africa, as yet unspoiled, with a wide sandy beach that stretches south as far as the eye can see.

Oukaimeden, at an altitude of 8,399 feet, nestles below the peak of Djebel Toubkal (13,665 feet) and advertises the highest ski lift in Africa. (I am curious to see the list of African ski lifts.) The drive through the valleys and gorges is beautiful, and the food is excellent. Skiers often stay on until April.

FROM NOTES TAKEN IN THAILAND

PROSE, SPRING 1972

I SOON LEARNED not to go near the windows or to draw aside the double curtains in order to look at the river below. The view was wide and lively, with factories and warehouses on the far side of the Chao Phraya, and strings of barges being towed up and down through the dirty water. The new wing of the hotel had been built in the shape of an upright slab, so that the room was high and had no trees to shade it from the poisonous onslaught of the afternoon sun. The end of the day, rather than bringing respite, intensified the heat, for then the entire river was made of sunlight. With the redness of dusk everything out there became melodramatic and forbidding, and still the oven heat from outside leaked through the windows.

Brooks, teaching at Chulalongkorn University, was required as a Fulbright Fellow to attend regular classes in Thai; as an adjunct to this he arranged to spend much of his leisure time with Thais. One day he brought along with him three young men wearing the bright orange-yellow robes of Buddhist monks. They filed into the hotel room in silence and stood in a row as they were presented to me, each one responding by joining his palms together, thumbs touching his chest.

As we talked, Yamyong, the eldest, in his late twenties, explained that he was an ordained monk, while the other two were novices. Brooks then asked Prasert and Vichai if they would be ordained soon, but the monk answered for them.

"I do not think they are expecting to be ordained," he said quietly, looking at the floor, as if it were a sore subject all too often discussed among them. He glanced up at me and went on talking. "Your room is beautiful. We are not accustomed to such luxury." His voice was flat; he was trying to conceal his disapproval. The three conferred briefly in undertones. "My friends say they have never seen such a luxurious room," he reported, watching me closely through his steel-rimmed spectacles to see my reaction. I failed to hear.

They put down their brown paper parasols and their reticules that bulged with books and fruit. Then they got themselves into position in a row along the couch among the cushions. For a while they were busy adjusting the folds of their robes around their shoulders and legs.

"They make their own clothes," volunteered Brooks. "All the monks do."

I spoke of Ceylon; there the monks bought the robes all cut and ready to sew together. Yamyong smiled appreciatively and said: "We use the same system here."

The air-conditioning roared at one end of the room and the noise of boat motors on the river seeped through the windows at the other. I looked at the three sitting in front of me. They were very calm and self-possessed, but they seemed lacking in physical health. I was aware of the facial bones beneath their skin. Was the impression of sallowness partly due to the shaved eyebrows and hair?

Yamyong was speaking. "We appreciate the opportunity to use English. For this reason we are liking to have foreign friends. English, American; it doesn't matter. We can understand." Prasert and Vichai nodded.

Time went on, and we sat there, extending but not altering the subject of conversation. Occasionally I looked around the room. Before they had come in, it had been only a hotel room whose curtains must be kept drawn. Their presence and their comments on it had managed to invest it with a vaguely disturbing quality; I felt that they considered it a great mistake on my part to have chosen such a place in which to stay.

"Look at his tattoo," said Brooks. "Show him."

Yamyong pulled back his robe a bit from the shoulder, and I saw the two indigo lines of finely written Thai characters. "That is for good health," he said, glancing up at me. His smile seemed odd, but then, his facial expression did not complement his words at any point.

"Don't the Buddhists disapprove of tattooing?" I said.

"Some people say it is backwardness." Again he smiled. "Words for good health are said to be superstition. This was done by my abbot when I was a boy studying in the *wat*. Perhaps he did not know it was a superstition."

We were about to go with them to visit the *wat* where they lived. I pulled a tie from the closet and stood before the mirror arranging it.

"Sir," Yamyong began. "Will you please explain something? What is the significance of the necktie ?"

"The significance of the necktie?" I turned to face him. "You mean, why do men wear neckties?"

"No. I know that. The purpose is to look like a gentleman."

I laughed. Yamyong was not put off. "I have noticed that some men wear the two ends equal, and some wear the wide end longer than the narrow, or the narrow longer than the wide. And the neckties themselves, they are not all the same length, are they? Some even with both ends equal reach below the waist. What are the different meanings?"

"There is no meaning," I said. "Absolutely none."

He looked to Brooks for confirmation, but Brooks was trying out his Thai on Prasert and Vichai, and so he was silent and thoughtful for a moment. "I believe you, of course," he said graciously. "But we all thought each way had a different significance attached."

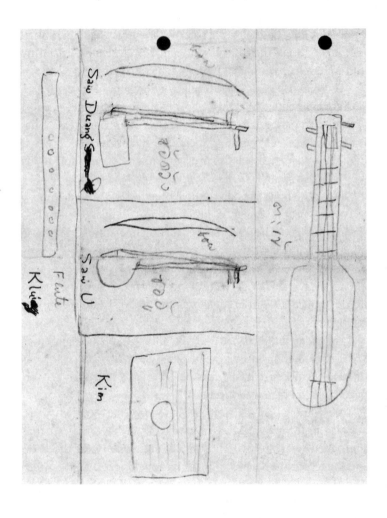

A page from Bowles' Thailand notebook, with drawings of local instruments

As we went out of the hotel, the doorman bowed respectfully. Until now he had never given a sign that he was aware of
my existence. The wearers of the yellow robe carry weight in
Thailand.

A few Sundays later I agreed to go with Brooks and our
friends to Ayudhaya. The idea of a Sunday outing is so repellent
to me that deciding to take part in this one was to a certain
extent a compulsive act. Ayudhaya lies less than fifty miles
up the (Chao Phraya from Bangkok. For historians and art-
collectors it is more than just a provincial town; it is a period
and a style – having been the Thai capital for more than four
centuries. Very likely it still would be, had the Burmese not laid
it waste in the eighteenth century.

Brooks came early to fetch me. Downstairs in the street
stood the three bhikkus with their book bags and parasols. They
hailed a cab, and without any previous price arrangement (the
ordinary citizen tries to fix a sum beforehand) we got in and
drove for twenty minutes or a half-hour, until we got to a bus
terminal on the northern outskirts of the city.

It was a nice, old-fashioned, open bus. Every part of it rattled, and the air from the rice fields blew across us as we pieced
together our bits of synthetic conversation. Brooks, in high
spirits, kept calling across to me: "Look! Water buffaloes!" As
we went further away from Bangkok there were more of the
beasts, and his cries became more frequent. Yamyong, sitting
next to me, whispered: "Professor Brooks is fond of buffaloes?" I
laughed and said I didn't think so.

"Then?"

I said that in America there were no buffaloes in the fields,
and that was why Brooks was interested in seeing them. There
were no temples in the landscape, either, I told him, and added,
perhaps unwisely: "He looks at buffaloes. I look at temples."
This struck Yamyong as hilarious, and he made allusions to it
now and then all during the day.

The road stretched ahead, straight as a line in geometry,
across the verdant, level land. Paralleling it on its eastern side

was a fairly wide canal, here and there choked with patches of enormous pink lotuses. In places the flowers were gone and only the pods remained, thick green disks with the circular seeds embedded in their flesh. At the first stop the bhikkus got out. They came aboard again with mangosteens and lotus pods and insisted on giving us large numbers of each. The huge seeds popped out of the fibrous lotus cakes as though from a punchboard; they tasted almost like green almonds. "Something new for you today, I think," Yamyong said with a satisfied air.

Ayudhaya was hot, dusty, spread-out, its surrounding terrain strewn with ruins that scarcely showed through the vegetation. At some distance from the town there began a wide boulevard sparingly lined with important-looking buildings. It continued for a way and then came to an end as abrupt as its beginning. Growing up out of the scrub, and built of small russet-colored bricks, the ruined temples looked still unfinished rather than damaged by time. Repairs, done in smeared cement, veined their façades.

The bus's last stop was still two or three miles from the center of Ayudhaya. We got down into the dust, and Brooks declared: "The first thing we must do is find some food. They can't eat anything solid, you know, after midday."

"Not noon exactly," Yamyong said. "Maybe one o'clock or a little later."

"Even so, that doesn't leave much time," I told him. "It's quarter to twelve now."

But the bhikkus were not hungry. None of them had visited Ayudhaya before, and so they had compiled a list of the things they most wanted to see. They spoke with a man who had a station wagon parked nearby, and we set off for a ruined *stupa* that lay some miles to the south-west. It had been built atop a high mound, which we climbed with some difficulty, so that Brooks could take pictures of us standing within a fissure in the decayed outer wall. The air stank of the bats that lived inside.

When we got back to the bus stop, the subject of food arose once again, but the excursion had put the bhikkus into such a state of excitement that they could not bear to allot time for anything but looking. We went to the museum. It was quiet; there were Khmer heads and documents inscribed in Pali. The day had begun to be painful. I told myself I had known beforehand that it would.

Then we went to a temple. I was impressed, not so much by the gigantic Buddha which all but filled the interior, as by the fact that not far from the entrance a man sat on the floor playing a *ranad* (pronounced *lanat*). Although I was familiar with the sound of it from listening to recordings of Siamese music, I had never before seen the instrument. There was a gradated series of wooden blocks strung together, the whole slung like a hammock over a boat-shaped resonating stand. The tones hurried after one another like drops of water falling very fast. After the painful heat outside, everything in the temple suddenly seemed a symbol of the concept of coolness – the stone floor under my bare feet, the breeze that moved through the shadowy interior, the bamboo fortune sticks being rattled in their long box by those praying at the altar, and the succession of insubstantial, glassy sounds that came from the *ranad*. I thought: if only I could get something to eat, I wouldn't mind the heat so much.

We got into the center of Ayudhaya a little after three o'clock. It was hot and noisy; the bhikkus had no idea of where to look for a restaurant, and the idea of asking did not appeal to them. The five of us walked aimlessly. I had come to the conclusion that neither Prasert nor Vichai understood spoken English, and I addressed myself earnestly to Yamyong. "*We've got to eat.*" He stared at me with severity. "We are searching," he told me.

Eventually we found a Chinese restaurant on a corner of the principal street. There was a table full of boisterous Thais drinking *mekong* (categorized as whiskey, but with the taste of cheap rum) and another table occupied by an entire Chinese family. These people were doing some serious eating, their faces buried in their rice bowls. It cheered me to see them: I was faint, and had half expected to be told that there was no hot food available.

The large menu in English which was brought us must have been typed several decades ago and wiped with a damp rag once a week ever since. Under the heading SPECIALITIES were some dishes that caught my eye, and as I went through the list I began to laugh. Then I read it aloud to Brooks.

"Fried Sharks Fins and Bean Sprout
Chicken Chins Stuffed with Shrimp
Fried Rice Birds
Shrimps Balls and Green Marrow
Pigs Lights with Pickles
Braked Rice Bird in Port Wine
Fish Head and Bean Curd"

Although it was natural for our friends not to join in the laughter, I felt that their silence was not merely failure to respond; it was heavy, positive.

A moment later three Pepsi-Cola bottles were brought and placed on the table. "What are you going to have?" Brooks asked Yamyong.

"Nothing, thank you," he said lightly. "This will be enough for us today."

"But this is terrible! You mean no one is going to eat anything?"

"You and Mr. Bowles will eat your food," said Yamyong. (He might as well have said "fodder.") Then he, Prasert, and Vichai stood up, and carrying their Pepsi-Cola bottles with them, went to sit at a table on the other side of the room. Now and then Yamyong smiled sternly across at us.

"I wish they'd stop watching us," Brooks said under his breath.

"They were the ones who kept putting it off," I reminded him. But I did feel guilty, and I was annoyed at finding myself placed in the position of the self-indulgent unbeliever. It was almost as bad as eating in front of Moslems during Ramadan.

We finished our meal and set out immediately, following Yamyong's decision to visit a certain temple he wanted to see. The taxi drive led us through a region of thorny scrub. Here and there, in the shade of spreading flat-topped trees, were great round pits, full of dark water and crowded with buffaloes; only their wet snouts and horns were visible. Brooks was already cry-ing: "Buffaloes! Hundreds of them!" He asked the taxi driver to stop so that he could photograph the animals.

"You will have buffaloes at the temple," said Yamyong. He was right; there was a muddy pit filled with them only a few hundred feet from the building. Brooks went and took his pic-tures while the bhikkus paid their routine visit to the shrine. I wandered into a courtyard where there was a long row of stone Buddhas. It is the custom of temple-goers to plaster lit-tle squares of gold leaf onto the religious statues in the *wats*. When thousands of them have been stuck onto the same sur-face, tiny scraps of the gold come unstuck. Then they tremble in the breeze, and the figure shimmers with a small, vibrant life of its own. I stood in the courtyard watching this quivering along the arms and torsos of the Buddhas, and I was reminded of the motion of the bo tree's leaves. When I mentioned it to Yamyong in the taxi, I think he failed to understand, for he replied: "The bo tree is a very great tree for Buddhists."

Brooks sat beside me on the bus going back to Bangkok. We spoke only now and then. After so many hours of resisting the heat, it was relaxing to sit and feel the relatively cool air that blew in from the rice fields. The driver of the bus was not a believer in cause and effect. He passed trucks with oncoming traffic in full view. I felt better with my eyes shut, and I might even have dozed off, had there not been in the back of the bus a man, obvi-ously not in control, who was intent on making as much noise as possible. He began to shout, scream, and howl almost as soon as we had left Ayudhaya, and he did this consistently throughout the journey. Brooks and I laughed about it, conjecturing whether he were crazy or only drunk. The aisle was too crowded for me to be able to see him from where I sat. Occasionally I glanced at the other passengers. It was as though they were entirely unaware of the commotion behind them. As we drew closer to the city, the screams became louder and almost constant.

"God, why don't they throw him off?" Brooks was beginning to be annoyed.

"They don't even hear him," I said bitterly. People who can tolerate noise inspire me with envy and rage. Finally I leaned over and said to Yamyong: "That poor man back there! It's incredible!"

"Yes," he said over his shoulder. "He's very busy." This set me thinking what a civilized and tolerant people they were, and I marveled at the sophistication of the word "busy" to describe what was going on in the back of the bus.

Finally we were in a taxi driving across Bangkok. I would be dropped at my hotel and Brooks would take the three bhikkus on to their *wat*. In my head I was still hearing the heartrending cries. What had the repeated word patterns meant?

I had not been able to give an acceptable answer to Yamyong in his bewilderment about the significance of the necktie, but perhaps he could satisfy my curiosity here.

"That man in the back of the bus, you know?"

Yamyong nodded. "He was working very hard, poor fellow. Sunday is a bad day."

I disregarded the nonsense. "What was he saying?"

"Oh, he was saying: 'Go into second gear,' or 'We are coming to a bridge,' or 'Be careful, people in the road.' Whatever he saw."

Since neither Brooks nor I appeared to have understood, he went on. "All the buses must have a driver's assistant. He watches the road and tells the driver how to drive. It is hard work because he must shout loud enough for the driver to hear him."

"But why doesn't he sit up in the front with the driver?"

"No, no. There must be one in the front and one in the back That way two men are responsible for the bus."

It was an unconvincing explanation for the grueling sounds we had heard, but to show him that I believed him I said: "Aha! I see."

The taxi drew up in front of the hotel and I got out. When I said good bye to Yamyong, he replied, I think with a shade of aggrievement: "Good bye. You have left your lotus pods on the bus."

Fez: Behind the Walls

Journal 1984; Barry Brukoff 'Morocco', 1991

I F YOU CAME down out of the mountains from Ouezzane, you saw it far below – a whitish-gray spot ringed with green, which from that distance was unrecognizable as a city; it might have been a quarry or a simple discoloration in the plain. As you swung around the curves on your way down the flank of Djebel Zalagh, the perspective remained the same, but the spot broadened constantly and a definite line separating the gray part from the green became visible: it was the wall surrounding the Medina. Within were the tens of thousands of cube-shaped structures, their pattern varied here and there by the thin prism of a minaret reaching above them. Outside the line were the fruit orchards and olive groves that brought the country to the very foot of the wall, enclosing the city within a solid frame of verdure, so that from this vantage point it was like a white bouquet tightly encased in leaves. In the past two decades the city has burst through its confines at several points and grown new additions outside the ramparts. But from above it looks much the same.

To call Fez one of the great cities of the world might seem to some a generous gesture. It is not commercially or industrially important; it is no longer a cultural or political center; it does not even have the most impressive examples of its own architectural style (which are not to be found in Morocco at all, but in Spain). Unlike other cities which enjoyed their period of greatness in remote times, and which are judged worthy of more or less attention according to the number of historical vestiges they contain, Fez does not have to rely upon its ancient structures for its claim to importance. Its interest lies not so much in relics of the past as in the life of the people there; that life *is* the past, still alive and functioning. It would be difficult to find another city anywhere in which the everyday vicissitudes of medieval urban life can be studied in such detail. How much longer this will remain true depends upon how quickly the Moroccans can implement their plans to industrialize the nation, since the economy of Fez is based primarily on the market for its hand-made goods. Here is a city of more than half a million people who spend their time at such occupations as hammering and chasing brass and copper, tanning and tooling leather, carding, spinning and weaving wool, and all the other slow processes whereby the raw materials of the land are transformed into artifacts. (These objects, originally designed for the Moroccan market, are now made with the tourist trade in mind, and there is a corresponding deterioration in their workmanship.)

The visitor senses something in Fez which he describes as a feeling of mystery; that is as good a way as any of describing the impression the city makes. There is no doubt that to the person with a little imagination that impression is very strong: the city seems inexhaustible, incredibly complex, and vaguely menacing. It is possible that the visitor will also find it beautiful, although this is by no means certain. Fez is not a city that everyone can like. Many travelers have a negative reaction to its dark twisting alleys, teeming with people and animals. Anyone subject to claustrophobia may well find it only a nightmarish welter of tunnels, dead-end passageways and windowless walls. To grasp the fascination of the place one has to be the sort of person who enjoys losing himself in a crowd and being pushed along by it, not caring where to or for how long. He must be able to attain relaxation in the idea of being helpless in the midst of that crowd, he must know how to find pleasure in the out-landish, and see beauty where it is most unlikely to appear.

One of the city's chief attractions (for the visitor) is also one of its major annoyances (for the inhabitants): its ancient wall. In some places people have done what was formerly unthinkable; they have built houses outside the ramparts. These miles of walls, without which Fez could not have existed, are beginning to stifle the city. There are not many gates, and to get out it is necessary often to make long detours. With the passage of time the wall seems destined to be reduced to a few vestiges of itself. New gateways will be cut through from the crowded interior to the open spaces outside. Eventually whatever is left of the wall will be lost in the new structures made inevitable by the fast-growing population and the unfolding of the city's economy. For the moment, however, the wall provides a precise demarcation between outside and inside. Automobiles can go through certain gates, but nowhere is it possible for them to continue very far. The ingenuous motorist who imagines that because he has got in, he is going to be able to go on, is in for a sad surprise. The street, narrow from the beginning, is suddenly allowing the walls to touch the car on both sides, and he has got to go back where he came from, but in reverse.

There is a good deal of frustration involved in the process of enjoying Fez. The blank wall is its symbol, but it is this very secretiveness which gives the city its quality. The Fassi feels intuitively that everything should be hidden: the practice of his religion, his personal possessions (including his womenfolk) and above all his thoughts. If anyone besides him knows what he really thinks, he is already compromised, at a disadvantage, since his mind functions largely in terms of strategy. Moroccans in general are not an "oriental" people, but the bourgeois of Fez are.

I HAVE NOTICED that the inhabitants have a minimal interest in what exists immediately outside the limits of their city. The dozen miles or so of high ramparts have consistently shut out not only the Berber's unwelcome person, but also his incompatible African culture. Some years ago I was working on a project for the Rockefeller Foundation, recording folk and art music throughout the country. This had to be done in collaboration with the Moroccan government. Inevitably, I came to Fez and presented my credentials to the *katib* of the governor. "Folk music!" he snorted. "I detest folk music! It is precisely this sort of thing that we are doing our best to stamp out."

Nevertheless, since he was a Moroccan and I was a foreigner in his country, he also felt it incumbent upon him to give me some sort of assistance, so that eventually I found myself talking with a group of young musicians who played *chaabiya* or popular urban music. One of them politely asked me in which city I had so far made most of my recordings. I said that the great majority of them had been made not in any city, but in the country. My answer seemed to bewilder him. "In the country? But there is no music in the country."

I said that my experience had been that there was music practically everywhere in Morocco. He smiled. "Oh, you mean the Berbers! I've never heard any of their music."

"Surely you must have," I said. "You can hear it only a short distance from here, up that way, down that way – (I pointed) around Tahala or Rhafaii, for instance."

He smiled again, this time at my ignorance. "Nobody ever goes to such places," he said categorically. Aware of that, I still feigned innocence. "Why not?" I demanded.

"Because there's nothing there. The people are like savages."

The Fassi is a metropolitan, bourgeois in his habits and isolationist in his attitude; he also has the reputation of being a hard man to beat in a business deal, which makes him not entirely popular with his compatriots. There is no doubt that he has an element of arrogance in his character. Aware that his city was the cultural hub of all North Africa, he has been content to let others come to him in order to learn. Civilization ended at the gates of the Medina; outside was the wilderness.

From its earliest days the growth of the city has followed a particular pattern which might have been expected to destroy it rather than to play a part in its development. The place seems to carry the element of dissension within its very foundations. It has been a schizophrenic city from the outset, when, early in the ninth century, Idriss II founded the two communities which formed its original nucleus. Each time its two parts have been unified, a rival town has sprung into existence next door, an entity which in its turn had to be subdued and ultimately amalgamated. And, from without, the place has been besieged, flooded, pillaged, burned and bombarded so often that it seems incredible there should be anything at all left of it, much less the architecturally homogeneous mass that it is. Through the centuries, the reigning dynasties have been obliged to wage war against its inhabitants in order to make them recognize their sovereignty. Being prepared for a siege is so much a part of the pattern of life that some middle- and upper-class citizens are inclined to keep a large supply of staple foods in their houses, "just in case."

The conditions responsible for this display of mass anxiety have not changed basically in the eleven hundred years since the founding of the city. One could use Fez as an object lesson to illustrate the play of forces in the city-versus-country struggle that operates throughout Morocco and determines much of its character. Fez was built at a natural crossroads, the spot where the route from the Sahara to the Mediterranean coast intersects the east-west passage between Algeria and the Atlantic. To impose an economic stranglehold on the newly conquered land it was imperative that the Arabs control these principal arteries of transit. Automatically, Fez became the strategic center, the command of which was a sine qua non for the administration of the entire region. Within the walls there grew up a prosperous commercial city with an imported Semitic culture, while directly outside in the surrounding hills, in full view of the town, lived the infinitely less evolved Berbers, upon whose precarious good will the urban dwellers' peace of mind largely depended. The pagan Berbers accepted the new monotheistic religion of Islam, but clashes between two such dissimilar groups were inevitable.

Despite the government's efforts to create a more homogenous population, the friction still persists.

THE STREET GOES down and down, always unpaved, nearly always partially hidden from the sky. Sometimes it is so narrow as to permit only one-way foot traffic; here the beasts of burden scrape their flanks on each side as they squeeze through, and you have to back up or step quickly into a doorway while they pass, the drivers intoning: "*Balak, balak, balak ...*" Here is the bitter earth odor of new pottery, here the rank smell of hides being tanned, or the stench of a butcher's stall where the meat, black with flies, ripens in a shaft of dusty sunlight that points like an accusing finger down through the meshes of the latticework. In dark recesses like grottoes are mosaic fountains where women and girls scream invective as they fill their pails and the dust under their feet turns to mud. Then you are walking under an elaborately carved portal hung with ancient bronze lanterns, and you smell the feline scent of fig-trees. A cascade of water rumbles nearby, but it is behind a wall and you never catch a glimpse of it.

Even in the heart of the city a surprising amount of space is devoted to private gardens. As he follows the winding, shut-in streets, the passer-by cannot divine the presence of the pleasure spots behind the high walls. But they are there, and for those who are lucky enough to possess them, they add immeasurably to the charm of living in Fez.

From the street a house is a high wall with a door somewhere along its uneven length and possibly a handful of tiny grilled peepholes sprinkled in a haphazard design across its surface. Some thirty feet above the ground there may be a huge cedar beam sprouting from the façade at a forty-five-degree angle and supporting a triangular bay that juts out high above the street, providing the *raison d'être* for that vast expanse of virtually empty wall below it. With the exception of the door, which is usually studded in a mosaic of brass nail-heads, there is no suggestion of decoration or even of a preoccupation with the kind of surface given to the adobe or plaster that covers the wall.

Fez El Bali, 1947 (PB)

The inside of the house is another matter. When you step into the glittering tile and marble interior of a prosperous Fez dwelling, with its orange trees and its fountains, and the combined pastel and hard-candy colors glowing from the rooms around the courtyard, you are pleased that there should be nothing but the indifferent anonymity of a blank wall outside – nothing to indicate the existence of this very private, remote and brilliant world within. A noncommittal expanse of earthen wall in the street hides a little Alhambra of one's own, a miniature paradise totally shielded from the gaze of the world.

In the less sumptuous homes, the door necessarily opens directly upon the patio. Nevertheless, even here from the street nothing is visible but a short blind corridor that makes a right-angle turn before opening into the courtyard. This is invariable. Whether the women are visible or hidden, their presence and collective personality are constantly suggested by the diaphanous curtains of white muslin that hang across the doorways and around the canopied beds; it is impossible to imagine the color schemes in the rooms, either, save in relation to the women who live in them. The men are in and out of the house, day and night – but the women literally pass their lives inside the house, and this is evident.

A courtyard may have as many as three galleries that go part or all the way around it; the rooms can be reached only by going along the galleries. Stairways are steep, inlaid with mosaics of very small titles, and sometimes tipped with white marble treads. The house looks in upon itself; the focus of attention is the stone basin of water in the center. The women must have total protection from the world without. The architect, having provided this, is then free to become decorator, and can concentrate his attention upon the delights of applied geometric design in plaster filigree, carved wood and paint. A large house may have several separate patios, each one multiple-storied and with many rooms; a humble house has a central open space with two or three rooms giving onto it. The very poor sometimes live in rooming-houses, each family occupying one room and having the use of that section of the gallery outside the door, conditions which necessarily give rise to disputes about rights to space and violation of private property.

Fez is still a relatively relaxed city; there is time for everything. The retention of this classic sense of time can be attributed, in part at least, to the absence of motor vehicles in the Medina. If you live in a city where you never have to run in order to catch something, or jump to avoid being hit by it, you are likely to have preserved a natural physical dignity that is not a concomitant of contemporary life; and if you still have that dignity, you want to go on having it. So you see to it that you have time to do whatever you want to do; it is vulgar to hurry.

For all their religious orthodoxy and outward austerity, the people of Fez are not ashamed to be hedonists. They love the sound of a fountain splashing in the courtyard; on the coals of their braziers they sprinkle sandalwood and benzoin; they have a passion for sitting on a high spot of ground at twilight and watching the slow change of light, color and form in the landscape. Outside the ramparts are innumerable orchards, delightful little wildernesses of canebrake, where olive and fig trees abound. It is the custom of families to out there on a late afternoon with their rugs, braziers and tea equipment. One discovers groups of such picnickers in the most secluded corners of the countryside, particularly on the northern slopes above the valley. Not long ago on one of my walks I came across a family spread out in the long grass. They were sitting quietly on their reed mats, but something in their collective attitude made me stop and observe them more closely. Then I saw that surrounding them at a radius of perhaps a hundred feet was a circle of bird cages, each supported by a stake driven into the ground. There were birds in all the cages and they were singing. The entire family sat there happily, listening. As urbanites in other places carry along their radios, they had brought their birds with them from the town, purely for entertainment.

The changes brought about during the past fifty-three years since I first saw Fez are relatively superficial; none has been so drastic as to alter its image. The Medina is protected by the form of the land on which it is built; its topography is roughly funnel-shaped, and it is not likely to be bulldozed like so much of Cairo in the time of Abdel Nasser. Yet with the increasing poverty in the region the city clearly cannot continue much longer in its present form. Those of the original inhabitants who can afford it are moving to Casablanca, leaving the Medina at the mercy of the impoverished rustics replacing them. A house which formerly sheltered one family now contains ten or twelve families, living, it goes without saying, in unimaginable squalor. The ancient dwellings are falling rapidly into disrepair. And so at last, it is the people from outside the walls who have taken over the city, and their conquest, a natural and inevitable process, spells its doom. That Fez should still be there today, unchanged in its outward form, is the surprising phenomenon.

AN ISLAND OF MY OWN

SAN FRANCISCO CHRONICLE, 1985

L IKE MOST PEOPLE, I have always been certain there was a place somewhere on this planet that could provide the necessary respite from all reminders of present-day chaos and noise, a place to which one could escape and, having escaped, shut the figurative door, there to breathe pure air and hear only the sounds provided by natural forces. So it was with tremulous excitement that I first saw the little island of Taprobane, in Weligama Bay off the south coast of Sri Lanka. Here was a site that seemed to have all the requisite qualities: it was scarcely more than a hummock of black basalt rising above the waves of the Indian Ocean, yet was heavily covered with high trees that left visible only a glimpse of the house at its summit. I had never seen a place that looked so obviously like what I was searching for. And I felt that it was aware of me, that it silently beckoned, sending forth a wordless message that meant: come, you'll like it here.

Three years later, I signed the necessary documents and became the owner of this tiny parcel of paradise. The erstwhile proprietor, a rubber planter named Mr. Jinadasa, also bred race-horses and bet on them. When a horse in which he had great confidence failed to justify his hopes, he found himself in immediate need of cash. My informant in Sri Lanka wired me in Madrid, and as soon as the news arrived I rushed out to cable the money.

I inherited a couple who were resident gardener and maid, and who continued their work as if they were still in the employ of Mr. Jinadasa. In aspects they had worked for several owners, scarcely knowing them apart, and were aware only that their employer must be addressed as Master. The island had belonged to various people in the recent past, and none of them had kept it very long. It was a pleasure dome, a place they used for weekend parties. The only person who had actually lived there was the Comte de Mauny Talvande, who had built the house and furnished it after reclaiming the island from its former status as the local cobra-dump. (All cobras found in the region were put into sacks, carried across to the island and left there, since in Sri Lanka one doesn't kill snakes.) In order to settle in, I needed to buy only new mattresses for the beds, and lamps and kitchenware. The furniture, made of the heaviest kinds of tropical wood, was well-nigh immovable.

Finding a good cook was the greatest initial challenge, but eventually, in the nearby town of Matara, I unearthed a man who had been chef in a hotel. At the same time I discovered that no cook would work without an assistant, so I was obliged to take on two men. The cook cooked; the extra man served at table and washed dishes. Indeed, each employee in the house had a very precise idea of what his work involved, and it was impossible to get any of them to perform an act he considered to be outside his domain. The maid polished the furniture and filled bowls with orchids. The gardener fetched things from the market in the village on the mainland. Another man, a Hindu, came twice a day to empty the latrines, as there was no running water on the island. Life moved like clockwork; there were no complications.

For me, much of the joy of living on Taprobane had to do with lying in bed at night listening to the sound of the big waves booming against the cliffs below, and the more distant, subdued sound of the same waves breaking on the sand along the great curved beach. I couldn't conceive of a greater luxury then, nor can I now. The subsidiary luxuries consisted of early tea along with an assortment of fruit (served in bed), a real English breakfast at nine and, at midday, a curry the like of which I've not eaten elsewhere. The cook provided twenty side dishes for each meal (including marunga leaves which, sprinkled over coconut cream, gave the food an irresistible flavor). At night the men would go down to the rocks and catch enough lobsters for the next day's curry. When the lobsters were too few, we made do with spearfish, the local equivalent of pompano, and equally delectable.

Only once was this tranquil existence significantly disrupted. What happened was that the government of Sri Lanka came to an agreement with Peking whereby China would receive the totality of Sri Lanka's rubber crop in return for specified quantities of China's rice. The rice arrived, but it had been lying in damp warehouses for so long that it was rancid. When one tried to cook it, it gave off an unbelievably powerful stench; it was inedible. All the Sinhalese were complaining, but there was no help for it. The only solution was to comb the shops in all towns along the coast for boxes of English rice and hoard them and, when the shops were empty, which they soon were, to go more than a hundred miles to Colombo and bring back all one could find. Only thanks to such efforts did the curry continue to be as good as ever.

For the most part, however, life on Taprobane was trouble-free. The ocean was languorously warm, and the sharks left alone. You could see them a few hundred feet away as they patrolled the reef, but they never ventured inside. Occasionally a gigantic tortoise that lived among the rocks on the south-west side of the island would rise to the surface and remain there, a floating boulder. If one swam toward it, it quickly submerged, 'Old' Benedict the gardener told me one day, indicating its domed back.

The catamarans bearing fishermen streamed past the island before sunrise and returned en masse at sunset, oars and sail giving them speed. And just as regularly, each daybreak flocks of crows arrived to chase away the hordes of bats that spent

Paul Bowles at work on *The Spider's House*, his third novel, on Taprobane, 1955.

each night hanging from the trees outside the windows. The bats were surprisingly big, often with a wingspread of three feet. Their bodies were covered with dark, russet-colored hair and their teeth looked very sharp when you flashed a light into a tree and saw them hanging above you. They were fruit-eating animals and entirely innocuous, even with respect to the vegetation; the big trees on the mainland where they gathered in daytime were burned white by their dung, and nothing grew in the immediate vicinity, but for some reason they did not excrete at night.

It was the crows that saved my trees. They came in great numbers at dawn for no purpose that I could discern other than to drive away the bats. Once they had done that and remarked about it with each other for a while, they flew back to the mainland. But the bats never returned until dark.

The central room of the house was 30 feet high, with a cupola at the top that let the wind blow in from all sides, so that even though the air was hot there was always a breeze moving through the room. The voluptuous breeze and the sounds of the sea made an after-lunch siesta inevitable. I missed two or three hours of the afternoon, but how fine it was when the cook's assistant arrived from behind the curtains at five o'clock saying, "tea, Master," and put the tray down on the bed, and I drank the tea still listening to the pounding waves.

Then it was time for a late-afternoon dip in the sea, when Benedict would return with provisions from the village along with two men who waded through the waves carrying tanks of water on their heads. Benedict did not like to be out after dark. Although he claimed to be a Catholic, he shared some of the superstitions of the uneducated Buddhist coastal population. He was particularly afraid of meeting a black dog on the road. According to him, all black dogs were evil spirits and should be avoided. I knew that the island had been cleared of snakes several decades earlier, and I had never seen a sign of the presence of venomous spiders or scorpions. Nevertheless, one evening the cook on his way to the kitchen stepped barefoot on a large centipede. He cried out, dropped the tray he was carrying and fell to the floor unconscious. Benedict, having been called from below, came with a "cobra stone," made an incision in the foot and rubbed the stone over it for some minutes. When the cook had revived, I asked to see the stone, but Benedict did not want me to touch it. In his hand it looked something like a sponge, light and porous. This miniature drama became in retrospect a major event, so uneventful was the passage of the days and weeks.

Time moved swiftly, imperceptively, on the island. Had it not been for two things, unrelated but equally important, I could have prolonged my sojourn there indefinitely. The first was that at the end of June the south-west monsoons arrived, so that during the high seas of the summer months Taprobane was uninhabitable. The other was the Sri Lankan law that required every foreigner who remained in the country six months or more to pay a high tax on his global income. Since I generally went to Taprobane around Christmas, I had to arrange my return to Europe for mid-June. Taprobane was not a permanent escape, then, but for half of each year it was idyllic.

Of course, no idyll is without its irony. When I finally did sell the island, the proceeds were impounded by the Finance Control of Sri Lanka, so that I have never seen any of my money. One can't always win – but one can always remember.

TANGIER

INDEPENDENT ON SUNDAY, 1990

WHEN THE JOURNALIST Robert Ruark spent a weekend in Tangier, his first report in the *New York World-Telegram* bore the following heading: "Tangier, Sinkhole of Iniquity". With such a flamboyant fanfare, it is not surprising that scores of lesser men of the Press should subsequently come in search of publishable proofs of iniquity. What they couldn't find, they invented with gusto.

For a long time, Tangier was enthusiastically dubbed The Sin City of the World. This probably helped the local economy, but at the cost of disappointing thousands of eager tourists. The appraisal in *The Rough Guide to Morocco* (1987) seems a lot more accurate: "... a tricky place for first arrivals, but once you've got the feel of it, can still be a lively and very likeable town ... with an enduring capacity for craziness."

The mention of craziness strikes me as apt. People are likely to behave in inexplicable ways. Residents are prone to blame everything on the east wind, just as unaccountable behavior in Provence is explained by the mistral – it is even considered to be a mitigating circumstance in a case of murder.

Here the wind accounts for undue nervousness and bad temper, but I suspect that whatever murders are committed while it is blowing would have been committed anyway. The month-long fast of Ramadan seems more likely to result in violent behavior than exposure to the wind – even though it can blow with gale force, day and night, for a week without surcease.

When I first arrived in Tangier, although it was primarily a port, there was no breakwater and no dock. The ferry from Gibraltar would cast anchor in the harbor, and passengers were rowed ashore in a dinghy.

The railway station was outside the town among the sand dunes; you reached it by a boardwalk that ran along parallel to the beach. If it was raining, you could hire a carriage drawn by one weak horse, which you hoped would get you to your train.

The Medina, a compact collection of buildings enclosed by ramparts, never ceased to fascinate me. Like the sea, it was always there but always different from what it had been the moment before. The dramas played by the Muslims in its labyrinthine passageways were like the inventions of an inspired playwright.

The town was so small and closely knit that from the Grand Socco, its center, I could walk in a half-hour to my house on the Old Mountain and be completely in the country, where the only sounds were the crickets and the wind in the trees.

The only Moroccans to be seen on the beach in those years were peasants riding their donkeys, coming into town for the market. The Tangerines considered the sun poisonous and did what they could to keep out of it. It was only later that a few young men were courageous enough to imitate the French, who had no scruples about swimming and lying on the sand in the sunlight. And it was still later that women began to venture (fully dressed) into the waves.

In the Medina the only sounds were human voices. The radio with its distorting amplifier had not yet arrived. For those who wanted music there were ancient wind-up gramophones to be rented by the hour. They were delivered by small boys who wore the flaring horns over their heads like huge morning glories and were thus often unable to see where they were going.

The Zoco Chico, in the center of the Medina, surrounded by cafés on all sides, presented a symphony of hundreds of conversations. In the early 1930s the clientele thinned out after midnight, but after the war, in the 1940s – when Tangier was packed with tourists and foreign residents – the cafés were busy until dawn; exhausted party-goers then arrived to take black coffee before retiring.

Those were the liveliest years for the town. Dollars and pounds fetched more than twice as many francs or pesetas in the International Zone as they did in Paris or Madrid (or Casablanca, for that matter). With a dollar account here, one could live in Paris on francs changed in one's Tangier bank, at the rate of 550 per dollar instead of 220. There were money changers throughout the town, displaying blackboards on which the latest rates were chalked. A few people rushed from one to another all day, buying and selling currencies, and managing thus to eke out a living; I never understood exactly how.

The only legal tender accepted by the canny peasant women who sold fruit, vegetables and eggs under the trees in the Grand Socco was silver. One had to change one's European money for silver Hassani coins before marketing.

Smuggling was a way of life in this laxly governed port, and I knew a man who persuaded a cobbler to make him shoes with elevated heels. Into each heel he put a half-kilo of gold bullion, enabling him to leave Tangier with an entire kilo, in order to sell it elsewhere at a good profit – or so he claimed. I found it difficult to believe that the difference in the price would have made it worth his while.

But some people seemed to attribute magical powers to the International Zone, administered for three decades by a fractious committee of Western European powers. It excited people to feel that they were in no country, that the zone was a kind of no-man's land where everyone did as they pleased, and where there was no interference by the law. And it is true that the town had an aura of general permissiveness, to an extraordinary degree. I had never seen anything quite like it before, nor have I since.

The old Tangier I had known in 1931 did not last. When I returned after the war in 1947 it was scarcely recognizable.

Apartment houses had gone up, trees had been done away with, streets had been cut through the outlying countryside. In the Medina, new façades had been given to the houses – in every case destroying the Moorish arch over the entrance door, thus depriving the streets of visual charm.

But most Moroccans are entirely indifferent to such details. They admire that which is new, regardless of its appearance. Apart from a few ancient buildings in the casbah, the only place I can think of which has not undergone modernizing alterations is a small café in the Marshan district at the edge of a high cliff above the sea. In the thirties I used to go there during Ramadan and play Lotto, and it was there that I learnt to count in Arabic.

This little establishment, bearing a sign identifying it as *La Guinguette Fleurie*, was run by an elderly Frenchman. What is astonishing is that after nearly 60 years it should still look the same, should still be its delightful self, with its series of terraces leading down to the edge of the cliff. Seagulls sail and turn in the wind, and occasionally a tanker moves slowly on its way to or from the Straits of Gibraltar. Now the place belongs to Moroccans and has no sign outside, but everyone knows it as the Café Hafa, or Cliff Café. If you were not certain of where it is, you would never find it.

In the years since I first came to Tangier and was captured by its charm, the town of 60,000 inhabitants has become a city of ten times that number and, judging by the widespread construction going on now, it will continue to expand as long as the present surge of prosperity lasts. Compared to most cities, it is still a pleasant place to live – but the Tangier I know exists only in memory.

VIEWS OF TANGIER

INTRODUCTION TO JELLEL GASTELLI'S BOOK,
'VUES CHOISIES', 1991

THERE WAS THE QUESTION of finding *djenoun* in Tangier.
Informal talks with members of the police force showed
that there was no possibility of unearthing such creatures
within a twenty kilometer radius of the town. It was explained
that they cannot live in proximity to iron or steel, which means,
for one thing, that where there are motorized vehicles these evil
spirits will not be found. The streets of Tangier have more cars
in them each year. And now, as an added precaution the masons
even include iron bars inside the walls of the buildings. "So
there is absolutely no danger of coming across a *djinn* in the city,
regardless of what ignorant people may tell you." Housemaids,
who come from the country, have all kinds of backward notions,
and even though they watch television every day, they still
think that *djenoun* live in the kitchen drainpipes, and refuse
to use hot water in the sink, for fear of annoying them. This
is understandable, since in the places where they lived before
coming to Tangier, it is said that *djenoun* are ubiquitous, and
are able to transform themselves not only into animals, but into
human beings as well. This possibility makes any unfamiliar
figure immediately suspect.

"Wherever there are many trees you have to be careful.
You've probably noticed that they're getting rid of the trees as

fast as they can. Tangier is a modern town. You can't have big trees all along the streets if you want a modern city. There's no room for them, and besides, it doesn't look right. Tangier is a place for tourists, and tourists want to see everything looking new and modern, the same as in their own countries. We've got one good restaurant here. It's called Big Mac, and the tourists always go there. We need more places like that. I think next year there'll be another. Of course, there are smaller places where they can go for a *casse-croûte*, like Sandwich Pourquoi Pas or Sandwich Picasso."

When the winter rains have been very heavy, some houses slide down the cliffs into the sea.

The wind sweeps back and forth over Tangier, first in one direction and then in another. The strong currents in the strait and sea carry away the bodies of those who drown.

If you live in the Casbah your house will be wet. If on the Marshan or the Mountain, it will simply be very damp. Tangier is a city where everyone lives in a greater or lesser degree of discomfort. There is always the threat that something will cease functioning as it should.

In summer the water is cut off. In winter the streets are flooded. There is no money to repair the potholes which make driving hazardous.

"When my boy was five, he went to his teacher and said: If I give you a dirham every day, will you give me good marks at the end of the term ? He didn't need to go to school, he already knew what life is about. He went two or three years, and then I took him out. He learned much more at home, watching television."

There is no public park in Tangier, nor any municipal bus system. A fleet of white Mercedes taxis takes the place of buses. There are struggles in the street among people hoping to get inside these cars, since each car can accommodate only six or seven passengers at a time.

THE HAKIMA

INTRODUCTION TO WILLIAM BETSCH'S BOOK,
'THE HAKIMA: A TRAGEDY IN FEZ', 1991

FEZ IS THE PLACE where nothing is direct. Going into the Medina is not like entering a city; it is more like becoming a participant in a situation whose meaning is withheld. There is a sense of deviousness and accompanying intrigue in the air, and the inhabitants do little to mitigate this impression. The enclosing ramparts were built high to protect the town-dwellers from the Berber enemy outside, and I remember that in 1931 the gates in the north wall were shut after sunset. The people were convinced that bands of robbers lurked outside, waiting to pounce on anyone who failed to get back inside through the gates before nightfall. They seemed, however, to be almost equally afraid of each other. I recall the difficulties involved in trying to walk through the Medina at night. Between one quarter and the next there were huge doors that were shut and bolted, to prevent those living on one side from getting into the neighboring section. It was necessary to find the watchman and persuade him to let me through. Then somewhat farther along I would come up against another such barrier.

Of all the entrance gates piercing the enclosing wall of the Medina, there is only one, Bab Fteuh, that permits the passage of a vehicle. The vehicle will have to be parked not far inside, there being no question of proceeding beyond the point where the street narrows into the footpath typical of the alleys of the city. The town was built for those going on foot and on the backs of animals. Fortunately, it has not yet been rebuilt to allow the passage of motorized traffic. As to the other gates, once inside them the only way to go is down. The topography of the place can be likened to that of a funnel. From Bab Bou Jeloud, the western doorway into the Medina, there are only two main alleys, the Talaa Kebira and the Zekak al Hajar. It's possible to find a few other very circuitous routes: unlike the two principal alleys lined with shops, these pass through residential quarters. But they all lead toward the maw of the city down below.

When I first walked in the alleys of Fez, I saw that the men were different from other Moroccans. Many of them were pallid, even sickly. I often had the impression that they aspired to invisibility, as if not being certain of their identity, they would have preferred to slip unnoticed through the city. From their appearance I deduced, and I think correctly, that the Medina must be an unhealthy place in which to live.

The Ahal Fas are not loved by their countrymen. You hear that they are greedy, hypocritical, dishonest, treacherous, and abysmally vicious. There is no outrageous sexual behavior that has not been attributed to the people of Fez. If they are a quarter as evil as they are made out to be by other Moroccans, then they must be very bad indeed. Happily it has not been my personal experience to find them so. But over the years the defamatory tales have managed to throw a faint pall of ambiguity over the town, so that notwithstanding what I knew, I sometimes found myself wondering how much truth, if any, there was in the legend supplied by non-Fassi Moroccans.

It seems clear that the unpopularity of the natives of Fez is due at least partially to their having been an urban population in contrast to the vast majority of other Moroccans, whose mentality was much closer to being a rustic one. The money of the country was concentrated here, as of course was the commerce. There is not much doubt that the original motivation for the widespread dislike of the city and its inhabitants was simply envy, although few Moroccans, even today, would agree.

Much of the pleasure I got from living in Fez in the early days had to do with being at one moment outside under the olive trees with the sheep, and at the next penetrating the ramparts. Because of repeated experiences which have not become permanent memories, I connect passing through certain gates with specific hours of the day. Bah Bou Jeloud is bright in the morning sun. The archway is tiled on one face in royal blue and on the other in emerald green. There are storks standing atop the minaret of the mosque directly ahead. The hot light of noon belongs to Bab Dekaken with its vista of the crowds filling the huge dusty enclosure of the Makina. Bah Segma I loved to go through just as the sun dropped below the flat Western horizon at my back. Perhaps because of the knowledge that as recently as the end of the First World War the top of the arch of Bab Mahrouk was often decorated with the severed heads of those who had expressed their opposition to the regime, dusk seemed the right hour to walk beneath its wide arch. And I associate Bab Guissa with rainy nights, when the faint sense of menace hanging over the city moved palpably closer, and although no less faint, became somehow more real. It was a fine sensation to slide downward into the city through the mud of the alleys, breathing the wine-like odor of the olive presses, knowing that after uncounted turns to left and right I would emerge into the Souk Attarine, where there were a few lights and a few people standing under the dripping latticework overhead.

I know that now Fez has fallen upon evil days, and is no longer the same. The cultural and commercial capital is disintegrating. The people who might have held it together have left their great houses and moved to Casablanca, and the city now belongs to the very poor who, because of the desperate and violent tenor of their life, can only ensure its more rapid destruction.

THE SKY

FROM VITTORIO SANTO'S BOOK,
'PORTRAITS NUDES CLOUDS', 1993

THE MOOD OF A SCENE we play in our lives is determined largely by the light projected upon us from above. As master electrician, the sky furnishes an endless variety of lighting effects for our actions, helping to mold even the emotions that accompany them. There is the slow dimming of twilight for the exchange of intimacies, the flooding sunlight of a spring morning, for feeling unreasoned delight, the blackness of night when no light falls from the sky and each one becomes the victim of his own fantasies, the gray, indifferent light of the covered sky in summer; an encouragement to indolence. How can we tell to what extent our actions have been determined by the light which enveloped us while we performed them?

But such indirect effects pale beside the unsurpassable spectacle of the sky itself as it produces them. It is generally agreed that the most astonishing and grandiose visions that a human being can imagine take place in the sky.

It's merely a question of watching; the sky will perform. Nevertheless there must be something there to watch, something that moves. This will be some form of moisture: probably clouds, or even rain or mist. The movements, formations and conjunctions of these bodies of moisture constitute the show. A momentary glimpse of light from the sun can provide the excitement.

There are times when the sky consists of two distinct layers. The lower level contains ragged, dark clouds blowing fast and very low across the earth, while the upper regions are unaffected by the commotion below, and move, stately and slow, far above. It is not unusual for the two layers to be moving in opposing directions. A completely cloudless sky is static; it cannot provide a spectacle. The Saharan sky is like a blackboard on which nothing has been written. You can admire it for the intensity and luminosity of its blue, but you have no urge to watch it because you know that it will not change.

Storms, of course, can be magnificent, particularly in the tropics.

Sri Lanka's sunsets over the Indian Ocean before the monsoons rank high among the great celestial displays.

The night sky, just as much as the day sky, needs something moving, something for the eye to follow. I think of the poem by Alfred de Vigny, where silver-edged clouds race across the disc of the moon, causing dark shadows to move over the countryside.

A recurring nightmare: the earth's atmosphere has escaped into space, and we see that the sky has become permanently black.

Jane and Paul Bowles, New York, 1944

PAUL BOWLES, HIS LIFE

PREVIOUSLY UNPUBLISHED JOURNAL, 1986

The first sky he saw was the sky above New York.

Winters it snowed. The school was dark.

There was a song which went: "When you come back, if you do
come back."

It was addressed to the American soldiers in France.

There was a day when the children paraded in the street.

They sang "Marching through Georgia", a song of victory from
the Civil War.

Now it celebrated a different victory.

Kaiser Wilhelm would no longer haunt the children's dreams.

Summer meant sunshine and lakes and crickets.

The peaches dropped to the ground and were speared by the
stubble.

A day was invisible, had no hours.

The dark brought the voices of the night insects.

But school went on for many years. Discipline was strict.

The idea of escape took root and grew.

A night with thunder in the sky he packed his bag and left.

The *S.S. Rijndam* was old and slow. This was its last voyage.

Passengers for Boulogne went ashore in a dinghy, rocked by the
waves.

At dawn the empty streets of Paris were clean and shining.

This was fifty-seven years ago. Things are different now.

The excitements of Paris: Le Café du Dôme, La Mosquée.

Le Théâtre du Grand Guignol, le Bal Nègre de la Rue Blomet.

He worked for forty francs a week, and sometimes was hungry.

Then a girl he'd known from childhood came through Paris and
  saved him.

He wandered on the Côte d'Azur, in Switzerland,

And along the paths of the Schwarzwald.

He was happy, and he wrote words which he imagined made
  poems.

That winter in New York Aaron Copland told him: You should
  become a composer.

It will be difficult, he thought, but why not try?

Soon he was in Paris again. He admired Gertrude Stein.

She told him he was not a poet, so he stopped trying to be one.

This meant that he devoted himself only to music.

Miss Stein did not like the music either.

In Hannover he stayed with Kurt Schwitters.

He went with him to the city dumping ground

And they collected material for the Merzbau.

In Berlin he wrote music, and people shouted; *Fenster zu*!

In Paris they cried: *Fermez la fenêtre*!

In Tangier only Copland and the cicadas could hear him.

In the Sahara he fell in love with the sky

And knew that he would keep returning there.

In the spring he was in Agadir, where the food was not clean.

The doctors in Paris told him he had typhoid fever.

He lay for a month in the hospital. His mother came from New
  York.

When he was well they went to Spain and to Monte Carlo.

Winter came. He wanted the desert.

He took a house outside the oasis of Ghardaia.

He went to Tunisia on the back of a camel.

In Tunis he learned that he had no money.

Franklin D. Roosevelt had closed the banks. The dollar was not negotiable.

Friends in France wired him francs.

He arrived in Tangier with his python skin and seventeen jackal pelts.

He knew he must return to America, but first he sailed to Puerto Rico.

That way he stayed outside the cage a little longer.

In New York he thought only of Morocco.

Like a convict planning a prison break he prepared his escape.

And summer found him sailing toward the east. He stayed in Fez this time.

And though his parents awaited him in New York

He went to South America to see how it looked.

The forests and the mountains delighted him, but he did not stay.

He was in California writing music. He was in New York writing music.

Orson Welles wanted music for two plays, and he provided it.

Kristians Tonny and his wife arrived in New York.

Jane Auer appeared on the scene, and the four set out for Mexico.

The day after they arrived in Mexico City Jane disappeared.

Much later they heard she had gone to Arizona.

After a few months they went on to Guatemala. It was very fine.

He hurried to New York to orchestrate his first ballet.

He took Jane Auer to hear it played by the Philadelphia Orchestra.

Soon Jane Auer became Jane Bowles.

With too much luggage they boarded a Japanese ship and went
southward.

Then they were in Guanacaste with the monkeys and parrots

And they carried a parrot with them from Costa Rica to
Guatemala.

They were on the Côte d'Azur when Chamberlain visited
Munich.

They were in New York when Hitler marched eastward.

He was writing music for theater and film directors

And Jane was writing a novel.

They decided to go and live in Mexico. The hacienda was ten
thousand feet up.

When he had to fly to New York to work, Jane stayed behind.

The rooming-house where they lived that winter was run by the
poet Auden.

At half past six each morning Jane met the poet in the dining-
room.

Jane was a friend of Thomas Mann's daughter Erika.

And Auden had married her. They had things to talk about.

Soon they were back in Mexico. He was composing a *zarzuela*.

And Jane was writing a novel.

One day she came to the end of it.

The next day the Japanese bombed Pearl Harbor.

They went to Tehuantepec and listened to the marimbas.

He was still working on the *zarzuela*. He was also writing a
second ballet.

They went to New York and he became a music critic.

Jane's novel was published and Leonard Bernstein conducted
the *zarzuela*.

He went to Mexico and admired the new volcano Paricutin.

The Belgian Government-in-Exile commissioned music for a film on the Congo.

Collaborating with Salvador Dali, he wrote a third ballet.

Then he began to write short stories, and grew tired of writing theater music.

He went to Cuba and El Salvador. Jane was writing a play.

He stopped being a music critic, but continued to write music for Broadway.

One night he dreamed he was in Morocco. The dream made him very happy.

A publisher commissioned him to write a novel.

He decided to leave New York and go back to Morocco.

In Fez he began to write *The Sheltering Sky*.

He continued to write it as he moved here and there in the Sahara.

He met Jane in Tangier and took her to Fez.

A stream rushed by under their windows as they worked. He finished his novel.

He had already written music for Tennessee Williams' first Broadway success.

He was not surprised to learn that Tennessee wanted him for another play.

He went to New York and wrote the score.

After the opening he took Tennessee back to Morocco with him.

The weather was bad, and Tennessee stayed less than a month.

He and Jane were living at the Farhar in Tangier. Truman Capote arrived.

For six weeks he amused them at mealtimes.

There were many parties and picnics.

Jane worked in her cottage, but he did not know what she was writing.

He was chagrined to hear that the publishers did not want his
    book.

We expected a novel, they said, and this is not a novel.

So it was published first in London.

They went to England and stayed a few weeks in Wiltshire.

Jane wanted to spend the winter in Paris. He decided on Sri
    Lanka.

On the ship he started a novel about Tangier.

He went to stay on a tea plantation in the hills.

Where leopards hid behind rocks and carried off the dogs.

He took a boat across to Dhanushkodi in India.

India was hotter than Sri Lanka. He worked on his novel.

When he arrived in Paris, Jane was not ready to leave.

He was making an opera out of Garcia Lorca's *Yerma*.

This was for Libby Holman. They spent a month together in
    Andalusia.

Autumn in Fez. Winter and spring in the Sahara.

Jane wanted to return to Morocco.

He drove to the French frontier and picked her up.

But she liked Spain so much that they spent a month there.

She finished her play and went to New York.

He finished his novel and went to Bombay.

The Indian railways had suffered in the past two years.

In South India he was put into a screening camp

Along with twenty thousand Tamils caught while trying to
    escape to Sri Lanka.

But although they were there for months and years

He got out after two days, and went to Sri Lanka.

In midsummer he was in Venice. He was in Madrid when a
    wire came from Ceylon.

It was possible now to buy a small island off the coast of Sri Lanka.

He bought it and went to New York to write music for Jane's play.

In the summer he was in Rome, working on a film for Visconti.

He did not know what he was doing, but he did it anyway.

That winter in Tangier, while he had paratyphoid, William Burroughs came to see him.

It was a year before they got to know one another.

In the summer he started to write a third novel, this one about Fez.

It was half finished when he and Jane sailed

To pass the winter on Taprobane, the island off the coast of Sri Lanka.

Jane was not well. She was not happy there.

After two months she returned to Tangier.

He finished his novel and took a cruise to Japan.

Then he went back to Tangier and continued his work on the Garcia Lorca opera.

His parents came to visit him. They enjoyed Morocco. He was surprised.

He thought about his island, and decided to go to Sri Lanka and sell it.

The Suez Canal was blocked. He had to go via Cape Town.

He passed the winter at Taprobane and set sail for Mombasa.

While he was in Kenya Jane suffered a stroke.

He took her to England to be examined.

The doctors could do nothing, and they returned to Tangier.

Soon she became worse and had to go to London again. It was a bad time.

In Madeira her health grew worse. She was obliged to go to New York.

Tennessee, who loved her, came from Florida to meet her at the airport.

The Garcia Lorca opera was produced. It was not a success.

Libby Holman had worked very hard, but there was no director.

He and Jane went back to Tangier. But then a telegram came from Tennessee

Saying he needed music for a new play.

He sent him the script for *Sweet Bird of Youth*.

Part of the music was written in Tangier and part on the New York-bound ship.

The Rockefeller Foundation gave him a grant to record music in Morocco.

He spent six months taping music in the mountains, the desert and the city.

The following year he began to tape Moroccan story-tellers.

Jane seemed to be better, but she still could not see to work.

He took Allen Ginsberg to Marrakesh.

But they arrived the day the Medina burned.

The smoke from the bazaars and souks was heavy in the air.

Jane's health was now less good. They went twice to America, saw their parents.

Consulted doctors who might be of use. But no doctor could be of use.

In Tangier on the Monte Viejo he wrote his fourth novel.

He began to translate what Mohammed Mrabet recorded.

A publisher asked him to write a book about Cairo.

He did not want to do it, so he playfully suggested Bangkok.

The publisher agreed. He went to Bangkok via Panama. He was appalled.

You have arrived fifteen years too late, everyone told him.

The trees were gone. The klongs had been filled in. The air was foul.

After four months the Thai authorities forced him to leave.

In Tangier he found that Jane needed to be hospitalized.

He took her to Spain.

Then he agreed to go to California to teach.

He told his students that he was not a teacher and could not teach.

They laughed, thinking he was eccentric.

After the first semester he returned to Morocco.

Jane begged to be taken back to Tangier. The doctors advised against it.

Nevertheless he took her back with him because she was so unhappy.

It was a disaster. She would not eat, and grew weak and thin.

He admitted defeat and returned her to the hospital in Spain.

She remained there. She died there. Her grave is unmarked.

After that it seemed to him that nothing more happened.

He went on living in Tangier, translating from Arabic, French and Spanish.

He wrote many short stories, but no novels.

There continued to be more and more people in the world.

And there was nothing anyone could do about anything.

GLOSSARY

FROM THEIR HEADS ARE GREEN, 1963

AHOUACHE In the Grand Atlas and in territories to the south of it, a formal festival involving groups of dancers, singers and percussionists.

BAKHSHISH A gratuity.

BENDIR A large disc-shaped drum with one membrane.

BHIKKU A Buddhist monk.

BIDONVILLES The shanty towns that have grown up during the past three decades around the urban centers of North Africa. Not a geographically restrictive term.

BLED The countryside.

BUTAGAZ Butane gas, used for cooking.

CAID The chieftan of a tribe (or fraction of a tribe).

CAIQUE A rowboat or sailing boat.

CHEHADE The spoken sentence affirming the Islamic faith.

CHIKH The leader, in this case, of a group of folk musicians.

CICERONE A tourist guide.

COMEDOR The dining room in a small hotel.

COUSCOUS (properly COUSCSOU) A form of pasta, made by sprinkling drops of water over flour.

DAGOBA Buddhist burial mound.

DAHVEN The repeated backward and forward motion of the torso of a seated person.

DARBOUKA Large ceramic hand drum.

DHOTI A loincloth worn by men in India.

DJAOUI Resin for burning, especially with benzoin in it.

DJELLABA A hooded overgarment with sleeves. Formerly a man's garment, but now worn by both sexes.

FRAJA Mass dancing.

GANNEGA A small disc-shaped drum with a single fine membrane.

GITANOS Gypsies.

GOPURAM Ornamented tower at the gateway to a Hindu temple.

GUENNAOUA (singular GUENNAOUI) A religious brotherhood, most of whose members are of Sudanese extraction, descendents of slaves. Their choreographed ritual is useful in the curing of madness, seizures and scorpion stings. They also rid houses of undesirable spirits.

HAIK Woman's traditional outer covering, generally of fine white wool.

IMAM Leader of prayer in the mosque.

IMDYAZEN In certain Berber-speaking regions of Morocco, professional itinerant musicians.

IMOCHAGH Tamachek term for Touareg.

JOTEYA Second-hand market.

KATIB Secretary.

KHALIFA A deputy official.

KIF The fine leaves at the base of the flowers of the common hemp plant, chopped and mixed (ideally in a ratio of seven to four) with tobacco grown in the same earth.

KISSARIA In a Moslem town, the quarter of the souks devoted to the sale of textiles, clothing and luxury articles.

LITHAM The cloth worn over the lower half of a woman's face.

MAHIA Alcohol distilled from fruit.

MAJOUN In North Africa majoun is the word for jam. Used in its special sense it is the word for any sweet preparation eaten with the purpose of inducing hallucinations; its active ingredient is the hemp plant.

MEDINA The Arabic word for city. In North Africa it indicates in particular that part of any city which was built by the Moslems and was already in existence at the time of the arrival of the Europeans.

MEHARISTES Saharan military cavalrymen mounted on camels.

MEKTOUB Destiny.

MIJMAH A brazier.

MOTTOUI Leather pouch for carrying kif on one's person.

MOULOUD The holiday commemorating the birthday of the Prophet Mohammed; also the month in which it occurs.

MOUSSEM Seasonal festival held at the tomb of a saint.

MRUQ Sauce.

M'TARRBA The high narrow mattresses that line the walls of the rooms in a Moslem house.

MSKA A clear yellow gum resin.

NABOULA Bladder. Specifically a lamb's bladder, dried and softened, in which to store kif hermetically.

NARGILEH A water-pipe consisting of a jar and a hose with a mouthpiece.

PARADOR An inn. In Spain and Morocco a specific term for government-run tourist hostelries.

PASEO An avenue, generally with a strip of garden in the center.

PELOTON In French military usage, a detachment of soldiers.

PIRITH Buddhist purification ceremony.

QAHAOUAJI Tea-maker.

QSBAH Large reed transverse flute with a low register.

RHAITA Reed instrument, equivalent to oboe.

RONDA Card game, suggestive of gin rummy.

SEBSI Long thin pipe for smoking kif.

SEMOLINA Grains made from grinding any cereal. In North Africa the process is slow: drops of water are sprinkled over the surface of flour, and the resulting accretions are shaken until they are globular and of the desired size.

SOUK (properly SOUQ) The word is used throughout North Africa to mean a market. In the larger cities it has a second, more specific use in designating a street or quarter devoted to the buying and selling (and often the manufacture) of one given commodity.

SPANIOLINE Plural of SPANIOLI, a Spaniard.

TARBOOSH High-crowned skullcap, a fez.

TBOLA Plural of TBEL, North African side-drum, played with sticks.

TOB Mixture of straw and earth (and often manure) for masonry.

TOUBIB Doctor.

TSEUHEUR The theory and practice of black magic.

YMAKA The small black skullcap worn by male Jews.

ZAMAR Riffian double-reed musical instrument.

ZAOUIA The seat of a religious brotherhood, generally comprising a mosque, a school and the tomb of the sect's founder.

ZEBU The East Indian humped ox.

A BOWLES CHRONOLOGY

BY DANIEL HALPERN

Paul Bowles with Tennessee Williams – a photo taken during Williams' first visit to
Morocco in January 1949

CHRONOLOGY

1910 Born Paul Frederic Bowles on December 30 in Jamaica, Queens, New York City, the only child of Rena Winewisser and Claude Dietz Bowles. (Bowles family immigrated to New England in the seventeenth century; Paul's grandfather, Frederick Bowles, fought for the Union in the Civil War and settled in Elmira, New York. Rena Winewisser's grandfather was a German freethinker and political radical who came to the United States in 1848; her father owned a department store in Bellows Falls, Vermont, before moving family to a 165-acre farm near Springfield, Massachusetts.) Father is a dentist. The family lives at 108 Hardenbrook Avenue in Jamaica, the building where his father has his office and laboratory.

1911–15 Bowles learns to read by age four and keeps notebooks with drawings and stories, a habit that will continue throughout his childhood. His activities are strictly regimented by father. He spends summers with paternal grandparents in Glencora, New York, or at the Winewissers'.

1916–18 Family moves to 207 De Grauw Avenue in Jamaica in summer 1916. Bowles begins attending Model School in Jamaica the following year, entering at the second grade level. Mother reads him stories of Hawthorne and Poe. Beginning in 1918, Bowles goes to Manhattan twice a week for orthodontic treatment, which will continue for ten years; makes monthly visits to New York Public Library on 42nd Street, where Anne Carroll Moore, a family friend, is head of the children's department. Receives books from Moore and visits her Greenwich Village apartment. Father confiscates notebooks in a fit of rage. (Bowles would write in his autobiography: "This was the only time my father beat me. It began a new stage in the development of hostilities between us.")

1919 Bowles and parents catch influenza but survive worldwide epidemic. Father buys phonograph, collects classical recordings, and forbids his son from bringing jazz records into the house. Bowles continues to buy "dance" records. After family buys piano, Bowles studies theory, sight-singing, and piano technique. Writes "Le Carré: An Opera in Nine Chapters" about two men who exchange wives.

1920–21 Keeps diary filled with imaginary events and made-up characters. Writes daily "newspaper." Is promoted from fourth to sixth grade.

1922 Family moves to 34 Terrace Avenue in Jamaica. Bowles gives readings of his poems and stories after school. Buys first book of poetry, Arthur Waley's *A Hundred and Seventy Chinese Poems*.

1924 Graduates Model School and attends public high school in Flushing, New York. Appointed humor editor of *The Oracle*, the school magazine.

1925–26 Writes crime stories with the recurring character "the Snake-Woman" and reads them at the summer home of Anna, Jane, and Sue Hoagland, friends of the family in Glenora. Meets the Hoaglands' friend Mary Crouch (later Oliver). Transfers to Jamaica High School. Reads English writer Arthur Machen. Is deeply impressed by a performance of Stravinsky's *The Firebird* at Carnegie Hall. Shows talent in painting.

1927 Performs with the Phylo Players, an amateur theatrical group. Reads André Gide. Buys an issue of the Paris-based literary magazine *transition*, which has a major impact on him. Is promoted to poetry editor of *The Oracle*.

1928 Graduates Jamaica High School in January. The Hoagland sisters help him sell his paintings; when father refuses to support his artistic aspirations, mother pays for classes at the School of Design and Liberal Arts in New York. Bowles publishes poem "Spire Song" and prose poem "Entity" in *transition*. Spends summer working in the transit department of the Bank of Manhattan. Enters University of Virginia in the fall. Reads *The Waste Land*; discovers Prokofiev, Gregorian chant, Duke Ellington, and the blues. Experiments with inhaling ether. While home on winter break, attends one of the Aaron Copland–Roger Sessions Concerts of Contemporary Music, featuring music by Henry Cowell and George Antheil.

1929 Returns to University of Virginia in January and is hospitalized with conjunctivitis. Decides to move to Paris and obtains passport with the help of Sue Hoagland and Mary Oliver; tells virtually no one else of his plans. Arrives in Paris in April and works as a switchboard operator at the *Herald Tribune*. Mother refuses request to send money to Bowles made by a friend of Oliver's. Bowles receives 2,500 francs from Oliver and quits job; takes a short trip to Switzerland and Nice. Publishes poems in English and French in the Paris-based magazines *Tambour*, *This Quarter*, and *Anthologie du Groupe Moderne d'Art*. Visits northeastern France and Germany. Loses virginity on a camping trip with a Hungarian woman he had met the day before at the Café du Dôme; has sexual experience with Billy Hubert, a family friend. Accompanies Hubert to St.-Moritz and St.-Malo. Decides to return home and sails for New York on July 24. Works at Dutton's Bookshop and rents a room at 122 Bank Street. Begins writing "Without Stopping," fictional account of his travels in Europe.

1930 Meets Henry Cowell, who calls Bowles' musical compositions "frivolous" but writes a note of introduction to Aaron Copland. Moves to parents' home in order to use piano after Copland offers lessons in composition. Returns to University of Virginia in March. Hitchhikes to Philadelphia to attend Martha Graham's ballet *Le*

Sacre du Printemps on April 11; meets Harry Dunham, who will become a close friend. Decides to leave college after finishing out the term in June. Spends September and October with Copland at the Yaddo Arts Colony in Saratoga Springs, New York. Asked by college friend Bruce Morrissette to edit an issue of University of Virginia magazine *The Messenger*, solicits submissions from William Carlos Williams, Gertrude Stein, and Eduard Roditi, who becomes a lifelong friend and correspondent. Quarrels violently with parents in December.

1931 Sails for Europe on March 25. Shortly after arriving in Paris, looks up Gertrude Stein, with whom a friendship develops. Meets Jean Cocteau, Virgil Thomson, Ezra Pound, and Pavel Tchelitchew. Goes to Berlin with Copland at the end of April. Meets Jean Rhys, Stephen Spender, and Christopher Isherwood, who will give Bowles' surname to the heroine of his *Goodbye to Berlin*. Continues composition studies with Copland but dislikes Germany. Visits Kurt Schwitters in Hannover and is impressed with his studio; Bowles will soon incorporate one of Schwitters' abstract poems into his *Sonata for Oboe and Clarinet*. Writes to friend Daniel Burns that he feels his poems are "worth a large zero" and stops writing poetry for more than two years. Spends part of July with Stein and Alice B. Toklas in Bilignan, France, where they are joined by Copland; at Stein's suggestion, the two men visit Morocco, which enchants Bowles and frustrates Copland. They live in Tangier until early October. Bowles meets Claude McKay and the surrealist painter Kristians Tonny. After visiting Fez, Bowles writes to Morrissette, "Fez I shall make my home some day!" Travels in Morocco with Harry Dunham after Copland leaves; returns to Paris via Spain. Attends final Copland-Sessions concert on December 16 in London, where his *Sonata for Oboe and Clarinet* is performed.

1932 Taken ill during a ski trip in the Italian Alps. Travels with literary agent John Trounstine to Spain and Morocco. Returns in May to Paris, where he is hospitalized with typhoid. Bowles' songs are performed at Yaddo. After leaving hospital in July, travels in France, seeing Gertrude Stein for the last time and meeting mother and Daniel Burns at Morrissette's house near Grenoble. Completes *Sonata No. 1 for Flute and Piano*. Goes to Spain with mother and Burns; after their departure, stays with Virgil Thomson and the painter Maurice Grosser. Visits Monte Carlo, where he becomes friendly with George Antheil. In December, finishes *Scènes d'Anabase*, based on the poem by Saint-John Perse. Leaves for Ghardaïa, a town in the northern Sahara recommended by Antheil.

1933 Arrives in Ghardaïa and settles in nearby Laghouat, where he uses the harmonium in the town's church to compose a cantata, using his own French text. Travels around the Sahara and North Africa with George Turner, an American. Goes to Tangier, where he shares house with Charles Henri Ford, surrealist poet and editor of *View* with whom he has been friendly since 1930, and Djuna Barnes. Returns to United States after a three-week visit to Puerto Rico en route to New York City. *Sonatina for Piano* performed on WEVD in New York on June 18. Bowles has difficulty adjusting to life in America; on June 24, writes Thomson, "Certainly nobody hates New York more than I do." Writes short story "A Proposition." Writes song cycle *Danger de Mort* and *Suite for Small Orchestra* and score for Dunham's film *Bride of Samoa*. Publishes "Watervariation" and "Message" in pamphlet *Two Poems*, his first separate publication. Sublets apartment from Copland at 52 West 58th Street. Founds music publishing company Editions de la Vipère and publishes *Scenes from the Door*, songs based on passages from Stein's *Useful Knowledge*. *Sonatina for Piano* performed in December at the League of Composers' Concert, where Bowles meets John Latouche, who becomes a close friend.

1934 Bowles meets George Balanchine and Lincoln Kirstein, who are interested in commissioning a score for American Ballet Caravan. Hired as a secretary by Charles Williams, director of The American Fondouk, a foundation in Morocco working for the prevention of cruelty to animals. Pays for Atlantic passage by working as a guide for a stockbroker vacationing in Spain. Buys records of

North African music. His duties end in October and, after a brief stopover in Spain, he travels to Colombia; smokes marijuana for the first time while at sea. Falls ill from unpurified water and recuperates on a coffee plantation in the Colombian mountains. Returns to the United States, visiting Los Angeles and San Francisco, where he sees Henry Cowell; Cowell offers to publish Bowles' compositions in quarterly *New Music*.

1935 Accepts job as live-in companion to a wealthy Austrian invalid in Baltimore. Collaborates with painter Eugene Berman on an aborted ballet project. Quits job and returns to New York City. Receives commission to write score for Balanchine's *Yankee Clipper*. Allows his records of North African music to be reproduced for Béla Bartók. Writes music for Dunham's film *Venus and Adonis*, which is premiered at a screening and concert featuring several other works by Bowles. Scores two short films by Rudy Burkhardt and writes incidental music for *Who Fights the Battle?*, a play by Joseph Losey. Works as copyist for the Broadway composer Vernon Duke.

1936 With the help of Virgil Thomson, receives commission to write music for *Horse Eats Hat*, Edwin Denby's adaptation of a Eugène Labiche farce directed by John Houseman and Orson Welles and supported by the Federal Theater Project. Helps to found the anti-Franco Committee on Republican Spain. Article by Copland commends Bowles' music in *Modern Music* as "full of charm and melodic invention, surprisingly well-made in an instinctive and non-academic fashion." Bowles learns orchestration and works on score for production of Marlowe's *Doctor Faustus* directed by Welles.

1937 *Doctor Faustus* opens in January; Thomson praises the score in *Modern Music* as "Mr. Bowles' definite entry into musical big-time." In February, Bowles is introduced to Jane Auer (b. February 22, 1917) by John Latouche. Sees Auer the following week at E. E. Cummings' apartment; when Bowles and Kristians Tonny propose a trip to Mexico, Auer asks to join them, and Bowles goes to meet her parents the same evening. Orders 15,000 anti-Trotsky stickers to distribute in Mexico. Travels to Mexico by bus with Auer, Tonny, and Tonny's wife Marie-Claire Ivanoff. Auer falls ill with dysentery a week after arriving in Mexico and returns home without telling her companions. Bowles meets the composer Silvestre Revueltas, who leads an impromptu performance of his *Homanaje a García Lorca* for him. Works on pieces influenced by Mexican folk music. Travels to Tehuantepec and helps prepare for the town's May Day Festival, then visits Guatemala. At Kirstein's request, returns to New York to orchestrate Balanchine's *Yankee Clipper*. Auer invites him to spend a weekend with her in Deal Beach, New Jersey, after which she sees Bowles regularly. *Yankee Clipper* premieres in Philadelphia. Bowles begins writing music for opera *Denmark Vesey* (now lost), with libretto by Charles Henri Ford. The first act of *Denmark Vesey* is performed at a benefit for *The New Masses*.

1938 Bowles marries Auer on February 21. The couple honeymoon in Central America, then travel to Paris. Jane Bowles works on novel *Two Serious Ladies*. The Bowles meet Max Ernst and the painter and writer Brion Gysin, who will become a friend. Marriage is strained as Jane spends much of her time apart from Bowles. Couple separates briefly when Bowles goes to the south of France; Jane joins him after Bowles urges her by wire to do so. The Bowles rent a house for the summer in Eze-Village near Cannes. Returning to New York in the fall, they move into the Chelsea Hotel. Bowles is commissioned to write music for Houseman and Welles' production of William Gillette's *Too Much Johnson*; finishes score but when the production is canceled, transforms his music into the piece *Music for a Farce*. Nearly broke, moves with Jane to a cheaper apartment.

1939 Receives relief payments from the Federal Music Project. Joins the American Communist Party. Writes score for the Group Theater's production of William Saroyan's *My Heart's in the Highlands* and uses the money to rent a farmhouse on Staten Island, where he works on *Denmark Vesey* while Jane resumes writing *Two Serious Ladies*. Writes short story "Tea on the Mountain."

Mary Oliver moves in and becomes Jane's friend and drinking companion, causing Bowles to move out. Bowles rents a room in Brooklyn and invites Jane to live with him. Jane refuses and moves with Oliver to a Greenwich Village apartment; the Bowles continue to attend parties and social events together.

1940 Bowles and Jane move to the Chelsea Hotel in March. Bowles completes music for Saroyan's *Love's Old Sweet Song*, which begins trial run in Princeton on April 6. After being hired by the Department of Agriculture to write music for *Roots in the Soil*, a film about soil conservation in New Mexico, travels to Albuquerque with Jane and Jane's friend Bob Faulkner. Finishes score in June and goes to Mexico with Jane and Faulkner. Meets Tennessee Williams in Acapulco. Reluctantly moves to Taxco when Jane rents a house there without consulting him; Jane invites Faulkner to the house and begins a romantic relationship with Helvetia Perkins, an American woman working on a novel. Bowles returns to New York alone in September to compose music for the Theatre Guild's production of *Twelfth Night*, which opens on November 19. Bowles' score is a critical success; he receives a second Theatre Guild commission for Philip Barry's *Liberty Jones*, directed by Houseman. Jane arrives in New York on Christmas Day and rents a separate room at the Chelsea, where she is joined a few weeks later by Perkins.

1941 *Liberty Jones* opens on Broadway on February 5; the play and score receive negative reviews. Bowles writes music for Lillian Hellman's *Watch on the Rhine*. Attempts to quit Communist Party and is told that expulsion is the only means of leaving the organization. Writes *Pastorela*, an opera-ballet based on Mexican themes, for American Ballet Caravan. Lives with Jane at "artist's residence" on Middagh Street in Brooklyn Heights (other residents at the time include W.H. Auden and Benjamin Britten). Publishes obituary for Revueltas and essay "On Mexico's Popular Music" in *Modern Music*. Receives Guggenheim grant in March to compose an opera and travels to Taxco with Jane and Perkins. At the request of Katharine Hepburn, writes music for the play *Love Like Wildfire*, written by Hepburn's brother Richard. Meets Ned Rorem, who will become a friend and lifelong correspondent. *Pastorela* tours South America. Bowles meets Mexican painter Antonio Álvarez, who becomes close friend. Hospitalized with dysentery in September; recovers but falls ill with jaundice and recuperates at a sanitarium in Cuernavaca. Reads manuscript of Jane's *Two Serious Ladies* and suggests revisions.

1942 Works on light opera *The Wind Remains*, based very loosely on García Lorca's *Así que pasen cinco años*, in Mexico after Jane returns to New York to look for a publisher for *Two Serious Ladies*. Jane attempts suicide by slashing wrists but does not tell Bowles for many years. Bowles returns to United States with Álvarez, who is now partially paralyzed from a suicide attempt. Moves to apartment on 14th Street and Seventh Avenue and becomes acquainted with Marcel Duchamp, its previous occupant. Sees Jane often while maintaining separate household and finances. Debuts as music critic for the *New York Herald Tribune* on November 20; will contribute reviews regularly until 1946. Drafted for military service but dismissed after psychological examination.

1943 *The Wind Remains*, conducted by Leonard Bernstein with choreography by Merce Cunningham, premieres at the Museum of Modern Art on March 30. Jane Bowles' *Two Serious Ladies* is published on April 19 to mostly negative reviews. Composes incidental music for productions of John Ford's *'Tis Pity She's a Whore* and a stage adaptation of James Michener's *Tales of the South Pacific*. "Bluey: Pages from an Imaginary Diary," a section of his childhood notebooks, is published in *View*. Bowles meets Peggy Guggenheim, who organizes a recording of five of his pieces. Meets Samuel Barber, Gian-Carlo Menotti, and John Cage. Visits Canada with Jane.

1944 Writes music for Theatre Guild production of Franz Werfel's *Jacobowsky and the Colonel* (adapted by S. N. Behrman) and for *Congo*, a film directed by André Cauvin with script by John

Latouche; receives recordings of Congolese music from Cauvin that influence the score. Composes music for ballet *Colloque Sentimental*, produced by the Ballet Russe de Monte Carlo with sets by Salvador Dali, and incidental music for Williams' *The Glass Menagerie*.

1945 Moves to an apartment on West 10th Street; Jane and Perkins rent apartment in the same building. Edits special issue of *View* on Central and South America and the Caribbean, translating several articles and contributing an anonymous story supposedly taken from a Mexican magazine; story will be revised four years later as "Doña Faustina." Writes "The Scorpion," inspired by his reading of indigenous Mexican myths, later writing that "the objectives and behavior of the protagonists remained the same as in the beast legends. It was through this unexpected little gate that I crept back into the land of fiction writing." Travels to Central America with set designer and distant cousin Oliver Smith during summer. Publishes "The Scorpion" and writes "A Distant Episode." Translates Borges' story "The Circular Ruins." Develops close friendship with Australian composer Peggy Glanville-Hicks, who will set Bowles' texts to music and become a frequent correspondent.

1946 Writes music for *Blue Mountain Ballads*, with lyrics by Tennessee Williams. Works on translation of Sartre's play *Huis Clos*. Publishes "By the Water" in *View* and "The Echo" in *Harper's Bazaar*. Completes *Sonata for Two Pianos* and several theater scores. *No Exit*, Bowles' translation of *Huis Clos* directed by John Huston, opens on November 29 and is awarded Drama Critics' Award for the year's best foreign play.

1947 *Partisan Review* publishes "A Distant Episode." At a meeting with Dial Press about a possible collection of stories, Bowles is introduced to Helen Strauss, who agrees to be his agent. Hears from Strauss that Doubleday has offered an advance for a novel; Bowles signs contract and leaves for Morocco soon after. Writes "Pages from Cold Point" while at sea. Works on *The Sheltering*

Sky, spending the fall in Tangier. Although he will travel frequently to Europe, Asia, and the United States, Tangier will be Bowles' home for the rest of his life. Contacts Oliver Smith in New York and they agree to buy a house in the Casbah of Tangier together, which upsets Jane. Meets Moroccan artist Ahmed Yacoubi, who will become a close companion during the 1950s. Begins taking *majoun*, a jam made from cannabis; tries *kif*, which he will begin smoking regularly and in large quantities from the 1950s through the 1980s, when health problems force him to reduce his consumption to one cigarette a day. Goes to Fez in December.

1948 Crosses into Algeria and travels around the Sahara. Jane arrives in Tangier with her new lover. Edwin Denby arrives and the four visit Fez. Jane has adverse reaction to *majoun*, hallucinating and experiencing severe paranoia. Bowles finishes *The Sheltering Sky* in May; travels through Anti-Atlas Mountains with singer Libby Holman. Returns to New York alone in July. Doubleday rejects *The Sheltering Sky* and demands return of the advance. Several months later, English publisher John Lehmann reads *The Sheltering Sky* while visiting New York and agrees to publish it; James Laughlin of New Directions promises to bring out the American edition. Writes music for Williams' *Summer and Smoke*. *Concerto for Two Pianos, Winds, and Percussion* premieres in New York. Bowles becomes friends with Gore Vidal and Truman Capote. Jane develops an intense emotional attachment to a Moroccan woman named Cherifa that will last for many years. Bowles returns to Morocco, writing "The Delicate Prey" while at sea in December.

1949 Hosts Tennessee Williams and Williams' lover Frank Merlo. Travels in Sahara with Jane, who is impressed by the desert and writes her last completed story, "A Stick of Green Candy," in Taghit. Visits Paris for a performance of his *Concerto for Two Pianos and Orchestra*. John Lehmann publishes *The Sheltering Sky*. Bowles works on novel "Almost All the Apples Are Gone," which is never completed. In October, travels to England, where he is feted and introduced to Elizabeth Bowen, Cyril Connolly, and other British writers. New Directions publishes *The Sheltering Sky* in a small first printing on October 14, planning a second printing of 45,000 for the following year. Sails for Ceylon and begins writing a new novel, *Let It Come Down*.

1950 *The Sheltering Sky* enters the New York Times bestseller list on January 1; reviewing it for the *Times*, Tennessee Williams praises its "true maturity and sophistication." Bowles spends several months in Ceylon and South India, working on *Yerma*, an opera for singer Libby Holman based on the García Lorca play. Joins Jane in Paris, where she is working on her play *In the Summer House*; Jane goes to New York, hoping to see the play staged, and Bowles returns to Morocco and receives visit from Brion Gysin. John Lehmann publishes *A Little Stone*, omitting "The Delicate Prey" and "Pages from Cold Point" because of censorship concerns. American version, *The Delicate Prey and Other Stories*, includes the two stories and is published by Random House in November.

1951 Bowles buys Jaguar and hires Mohammed Temsamany as chauffeur; travels with Gysin through Morocco and Algeria. Works on *Let It Come Down* during summer in the mountain village of Chaouen; returns to Tangier in the fall and finishes the novel. Translation of R. Frison-Roche's *The Lost Trail of the Sahara* is published in August. Bowles leaves with Yacoubi for India in December.

1952 *Let It Come Down* published in February by Random House and by John Lehmann in England. Accused of spying by the Ceylonese government, Yacoubi and Bowles are detained for two days before being permitted to travel to Ceylon. Bowles makes offer to buy the island of Taprobane off the coast of Ceylon. Leaves with Yacoubi for Italy, where he plays a role in Hans Richter's film *8 x 8*. Agreement to buy Taprobane is sealed.

1953 Jane Bowles completes *In the Summer House*; having agreed to write music for the play, Bowles sails to New York with Yacoubi in March. Visits Jane at Libby Holman's house in Connecticut. Holman, infatuated with Yacoubi, convinces him to live with her, and Bowles returns to Tangier without completing score for *In the Summer House*. Writes *A Picnic Cantata*, with text by James Schuyler. Yacoubi returns to Tangier after quarreling with Holman. Bowles and Yacoubi go to Italy, where Bowles collaborates with Tennessee Williams on English adaptation of Visconti's film *Senso*. Bowles goes to Istanbul with Yacoubi to write travel essay for *Holiday*. They return to Italy in October and see Williams and Truman Capote before returning to Tangier amid rioting against the French. Bowles sails alone to United States, and completes music (now lost) for *In the Summer House* in time for its December 14 performance in Washington and its six-week Broadway run.

1954 Returns to Tangier, where he is soon joined by Jane. Falls ill with typhoid and sees Williams and Frank Merlo while convalescing. Receives brief visit from William Burroughs, who will live in Tangier for several years. Bowles begins writing *The Spider's House*, inspired by political upheaval in Morocco; moves for the summer with Yacoubi to a rented house overlooking the ocean and maintains strict schedule of writing. Transcribes Moghrebi tales told to him by Yacoubi. Moves to Casbah in fall. Bowles and Jane refuse to visit each other because of Bowles' suspicion of Cherifa and Jane's distrust of Yacoubi. Hoping to ease tensions by leaving Tangier, Bowles sails for Ceylon with Jane and Yacoubi in December.

1955 Works on *The Spider's House* at house on Taprobane; Jane dislikes the island, is unable to write, and returns to Tangier in March. Bowles finishes *The Spider's House* on March 16. Travels with Yacoubi in East Asia before returning to Tangier in June. Works on *Yerma*. Writes text for *Yallah*, a book of Saharan photographs taken by Peter Haeberlin. Writes to Thomson in September that "the possibility of being attacked is uppermost in every non-Moslem's mind ... I have taken an apartment until the first of October next year, but whether I'll be able to stick it out that long remains to be seen." Develops friendship with Francis Bacon. At Jane's request, agrees to give Casbah house to Cherifa. *The Spider's House* is published by Random House on November 14.

1956 In Lisbon, Bowles writes anonymous article on Portuguese elections for *The Nation*. Morocco gains independence on March 2, with Tangier remaining under international control; Bowles writes in *The Nation* that "in fact, if not officially, the integration of Tangier with the rest of Morocco has already taken place" and that Europeans "know better than to wander down into the part of town where they are not wanted." Bowles' parents visit during the summer. German edition of *Yallah* published in October by Manesse Verlag in Switzerland. Bowles travels to Ceylon with Yacoubi, arriving in late December.

1957 Needing money, attempts to sell Taprobane. English edition of *The Spider's House* brought out by Macdonald & Co. Bowles travels to Kenya to cover the Mau-Mau uprising for *The Nation*. Upon return to Morocco in May, discovers that Jane has suffered a stroke; rumors circulate of a violent reaction to *majoun* or poisoning by Cherifa. Receives visits from poets Allen Ginsberg, Peter Orlovsky, and Alan Ansen, who are drawn to Tangier in part because Bowles and Burroughs live there. Bowles posts bail after Yacoubi is arrested for alleged indecent behavior with an adolescent German boy. Takes Jane to London for treatment in August. Returning briefly to Morocco, Jane continues to have seizures and her psychological state deteriorates; she goes back to England and is admitted to a psychiatric clinic. Bowles and Yacoubi visit Jane in September. Bowles is hospitalized with Asiatic flu and writes "Tapiama" while suffering severe fever. Contracts pneumonia and pleurisy and is bedridden for three weeks; convalesces at the house of Sonia Orwell. Jane receives electric shock treatments. American edition of *Yallah* published by McDowell, Obolensky in October. Bowles convinces English publisher William Heinemann to bring out a story collection. Returns to Tangier with Jane and Yacoubi in November; Yacoubi is arrested and charged with "assault with intent to kill" the German boy.

1958 Police interrogate Bowles about Yacoubi and begin investigating Jane's relationship to Cherifa; the Bowles leave Tangier and Temsamany is repeatedly questioned about them. Taprobane is sold but Bowles is unable to take any of the proceeds of the sale out of Ceylon. The Bowles travel to Madeira, where Jane's condition improves. Yacoubi is acquitted in a trial lasting five minutes. Jane flies alone to New York in April. En route to the United States in June, Bowles finishes score for *Yerma*, which premieres at the University of Colorado on July 29. Jane enters psychiatric clinic in White Plains, New York, in October. Bowles goes to Los Angeles and quickly writes score for Milton Geiger's play *Edwin Booth*, directed by José Ferrer. Returns to New York; with Ned Rorem and John Goodwin, tries mescaline for the first time. Seeks financial support to record Moroccan folk music. Jane is released from the hospital and leaves the United States with Bowles in December, arriving in Tangier by the end of the year.

1959 Bowles travels to New York after he is asked to write the score for Williams' *Sweet Bird of Youth*, which opens on Broadway March 10. Sees Ginsberg frequently. Awarded Rockefeller Grant to record North African music and returns to Morocco. Heinemann publishes the story collection *The Hours After Noon* in May. Accompanied by Canadian painter and journalist Christopher Wanklyn and driver Mohammed Larbi, Bowles makes four trips to record in remote areas and takes extensive notes that form the basis of essay "The Rif, to Music." Near the end of the project, the Moroccan government forbids further recording, calling the endeavor "ill-timed."

1960 The Bowles move into separate apartments in the same building, the Inmeuble Itesa in Tangier. Bowles refuses offer of a year-long professorship from the English Department to Los Angeles State College.

1961 Tape-records and translates tales by Yacoubi, publishing "The Game" in *Contact* in May and "The Night Before Thinking" in *Evergreen Review* in September. Ginsberg returns to Tangier and encourages Bowles to write to Lawrence Ferlinghetti, publisher of City Lights Books, with a proposal for a collection of stories about kif-smoking which were written with the aid of kif; Ferlinghetti accepts enthusiastically.

1962 Bowles continues to record and translate stories told to him by Moroccans, a pursuit that will figure prominently in his later career. Meets Larbi Layachi, who tells Bowles autobiographical tales; under the pseudonym Driss ben Hamed Charhadi, Layachi's "The Orphan," transcribed and translated by Bowles, is published in *Evergreen Review*. Grove Press offers to publish Layachi's autobiography. When English publisher Peter Owen solicits a manuscript, Bowles collects essays and magazine pieces that will be published the following year as *Their Heads Are Green* (American edition is entitled *Their Heads Are Green and Their Hands Are Blue*); Peter Owen will be Bowles' primary English publisher for the rest of his career. *One Hundred Camels in the Courtyard* published by City Lights in September. Bowles returns with Jane to New York to write music for Williams' *The Milk Train Doesn't Stop Here Anymore*; visits parents in Florida and attends try-outs of *Milk Train* before returning to Tangier.

1963 Completes translation of Charhadi's *A Life Full of Holes*. Rents beach house at Asilah, a town south of Tangier, and spends several months there with Jane. Begins writing *Up Above the World*.

1964 *A Life Full of Holes* published by Grove Press in May. Working steadily, Bowles completes *Up Above the World* late in the year. Burroughs, Gysin, and Layachi leave Tangier for New York.

1965 Bowles and Jane visit the United States to visit Bowles' father, who has suffered a cerebral hemorrhage, and they consider buying a house in Santa Fe. Random House rejects *Up Above the World*. With Jane, Bowles returns to Tangier, where he learns that Simon & Schuster has accepted *Up Above the World*. Agrees to write book about Bangkok for Little, Brown. Begins to record and translate the spoken stories of Mohammed Mrabet, who becomes a close friend and regular visitor to Bowles' home.

1966 Film rights to not-yet published *Up Above the World* are sold to Universal Studios for $25,000 in February; the novel is published by Simon & Schuster on March 15 to mixed reviews. Bowles receives word in June that parents have died within a week of each other. Travels with Jane to New York, then sails alone for southeast Asia in July. Arrives in Bangkok in the fall and immediately dislikes the city. ("Most of Bangkok looked like the back streets of the nethermost Bronx relocated in a Florida swamp.") Goes to Chiangmai; records indigenous Thai music. Begins stage adaptation of story "The Garden."

1967 *Jilala*, an album featuring recordings of the Jilala religious brotherhood made by Bowles and Brion Gysin, is released in January. Bowles returns to Tangier in March after being informed that Jane's condition has worsened, her depression so severe that she can barely sleep or eat. Takes Jane to a clinic in Málaga, where she is treated until August. "The Garden" is performed in April at the American School in Tangier. Bowles abandons Bangkok book and returns advance. Translation of Mrabet's *Love With a Few Hairs* is published by Peter Owen in London; book is adapted for the BBC and shown on September 22 (American edition is brought out by George Brazillier in 1968).

1968 Peter Owen publishes story collection *Pages from Cold Point* in April. Jane returns to Málaga clinic for treatment. Bowles accepts teaching appointment in the English Department of San Fernando Valley State College in California, where he teaches a seminar on existentialism and the novel.

1969 Returns to Tangier, bringing Jane; Jane loses weight excessively and returns to the hospital in Málaga. Bowles signs contract to write autobiography for G.P. Putnam's Sons. Publication of Mrabet's *The Lemon* by Peter Owen (American edition, City

Lights, 1972) and *M'Hashish* by City Lights, both translated by Bowles.

1970 Poet Daniel Halpern, whom Bowles had met while teaching in California, starts the magazine *Antaeus*; Bowles is named founding editor. In May, Jane suffers stroke and her condition deteriorates, causing her to lose her vision. Premiere of Gary Conklin's film *Paul Bowles in the Land of the Jumblies* (retitled *Paul Bowles in Morocco* for English release and airing on CBS the following year) on December 10 in New York.

1971–72 Bowles begins translating the work of Mohamed Choukri, Moroccan writer, working from Choukri's Arabic texts. *Music of Morocco*, two-disc set taken from Bowles' recordings in the archives of the Library of Congress, is released. Black Sparrow Press brings out *The Thicket of Spring: Poems 1926–69*. Autobiography, *Without Stopping*, is published by G.P. Putnam's Sons on March 15, 1972. Bowles discovers the stories of Swiss expatriate writer Isabelle Eberhardt (1877–1904) and begins to translate them.

1973 Jane Bowles dies in Málaga clinic on May 4 with Bowles at her side. In the years following Jane's death, Bowles will travel outside of Morocco infrequently and will be increasingly confined to the Inmeuble Itesa (in part because of health problems); receives many visitors and, choosing not to install a telephone at his home, maintains extensive correspondence.

1974 Bowles publishes three translations: Choukri's *For Bread Alone* and *Jean Genet in Tangier*, and Mrabet's *The Boy Who Set the Fire*. Resumes writing own short stories after a hiatus of several years.

1975 Publishes translations of Mrabet's *Hadidan Aharam* and Eberhardt's *The Oblivion Seekers* in November. Stories "Afternoon with Antaeus," "The Fqih," and "Mejdoub" are collected in *Three Tales*, published by Frank Hallman in the fall.

1976–78 Black Sparrow Press publishes translations of Mrabet's *Look & Move On* and *Harmless Poisons, Blameless Sins* in 1976 and *The Big Mirror* in 1977; Bowles' story collection *Things Gone and Things Still Here* published in July 1977. Meets Millicent Dillon, who is working on a biography of Jane Bowles (*A Little Original Sin*, 1981).

1979 *Collected Stories 1939–76* is published by Black Sparrow with an introduction by Gore Vidal. Publication of translations *Tennessee Williams in Tangier* by Choukri and *Five Eyes*, collection of stories by Abdeslam Boulaich, Mrabet, Choukri, Layachi, and Yacoubi.

1980 Translation of Mrabet's *The Beach Café & The Voice* is published. Bowles begins working on *Points in Time*, long essay about Morocco in a genre that he calls "lyrical history."

1981–82 Premiere of Sara Driver's film *You Are Not I*, based on Bowles' story, on May 12, 1981, in New York. Story collection *Midnight Mass* is brought out by Black Sparrow Press in June 1981. *Next to Nothing*, collected poems, is published by Black Sparrow the same month. Bowles completes *Points in Time*, to be published in 1982 in England by Peter Owen (American edition, The Ecco Press, 1984). Teaches summer writing seminars in Tangier program of the School of Visual Arts in New York. One of his colleagues in the program is Regina Weinreich, who will make a documentary about him. Bowles discovers the work of Guatemalan writer Rodrigo Rey Rosa, one of his students, whose stories he begins to translate. Translation of Rey Rosa's *The Path Doubles Back* is published in November 1982.

1983–85 Bowles publishes unpunctuated "Monologue" stories in *The Threepenny Review* and *Conjunctions*. Translation of Mrabet's *The Chest* is published. Bowles travels to Bern, Switzerland, for medical treatment in summer 1984. Publication of *The Beggar's Knife*, stories by Rey Rosa translated by Bowles, and *She Woke Me Up So I Killed Her*, collection of translations from several authors.

1986–90 Translation of Mrabet's *Marriage with Papers* is published in 1986. Bowles suffers aneurysm in the knee and undergoes surgery in Rabat in September 1986. Meets the following year with director Bernardo Bertolucci, who is interested in adapting *The Sheltering Sky*. Begins keeping a diary, which will be published as *Days: Tangier Journal 1987–89*. Concert of Bowles' chamber music is performed in Nice. Story collection *Unwelcome Words* is published by Tombuctou Books. Shooting of *The Sheltering Sky* on location in Morocco begins in 1989. Bowles plays role of narrator, which includes on-screen appearance; becomes frustrated with Bertolucci's refusal to listen to his objections to the adaptation. Peter Owen brings out story collection *Call at Corazón* and Bowles' translation of Rey Rosa's *Dust on Her Tongue*. Bowles meets Virginia Spencer Carr, who will become his biographer. Travels to Paris for premiere of *The Sheltering Sky*; calls the film "awful." Exhibition "Paul Bowles at 80" mounted at the University of Delaware. *The Invisible Spectator*, biography by Christopher Sawyer-Lauçanno, is published by Grove Press; Bowles objects to the book and writes in *Antaeus*, "I wonder if he knows how deeply I resent his flouting my wishes." Robert Briatte's biography, *Paul Bowles: 2117 Tanger Socco*, is published in France.

1991–94 Translations of Mrabet's *Chocolate Creams and Dollars* and Rey Rosa's *Dust on Her Tongue* are published in the United States in 1992. Limited edition of essay *Morocco*, with photographs by Barry Brukoff, appears the following year. Bowles' vision is impaired due to glaucoma. Scores written for synthesizer are performed at productions of Oscar Wilde's *Salome* (1992) and Euripides' *Hippolytus* (1993) at the American School in Tangier. In April 1994, Bowles attends concert of his music at the Théâtre du Rond Point in Paris, which is recorded and released as *An American in Paris*. Spends a month in Atlanta for medical treatment at Emory University. Show of Bowles' photographs exhibited at the Boijmans van Beuningen museum in Rotterdam; *Paul Bowles Photographs: "How Could I Send a Picture into the Desert?"* is published. Canadian filmmaker Jennifer Baichwal visits Bowles and begins filming a documentary. *In Touch*, an edition of Bowles' letters edited by Jeffrey Miller, is published. Premiere of *Paul Bowles: The Complete Outsider*, documentary film by Catherine Warnow and Regina Weinrich.

1995 Premiere of *Halbmond*, adaptation of Bowles' stories "Merkala Beach" (alternate title of "The Story of Lahcen and Idir"), "Call at Corazón," and "Allal" by German film-makers Frieder Schlaich and Irene van Alberti, with Bowles introducing the film in an on-screen appearance. For the first time in decades, Bowles visits New York City for three days of concerts devoted to his music and a symposium at the New School for Social Research, September 19–21. Receives standing ovation at concert at Lincoln Center. Reunion with Burroughs and Ginsberg at Mayfair Hotel is filmed by Baichwal. *Paul Bowles: Music*, a collection of essays relating to his career as a composer, is published by Eos Music Press.

1996–98 Contributes essay to monograph on Tangier-based artist Claudio Bravo published in 1996. Makes final visit to the United States for medical treatment in 1996. *The Music of Paul Bowles*, performed by the Eos Orchestra under the direction of Jonathan Sheffer, is released by BMG/Catalyst. *Paul Bowles: Migrations*, performed by members of the Frankfurt-based Ensemble Moderne, is released by Largo. Mohamed Choukri's *Paul Bowles wa 'uzla Tanja*, a book hostile to Bowles, is published in Arabic in Morocco in 1996 and in French translation (*Paul Bowles, le reclus de Tanger*) the following year; in a 1997 interview in the Tangier weekly *Les Nouvelles du Nord*, Bowles says "there's no logic" to Choukri's accusatory assessment. Premiere of Baichwal's *Let It Come Down: The Life of Paul Bowles* at the 1998 Toronto International Film Festival. Millicent Dillon's *You Are Not I: A Portrait of Paul Bowles* is published in 1998. Edgardo Cozarinsky's *Fantômes de Tanger*, fictional film about post-war Tangier in which Bowles appears as himself, is released in France.

1999 Bowles transfers the majority of his literary papers to an archive at the University of Delaware. Owsley Browne's documentary *Night Waltz: The Music of Paul Bowles* is released. Bowles is hospitalized due to cardiac problems on November 7. Suffers heart attack in hospital and dies on November 18. Bowles' ashes are interred near those of his parents and grandparents at Lakemont Cemetery in Lakemont, New York.

Paul Bowles in Tangier, 1980s